THE NEW CIVIL RIGHTS MOVEMENT READER

The New CIVIL RIGHTS MOVEMENT READER

Resistance, Resilience, and Justice

edited by Traci Parker and
Marcia Walker-McWilliams

UNIVERSITY OF MASSACHUSETTS PRESS
Amherst and Boston

ISBN 978-1-62534-689-6 (paper)

Designed by Sally Nichols
Set in Minion Pro and Bebas Neue
Printed and bound by Books International, Inc.

Cover design by Sally Nichols
Cover photos: (top) Peter Pettus, *Participants, some carrying American flags, marching in the civil rights march from Selma to Montgomery, Alabama, 1965.* Courtesy Library of Congress.
(bottom) Flo Ngala, *Depictions of joy, love, and unity reject the trope that protest images must convey simple messages of spectacular conflict.* © Flo Ngala/The New York Times / Redux)

Library of Congress Cataloging-in-Publication Data

Names: Parker, Traci, editor. | Walker-McWilliams, Marcia, 1984–editor.
Title: The new civil rights movement reader : resistance, resilience, and
    justice / edited by Traci Parker and Marcia Walker-McWilliams.
Description: Amherst : University of Massachusetts Press, [2023] | Includes
    bibliographical references.
Identifiers: LCCN 2022045065 (print) | LCCN 2022045066 (ebook) | ISBN
    9781625346896 (paper) | ISBN 9781613769706 (epub)
Subjects: LCSH: African Americans—Civil rights—History—20th
    century—Sources. | Civil rights movements—United States—History—20th
    century—Sources. | African American political activists—History—20th
    century—Sources. | Political activists—United States—History—20th
    century—Sources. | United States—Race relations—History—20th
    century—Sources.
Classification: LCC E185.61 .N456 2023 (print) | LCC E185.61 (ebook) |
    DDC 323.1196/073—dc23/eng/20220920
LC record available at https://lccn.loc.gov/2022045065
LC ebook record available at https://lccn.loc.gov/2022045066

British Library Cataloguing-in-Publication Data
A catalog record for this book is available from the British Library.

CONTENTS

Chapter 4: Youth Activism in the Early 1960s   80

Chapter 5: Local Struggles   99

Chapter 6: The Struggles for Voting and Political Power in Mississippi and Alabama   127

Chapter 7: Economic Dimensions of the Civil Rights Movement   147

Chapter 8: Black Power   169

Chapter 9: Gender and Sexuality   210

Chapter 10: Culture and the Movement   251

Chapter 11: Black Power Politics and Reform in the 1970s and 1980s 270

Chapter 12: The Reach of the Civil Rights Movement 301

Chapter 13: The Black Freedom Movement in the Twenty-First Century 336

LIST OF FIGURES

PREFACE

The New Civil Rights Movement Reader introduces a new generation of students, many of whose understanding of civil rights activism has been largely shaped by the Black Lives Matter (BLM) movement, to the enduring questions, conditions, and legacies of the struggle for racial justice. This reader illustrates the arc of the struggle for Black freedom, humanity, and justice over much of the past century.

We are scholars of African American history who met as graduate students in the Department of History at the University of Chicago. We formed a strong bond as two Black women navigating the Ivy Tower and as graduate students on a Black history archiving project called Mapping the Stacks (thank you, Jacqueline Goldsby!) where we worked for several years processing archival collections at the Vivian G. Harsh Research Collection of Afro-American History and Literature at the Chicago Public Library. Under the tutelage of former senior archivist and civil rights activist Michael Flug, we gained a deep appreciation for archives and primary sources as living texts that help us better understand the past, present, and our possible futures.

In many ways, this reader is an homage to our journey through the archives. We began this project in 2015 in the early years of the Black Lives Matter movement. Eight years later, the purpose of this reader is just as, if not more, significant.

We would like to thank Cécile Yézou for her tireless, unwavering support of this reader and for her talents and expertise in tracking down permissions; contacting activists, authors, artists, archivists, and photographers; and editing substantial portions of the manuscript. She has been with the project since the beginning and has been essential to its completion. We are indebted to Mary Dougherty, our always encouraging and helpful editor, and Tricia Loveland, who patiently worked with us on the (very complex and tedious) financial aspects of securing permissions, as well as Rachael DeShano, Annette Wenda, Troy Zaher, Yara Akeh, and Angela Kwebiiha.

Finally, the reader would not be without the contributions of the numerous folks who have graciously permitted us to reprint their work and lent their assistance and support in securing the documents that are featured in this book: Mike Allard (MDAH), Ernest Allen, John Allison, John Anderies (WW LGBT CC), Linden Anderson (Schomburg), Wendy Appelle (Wylie Agency), Meliss Arteaga (Ms. Magazine), Khadijah Austin (MeToo—Tarana Burke), Dani Ayers (MeToo—Tarana Burke), Diana Bachman (Bentley Hist. Library, UMich), Roscoe Barnes III (Anne Moody), Maria Bell (Sterling Lord Literistic), Fred and Phyllis Blackwell, Donna Borden (LOC Veterans History Project), Sarah Breaux (Schulz), Emilyn Brown (Schlesinger), Tarana Burke, Angela Burton (University of Illinois Press), Mary Ann Cain (Margaret Burroughs), Diana Carey (Schlesinger), William Chafe (Duke U), Charles Cobb (Bob Moses), Renee Coleman (Ebony), Richard and Diane Copley, Fred Courtwright, Kerry D'Agostino (Curtis Brown), Kenneth Dawes (Chicago Review Press), Evan Patchen

Dellinger (and his three sisters!—Liberation estate), Edward Elbers (Alper), Uuka Elegba (NCOBRA), Ally Fell (Salky Literary Management), Cynthia Foster (U of S. Miss.), Daniel Friedan, John Gartrell (Duke University Archives—SNCC), Wendy Goff (NCOBRA), Jacqueline Goldsby (Yale), Richard Goldstein, Doris Goodnough (Orbis Books), Aram Goudsouzian, Jenissa Graham (Writer's House), Spencer Grant, Joi Gresham (Estate of Lorraine Hansberry), Michele Hadlow (Everett), Jacqueline Hamer Flakes (Fannie Lou Hamer), Shannon Harmer (Pars International Corp.), Megan Harris (LOC Veterans History Project), Peter Harvey (Lewis), Todd Harvey (American Folklife Center, LOC), Richard Hazboun (Pathfinder Press), Carrie Hintz (Emory), Melissa Holland (Kheel), Catherine Hosch (Chris Calhoun Agency), Winston Huff (Ebony), Calvin Hughes (T. Martin reps), Andrew Hunt (Hist. Professor—contact for Dellinger family), Mary Beth Jarrad (NYU Press), Ashley Johnson (Pittsburgh Courier), Michael Koncewicz (NYU), Brenda Lett (NCOBRA), Peter London (Harper Collins), Rachel Ludwig (D. Black Agency), Matthew Lutts (AP), Maria Marshall (SWGAP), Clifford Mason, Lynn Mason (PBS), Caitlin McCarthy (the Center), Michael McCullough (Duke Press), Julie McGarvie (D. Black Agency), James and Judy Meredith, Anne Moebes, Mari Morales-Williams (MeToo—Tarana Burke), Janet Moses (Bob Moses), Bill Mullen (Margaret Burroughs), Walter Naegle (Bayard Rustin), Diane Nash, Angelique Nelson (Chicago Defender), Debbie Paitchel (PMC/Variety), Lady Parada (the Center), Shawn J. Parry-Giles (Louis Farrakhan), Laura Peimer (Radcliffe), Laura Piasio (Hachette), Robert Platt (NYU), Deborah Porfido (McGee Media), Jackie Rader (Schulz), Barbra Ramos (AASC Press), Connie Robinson (NBH), Jesseca Salky (Murray), Yessenia Santos (Simon & Schuster), Robert Shatzkin (WW Norton), Monica Smith, Sasha Straus (Anne Moody), Lorraine Stuart (USM), Beau Sullivan (Penguin Random House), Amy Sun (PARS), Mary Sykes (WW Norton), Alaina Taylor (New York Review Books), Michael Thelwell, Scheherazade Tillet (ALWH), Eric Toller (Margaret Burroughs), Andy Uhrich (WUSTL), Karin Unger (Huey P. Newton Foundation), Alexandra Villaseran (NARA), Laura Visser-Maessen (Bob Moses), Morag Walsh (CPL), Jade Wong-Baxter (Goldin Literary Agency), Sarah Zimmerman (CPL), Rebecca Zorach (Margaret Burroughs), and Ayla Zuraw-Friedland (David Black Agency).

PREFACE FOR STUDENTS

In the summer of 2020, headlines and news stories across the country focused on the rise of protests against racial injustice and police brutality following the murders of Ahmaud Arbery, Breonna Taylor, George Floyd, Tony McDade, and so many others. A common theme throughout the coverage of these protests was the presence of students and young adults on the front lines, especially those from Black and Brown communities. An article in the *Baltimore Sun* stated, "Today's teenagers and college students came of age protesting gun violence, climate change and racial injustice. They say they have watched adults and elected leaders do nothing to tackle these issues. They are showing up on podiums and at police lines because they believe it will be up to their generation to solve these problems." And an *LA School Report* read, "The demonstrations gripping the nation are not new, but they're playing out against an unprecedented backdrop: a global pandemic that's under-scored existing inequities, disproportionately wreaked havoc on the health and livelihoods of communities of color and shut down America's K–12 and higher education systems. Black and Hispanic people are bearing the brunt of the economic fallout and resulting spike in unemployment. And black communities, in particular, represent an alarmingly dispropor-tionate number of coronavirus deaths."[1]

In 2020, the ascendance of the Black Lives Matter movement and the groundswell of activism against racial oppression and police brutality have drawn parallels to the civil rights movements of the 1950s and 1960s. In what ways are these two moments and movements connected? And in what ways are they different? At their core, the civil rights and Black Lives Matter movements demand racial justice. The civil rights movement was presented with the problem of Jim Crow—the legalized system of racial segregation and discrimination—that positioned African Americans as second-class citizens. It dismantled many legal compo-nents of the system, desegregating schools and public accommodations, outlawing employ-ment discrimination, and securing the passage of federal legislation, including the Civil Rights Act of 1964 and the Voting Rights Act of 1965. In the movement's aftermath, systemic racism persists—as evidenced by the various concerted efforts to undo and circumvent civil rights legislation and programs. In 2013, for example, the Supreme Court gutted the Voting Rights Act in *Shelby v. Holder*. The Court's decision has allowed for the resumption of Black voter disenfranchisement.

The Black Lives Matter movement, thus, is picking up where the civil rights movement left off. Learning from the past, protesters are leveraging sit-ins, picket lines, and boycotts to challenge police brutality and systemic racism. What is noticeably new is the use of social media—a medium that has facilitated the wide, and near-immediate, dissemination and participation in this grassroots movement. The Internet, cellular phones, and social media allow people to connect people across nations, cultures, and communities, providing tools to capture racial oppression and white supremacy and mobilize opposition. But the mere fact that today's students and young adults are still witnessing and battling racial injustice provides a point of continuity with the students and young adults who integrated schools, organized sit-ins, and fought for political, economic, and social justice.

This reader presents the civil rights movement in ways that may provide key lessons and strategies for current and future movements—not only those for racial justice but also those for LBGTQUIA rights, environmental justice, and women's rights, among others. It challenges the conventional narrative of a beginning point with southern demonstrations in the 1950s and an end point in 1968 with the death of Martin Luther King Jr. and rising prominence of Black Power. In *The New Civil Rights Movement Reader*, the dynamism of the movement is highlighted through chapters that reveal the intersections of race, place, gender, labor, culture, and strategy.

After an introduction, each chapter includes visual and textual primary sources. Primary sources are firsthand accounts from the people who had a direct connection with a particular event, issue, or topic. Examples of primary sources include newspapers, speeches, autobiographies and memoirs, diaries, interviews, letters, photographs, poems, music, film, and television shows of the time. Secondary sources, which are suggested at the end of each chapter, use primary sources to discuss and analyze a topic. These sources include books written by people not directly involved, textbooks, documentaries, journal articles, and essays.

In the introduction of each chapter, you will find a series of questions to facilitate your engagement with the primary and secondary sources that follow. You should use these questions to guide and inform readings and analysis on the events, themes, and debates of that particular moment. For example, in the book's first chapter, one question asked: What was African Americans' relationship to organized labor in the 1930s? You then should read the subsequent sources with this question in mind, so you can determine the contours and labor dimensions of the early civil rights movement—or, rather, the Black freedom movement in the decades before the *Brown v. Board of Education* decision and the Montgomery Bus Boycott, two events that historians argue started the civil rights movement. Understanding this, as you learn in subsequent chapters, immensely influenced the nature and direction of the civil rights movement in the 1950s and 1960s. While some questions, such as the example provided above, directly focus on the readings in a specific chapter, other questions will ask you to make connections across chapters. For example, while chapter 9 explores gender and sexuality in the movement, these topics are explored throughout the book. Therefore, questions posed in this chapter will draw on your reading and engagement with the issues of gender, sex, and sexuality as discussed in other sources, such as "Rosa Parks Recalls the Montgomery Bus Boycott" in chapter 3 or Gloria Richardson's "Focus on Cambridge" in chapter 5.

Similarly, the importance of youth in the movement is a theme that runs throughout the reader. While chapter 4 explicitly takes up youth activism in the early 1960s, the murder of Emmett Till as a flash point in the movement and the experiences of the Little Rock Nine as agents of integration in the 1950s are taken up in chapter 3. Documents in subsequent chapters look at the role of schoolchildren in the 1963 Birmingham struggle and the demands of college students for more Black students, faculty, and departments in the late 1960s. The busing controversy of the late 1960s and affirmative action cases of the 1970s also highlight the important ways in which students shaped and were shaped by civil rights struggles.

When answering the discussion questions, please note that there is not necessarily a right or wrong answer, just different ways of looking at a particular moment, topic, or debate. What is important, however, is that you can ground and defend your perspective using the presented sources.

NOTES

1. Liz Bowie, "Youth Leaders Stand on the Front Lines of Baltimore Protest," *Baltimore Sun*, June 6, 2020, https://www.baltimoresun.com/maryland/baltimore-city/bs-md-youth-leaders-20200606-uckjrdy wmzgtpi7n7k3jshsdp4-story.html; Taylor Swaak and Bekah McNeel, "'This Is a Revolution': Student Activists across the Country Take Their Place—on the Front Lines and Behind the Scenes—in Historic Protests," *LA School Report*, June 5, 2020, http://laschoolreport.com/this-is-a-revolution-student-activists-across-the-country-take-their-place-on-the-front-lines-and-behind-the-scenes-in-historic-protests/.

THE NEW CIVIL RIGHTS MOVEMENT READER

Introduction

On January 6, 2021, the Reverend Raphael Warnock made history when he was declared the first African American senator in the state of Georgia, defeating sitting U.S. senator Kelly Loeffler. A notable increase in registered voters due to efforts of Black women like Stacey Abrams helped turn the tide in Warnock's favor. That same day, as numerous Americans celebrated democracy, President Donald J. Trump declared once again that he had been robbed of his reelection before a group of his supporters. Per his instructions, they—many of whom were known white supremacists—marched to and rioted at the U.S. Capitol as Congress certified the election results in favor of President-Elect Joseph R. Biden. The riot left five people dead and many others injured. Seven days later, because of Trump's involvement, the House of Representatives impeached the president for a second time, marking the first time in U.S. history that a president had been impeached twice.

The stark contrast between the democratic political progress in Georgia and the assault on democracy in the nation's capital reveals the extent to which Black progress is often inextricably linked to a struggle against white supremacy. The events of January 6, 2021, served as a reminder to Americans that we must continue to reckon with multiple, often competing, ideas of what it means to be a democratic nation. In many ways, this reader is a testament to this challenge and the ways in which Black Americans have sought a more just and democratic society.

The New Civil Rights Movement Reader: Resistance, Resilience, and Justice offers the most inclusive, comprehensive assessment of the struggle for racial justice from the beginnings of the civil rights movement (including its roots in the 1930s labor movement) through the Black Lives Matter movement. It is unlike many other compilations of primary and secondary sources on the market because it is aimed at teachers and students alike. For instructors, this reader provides pedagogical tools and approaches and encourages them to move beyond the master narrative that centers Dr. Martin Luther King Jr., offers a top-down approach, focuses on the period of 1954 to 1968 (also known as the King years), and celebrates the movement's nonviolent ideology and tactics. Instructors can then present, or rather engage, the movement in ways that more accurately reflect recent historiography: a struggle led by ordinary people from all walks of life—Black and white, men and women, working class, poor, and middle class—who fought to eliminate the scourge of white supremacy in every facet of American life, not solely in schools or lunch counters but also in workplaces and political institutions.

Students are offered a large and diverse selection of primary sources—including oral histories, speeches, newspaper articles, literature, and music—that seek to excite, engage, and connect them to the past and present Black freedom movement. We hope that students will be able to "see" themselves in this ongoing struggle and learn from its lessons and goals. For example, we hope that African American girls and women will come to understand that they are progenies of key civil rights leaders such as Fannie Lou Hamer, Rosa Parks, Gloria Richardson, and Diane Nash and the ways that patriarchy and sexism tried to limit, albeit unsuccessfully, the influence and reach of Black women not only in the civil rights movement but also in studies on this subject. Also, in providing a variety of sources, students can hear from those women and members of the LGBTQIA community who were marginalized in the movement and its retellings.

Does the civil rights movement begin with the *Brown v. Board of Education* in 1954 striking down segregation in public schools and end with the assassination of Martin Luther King Jr. in Memphis in 1968? Do we frame the civil rights movement with iconic decisions, events, and figures, or do we consider enduring protests against segregation, discrimination, and racism well before and beyond these events as indicative of a longer, broader struggle for Black freedom, dignity, and equality? If we begin a study of the movement with the *Brown* decision, which overturned the separate-but-equal doctrine of the 1896 *Plessy v. Ferguson* case, how do we acknowledge and account for African American resistance to segregation and Jim Crow in schools, employment, and public accommodations prior to 1954, much of which provided painful lessons as well as possible pathways for change? On the other hand, if we extend the movement beyond the assassination of Martin Luther King Jr. and the grassroots organizing of the 1960s to analyze continued and new patterns of segregation and systemic inequalities, are we somehow diluting the concentration and impact of activism and movement building by African Americans in the movement over the course of the 1950s and 1960s?

Recent works on the civil rights movement have troubled the great men, great organization focus, and chronology. They examine the contributions and experiences of ordinary or lesser-known women and men, the battle for civil rights in the North and the West, and the struggles of Black freedom before the 1954 *Brown v. Board of Education* decision. On the issue of chronology, more and more scholars have embraced the "long civil rights movement" approach as conceptualized by historian Jacqueline Dowd Hall.[1] Hall sees the civil rights movement as a struggle that began with the Great Depression and the New Deal and continued until the 1970s, as well as occurring not only in the American South but throughout the nation.[2]

Using the long civil rights movement, this book challenges the master narrative and the top-down approach to the civil rights movement. The historian Hasan Kwame Jefferies aptly describes this narrative as a "fiction" that insists:

> The movement begins in 1954 when the U.S. Supreme Court concedes that segregation is wrong. It gains momentum when an interracial coalition, inspired by the court's bold action, engages in noble acts of nonviolent protest, ranging from bus boycotts to sit-ins. Dr. King leads this moral crusade and receives the unwavering support of Presidents John F. Kennedy and Lyndon B. Johnson, who put the full weight of the federal government, including the vast resources

of the FBI, behind it. It reaches its peak when northern whites learn the disgraceful extent of racial discrimination in the South and southern whites realize that racial prejudice is morally wrong. Then Congress passes landmark legislation designed to end racial discrimination. Unfortunately, African Americans are dissatisfied with the remarkable progress and undermine the movement by rejecting nonviolence, shunning well-meaning whites, and embracing Black Power. Finally, in 1968, Dr. King is killed, effectively ending the movement. But thankfully, by that time, America had essentially righted its racial wrongs, thereby leveling the playing field for future generations and paving the way for Barack Obama.[3]

As a result, this book decenters Dr. Martin Luther King Jr., yet still documents his invaluable influence on the nature and direction of the movement, it considers key Supreme Court cases and legislation but in a manner that doesn't suggest that these were primarily goals and accomplishments of the movement, and it reflects on the movement in the American South without implying that the movement did not occur elsewhere in the United States.

In taking this approach, this reader offers students a fuller picture of the civil rights movement. It reveals the ways that Jim Crow permeated every corner of the country, which the movement reflected geographically, and spotlights the intersections of race, class, gender, and sexuality in the inner workings of the movement. Additionally, this book exposes the civil rights movement's deep roots in the 1930s labor movement, employing the tactics of nonviolence but also self-defense, and shows that it was a national phenomenon that had an international reach. The movement, in fact, may have begun with the 1954 Supreme Court decision in *Brown v. Board of Education*, but, to some minds, it was the murder of Emmett Till and the Montgomery Bus Boycott that galvanized African Americans and facilitated the rise of the civil rights movement. Thereafter, African Americans leveraged their labor and purchasing power, built interracial and intraracial alliances, staged picket lines and protests, and mobilized informal and formal political campaigns. Their activism transformed a nation: it ended de jure segregation in public schools, enfranchised African American voters, advanced fair-employment practices, reconfigured the public sphere by opening retail and service establishments, "reformed the criminal justice system by eliminating all-white juries," and "refashioned neighborhoods by opening up housing on a nondiscriminatory basis."[4]

But, as this book also illustrates, the movement continued even after the assassination of Dr. King. In the late 1960s and 1970s, activists succeeded in implementing affirmative action, increased Black political representation, challenged racial capitalism in ways that gave rise to the War on Poverty and other antipoverty initiatives, and influenced the nature and direction of other movements that pushed America to confront gender and sexuality discrimination, imperialism and colonialism, xenophobia, health disparities, police brutality, and mass incarceration. By the 1980s and 1990s, hip-hop (an emerging musical genre), the AIDS pandemic, and the election of Ronald Reagan presented both new challenges and new methods of protest. The twenty-first century has birthed a new iteration of the Black freedom movement: Black Lives Matter. Founded by three Black queer women after the murder of Trayvon Martin in 2013, BLM seeks "to eradicate white supremacy and build local power to intervene in violence inflicted on Black communities by the state and vigilantes." It is a decentralized movement—meaning it is without a King-like figure—that "combat[s] and counter[s] acts" of racial terrorism and oppression, "create[s] space for Black imagination and innovation, and center[s] Black joy."[5]

We recognize that the foundations of Jim Crow in America were anchored in slavery and thus inscribed in the nation's earliest economic, legal, political, and social structures. African Americans found ways to resist enslavement and secure and protect their freedom and rights. Their striving for a better life—as an important ideological and pragmatic approach—offered African Americans a strategy by which to procure the collective safety and survival of the race in the face of white supremacy. Through economic, legal, political, and sociocultural means, Black Americans confronted and attempted to buck white supremacy.

This reader is organized into chronological and thematic chapters that explore various aspects of the civil rights movement, beginning with increased African American mobilization against racial discrimination as workers and consumers in the 1930s. Chapter 2 examines the World War II era as a hotbed of civil rights activism undergirded by the Double V campaign and an African American consciousness that challenged racism abroad and at home. The third chapter, "Galvanizing the Movement in the 1950s," touches on many of the well-known events of the southern civil rights movement, including *Brown v. Board of Education*, the murder of Emmett Till, the Montgomery Bus Boycott, and the Little Rock Nine. Chapter 4 explicitly takes up the role of young people and their intentional civil rights activism in early-1960s nonviolent direct action against segregation in public spaces and higher education. Chapters 5 and 6 focus on the dynamics of local civil rights struggles in Florida, South Carolina, Maryland, Alabama, Louisiana, and Mississippi, where challenges to segregation and disenfranchisement were mounted using nonviolent direct action and self-defense.

Chapter 7, "Economic Dimensions of the Civil Rights Movement," explores antipoverty efforts, fair-housing legislation, and worker demonstrations. Black Power as philosophy, organizing principle, and cultural movement is the focus of chapter 8. The next chapter engages gender and sexuality within the movement, specifically how women challenged subordination within the movement and how Black women theorized their intersectionality and oppression within and outside of civil rights and Black Power organizing. The experiences of Black gay and lesbian civil rights activists are also explored. Chapter 10 explores the pivotal roles of Black cultural production and consumption in the civil rights movement, from music and theater to television and fashion.

Efforts to reform education through school control, busing, and affirmative action in the 1970s and 1980s are paired with efforts to gain Black political power and representation during the same era in chapter 11. Chapter 12 explores the broad reach of the civil rights movement into other social justice movements and with efforts of Black American civil rights activists to connect their struggle to decolonization in African nations. This reader culminates with a chapter exploring Black civil rights and freedom struggles into the twenty-first century, including the movement for Black lives against police brutality and white supremacy.

Each chapter opens with an introduction exploring the major themes and questions posed by a set of primary source documents and the historical essays that follow. The introduction provides contextual knowledge for the chapter's focus and poses questions that students should consider when reading the documents and essays that follow. These questions can serve as the start or basis of in-class and online discussion forums. Some of the primary source documents may be familiar to students, such as President Barack Obama's speeches and Alicia Garza's "A Herstory of the Black Lives Matter Movement." Others like John Lewis's speech at the March on Washington in 1963 and Lorraine Hansberry's anonymous letters to the *Ladder* (the first nationally published lesbian publication), however, may be less familiar or altogether unknown.

While each chapter can be read on its own, this reader is constructed in such a way to help students analyze civil rights activism from different vantage points and categories of analysis over time. For example, chapter 4, "Youth Activism in the Early 1960s," documents the efforts of Black college students who resisted segregation in public spaces and higher education. But youth play pivotal roles in the movement prior and to and after the 1960s, and those voices are reflected in chapters throughout the reader. The Scottsboro Boys, Black Alabama teenagers accused of raping two white women in 1931, and Emmett Till's murder at the age of fourteen in 1955 for reportedly whistling at a white woman illustrated how young Black men in particular were subject to the racism embedded in social mores around race and gender in ways that stripped them of their rights and freedoms. In 1957, Black teenagers in Little Rock, Arkansas, integrated Central High School. Ten years later, Black students on college campuses were demanding Black Power, equal treatment, the creation of Black-studies departments, and the hiring of more Black faculty. And young people are on the front lines of today's movement for Black lives. Instructors might ask students to analyze or compare and contrast the role of youth in the movement over time.

Similarly, students might be prompted to see gender and sexuality engaged in multiple ways in this reader, beyond chapter 9's clear focus on these aspects. In the preceding chapters, Black women working and organizing in World War II as well as fears of miscegenation and interracial mixing that promoted white violence and undergirded concerns about school integration and the leadership of local activists like Gloria Richardson, Fannie Lou Hamer, Annie Devine, and Victoria Gray should raise questions and commentary about how gender and sexuality influenced civil rights activism and its opposition. In the chapters that follow, Shirley Chisholm's claims that sex discrimination impacted her more than race discrimination, the sexual harassment and assaults experienced by Anita Hill as well as Tarana Burke and other women of the MeToo movement, and the Black queer women who founded the Black Lives Matter movement provide opportunities for students to continue to engage, question, and analyze how gender and sexuality shape individual and collective notions of resistance, resilience, and justice. Other themes and categories of analysis—the law, geographic region, and strategies of resistance—may also help students make connections across time and location.

NOTES

1. See Jacqueline Dowd Hall, "The Long Civil Rights Movement and the Political Uses of the Past," *Journal of American History* 91, no. 4 (2005): 1233–63.
2. Some of the scholars who have embraced the long civil rights movement are Robert Self, Jeanne Theoharis, Martha Biondi, and Thomas Sugrue. Eric Arnesen, Clarence Lang, and Sundiata Keita Cha-Jua, among others, however, disagree with this approach. Arnesen, in particular, writes, "The movement was distinctive. It was significantly larger than its predecessors; it was visible nationally and consistently in a way unmatched by

earlier organizations; it attained a genuinely mass character; it provoked a violent backlash of unprecedented proportions; and it ultimately succeeded in toppling legalized segregation and enfranchising black Southerners." Eric Arnesen, "Reconsidering the Long Civil Rights Movement," *Historically Speaking* (April 2009): 34. For further reading on the chronology of the civil rights movement, see Sundiata Keita Cha-Jua and Clarence Lang, "The 'Long Movement' as Vampire: Temporal and Spatial Fallacies in Recent Black Freedom Studies," *Journal of African American History* 92 (Spring 2007): 265–88; Charles W. Eagles, "Toward New Histories of the Civil Rights Era," *Journal of Southern History* 66 (November 2000): 815–48; Adam Fairclough, "Historians and the Civil Rights Movement," *Journal of American Studies* 24 (December 1990): 387; Robert Korstad and Nelson Lichtenstein, "Opportunities Found and Lost: Labor, Radicals, and the Early Civil Rights Movement," *Journal of American History* 75, no. 3 (1988): 786–811; Clarence Lang, "Locating the Civil Rights Movement: An Essay on the Deep South, Midwest, and Border South in Black Freedom Studies," *Journal of Social History* 47 (December 2013): 371–400; Steven F. Lawson, "Freedom Then, Freedom Now: The Historiography of the Civil Rights Movement," *American Historical Review* 96 (April 1991): 456–71; Danielle L. McGuire and John Dittmer, *Freedom Rights: New Perspectives on the Civil Rights Movement* (Lexington: University Press of Kentucky, 2011); and Jeanne Theoharis and Komozi Woodard, eds., *Freedom North: Black Freedom Struggles Outside the South, 1940–1980* (New York: Palgrave Macmillan, 2003).

3. Hasan Kwame Jefferies, *Understanding and Teaching the Civil Rights Movement* (Madison: University of Wisconsin Press, 2019), 4–5.

4. Jefferies, *Understanding and Teaching the Civil Rights Movement*, 3.

5. "About—Black Lives Matter," Black Lives Matter website, https://blacklivesmatter.com/about/.

1

Labor and Civil Rights in the 1930s

How did the Great Depression and the New Deal impact African Americans? How did these events inform the labor movement and the Black freedom struggle? What was African Americans' relationship to organized labor in the 1930s? How did African Americans leverage the labor movement to push for civil rights?

Starting in 1910, the largest migratory movement of African Americans—known as the Great Migration—began. This movement involved the relocation of approximately six million Black southerners seeking to escape racial violence, limited economic and educational opportunities, and disenfranchisement to northern and western cities. Their migration facilitated the emergence of thriving Black enclaves that exalted Black culture in northern and western cities such as Harlem (in New York) and Bronzeville (on the South Side of Chicago). In these locales, African Americans had better chances to secure skilled and fairly well-paid jobs, receive better schooling, and participate in politics. Yet regardless of location, Black migrants continued to face racism and discrimination in employment, education, medical care, housing, and policing. As such, African Americans routinely used direct action, organizing boycotts, pickets, and sit-in campaigns, to realize first-class citizenship.

For those who remained in the South, the realities of Jim Crow segregation continued to constrict Black life in the 1930s, especially Black economic opportunity. Long before the onslaught of the Great Depression in the late 1920s, African Americans encountered forms of rural poverty as sharecroppers and tenant farmers and urban poverty as underpaid industrial and domestic workers without adequate housing and city services.

The Great Depression, however, worsened an already bleak situation. During this economic crisis, African Americans routinely faced high unemployment levels of 50 percent, compared to a high of 25 percent for Americans on the whole; they not only were terminated from their menial jobs but also found their jobs—typically referred to as "Negro work"—reassigned to whites. African Americans thus often found themselves impoverished, homeless, and starved.

Not only did the Great Depression economically cripple African Americans, but it also altered the terrain upon which African Americans struggled for economic advancement and civil rights. Initially, President Franklin D. Roosevelt's New Deal offered a glimmer of hope. African Americans, however, soon found that the program offered them little to no relief. The New Deal deemed African Americans ineligible due to their lack of landownership and steady wages. Too, racist segregationists administered the program, and, even when African Americans finally became eligible, these administrators unsurprisingly gave preference to whites for employment and relief assistance.

In response, African Americans employed various strategies to protest Jim Crow in employment and organize for greater economic, civil, and political rights. A number of labor unions in the American Federation of Labor (AFL) excluded Blacks from membership. Thus, one strategy that African Americans used was to create labor unions open to or that catered to Black workers, such as A. Philip Randolph's Brotherhood of Sleeping Car Porters. Laborers frustrated by the AFL's refusal to organize unskilled and semiskilled industrial workers established the Congress of Industrial Organizations (CIO). Led by Communists in its early years, the CIO welcomed African American and women workers when the AFL refused. In this prolabor milieu, this chapter reveals, African Americans organized under the CIO found a space and new support to effectively challenge race and economic discrimination in the workplace. The Southern Tenant Farmers Union (STFU), an interracial union made up of Black and white agricultural workers, also emerged in the American South in 1934. African Americans courted, utilized, and in some instances adopted the stance of the political Left, most notably the Communist Party, which proved open to acknowledging racism and organizing as a way of building class solidarity between whites and Blacks. Even those who did not adopt the stance of the Communist Party continued to call out the United States by questioning how the nation planned to recover from the Great Depression if its most marginalized citizens were continuously left behind. African Americans also chose to put pressure on companies who relied upon Black consumerism but failed to employ Blacks, as evidenced in the "Don't Buy Where You Can't Work" campaigns of the 1930s. All of these strategies and approaches would later be employed during and immediately following the Second World War.

DOCUMENT 1.1
"Race Loses Jobs to Whites" (1931)

Robert S. Abbott founded the *Chicago Defender*, "The World's Greatest Weekly," newspaper in 1905 to provide a voice for African Americans that would challenge Jim Crow and feature stories by and about African Americans. The *Chicago Defender* became a major proponent of the Great Migration and often featured articles imploring African Americans to leave the South.

In this article, the *Defender* reports the impact of the Great Depression on African American workers.

> The National Urban League's monthly check on employment conditions among our Race shows that wages have dropped decidedly in all sections of the country, that whites continue to supercede our workers in hotels, and that new people have moved into northern and southern cities from neighboring rural areas. . . .

In Spartanburg, S.C., wages dropped from 5 to 20 per cent. A monthly wage of $30 for domestics in Seattle is common, and men in the lumbering camps are paid as little as 18 cents per hour. In Richmond construction laborers have been reduced from 35 to 20 and 25 cents per hour. Only by accepting reduced wages of from 10 to 20 per cent have we been able to keep jobs in Grand Rapids.

In the New York area wages for domestics and common laborers have shown similar curtailment. Women recently employed in an important business establishment are working for less than whites who formerly held the job, and doing more work than it ordinarily entails. In some places men are paid considerably less than whites working alongside of them.

Cutting of prices was resorted to in South Carolina by a cleaning and dyeing establishment run by whites, when a similar business was opened by Negroes employing ten workers. In at least two cities on the Pacific coast white girls are now waiting in hotels in the place of our men. Attempts are being made to crystallize sentiment against continuing the policy of employing our bellmen and waiters in hotels in certain sections of the South. When department stores in Richmond discontinued their delivery service and entered into contracts with express companies to handle their packages a number of our drivers lost their jobs.

Strangers are moving into Denver, Detroit, Atlanta, Akron, Boston and Philadelphia. Some reports indicate a movement to the farms from cities, but the largest movement appears to be in the opposite direction

Source: "Race Loses Jobs to Whites," *Chicago Defender*, May 30, 1931.

DOCUMENT 1.2

"Don't Buy Where You Can't Work" Demonstration (1941)

This document is a photograph of a "Don't Buy Where You Can't Work" protest on 134th Street in Harlem in 1941. Adam Clayton Powell, a prominent civil rights leader and future congressman, leads the protest. As pastor of the Abyssinian Baptist Church, Powell helped lead the fight for jobs and affordable housing in New York City and eventually became the first Black U.S. congressman from the state of New York. The "Don't Buy" movement was a Black consumer campaign that demanded white-collar work in sales and offices in businesses located in African American enclaves. It began in Chicago 1929 and quickly spread to other cities, including Harlem, Baltimore, Cleveland, Detroit, Richmond, and Washington, D.C. It is said to have secured thousands of white-collar and skilled jobs for African Americans in the 1920s and 1930s.

Source: Morgan and Marvin Smith, *Don't Buy Where You Can't Work*, 1941, photograph, Schomburg Center for Research in Black Culture, New York Public Library. Photograph © Morgan and Marvin Smith. Courtesy of Monica P. Smith.

DOCUMENT 1.3

Attorney Samuel Leibowitz with the Scottsboro Boys (ca. 1933)

In the early 1930s, nine African American teenagers were accused of raping two white women in Scottsboro, Alabama. Despite scant evidence, the Scottsboro Boys were tried in court, and eight of them were found guilty and sentenced to death in 1931. Both the National Association for the Advancement of Colored People (NAACP) and the American Communist Party jockeyed for the opportunity to represent the Scottsboro Boys in appeals cases. The American Communist Part's legal arm, the International Labor Defense, ultimately represented the Scottsboro Boys. After multiple appeals and trials, the convictions of some of the Scottsboro Boys were overturned due to injustices in the legal system—lack of adequate counsel, fair sentencing, the trying of minors as adults, and systemic exclusion of African American jurors. The remaining Scottsboro Boys served prison terms into the late 1940s.

Clockwise: Olen Montgomery, Clarence Norris, Andrew Wright, Willie Roberson, Ozzie Powell, Leroy Wright, Charlie Weems, Eugene Williams, and Haywood Patterson.

Source: *Attorney Samuel Leibowitz with the Scottsboro Boys*, ca. 1933, photograph. Morgan County Archives, Decatur, Alabama.

Angelo Herndon, *The Scottsboro Boys* (1937)

Angelo Herndon was an African American labor organizer who supported the Communist Party's efforts to defend the Scottsboro Boys. Attracted to the Alabama Communist Party's interracial makeup and antiracist stance, Herndon became familiar with the injustice of the southern legal system when he was arrested in 1932 for organizing a peaceful demonstration of unemployed workers in Atlanta. The Communist Party's International Labor Defense aided Herndon's defense, but he was found guilty and sentenced to two years in a chain gang. Herndon was just twenty years old at the time.

Upon his release, he continued to be active in the Community Party and in 1937 served as national head of the Young Communist League. That same year, he wrote "The Scottsboro Boys: Four Freed! Five to Go!" pamphlet to keep the spotlight on the Scottsboro Boys' case and help raise money for their defense fund.

EUGENE WILLIAMS, Roy Wright, Willie Roberson and Olen Montgomery are free! Let this victory and great cause for jubilation hasten on the struggle for the freedom of the other five boys.

Six years of unyielding struggle of the Negro people, of their supporters, and of friends of democracy and justice the world over—in the U. S. A., London, Moscow, Berlin, Cuba, Mexico and Spain—have wrenched from the hands of Alabama's feudal despots four more intended victims of the rope and faggot.

Congratulations, International Labor Defense, the Communist Party, and the Young Communist League. Congratulations to the organizations of the united Scottsboro Defense Committee, the National Association for the Advancement of Colored People, the League for Industrial Democracy, the Church League for Industrial Democracy (Episcopal), the I.L.D., the Methodist Federation for Social Service and the American Civil Liberties Union. You have scored a smash-hit victory for Negro rights and the preservation of civil liberties.

We of the Young Communist League are proud that we have played a leading role in this noble cause for justice and democracy. In expressing our greetings to the Scottsboro boys and their defenders, we pledge our continued efforts in mobilizing every possible force in the fight for the freedom of the other five. We shall be ever vigilant in bringing to the consciousness of all youth the shameful crime of Scottsboro. We will leave no stone unturned in the fight for the liberation of the Negro people from the rule of Southern landlord oppression.

Alabama's attempt to perpetuate the slave system by framing nine Negroes met with universal opposition from those who have been outraged by this crude type of injustice. The liberty-loving people of the world chorused in repeated determination: *The Scottsboro boys shall not die!* The hundreds and thousands of mass meetings, demonstrations and other dramatic actions struck a ringing blow at Alabama's system of human bondage. The compelling force generated through the organized might of millions wrung from their bloodstained hands this glorious, but partial, victory.

On July 25, 1937, after six long years of endless and tireless work for the freedom of the Scottsboro boys, the news which flashed around the world that four of the boys had been freed came as a thunderbolt of joy and happiness to the hearts of millions. In Harlem, New York, many Negro mothers, who had untiringly followed the Scottsboro case from its beginning, wept for sheer joy. Kerchiefs in hand, they dabbed away almost incessantly at the tears that flowed freely until their warm hearts tired from the excitement. In their happiness, they expressed their kindred feeling of brotherhood with all the members of their race who are degraded and crushed by the iron heel of Southern barbarism. . . .

RELEASING FOUR TO MURDER FIVE

. . . Yes, the whole world knows that the Scottsboro boys are not guilty. Nobody will be fooled by the insidious move of releasing four in order to murder the other five.

Victoria Price lied defiantly for six years. She swore by the Bible and everything else, as only a disreputable character like her would do, that all nine of the boys raped her in succession. According to her story at the first and other trials that followed, she was thrown on top of sharp jagged rock, in the open gondola car in which they were riding, and the nine Negroes ravished her one after the other. Clearly the State of Alabama now admits that she was giving false testimony.

Dr. D. R. Bridges, who examined her, testified that there was no evidence of scratches or cuts on her back, nor of such injuries as would be expected after such an experience. It seems rather interesting in view of the fact that she claimed to have fought back vigorously in trying to keep the Negroes off, that there were no bruises or scratches on her back—a remarkable back she has! The examination of Victoria Price by Dr. Bridges on the day of the alleged rape indicated that she had not had intercourse for at least twenty-four hours.

Dr. Bridges also testified that she was calm and showed no signs of excitement such as would be inevitable after mass rape.

RUBY BATES DECLARES BOYS INNOCENT

Ruby Bates, who repudiated her previous testimony, blasted the whole frameup when she testified that neither she nor Victoria Price had been touched by the nine Negroes. Since then Ruby Bates has been working for the freedom of the Scottsboro boys. . . .

But the State of Alabama concurred in Victoria Price's perjured testimony and held her up as a glowing example of true white womanhood. Upon the words of a habitual prostitute, whose purity of womanhood and character had long passed into obscurity, the lynchers sought to snuff out the lives of nine black boys.

The trial was a farce, as all the others have proved to be. Guilty or innocent, Alabama wanted nothing short of the death penalty. On April 8, 1931, an all-white jury found the boys guilty, and Judge Hawkins set the date of execution for July 10.

A UNITED WORLD-WIDE STRUGGLE

It was at this time that the I.L.D. stepped in and demanded a halt to this attempted wholesale massacre. . . .

Joseph R. Brodsky, chief counsel for the I.L.D., went down to Alabama and made application for the arrest of judgment against the boys. Upon his arrival, he was met by a howling mob of lynchers. In his efforts to have the convictions set aside, Hawkins immediately overruled Brodsky's request. Brodsky took exception to the judge's ruling, whereupon the judge overruled his exception. Brodsky then countered with an exception to Hawkins' decision overruling his previous request to except.

The judge became so angry that he made a grand exit through the rear door of the courtroom. In all the confusion, Brodsky turned round, and was suddenly seized by a husky man who said:

"Come on, yah Jew bitch! We'll show you how to defend nigger rapers."

When the execution date, July 10, was set aside, the I.L.D. mobilized all of its forces for a fight to the finish. J. Louis Engdahl, late chairman of the I.L.D., with Mother Ida Wright, toured twenty-six European countries on behalf of the Scottsboro boys. . . .

The Communist Party and the Young Communist League were the great stimulating forces which brought Scottsboro before the broad masses of organized labor. In cooperation with the I.L.D., the question of Negroes serving on juries was raised for the first time. Because this question struck at the root of Negro oppression, and because of the mass fight carried on around it, the United States Supreme Court was forced to reverse the convictions of the Scottsboro boys for the second time. Like the infamous Dred Scott decision, in which the Negro-hating Judge Taney ruled that a Negro "has no rights a white man is bound to respect," Scottsboro became the beacon light and symbol of the struggle of the Negro for complete freedom. . . .

Just as the pioneers of 1776 blazed the trails in search of democracy, freedom and a decent world for human beings to live in, so the Communists were the spearheads who first threw their support around the Scottsboro case. Communists recognized that in order to wage an effective fight it was necessary to expose and publish abroad the denial of elementary human justice, the inhuman exploitation which are invariably imposed upon the Negro by the bourbon ruling class of the South. . . .

THE FIVE OTHERS MUST GO FREE

. . . Communists pledge their continued support to the fight for the vindication of the other boys. One important victory has been won. This should stimulate even more and greater activity on the part of all who have thus far helped to make possible this partial victory. Those desiring to maintain liberty and democracy should redouble their efforts on behalf of the five Scottsboro boys who must be freed. . . .

To the youth of our generation Scottsboro is a tragic lesson of what a future under reaction would hold in store. It spells death especially to the younger Negro generation. But through the victory of Scottsboro, a future which is bright with hope, confidence and the attributes of man's ability to abolish exploitation of man by man, can be realized. . . .

Source: Angelo Herndon, *The Scottsboro Boys: Four Freed! Five to Go!* (New York: Workers Library, 1937). Courtesy of the *People's World*.

Nate Shaw Discusses Sharecropping (1974)

Nate Shaw, whose real name was Ned Cobb, was an African American tenant farmer in Tallapoosa County, Alabama. His struggles to succeed as a tenant farmer and his involvement in the Sharecroppers' Union in the early twentieth century are detailed in his autobiography, *All God's Dangers: The Life of Nate Shaw* (as told to historian Theodore Rosengarten), published in 1974. The following is an excerpt from this book.

Then I moved to Mr. Gus Ames', 1908. Mr. Ames' land was a little better than Mr. Curtis's, but it was poor. Worked his pet land hisself and whatever he made off me, why, that was a bounty for him. I didn't make enough there to help me.

Hannah was dissatisfied at it, too. We talked it over and our talk was this: we knew that we weren't accumulatin nothin, but the farmin affairs was my business, I had to stand up to em as a man. And she didn't worry me bout how we was doin—she knowed it weren't my fault. We was just both dissatisfied. So, we taken it under consideration and went on and she was stickin right with me. She didn't work my heart out in the deal. I wanted to work in a way to please her and satisfy her. She had a book learnin, she was checkin with me at every stand. She was valuable to me and I knowed it. And I was eager to get in a position where I could take care of her and our children better than my daddy taken care of his wives and children.

Mr. Curtis and Mr. Ames both, they'd show me my land I had to work and furnish me—far as fertilize to work that crop, they'd furnish me what *they* wanted to; didn't leave it up to me. That's what hurt—they'd furnish me the amount of fertilize they wanted regardless to what I wanted. I quickly seed, startin off with Mr. Curtis in 1907, it weren't goin to be enough. First year I worked for him and the last year too he didn't allow me to use over twenty-two hundred pounds of guano—it come in two-hundred-pound sacks then—that's all he'd back me up for all the land I worked, cotton and corn. It was enough to start with but not enough to do any more. Really, I oughta been usin twice that amount. Told him, too, but he said, "Well, at the present time and system, Nate, you can't risk too much."

I knowed I oughta used more fertilize to make a better crop—if you puts nothin in you gets nothin, all the way through. It's nonsense what they gived me—Mr. Curtis and Mr. Ames, too—but I was a poor colored man, young man too, and I had to go by their orders. It wasn't that I was ignorant of what I had to do, just, "Can't take too much risk, can't take too much risk." Now if you got anything that's profitable to you and you want to keep it and prosper with that thing, whatever it is, however you look for your profit—say it's a animal; you're due to look for your profit by treatin him right, givin him plenty to eat so he'll grow and look like somethin. Or if you fertilize your crop right, if you go out there and work a row of cotton—that's evidence of proof—I have, in my farmin, missed fertilizin a row and it stayed under, too. Them other rows growed up over it and produced more. If you don't put down the fertilize that crop aint goin to prosper. But you had to do what the white man said, livin here in this country. And if you made enough to pay him, that was all he cared for; just make enough to pay him what you owed him and anything he made over that, why, he was collectin on his risk. In my condition, and the way I see it for everybody, if you don't make enough to have some left you aint done nothin, except givin the other fellow your labor. That crop out there goin to prosper enough for him to get his and get what I owe him; he's makin his profit but he aint goin to let me rise. If he'd treat me right and treat my crop right, I'd make more and he'd get more—and a heap of times he'd get it all! That white man gettin all he lookin for, all he put out in the spring, gettin it all back in the fall. But what am I gettin for my labor? I aint gettin nothin. I learnt that right quick: it's easy to understand if a man will look at it.

I worked four years on halves, two with Mr. Curtis. I was just able when I moved from his place to leave him paid. What did I have left? Nothin. Of course, if I'm left with nothin, no cash in my pocket, I can look back and say what I paid for I got. But what little I did get I had to work like the devil to get it. It didn't profit me nothin. What little stuff I bought to go in my house—it set in my house! What is that worth to me in my business out yonder? It aint prosperin me noway in my work. I'm losin out yonder to get a little in my house. Well, that's nothin; that aint to be considered. You want some cash above your debts; if you don't get it you lost, because you gived that man your labor and you can't get it back.

Now it's right for me to pay you for usin what's yours—your land, stock, plow tools, fertilize. But how much should I pay? The answer ought to be closely seeked. How much is a man due to pay out? Half his crop? A third part of his crop? And how much is he due to keep for hisself? You got a right to your part—rent; and I got a right to mine. But who's the man ought to decide how much? The one that owns the property or the one that works it?

Source: Theodore Rosengarten, "Nate Shaw Discusses Sharecropping," in *All God's Dangers: The Life of Nate Shaw* (New York: Alfred A. Knopf, 1974), 107–8. Excerpt(s) from *All God's Dangers* by Theodore Rosengarten, copyright © 1974 by Theodore Rosengarten and the Estate of Ned Cobb. Used by permission of Alfred A. Knopf, an imprint of the Knopf Doubleday Publishing Group, a division of Penguin Random House LLC. All rights reserved.

DOCUMENT 1.6

Southern Tenant Farmers Union (1937)

A meeting of the Southern Tenant Farmers Union near Parkin, Arkansas, is the subject of this photograph. The Southern Tenant Farmers Union was an interracial union of Black and white sharecroppers and tenant farmers who sought to organize for better terms with landowners who benefited from New Deal programs, while landless farmers received no benefits.

Source: Louise Boyle, *Black and White STFU Members Including Olin Lawrence, Seated in Front, Listen to Norman Thomas Speak Outside Parkin, Arkansas, on September 12, 1937*, 1937, photograph, Southern Tenant Farmers Union Photographs, 1937 and 1982, the Kheel Center for Labor-Management Documentation and Archives, Catherwood Library, Cornell University.

DOCUMENT 1.7

A. Philip Randolph, "The Pullman Company and the Pullman Porter" (1925)

An excerpt from A. Philip Randolph's "The Pullman Company and the Pullman Porter" published in the *Messenger*, an African American magazine founded in New York City in 1917 by Randolph and Chandler Owen, is below. This article was published one year after the founding of the Brotherhood of Sleeping Car Porters, the labor union led by African Americans and part of the American Federation of Labor, and details the working conditions of Pullman Porters. Pullman Porters were African American men hired to serve passengers on overnight trains for the Pullman Company, a railroad company founded by George Pullman in 1867. Pullman Porters largely catered to white passengers but were well-known and respected in African American communities because they relayed important information about conditions of Black life across the country.

Pullman porters are efficient. They are loyal. They are honest. They are faithful. This, the company admits. Not only does the company admit it, but praises the porters to the highest.

Listen to the Pullman Company for itself on the porters' honesty. Note the following items, appearing in the column entitled "Honesty's Honor Roll," in the *Pullman News*, a monthly magazine of the company, of March, 1925:

Honesty's Honest Roll

Porter J.E. Avery (Jacksonville) was highly complimented for turning in a wallet whose contents aggregated $750, of which $250 was cash and the remainder endorsed drafts.

Porter E. Hutchinson (Chicago Western) found $180 in a vestibule on the "Overland Limited" soon after leaving Chicago recently, and on arrival at San Francisco deposited it at the Pullman Office.

Porter W.T. Davis (Chicago Southern) found a purse containing $60 on the "Floridian" and was given $10 for his honesty by the owner.

Porter G.W. Tisdale (Nashville) was rewarded for turning in a purse containing $55.

And this is a general thing. One may find in practically every issue of the *Pullman News* the mention of porters for honesty. I need not remark that it is a commonplace that honest workers are an asset to any institution. The Pullman company undoubtedly realizes this, else it wouldn't praise its employees for honesty. But it does little to make the porters honest save by putting their names on the Honesty's Honor Roll, a reward of too unsubstantial a character to merit appreciation. The policy of the Pullman Company has been to reward their porters with praise and flattery only. But the porters want more than kind words.

Pullman Porters Synonymous with Pullman Company

Well does the Pullman Company know that the Pullman porter is synonimous with the Pullman Company. When one speaks of the Pullman Company, the first image which comes to mind is the porter with his white coat, cap and brush. In fact, it is a matter of common knowledge that the chief commodity which the Company is selling is *service*, and that service is given by the Pullman porters. For comfort, ease and safety, the traveling public looks to the porter. Children, old, decrepit and sick persons, are put in his charge. And the history of the Company shows that he has been a responsible custodian, ever vigilant, tender and careful of the well-being of his passengers. His every move and thought are directed toward the satisfaction of the slightest whim of restless and peevish passengers.

And ofttimes this service is rendered under the most trying conditions. Many a porter is doing duty though he has not slept in a bed for two or three nights at a time. Nor has he had adequate food. Despite the requirements that he be clean, he is often doubled and trebled back without ample time to give his body proper cleansing.

Treated Like Slaves

But despite the long, devoted, patient and heroic service of the Pullman porter to the Pullman Company, despite the fact that the fabric of the company rests upon his shoulders, despite the fact that the Pullman porter has made the Company what it is today, the Company, callous and heartless as Nero, treats him like a slave. In very truth, the Pullman porter has no rights which the Pullman Company is bound to respect. So far as his manhood is concerned, in the eyes of the Company, the porter is not supposed to have any. When he is required to report in the district offices to answer to some complaint, he is humiliated in being compelled to stand for two or three hours before the district officials decide to consider him, while there he is insulted by some sixteen-year-old whipper snapper messenger boy who arrogantly snaps out: "What d'you want, George." This may be a porter who has been in the service some thirty or forty years, trenching hard upon the retirement period. But what does that matter? He is only a Pullman porter. His lot is hapless. In obedience to the holy writ, when he is slapped on one side of the cheek, he is expected to turn the other one. And if, perchance, under the cross of oppression, of bitter insult and brutal exploitation, he should assert his rights as a man, immediately he is branded as a rattled brain radical, and hounded and harassed out of service. Many a tragic and pitiful case may be cited of porters who committed the lese majeste of challenging the injustice of an Assistant District Superintendent, being deliberately framed in order to secure a pretext for persecuting him until his life becomes more miserable than a dog's, and is driven to resign. And this porter may be one who has not only rendered exemplary service to the Company but has seen a score or more years on the road.

Framing Up Porters

There are many ways in which to "get" a porter. A porter must be examined, unlike any other worker on the railroad, once every year. Many of them speak bitterly of this method of humiliation and abuse. If a porter is pronounced unfit, he may be retired or fired. Whenever the Company wants to "can" a porter who has the impudence to "speak up" for his rights and the rights of the men, the examining doctor, paid by the Company, finds it necessary to give this particular porter a *very rigid* examination, and he does not *pass*. He is politely told that, on account of the report of the doctor's examination, his (the porter's) services are no longer required. Porter after porter avers this to be a fact . . . If a man is up to be retired or fired, as a result of a Company doctor's examination, he should have the right to file a report of an examination in a first class hospital on his case. And the report of the examination in the hospital should be considered final and decisive. But in fact, the porters should not be subject to a physical examination every year at all. It is unnecessary, discriminatory and hence, unfair. In this connection it is interesting to note that some of the porters objected to a certain Company doctor, and suggested that the Company employ U. Conrad Vincent, a colored physician of high standing, and, incidentally, a former Pullman porter with an excellent record card, but the Company balked. Why? Guess? It may not be so easy to frame a porter though annual physical examinations. The only remedy for this situation is organization. If, when a porter is told that he is unfit for any future service, he could say to the Company, "Well, I will report the matter to my union," a very different attitude would be assumed toward him. It is because the Pullman conductors have their own union that they are not subjected to the degrading ordeal of these yearly physical examinations. It must be remembered too, that there are only one-fourth as many Pullman conductors as Pullman porters. But their interests and rights are not disregarded as the porters are, because they are organized . . .

Porter's Word Regarded of No Value

A classic instance in point is the case of a porter who was accused by a woman passenger of having hugged her at two o'clock in the night. She claimed that she screamed and stuck him with a hat pin, that he hollered, but no one came or awoke. This, too, was in a ten section car. She never reported the incident until seven o'clock in the morning to the trainman. The porter denied it. The trainman and the Pullman conductor wrote the woman's report to the Pullman office. The case hung on for six months. One morning one of the members of the Grievance Committee, under the Employee Representation Plan, was commanded to come to the office and sit on the case. This porter had been up two nights on the road. When he appeared in the office before the nine men sitting on the case, he pleaded that he was unfit to deliberate on the matter; that he needed rest. "To insist upon my passing judgment on this case, indicates," said the porter, "that either you undervalue your own ability or you over value mine, because you expect me to do in a few minutes what it has taken you six months to do, and you still have not finished." This porter member of the Grievance Committee maintained that it was ridiculous to think that a porter would hug a woman in a ten section car, that a woman could scream and not awaken the passengers or the Pullman conductor who was asleep in a berth two spaces away; and that the porter could yell and not be heard. The accused porter had requested the officials to examine him stripped for the pin prick, but this was not done. The porter-member of the Grievance Committee pointed out that the Company was doing to the porter what a mob in the South would not do to its victim, namely, it was trying and convicting him without his accuser identifying him. He also contended that the woman might have dreamt that some one was hugging her, and the next morning put it on the porter, the most defenseless person on the car. This porter was fired after he had walked the streets for six months. The porter-member of the Grievance Committee was forthwith framed-up and fired because of his manly attitude in fight for the accused porter. He is one of the responsible citizens of New York. Such rank injustice cries out to high heaven for redress! But there is none except through organized action.

Source: A. Philip Randolph, "The Pullman Company and the Pullman Porter,"
Messenger VII, no. 9 (September 1925).

Mary McLeod Bethune, "What Does Democracy Mean to Me?" (1939)

Mary McLeod Bethune's address "What Does Democracy Mean to Me?" examines the meaning of democracy and citizenship for African Americans in the early twentieth century. Bethune delivered this address while serving as a panelist on NBC Radio's public affairs broadcast, *America's Town Meeting of the Air.* Here, she, and other panelists, were asked to consider the question: What does American democracy mean to me? The program aired on November 23, 1939, twelve weeks after the Second World War began.

Four years prior to this speech, Bethune founded the National Council for Negro Women (NCNW), a national coalition of African American women's organizations. It became one of the most influential organizations during the civil rights movement. In addition to the NCNW, Bethune served as the eighth president of the National Association for Colored Women (founded in 1896) from 1924 to 1928 and was a national adviser to President Franklin D. Roosevelt's Division of Negro Affairs of the National Youth Administration from 1936 to 1943. Impressed by her work, Roosevelt considered her one of his foremost advisers and appointed her to the Federal Council of Negro Affairs, also known as the Black Cabinet. Bethune also is well known for establishing the Daytona Educational and Industrial Training School for Negro Girls in Daytona Beach, Florida, in 1904. This school is now Bethune-Cookman University.

Democracy is for me, and for 12 million black Americans, a goal towards which our nation is marching. It is a dream and an ideal in whose ultimate realization we have a deep and abiding faith. For me, it is based on Christianity, in which we confidently entrust our destiny as a people. Under God's guidance in this great democracy, we are rising out of the darkness of slavery into the light of freedom. Here my race has been afforded [the] opportunity to advance from a people 80 percent illiterate to a people 80 percent literate; from abject poverty to the ownership and operation of a million farms and 750,000 homes; from total disfranchisement to participation in government; from the status of chattels to recognized contributors to the American culture.

As we have been extended a measure of democracy, we have brought to the nation rich gifts. We have helped to build America with our labor, strengthened it with our faith and enriched it with our song. We have given you Paul Lawrence Dunbar, Booker T. Washington, Marian Anderson and George Washington Carver. But even these are only the first fruits of a rich harvest, which will be reaped when new and wider fields are opened to us.

The democratic doors of equal opportunity have not been opened wide to Negroes. In the Deep South, Negro youth is offered only one-fifteenth of the educational opportunity of the average American child. The great masses of Negro workers are depressed and unprotected in the lowest levels of agriculture and domestic service, while the black workers in industry are barred from certain unions and generally assigned to the more laborious and poorly paid work. Their housing and living conditions are sordid and unhealthy. They live too often in terror of the lynch mob; are deprived too often of the Constitutional right of suffrage; and are humiliated too often by the denial of civil liberties. We do not believe that justice and common decency will allow these conditions to continue.

Our faith envisions a fundamental change as mutual respect and understanding between our races come in the path of spiritual awakening. Certainly there have been times when we may have delayed this mutual understanding by being slow to assume a fuller share of our national responsibility because of the denial of full equality. And yet, we have always been loyal when the ideals of American democracy have been attacked. We have given our blood in its defense—from Crispus Attucks on Boston Commons to the battlefields of France. We have fought for the democratic principles of equality under the law, equality of opportunity, equality at the ballot box, for the guarantees of life, liberty and the pursuit of happiness. We have fought to preserve one nation, conceived in liberty and dedicated to the proposition that all men are created equal. Yes, we have fought for America with all her imperfections, not so much for what she is, but for what we know she can be.

Perhaps the greatest battle is before us, the fight for a new America: fearless, free, united, morally re-armed, in which 12 million Negroes, shoulder to shoulder with their fellow Americans, will strive that this nation under God will have a new birth of freedom, and that government of the people, for the people and by the people shall not perish from the earth. This dream, this idea, this aspiration, this is what American democracy means to me.

Source: Mary McLeod Bethune, "What Does Democracy Mean to Me?"
America's Town Meeting of the Air, NBC, November 23, 1939.

FURTHER READING

Arnesen, Eric. *Brotherhoods of Color: Black Railroad Workers and the Struggle for Equality*. Cambridge, MA: Harvard University Press, 2002.

———. *Waterfront Workers of New Orleans: Race, Class, and Politics, 1863–1923*. New York: Oxford University Press, 1991.

Bates, Beth Tompkins. *Pullman Porters and the Rise of Protest Politics in Black America, 1925–1945*. Chapel Hill: University of North Carolina Press, 2001.

Bynum, Cornelius L. *A. Philip Randolph and the Struggle for Civil Rights*. Urbana: University of Illinois Press, 2010.

Carter, Dan T. *Scottsboro: A Tragedy of the American South*. Baton Rouge: Louisiana State University Press, 2007.

Clark-Lewis, Elizabeth. *Living in, Living Out: African American Domestics in Washington, D.C., 1910–1940*. Washington, DC: Smithsonian Institution Press, 1994.

Cohen, Lizabeth. *Making a New Deal: Industrial Workers in Chicago, 1919–1939*. Cambridge: Cambridge University Press, 2014.

Foner, Philip Sheldon. *Organized Labor and the Black Worker, 1619–1981*. Chicago: Haymarket Books, 2018.

Goldfield, Michael. *The Southern Key: Class, Race, and Radicalism in the 1930s and 1940s*. Oxford: Oxford University Press, 2020.

Greenberg, Cheryl Lynn. *"Or Does It Explode?": Black Harlem in the Great Depression.* Oxford: Oxford University Press, 1997.

Grossman, James R. *Land of Hope: Chicago, Black Southerners, and the Great Migration.* Chicago: University of Chicago Press, 1989.

Harris, William H. *The Harder We Run: Black Workers since the Civil War.* Oxford: Oxford University Press, 1982.

Honey, Michael K. *Black Workers Remember: An Oral History of Segregation, Unionism, and the Freedom Struggle.* Berkeley: University of California Press, 2001.

———. *Sharecropper's Troubadour: John L. Handcox, the Southern Tenant Farmers' Union, and the African American Song Tradition.* New York: Palgrave Macmillan, 2013.

Kelley, Robin D. G. *Hammer and Hoe: Alabama Communists during the Great Depression.* Chapel Hill: University of North Carolina Press, 2006.

King, Shannon. *Who's Harlem Is This, Anyway?: Community Politics and Grassroots Activism during the New Negro Era.* New York: New York University Press, 2015.

Letwin, Daniel. *The Challenge of Interracial Unionism: Alabama Coal Miners, 1878–1921.* Chapel Hill: University of North Carolina Press, 1998.

Moreno, Paul D. *Black Americans and Organized Labor: A New History.* Baton Rouge: Louisiana State University Press, 2007.

Phillips, Kimberley L. *AlabamaNorth: African American Migrants, Community, and Working Class Activism in Cleveland, 1915–45.* Urbana: University of Illinois Press, 1999.

Sitkoff, Harvard. *A New Deal for Blacks: The Emergence of Civil Rights as a National Issue; The Depression Decade.* New York: Oxford University Press, 2009.

Skotnes, Andor. *A New Deal for All? Race and Class Struggles in Depression-Era Baltimore.* Durham, NC: Duke University Press, 2012.

Sullivan, Patricia. *Days of Hope: Race and Democracy in the New Deal Era.* Chapel Hill: University of North Carolina Press, 2014.

Trotter, Joe William, Jr. *Coal, Class, and Color: Blacks in Southern West Virginia, 1915–32.* Urbana: University of Illinois Press, 1990.

———. "From a Raw Deal to a New Deal." In *To Make Our World Anew,* edited by Robyn D. G. Kelley and Earl Lewis, 131–66. Oxford: Oxford University Press, 2000.

———. *Workers on Arrival: Black Labor in the Making of America.* Oakland: University of California Press, 2019.

Watts, Jill. *The Black Cabinet: The Untold Story of African Americans and Politics during the Age of Roosevelt.* New York: Grove Press, 2020.

Weiss, Nancy. *Farewell to the Party of Lincoln: Black Politics in the Age of FDR.* Princeton, NJ: Princeton University Press, 1983.

Woodruff, Nan. *American Congo: The African American Freedom Struggle in the Delta.* Cambridge, MA: Harvard University Press, 2009.

Zieger, Robert H. *For Jobs and Freedom: Race and Labor in America since 1865.* Lexington: University Press of Kentucky, 2007.

2

World War II

During the Second World War, how did African Americans conceptualize the relationship between fascism and colonization abroad and the fight against racism at home? What were the goals and strategies of the civil rights movement in the 1940s? In what ways did it build upon and divert from Black workers' struggles in the 1930s?

This chapter reveals aspects of the Black freedom struggle during World War II and the early Cold War era. The Second World War was a major turning point in the Black freedom struggle and was leveraged to spotlight racial discrimination and segregation and make claims to citizenship by African Americans. In fact, the civil rights activism of this period would directly influence local and national civil rights struggles in the 1950s and 1960s.

Recall, in the decade prior to the Second World War, African Americans were involved in civil rights unionism, a national movement that simultaneously pressed for workplace rights and civil rights. When the United States entered the war, after the bombing of Pearl Harbor, African American men were drafted and voluntarily enlisted in the war, while Black women joined the Women's Army Corps and other women's auxiliary groups. On the home front, Black men and women kicked off the second wave of the Great Migration, flocking to urban industrial centers in the Midwest, Northeast, and California as well as to Florida, all of which boasted opportunities in defense-industry employment.

Yet racial discrimination and segregation persisted, leaving many African Americans to ask, "Should I sacrifice to live 'half-American'?" This question spawned a new civil rights agenda and a new militancy that leveraged civil rights unionism, grassroots activism, and a keen understanding and manipulation of the federal government's need to maintain peaceful race relations in order to win the war. In other words, racial segregation and discrimination in the military, employment, and housing served only to highlight for African American the juxtaposition of fighting in a war against fascism when the promises of democracy rang hollow at home.

This realization prompted African Americans to challenge Jim Crow consistently and effectively during the war. In 1941, A. Philip Randolph and Bayard Rustin organized the March on Washington (MOW) movement, which ultimately pressured the United States to desegregate the armed forces and defense industries. The following year, the Double V campaign, an initiative of the *Pittsburgh Courier*, spotlighted the contradictions of the country's involvement in a war against fascism and the failures of American democracy as it concerned African Americans. The Double V campaign promoted victory against fascism abroad and victory against racism at home, especially regarding discrimination and racism in employment, housing, and the armed forces. True integration in the armed forces, however, would not come until President Harry S. Truman signed Executive Order 9981, which desegregated the armed forces during the Korean War.

Black organizations also grew and expanded, while unionization increased during the war. The National Association for the Advancement of Colored People, for example, increased from fifty thousand to more than four hundred thousand members from 1940 to 1945. In March 1942, African American and white student activists founded the Congress of Racial Equality in Chicago. CORE organized what some believe to be the first sit-in movement against racial segregation and discrimination in public accommodations in May 1942. Early the following year, in early 1943, Howard University students under the leadership of Pauli Murray sparked a citywide movement to protest Jim Crow in Washington, D.C., when they sat in at the Little Palace Cafeteria, not far from the university.

Not all confrontations with racism were nonviolent, however. During the war, dramatic population increases in urban centers, as a result of the Second Great Migration, worsened competition over employment and housing between Black and white Americans. This combined with the persistence of virulent racism incited violent race riots during wartime. In 1943 alone, urban upheavals erupted in Detroit, becoming one of the bloodiest race riots in the nation's history; Harlem; Los Angeles (better known as the Zoot Suit Riots); Mobile, Alabama; Columbia, Tennessee; and Beaumont, Texas.

DOCUMENT 2.1

A. Philip Randolph, "The Call to Negro America to March on Washington" (1941)

In 1941, labor leader and civil rights activist A. Philip Randolph called for a March on Washington to protest racial segregation and discrimination in defense-industry jobs, housing, and the armed forces. News of the march persuaded President Franklin D. Roosevelt to issue Executive Order 8802, which effectively ended racial discrimination in the employment of workers in defense industries. Even after this accomplishment, the movement—known as the March on Washington movement—continued its mission against racial discrimination and violence and remained a leading force in the civil rights battles of the 1940s. MOW would serve as a model for the 1963 March on Washington for Jobs and Freedom, where Dr. Martin Luther King Jr. delivered his famous speech "I Have a Dream" in Washington, D.C.

> We call upon you to fight for jobs in National Defense. We call upon you to struggle for the integration of Negroes in the armed forces. . . .
>
> We call upon you to demonstrate for the abolition of Jim-Crowism in all Government departments and defense employment.

This is an hour of crisis. It is a crisis of democracy. It is a crisis of minority groups. It is a crisis of Negro Americans. What is this crisis?

To American Negroes, it is the denial of jobs in Government defense projects. It is racial discrimination in Government departments. It is widespread Jim-Crowism in the armed forces of the Nation.

While billions of the taxpayers' money are being spent for war weapons, Negro workers are finally being turned away from the gates of factories, mines and mills— being flatly told, "NOTHING DOING." Some employers refuse to give Negroes jobs when they are without "union cards," and some unions refuse Negro workers union cards when they are "without jobs."

What shall we do?
What a dilemma!
What a runaround!
What a disgrace!
What a blow below the belt!

Though dark, doubtful and discouraging, all is not lost, all is not hopeless. Though battered and bruised, we are not beaten, broken, or bewildered.

Verily, the Negroes' deepest disappointments and direst defeats, their tragic trials and outrageous oppressions in these dreadful days of destruction and disaster to democracy and freedom, and the rights of minority peoples, and the dignity and independence of the human spirit, is the Negroes' greatest opportunity to rise to the highest heights of struggle for freedom and justice in Government, in industry, in labor unions, education, social service, religion, and culture.

With faith and confidence of the Negro people in their own power for self-liberation, Negroes can break down that barriers of discrimination against employment in National Defense. Negroes can kill the deadly serpent of race hatred in the Army, Navy, Air and Marine Corps, and smash through and blast the Government, business and labor-union red tape to win the right to equal opportunity in vocational training and re-training in defense employment.

Most important and vital of all, Negroes, by the mobilization and coordination of their mass power, can cause PRESIDENT ROOSEVELT TO ISSUE AN EXECUTIVE ORDER ABOLISHING DISCRIMINATIONS IN ALL GOVERNMENT DEPARTMENT, ARMY, NAVY, AIR CORPS AND NATIONAL DEFENSE JOBS.

Of course, the task is not easy. In very truth, it is big, tremendous and difficult.

It will cost money.
It will require sacrifice.
It will tax the Negroes' courage, determination and will to struggle. But we can, must and will triumph.

The Negroes' stake in national defense is big. It consists of jobs, thousands of jobs. It may represent millions, yes hundreds of millions of dollars in wages. It consists of new industrial opportunities and hope. This is worth fighting for.

But to win our stakes, it will require an "all-out," bold and total effort and demonstration of colossal proportions.

Negroes can build a mammoth machine of mass action with a terrific and tremendous driving and striking power that can shatter and crush the evil fortress of race prejudice and hate, if they will only resolve to do so and never stop, until victory comes.

Dear fellow Negro Americans, be not dismayed by these terrible times. You possess power, great power. Our problem is to harness and hitch it up for action on the broadest, daring and most gigantic scale.

In this period of power politics, nothing counts but pressure, more pressure, and still more pressure, through the tactic and strategy of broad, organized, aggressive mass action behind the vital and important issues of the Negro. To this end, we propose that ten thousand Negroes MARCH ON WASHINGTON FOR JOBS IN NATIONAL DEFENSE AND EQUAL INTEGRATION IN THE FIGHTING FORCES OF THE UNITED STATES.

An "all-out" thundering march on Washington, ending in a monster and huge demonstration at Lincoln's Monument will shake up white America.

It will shake up official Washington.

It will give encouragement to our white friends to fight all the harder by our side, with us, for our righteous cause.

It will gain respect for the Negro people.

It will create a new sense of self-respect among Negroes.

But what of national unity?

We believe in national unity which recognizes equal opportunity of black and white citizens to jobs in national defense and the armed forces, and in all other institutions and endeavors in America. We condemn all dictatorships, Fascist, Nazi and Communist. We are loyal, patriotic Americans all.

But if American democracy will not defend its defenders; if American democracy will not protect its protectors; if American democracy will not give jobs to its toilers because of race or color; if American democracy will not insure equality of opportunity, freedom and justice to its citizens, black and white, it is a hollow mockery and belies the principles for which it is supposed to stand. . . .

Today we call on President Roosevelt, a great humanitarian and idealist, to . . . free American Negro citizens of the stigma, humiliation and insult of discrimination and Jim-Crowism in Government departments and national defense.

The Federal Government cannot with clear conscience call upon private industry and labor unions to abolish discrimination based on race and color as long as it practices discrimination itself against Negro Americans.

Source: A. Philip Randolph, "Call to Negro America to March on Washington for Jobs and Equal Participation in National Defense," *Black Worker* 14 (May 1941).

DOCUMENT 2.2

"Executive Order 8802: Prohibition of Discrimination in the Defense Industry" (1941)

The threat of the March on Washington in 1941 prompted President Franklin D. Roosevelt to issue Executive Order 8802 to appease labor and civil rights leader A. Philip Randolph and the March on Washington movement. Roosevelt rightly reasoned that any racial unrest would undermine and hinder America's fight against fascism abroad. Executive Order 8802 banned discriminatory employment practices in defense industries and established the Fair Employment Practices Committee. The FEPC was tasked with educating industries and investigating complaints of discrimination. As a result, "African Americans in federal jobs reportedly increased from 60,000 in 1941 to 200,000 in 1945," although workers of color continued to encounter racial segregation and discrimination in the workplace.[1]

REAFFIRMING POLICY OF FULL PARTICIPATION
IN THE DEFENSE PROGRAM BY ALL PERSONS, REGARDLESS
OF RACE, CREED, COLOR, OR NATIONAL ORIGIN, AND
DIRECTING CERTAIN ACTION IN FURTHERANCE OF
SAID POLICY

June 25, 1941

WHEREAS it is the policy of the United States to encourage full participation in the national defense program by all citizens of the United States, regardless of race, creed, color, or national origin, in the firm belief that the democratic way of life within the Nation can be defended successfully only with the help and support of all groups within its borders; and

WHEREAS there is evidence that available and needed workers have been barred from employment in industries engaged in defense production solely because of considerations of race, creed, color, or national origin, to the detriment of workers' morale and of national unity:

NOW, THEREFORE, by virtue of the authority vested in me by the Constitution and the statutes, and as a prerequisite to the successful conduct of our national defense production effort, I do hereby reaffirm the policy of the United States that there shall be no discrimination in the employment of workers in defense industries or government because of race, creed, color, or national origin, and I do hereby declare that it is the duty of employers and of labor organizations, in furtherance of said policy and of this order, to provide for the full and equitable participation of all workers in defense industries, without discrimination because of race, creed, color, or national origin;

And it is hereby ordered as follows:

1. All departments and agencies of the Government of the United States concerned with vocational and training programs for defense production shall take special measures appropriate to assure that such programs are administered without discrimination because of race, creed, color, or national origin;

2. All contracting agencies of the Government of the United States shall include in all defense contracts hereafter negotiated by them a provision obligating the contractor not to discriminate against any worker because of race, creed, color, or national origin;

3. There is established in the Office of Production Management a Committee on Fair Employment Practice, which shall consist of a chairman and four other members to be appointed by the President. The chairman and members of the Committee shall serve as such without compensation but shall be entitled to actual and necessary transportation, subsistence and other expenses incidental to performance of their duties. The Committee shall receive and investigate complaints of discrimination in violation of the provisions of this order and shall take appropriate steps to redress grievances which it finds to be valid. The Committee shall also recommend to the several departments and agencies of the Government of the United States and to the President all measures which may be deemed by it necessary or proper to effectuate the provisions of this order.

Franklin D. Roosevelt

THE WHITE HOUSE,
JUNE 25, 1941.

Source: Franklin D. Roosevelt, "Executive Order 8802 Dated June 25, 1941, Prohibiting Discrimination in the Defense Program," 1941, *Executive Orders, 1862–2011*, General Records of the United States Government, Record Group 11, National Archives and Records Administration.

NOTES

1. A. Philip Randolph, "Call to Negro America to March on Washington for Jobs and Equal Participation in National Defense," *Black Worker* 14 (May 1941).

James G. Thompson, "Should I Sacrifice to Live 'Half-American?' Suggest Double VV for Double Victory against Axis Forces and Ugly Prejudices on the Home Front" (1942)

James G. Thompson, a reader of the *Pittsburgh Courier*, one of the largest African American newspapers in the country, inspired the Double V campaign in 1942. Thompson was a twenty-six-year-old defense worker in Wichita, Kansas. Like many African Americans during the Second World War, Thompson was hired to work in an aircraft manufacturing company, not on the factory floor as white workers did; instead, he was relegated to the factory cafeteria. In his letter to the *Pittsburgh Courier*, Thompson recognizes the sacrifices of millions of African Americans in World War II who were still being treated as second-class citizens. He thus speaks to the contradictions of American democracy and the nation's participation in the battle to end fascism abroad. At the end of his letter, Thompson calls for a Double V campaign, with the first *V* standing for victory against enemies abroad and the second *V* representing victory against enemies at home.

> (*EDITOR'S NOTE: A YOUNG MAN, CONFUSED AND BEFUDDLED BY ALL OF THIS DOUBLE TALK ABOUT DEMOCRACY AND THE DEFENSE OF OUR WAY OF LIFE, IS ASKING, LIKE OTHER YOUNG NEGROES, SOME VERY PERTINENT QUESTIONS. WE REPRINT THIS LETTER IN FULL BECAUSE IT IS SYMBOLIC.*)

DEAR EDITOR:

Like all true Americans, my greatest desire at this time, this crucial point of our history; is a desire for a complete victory over the forces of evil, which threaten our existence today. Behind that desire is also a desire to serve, this, my country, in the most advantageous way.

Most of our leaders are suggesting that we sacrifice every other ambition to the paramount one, victory. With this I agree; but I also wonder if another victory could not be achieved at the same time. After all the things that beset the world now are basically the same things which upset the equilibrium of nations internally, states, counties, cities, homes and even the individual.

Being an American of dark complexion and some 26 years, these questions flash through my mind: "Should I sacrifice my life to live half American?" "Will things be better for the next generation in the peace to follow?" "Would it be demanding too much to demand full citizenship rights in exchange for the sacrificing of my life? Is the kind of America I know worth defending? Will America be a true and pure democracy after this war? Will Colored Americans suffer still the indignities that have been heaped upon them in the past? These and other questions need answering; I want to know, and I believe every colored American, who is thinking, wants to know.

This may be the wrong time to broach such subjects, but haven't all good things obtained by men been secured through sacrifice during just such times of strife.

I suggest that while we keep defense and victory in the forefront that we don't lose sight of our fight for true democracy at home.

The V for victory sign is being displayed prominently in all so-called democratic countries which are fighting for victory over aggression, slavery and tyranny. If this V sign means that to those now engaged in this great conflict then let we colored Americans adopt the double VV for a double victory. The first V for victory over our enemies from without, the second V for victory over our enemies from within. For surely those who perpetrate these ugly prejudices here are seeking to destroy our democratic form of government just as surely as the Axis forces.

This should not and would not lessen our efforts to bring this conflict to a successful conclusion; but should and would make us stronger to resist these evil forces which threaten us. America could become united as never before and become truly the home of democracy.

In way of an answer to the foregoing questions in a preceding paragraph I might say that there is no doubt that this country is worth defending; things will be different for the next generation; colored Americans will come into their own, and America will eventually become the true democracy it was designed to be. These things will become a reality in time; but not through any relaxation of the efforts to secure them.

In conclusion let me say that though these questions often permeate my mind, I love America and am willing to die for the America I know will someday become a reality.

JAMES G. THOMPSON

Source: James G. Thompson, "Should I Sacrifice to Live 'Half American?,'" letter to the editor, *Pittsburgh Courier*, January 31, 1942. Courtesy of Pittsburgh Courier Archives.

Double V Campaign Emblem (ca. 1942)

Proposed by *Pittsburgh Courier* reader James G. Thompson, the Double V campaign was a slogan that advocated for victory abroad against fascism and victory at home against Jim Crow. The *Pittsburgh Courier* published the Double V insignia on its front page on February 7, 1942, announcing "Democracy at Home-Abroad." African Americans immediately and overwhelmingly embraced the call—so much so that several Black soldiers were said to have carved the emblem into their chests.

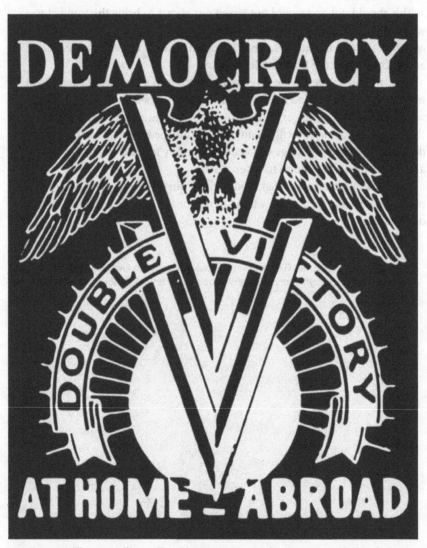

Source: Wilbert L. Holloway, "Double V Campaign," 1942, illustration, *Pittsburgh Courier.*
Courtesy of Pittsburgh Courier Archives.

DOCUMENT 2.5

Pauli Murray, "Jim Crow in the Nation's Capital" (1987)

In April 1943, Howard University law student Pauli Murray led a sit-in protest against Jim Crow at the Little Palace Cafeteria, a Greek-owned restaurant, in Washington, D.C. The Little Palace Cafeteria was one of the handful of "Whites-Only" eateries in the mostly Black community surrounding Howard University. To complement the sit-in, students picketed with signs that read "Our Boys, our Bonds, our Brothers are Fighting for You! Why Can't We Eat Here?" "We Die Together—Why Can't We Eat Together?" and "There's No Segregation Law in D.C. What's Your Story Little Palace?" Within forty-hours, restaurant owners capitulated to protesters' demands and began serving Black customers.[1] It is notable that this sit-in occurred more than fifteen years prior to the Greensboro sit-in in February 1960, which historians have credited for instigating the 1960s student sit-in movement.

. . . Washington was seen by many as the symbolic capital of the nations allied against the Axis, and its advocacy of war aims such as the Four Freedoms made it the logical place for Negro activists to press their claims for equality. At the same time, the city epitomized the great gap between official United States war propaganda and racial practices within our own borders. Segregation in the nation's capital was an especially galling indignity. Aside from some government cafeterias and the YWCA cafeteria at Seventeenth and K streets, N.W., Union Station was the only place in downtown Washington where a Negro could get a meal or use rest room facilities. Although the city had no segregation ordinance requiring separation of the races, Negroes were systematically barred from hotels, restaurants, theaters, movie houses, and other places of public accommodation. Ironically, streetcars and buses were not segregated.

In contrast to this rigid pattern of separation, the faculty of Howard University was integrated, and its graduate and professional schools had a sprinkling of white students. . . . The concentration and accessibility of . . . scholars on a small campus was both intellectually stimulating and a powerful affirmation of human dignity and equality, which communicated itself to the student body.

In 1942 some two thousand students from forty-five states and twenty-four foreign countries were enrolled at the university, young people who for the most part came from middle-class Negro homes and achieving families. Over half were from northern and border states or midwestern and western communities, and many had never before been exposed to segregation in public facilities. Unaccustomed to southern patterns of racial etiquette, these students were unprepared for the insults and humiliations that descended upon them when they left campus and went downtown to see a movie or stopped at a soda fountain while shopping. Conscious of wartime appeals for sacrifice on behalf of freedom, they were unwilling to accept Jim Crow as an unalterable way of life.

The tensions produced by segregation in Washington were aggravated by steadily mounting evidence of the ill treatment Negroes were receiving in the armed forces. . . .

Ideas about the use of nonviolent resistance to racial injustice, modeled on Gandhi's movement in India, were in the air. A. Philip Randolph announced publicly in late December 1942 that the March on Washington Movement was considering a campaign of civil disobedience and non-cooperation. . . .

The spark that ignited campus civil rights activity was the arrest in January 1943 of three sophomore women who had been overcharged for hot chocolate in a United Cigar store on Pennsylvania Avenue. Ruth Powell from Massachusetts and Marianne Musgrave and Juanita Morrow from Ohio had sat down at the counter and ordered the hot drinks. When they were refused, they asked for the manager and were told he was out. They said they would wait for him, still maintaining their seats at the counter. Two policemen were summoned, who, after questioning the students, told the waitress to serve them. When she brought their checks they discovered they had been charged twenty-five cents for each cup of chocolate instead of the usual ten cents. The young women placed thirty-five cents on the counter and started to leave, whereupon they were arrested, held until the arrival of a police wagon, carted off to jail, searched, and thrown into a cell with prostitutes and other criminal suspects. "The policeman who arrested us," Ruth reported later, "told us we were being taken in for investigation because he had no proof that we weren't '*subversive agents*'!"

After several hours Dean Elliott was notified and the young women were discharged in her custody. No charge was lodged against them, the purpose of their arrest having been intimidation, but the incident unleashed a torrent of resentment within the student body.

. . . [A] Civil Rights Committee was formed under the sponsorship of the Howard Chapter of the NAACP to bring about equal accommodations in the city of Washington. A survey of local laws unearthed a civil rights bill for the District of Columbia (H.R. 1995) recently introduced into the House of Representatives by Congressman William A. Rowan from Illinois, and a companion bill (S. 442) introduced into the Senate by Senator Warren Barbour from New Jersey. One of our activities was to educate the campus community on the existence of this pending legislation so that students could lobby their home-state representatives through visits and letters urging support of the bills.

The major excitement, however, centered on the work of the Direct Action subcommittee, chaired by Ruth Powell. Its purpose was "to enroll students who will participate in small carefully planned demonstrations for equal rights in the District of Columbia." . . . [A] group of students surveyed public eating places in the neighboring, mostly Negro community on Northwest U Street that still catered to the "White Trade Only." One of the most notorious of these lily-white establishments was the Little Palace Cafeteria, located at the busy intersection of Fourteenth and U streets, N.W., and run by a Mr. Chaconas. Because of its strategic location, the Little Palace had long been a source of mortification for countless unsuspecting Negroes, who entered it assuming that at least they would be served in the heart of the Negro section of the city.

The Little Palace Cafeteria was selected as our first target. For a week prior to our move against the cafeteria we held campus pep rallies and drummed up support for our effort through noon-hour broadcasts from the tower of Founder's Library. We decorated hot-chocolate cups and used them around campus as collection cans to solicit the funds we needed for paper, postage, and picket signs. We held a midweek Town Hall meeting and brought in experienced political leaders—Thomasina Johnson, legislative representative of Alpha Kappa Alpha Sorority, and Albert B. Herman, political aide to Senator Barbour—to lead a forum on civil rights legislation and methods of achieving it. We conducted classes on the legal aspects of picketing and disorderly conduct in the District of Columbia, spent hours in small groups discussing public decorum, anticipating and preparing for the reactions of the black public, the white public, white customers, and white management respectively. We stressed the importance of a dignified appearance, and the subcommittee directed that all participants dress well for the occasion. We also pledged ourselves to exemplary nonviolent conduct, however great the provocation.

Finally, on April 17, a rainy Saturday afternoon, we assembled on campus and began to leave the Howard University grounds in groups of four, about five minutes apart, to make the ten-minute walk to the Little Palace Cafeteria. The demonstration was limited to a carefully selected group of volunteers—less than twenty students—who felt confident they could maintain self-restraint under pressure. As each group arrived, three entered the cafeteria while the fourth remained outside as an "observer." Inside, we took our trays to the steam table and as soon as we were refused service carried our empty trays to a vacant seat at one of the tables, took out magazines, books of poetry or textbooks, notebooks and pencils, and assumed an attitude of concentrated study. Strict silence was maintained. Minutes later the next group arrived and repeated the process. Outside, the observers began to form a picket line with colorful signs reading "Our Boys, our Bonds, our Brothers are Fighting for you! Why Can't We Eat Here?"; "We Die Together—Why Can't We Eat Together?"; "There's No Segregation Law in D.C. What's Your Story, Little Palace?" Two pickets carried posters (prepared for the War Manpower Commission by the Office of War Information) depicting two workers—one black and the other white—working together as riveters on a steel plate. The inscription on the poster read "UNITED WE WIN!"

My heart thumped furiously as I sat at a table awaiting developments. The management was stunned at first, then after trying unsuccessfully to persuade us to leave, called the police. Almost immediately a half-dozen uniformed officers appeared. When they approached us we said simply, "We're waiting for service," and since we did not appear to be violating any law, they made no move to arrest us.

After forty-five minutes had passed and twelve Negro students were occupying most of the tables of the small cafeteria, Chaconas gave up and closed his restaurant eight hours earlier than his normal closing time. Those of us who were inside joined the picket line and kept it going for the rest of the afternoon. Chaconas told reporter Harry McAlpin, who covered the demonstration for the *Chicago Defender*: "I'll lose money, but I'd rather close up than practice democracy this way. The time is not ripe." When Juanita Morrow, a journalism student, interviewed Chaconas several days later, he admitted that he had lost about $180 that Saturday afternoon and evening, a considerable sum for a small business.

Actually, the incident did not arouse the furor we had feared but revealed the possibilities for change. When told why the place was closed and being picketed, a white customer named Raymond Starnes, who came from Charlotte, North Carolina, said, "I eat here regularly, and I don't care who eats here. All I want is to eat. I want the place to stay open. After all, we are all human." Another white bystander, asked what he thought of the students' action, replied, "I think it's reasonable. Negroes are fighting to win this war for democracy just like whites. If it came to a vote, it would get my vote."

When Chaconas opened his place on Monday morning, our picket line was there to greet him, and it continued all day. Within forty-eight hours he capitulated and began to serve Negro customers. We were jubilant. Our conquest of a small "greasy spoon" eating place was a relatively minor skirmish in the long battle to end segregation in the nation's capital—a battle that was ended by a Supreme Court decision ten years later—but it loomed large in our eyes. We had proved that intelligent, imaginative action could bring positive results and, fortunately, we had won our first victory without an embarrassing incident. (One other small restaurant in the area was desegregated that spring before final examinations and summer vacation interrupted our campaign.)

Significantly, the prominent role of women in the leadership and planning of our protest was a by-product of the wartime thinning of the ranks of male students. Twelve of the nineteen Howard University demonstrators at the Little Palace on April 17 were female. (The twentieth demonstrator was Natalie Moorman . . . from Arlington, Virginia. . . . Armed with an umbrella and a commanding voice, she regularly rode the bus from the District to its Arlington suburb and challenged bus drivers to try to enforce segregation under Virginia law. . . .)

Source: Pauli Murray, *Song in a Weary Throat: Memoir of an American Pilgrimage* (New York: W. W. Norton, 1987), 258–62, 266–70. Copyright © 1987 by the Pauli Murray Foundation. Introduction copyright © 2018 by Patricia Bell-Scott. Used by permission of Liveright Publishing Corporation.

NOTES

1. Rosalind Rosenberg, *Jane Crow: The Life of Pauli Murray* (Oxford: Oxford University Press, 2017), 127.

Billboard Protesting Black Occupancy of the Sojourner Truth Homes (1942)

This document illustrates the resistance that African Americans faced in Detroit when attempting to integrate the Sojourner Truth Homes in Detroit. Conflict between Blacks and white over segregation in housing and employment led to the 1943 Detroit race riot. The Detroit riot, one of three that occurred during the summer of 1943, resulted from intense competition over jobs and housing. It lasted three days during which thirty-four people were killed, more than four hundred people were injured, and an estimated eighteen hundred were arrested.

Source: Arthur S. Siegel, *Detroit, Michigan. Riot at the Sojourner Truth Homes, a New U.S. Federal Housing Project, Caused by White Neighbors' Attempt to Prevent Negro Tenants from Moving In. Sign with American Flag "We want white tenants in our white community," Directly Opposite the Housing Project*, 1942, photograph, Farm Security Administration/Office of War Information Black-and-White Negatives, Prints & Photographs Division, Library of Congress, https://www.loc.gov/item/2017844754/.

DOCUMENT 2.7

Ruth Miller, El Segundo Plant of the Douglas Aircraft Company (ca. 1939–1944)

Ruth Miller works on an aircraft at the El Segundo Plant of the Douglas Aircraft Company in Los Angeles, California, in this photograph. Miller was one of many African American women who secured employment in wartime defense industries by the end of the Second World War. Some women of color left the Jim Crow South and migrated to northern and western states such as California, where employment in shipyards and factories freed them from oppressive and often dangerous domestic service jobs. African American women like Miller, however, were the last group to be hired and routinely paid less than white men, white women, and African American men.

Source: *Ruth Miller, El Segundo Plant of the Douglas Aircraft Company*, ca. 1939–44, photograph, Schomburg Center for Research in Black Culture, Photographs and Prints Division, New York Public Library, https://digitalcollections.nypl.org/items/510d47dd-c6a0-a3d9-e040-e00a18064a99.

Brigadier General Benjamin O. Davis Watches a Signal Corps Crew Erecting Poles (1944)

Brigadier General Benjamin O. Davis, the first African American to rise to this rank in the regular army and in the U.S. armed forces, is featured in this photograph. In it, he watches a signal corps crew erect poles in France in August 1944. Brigadier General Davis entered the military in July 1898 during the Spanish-American War. He also served as a professor of military science and tactics at Wilberforce University in Ohio and Tuskegee Institute in Alabama and was assigned to the National Guard before entering the Second World War, where he was influential in advancing integration in the armed forces. During his military career, he was awarded the Bronze Star Medal and the Distinguished Service Medal. His son, Benjamin O. Davis Jr., trained as a Tuskegee Airmen during World War II and would also have a decorated military career.

Source: *Brigadier General Benjamin O. Davis Watches a Signal Corps Crew Erecting Poles, Somewhere in France,* August 8, 1944, photograph, National Archives and Records Administration, https://www.archives.gov/files/research /african-americans/ww2-pictures/images/african-americans-wwii-217.jpg.

DOCUMENT 2.9

Lieutenant Colonel Harold Brown on Being a Tuskegee Airman (2010)

The following is an excerpt from an oral history of Lieutenant Colonel Harold Brown, a Tuskegee Airmen who was captured as a prisoner of war and rescued by the advancing U.S. Army a couple months later. Lieutenant Colonel Brown was one of nearly one thousand African Americans trained at Tuskegee Institute between 1941 and 1946, commissioned as an officer in the U.S. Army Air Corps in 1944, and a celebrated Red Tail, a Tuskegee Airman who flew a P-51 Mustang fighter plane emblazoned with bright-red tails. The Tuskegee Airmen were the first Black military aviators (of the 332nd Expeditionary Operations Group) in the U.S. armed forces and thus became the most famous group of African American men to serve in World War II. These airmen received three distinguished unit citations for action over Sicily in May and June 1943; successful air strikes against Monte Cassino, Italy, in May 1944; and a bomber escort mission that shot down three enemy jets in March 1945. Several airmen were awarded Silver and Bronze Stars, Purple Hearts, Air Medals, and other commendations.

REBECCA WIGGENHORN: . . . First question, were you drafted or did you enlist?

HAROLD BROWN: No. I enlisted.

REBECCA WIGGENHORN: Okay. Where were you living at the time that you enlisted?

HAROLD BROWN: Minneapolis, Minnesota.

REBECCA WIGGENHORN: Okay. And why did you do that? Why did you join?

HAROLD BROWN: I wanted to become a military fighter pilot.

REBECCA WIGGENHORN: Okay. Why did you pick the service branch you joined?

HAROLD BROWN: Well, at that time, the Air Force—it wasn't the Air Force then, it was the Army Air Corps—those were the only people training military fighter pilots.

REBECCA WIGGENHORN: Okay. Do—do you recall your very first days in service?

HAROLD BROWN: Well, after taking all the exams and so forth to qualify for flight training, I had about a three- or a four-month wait to find out if I had been selected; and they notified me in December of 1944 that I had been selected and advised me to immediately enlist, and they would send all of the appropriate paperwork that would cause me to go down to Tuskegee.

REBECCA WIGGENHORN: Uh-huh.

HAROLD BROWN: . . . Well, going from the good state of Minnesota down to the deep south of Biloxi, Mississippi, in 1944—it was the first time that I had been South in my life—it was a rude awakening, and you can imagine what was going on down there with segregation being not only by tradition but by law, but that was right down into the bowels of the South, so it was interesting, to say the least.

REBECCA WIGGENHORN: Tell me about that experience. What did you experience in boot camp and during your training there?

HAROLD BROWN: Well, I was only there for just six weeks, and there were about 600 of us that was sent there, and they had just started doing that. Prior to that, they were going straight to Tuskegee for flight training, but they changed things around. . . . [W]e were on one side of the field, completely segregated from everyone else on the field, and they just took us through, oh, some regular boot training, and then they retested all of us again, and then it was a result of the retesting that would determine whether or not you would go up to Tuskegee for flight training. And I was in the group of about a couple hundred of us that passed the second retesting; and after another few weeks, we were sent from Biloxi up to Tuskegee Institute up in Tuskegee, Alabama.

. . .

REBECCA WIGGENHORN: Uh-huh.

HAROLD BROWN: And they put us through a rather rigorous curriculum, and the length of time you stayed in the curriculum was dependent upon the score that you made in the testing, . . . and we had the regular instructors and whatnot right there at the institute who were teaching all of the classes and things, and we were just going there taking college training. And it was a designated curriculum that they had established for us only because we did not have any college education, at least most of us didn't. You see, prior to this time, you had to have four years of college to even think about going into military flight training. Then they reduced it to two years, and they still weren't getting enough people, so they reduced it to high school, assuming that you could pass the intelligence test and pass the physical test. So I was in that category, and I was fresh out of high school, 17 years old, when I applied for this. So for us young guys coming in, without college experience, then they sent us through a college training detachment, and we got four, five, six months of college training. I got the few days past the four months of college training at Tuskegee, and then they sent me out to the Air Force base, which is about eight miles north of Tuskegee.

. . .

HAROLD BROWN: . . . [I]t was May 23rd of 1944 when we graduated. From there, we went into a fighter training down in Walterboro, South Carolina, for approximately 60 to 70 days. We were flying the P-47 at that time. And then after we finished fighter training, then they shipped us overseas. . . . I arrived . . . [at my base in Foggia, Italy] in September of 1944.

HAROLD BROWN: Do you remember arriving there and can you tell me what it was like when you got there, how you felt?

HAROLD BROWN: Well, it was new. It was foreign to us. Our first trip overseas. At the time, I was 19 years old. . . . So it was all just a great big experience, exciting, looking forward to what we were going to do, with a certain amount of apprehension, of course—we would be flying combat, escorting the heavy bombers from Italy up into Germany. . . .

REBECCA WIGGENHORN: Was—was—how many of you were there at that point, approximately?

HAROLD BROWN: Well, they trained the total of a thousand people down—pilots down in Tuskegee; and from July 1941 to July 1946, a thousand pilots were trained. Out of that thousand pilots, 450 of us were selected as fighter pilots to go overseas, and we fought the war over in the European theatre. The other pilots stayed in the States and became bomber pilots, and they were just getting ready to be shipped to the Far East when the war ended, so the other 550 pilots didn't get the opportunity to go overseas to fight the war. It ended before they got there. . . .

REBECCA WIGGENHORN: So you saw quite a bit of combat during that time?

HAROLD BROWN: Well, I flew 30 missions, and I was shot down twice. And on my 30th mission, I became a POW at that time. . . . My 30th mission, we were on a strafing mission up close to Linz, Austria, and that's the one that I got shot down on—

REBECCA WIGGENHORN: Okay.

HAROLD BROWN:—and bailed out of the aircraft and was picked up about 30 minutes later, walked back to the last little village that we had strafed, and that was rather interesting because they always told you to get as far away from the target as possible, primarily because there's a lot of angry people down there when you are shooting up the town. . . . [T]hey picked me up, a couple of constables, and walked me back to the village, and we were met by a mob of some 30, 35 people, very, very angry people. . . . [T]hey got ready to hang me, and a constable came up behind me and held the people at bay and put me behind them, and we walked about a block or so back up into the village to a little pub with them following, hollering and screaming. We barricaded ourselves in there, and they finally dispersed, and around midnight or so we left. We left the little pub out the back door and walked several kilometers down to another little village; and then from there, to another little village where they called someone in the military and, oh, two or three hours later a couple of soldiers came up and picked me up; and then they took me to another little village where they put me in a small cell where I stayed for about three or four days.

REBECCA WIGGENHORN: What was that experience like for you? Were you—were you scared?

HAROLD BROWN: I was scared as hell. . . . You don't know what's going to happen. You don't know the language. Every time, you know, they would walk up to the cell, I'm wondering, well, what are they—what are they going to do to me now, you know? . . . [F]rom that point on, it took us about eight, nine days of traveling on all the various modes of transportation, buses, trains, trucks, and everything, because they were taking us from that little village all the way up to Nuremberg to where the big interrogation center was, and it took us just about eight days to get there. . . .

REBECCA WIGGENHORN: What was that—what was that interrogation like?

HAROLD BROWN: Well, it was interesting, to say the least. The first time I went in, my interrogator was a major in the German Army. He spoke perfect English, and he had gone to school over in—over in England, and so he asked me a series of questions, and, of course, we were always trained, no, nope, you don't answer. All you do is just give them your name, rank, and serial number, and that was what I was doing. . . . [H]e brought me back in the next day, and—and he looked at me, and he says, well, Harold, he says, I don't believe there's anything you can tell me that I don't know. And I thought, well, that was strange, so he took me into another room, and there he had four great big blue notebooks. On one notebook it was 332, which was our fighter group, the 332nd Fighter Group. Then he had the 99th Fighter Squadron, the 100th Fighter Squadron on another big notebook, the 301st and 302nd, all of our squadrons. So he says you were in the 99th Fighter Squadron, weren't you? And I wondered, well, how in the world did he know that? And he says, the reason why I know is because the airplane that you crashed is—the numbers on that aircraft was A32, and we know that it's only the 99th that has the A in front of their numbers—which was the case. So, you know, again, name, rank, serial number, and I just kind of looked at him and, you know, smiled. He says, yeah, yeah, I know. So we went through a series of things like this, and then he said, well, I am sending you back to the camp. I'm through with you. . . . [H]e says, when you get in—in prison camp, you know, don't try to escape but don't give the guards any reason to shoot you. He says, the war isn't going to go on much longer, and he says, there isn't any doubt that it's just a matter of time before the Germans' Army is going to have to surrender, and he wished me luck. . . . [A]t that point they then sent me about 10 miles down to the big POW camp, and this was—Stalag Luft VII A was the prison camp up in Nuremberg, and there is where I was interred.

REBECCA WIGGENHORN: How long were you there then?

HAROLD BROWN: Well, we were only there for approximately a little over two weeks. . . . They had the whole prison divided up into sections, and they had about 200 men in each one of these little, you know, sections, and there was a total of 10,000 of us there in Nuremberg, so I spent the rest of the time with [George Iles], which was nice, you know, seeing my—seeing a good friendly face, and someone who was, you know, a dear friend, but we spent the rest of the time together in the POW. But after we had been there for about two weeks, the Americans, who were getting close—so they said they had to evacuate us—so they evacuated all 10,000 of us, and we had to walk from Nuremberg down to Moosburg which was—it took us just about two weeks to walk that distance, and you can imagine a string of 10,000 men in groups of 200, you know. We were quite a mob, you know, walking. And in the evening they would just put us on some farm and—with a couple of guards around 2 or 300 of us, and the next morning, you know, we were off walking again, but that was not bad. . . .

REBECCA WIGGENHORN: Were you awarded any medals or citations for your time over there?

HAROLD BROWN: Oh, I received the Air Medal with two Oakleaf clusters, and then our group escorted—the 15th Air Force made one trip to Berlin. I think it was primarily to say that they had bombed Berlin. There was only one wing of B-17s we had, and it was the only heavy bomber that had the range to go to Berlin, and that was a 1,600-mile round-trip, and even the fighters had to have oversize wingtips with fuel in order to escort them up and back. It was the longest mission that the 15th Air Force flew, and our 332nd group was not originally assigned to fly that mission, but by this time we had created quite a reputation, and most of the bomber boys were actually asking for us. They were requesting us as their escort on their regular bombers 'cause B.O. Davis, who was our commander, he was a West Pointer, came out of West Point in 1936, wanted the Air Force but his father was a brigadier general at the time, and they denied him then, you know, because he's an Afro-American, he was denied that request. So when they opened up flying to us, then he was one [of] the first ones that they brought in, and being a West Pointer—as a matter of fact, the only West Pointer, he spent four years at West Point, and no one even spoke to him except in an official capacity. He lived by himself the entire four years while he was at West Point, but nevertheless he was our commander, and he was a colonel by this time, and he was very, very strict, and he made it very clear—I remember when I got there—he said you are here for one reason. Your mission is to protect the bombers; and if you ever leave these bombers unprotected, going off looking for personal victories or aerial victories, he said, don't come back because I'll court-martial you. So that was our job. As fighter pilots, you were to escort those bombers. Your job was to get them up there, drop the bombs over target, and get them back home safely. So the only time we ever engaged the enemy was when the enemy engaged us, and we just stuck with the bombers. Well, and that became our big reputation, because it wasn't happening that—that much with many of the other fighter groups. And we were all in just one fighter group, the Red Tails of 332nd Fighter Group, and—so we got quite a reputation. So there were times when they would—on a tough mission, they would say, hey, who's our escort? Well, the Red Tails. Hey, great. If it wasn't the Red Tails, they would request us. Sometimes they would, you know, reassign us. Sometimes they wouldn't, but they did on the trip to Berlin. They asked who was escorting, and there was a couple of other groups that was on the escort, but one of the third groups, they asked that they be replaced by us. So they reassigned one of the fighter groups and put us in their place, primarily because of the bomber pilots' request, so this is how we flew that mission. That was the big mission where we ran into something like—something like 40, 50 Me 262s, which were the new jet aircraft that the Germans had built, extremely fast. And, unfortunately, they didn't mass produce them, or it would have prolonged the war a little bit; but, nevertheless, we shot down several of them. We had several damages. We got the aircraft back, and for that mission they gave us a Presidential Unit Citation to the fighter group. So along with the Air Medal and two clusters, we also got the Presidential Unit Citation.

. . .

REBECCA WIGGENHORN: Wow. Let me ask you this: While you were in the service, did you make any close friends that you still stay in contact with?

HAROLD BROWN: In the military?

REBECCA WIGGENHORN: Yes.

HAROLD BROWN: Oh, we're all friends. Matter of fact, we have a—we have a big organization. It's a national organization that was formed in 1975, and the national organization was the Tuskegee Airmen, and we had the national, but then we had chapters, and we got chapters—we must have about 30-some chapters located throughout the United States. And every year we have the national meeting of—of the Tuskegee Airmen, and we either have it—we rotate. It's—in the west, we have the western sector, the central sector, and the eastern sector. This year, it's going to be in the central, down in San Antone starting in—I believe it's in August. . . .

. . . So this has been going on since 1975. Now, I don't attend every meeting. I used to attend a lot of them, but—but what they did is they—we were a dying organization, so they decided to have other people become members of the Tuskegee Airmen, people who were not originally there, and they have four categories of people. One, there is a category involving descendants of Tuskegee Airmen, and they can immediately become members. Then there's another one that will handle people who are in the Air Force presently, and they can join. And then there are two others, and I can't remember what the categories are. So now even though we may have some seven, eight hundred people all as members of the Tuskegee Airmen, there's only a small fraction of them that were all part of the original Tuskegee Airmen, because death has, you know, caught up with so many of them. So out of the thousand pilots, we're estimating that there probably isn't much, many more than a hundred at the maximum that are left, but for every pilot, there was a approximately 10 people on the ground supporting us. So there's probably was originally close to 10,000 ground personnel, and we figured that now those numbers are probably down to something less than 4—three to four hundred people. So out of the original almost 11, 12,000 people who was all a part of this effort, it's now down to nothing more but something less than a hundred pilots and something less than 300 ground support people. But we had everything. We had our own hospital, our own MPs, our own cooks, mechanics, radiomen, armament men. We were actually a self-contained Air Force during those early days when we were all segregated, and we had—everything was, you know, Afro-American. . . .

Source: Harold H. Brown (Tuskegee Airman), interview by Rebecca Wiggenhorn, May 15, 2010. Veterans History Project, Library of Congress, https://memory.loc.gov/diglib/vhp-stories/loc.natlib.afc2001001.76178/transcript.

DOCUMENT 2.10

Executive Order 9981 Desegregates Armed Forces (1948)

On July 26, 1948, President Harry S. Truman issued Executive Order 9981, a mandate that outlawed discrimination "on the basis of race, color, religion, or national origin" in the U.S. armed forces. The order not only mandated equal treatment and opportunity in the armed forces but also commanded all executive-level and federal government agencies to cooperate fully and established an oversight committee. Executive Order 9981 was the result of ongoing pressure from African Americans (indeed, activists threatened to boycott a draft law then under consideration) and "To Secure these Rights: The Report of the President's Committee on Civil Rights," an account that detailed civil rights abuses against African Americans and suggested ways to improve civil rights and liberties in the United States. As a result of the order, 95 percent of all African American soldiers were serving in integrated units in October 1953, and less than one year later, in September 1954, the last all-Black military units were disbanded. The armed forces thus became the first sector of American society to abandon segregation.

ESTABLISHING THE PRESIDENT'S COMMITTEE ON EQUALITY OF TREATMENT AND OPPORTUNITY IN THE ARMED FORCES

WHEREAS it is essential that there be maintained in the armed services of the United States the highest standards of democracy, with equality of treatment and opportunity for all those who serve in our country's defense:

NOW, THEREFORE, by virtue of the authority vested in me as President of the United States, by the Constitution and the statutes of the United States, and as Commander in Chief of the armed services, it is hereby ordered as follows:

1. It is hereby declared to be the policy of the President that there shall be equality of treatment and opportunity for all persons in the armed services without regard to race, color, religion or national origin. This policy shall be put into effect as rapidly as possible, having due regard to the time required to effectuate any necessary changes without impairing efficiency or morale.

2. There shall be created in the National Military Establishment an advisory committee to be known as the President's Committee on Equality of Treatment and Opportunity in the Armed Services, which shall be composed of seven members to be designated by the President.

3. The Committee is authorized on behalf of the President to examine into the rules, procedures and practices of the armed services in order to determine in what respect such rules, procedures and practices may be altered or improved with a view to carrying out the policy of this order. The Committee shall confer and advise with the Secretary of Defense, the Secretary of the Army, the Secretary of the Navy, and the Secretary of the Air Force, and shall make such recommendations to the President and to said Secretaries as in the judgment of the Committee will effectuate the policy hereof.

4. All executive departments and agencies of the Federal Government are authorized and directed to cooperate with the Committee in its work, and to furnish the Committee such information or the services of such persons as the Committee may require in the performance of its duties.

5. When requested by the Committee to do so, persons in the armed services or in any of the executive departments and agencies of the Federal Government shall testify before the Committee and shall make available for the use of the Committee such documents and other information as the Committee may require.

6. The Committee shall continue to exist until such time as the President shall terminate its existence by Executive order.

Harry Truman

THE WHITE HOUSE
JULY 26, 1948

Source: Harry Truman, "Executive Order 9981 of July 26, 1948: Desegregation of the Armed Forces," General Records of the United States Government, Record Group 11 (1948), National Archives and Records Administration, https://www.archives.gov/milestone-documents/executive-order-9981#transcript.

FURTHER READING

Adams Early, Charity. *One Woman's Army: A Black Officer Remembers the WAC*. College Station: Texas A&M University Press, 1995.

Bolzenius, Sandra M. *Glory in Their Spirit: How Four Black Women Took on the Army during World War II*. Urbana: University of Illinois Press, 2018.

Bynum, Cornelius L. *A. Philip Randolph and the Struggle for Civil Rights*. Urbana: University of Illinois Press, 2010.

Eschen, Penny von. *Race against Empire: Black Americans and Anticolonialism, 1937–1957*. Ithaca, NY: Cornell University Press, 1997.

Honey, Maureen. *Bitter Fruit: African American Women in World War II*. Columbia: University of Missouri Press, 1999.

Kelley, Robyn D. G. *Race Rebels: Culture, Politics, and the Black Working Class*. New York: Free Press, 1994.

Kersten, Andrew Edmund. *A. Philip Randolph: A Life in the Vanguard*. Lanham, MD: Rowman & Littlefield, 2007.

Kimble, Lionel, Jr. "I Too Serve America: African American Women Workers in Chicago, 1940–1945." *Journal of the Illinois State Historical Society* 93, no. 4 (2000–2001): 415–34.

Korstad, Robert, and Nelson Lichtenstein. "Opportunities Found and Lost: Labor, Radical and the Early Civil Rights Movement." *Journal of American History* 75, no. 3 (1998): 786–811.

Lucander, David. *Winning the War on Democracy: The March on Washington Movement, 1941–1946*. Urbana: University of Illinois Press, 2014.

Meier, August, and Elliot Rudwick. *Along the Color Line: Explorations in the Black Experience*. Urbana: University of Illinois Press, 1976.

Moye, J. Todd. *Freedom Flyers: The Tuskegee Airmen of World War II*. Oxford: Oxford University Press, 2012.

Mullenbach, Cheryl. *Double Victory: How African American Women Broke Race and Gender Barriers to Help Win World War II*. Chicago: Chicago Review Press, 2013.

Roberts, Gene, and Hank Klibanoff. *The Race Beat: The Press, the Civil Rights Struggle and the Awakening of a Nation*. New York: Alfred A. Knopf, 2007.

Rosenberg, Rosalind. *Jane Crow: The Life of Pauli Murray*. Oxford: Oxford University Press, 2017.

Shockley, Megan. *"We Too Are Americans": African American Women in Detroit and Richmond, 1940–54*. Urbana: University of Illinois Press, 2003.

Williams, Rachel. *Run Home if You Don't Want to Be Killed: The Detroit Uprising of 1943*. Chapel Hill: University of North Carolina Press, 2021.

3

Galvanizing the Movement in the 1950s

What was the watershed moment of the civil rights movement? Was it the Supreme Court's overturning of the "separate but equal" doctrine in *Brown v. Board of Education of Topeka, Kansas*; the murder of young Emmett Till; or the Montgomery Bus Boycott? In what ways did legal challenges to Jim Crow segregation dominate civil rights activism from the late 1940s through the 1950s? What gains emerged from these legal challenges, and what barriers to full citizenship remained?

The post–Second World War era witnessed three major changes that would influence the emergence, nature, and direction of the civil rights movement: first, anticommunist sentiment undermined and even overturned many of the gains made by workers in the 1930s; second, the United States experienced a reconversion and reconsolidation of racial discrimination (for example, lynching and violence against African Americans—especially those returning from war—became commonplace); and third, new attention was being paid to the United States, as the world was watching and questioning whether it was living up to its own ideals of democracy. Racial segregation and discrimination, the country's critics rightly argued, contradicted and undermined American democracy and frankly made the nation look hypocritical.

As a result, the movement to end racial segregation and discrimination received assistance —sometimes begrudgingly—from the federal government. Starting with President Harry S. Truman, the federal government began addressing domestic racism in a manner not seen since the Reconstruction era. Truman was willing to tackle racism because of pressure from civil rights activists, and he also believed that African American voters would be crucial to his reelection in 1948. The international gaze and the Cold War were also concerns for the Truman administration, as the legal challenges to Jim Crow could have a significant impact on perceptions of U.S. racial democracy abroad.

Equally important were the legal successes and the unprecedented number of people now engaged in the struggle to end Jim Crow. To many scholars, the *Brown* case was the legal turning point in the struggle for Black equality. The fate of Emmett Till and the

Montgomery Bus Boycott, then, were the psychological turning points in the movement in that hundreds of thousands of ordinary folks—Black and white, men and women, old and young—became willing to put their lives at risk for Black freedom.

The road to the *Brown* decision was paved with other cases brought before the Supreme Court by the NAACP Legal Defense and Educational Fund. In its first years of existence, the NAACP-LDEF won several landmark cases: *Smith v. Allwright* (1944) ruled white primaries unconstitutional, *Morgan v. Virginia* (1946) declared Virginia's state law enforcing segregation on interstate buses to be unconstitutional, and *Shelley v. Kraemer* (1948) outlawed restrictive covenants. In *Sipuel v. Board of Regents of the University of Oklahoma* (1948), *McLaurin v. Oklahoma State Regents for Higher Education* (1950), and *Sweatt v. Painter* (1950), the Court decided against segregation in higher education.

One year after the *McLaurin* and *Sweatt* decisions, African American parents filed suits against segregated school systems in Kansas, South Carolina, Virginia, Delaware, and the District of Columbia. They asked the courts to apply the qualitative test of the *Sweatt* case to elementary and secondary schools and to declare the "separate but equal" doctrine invalid in public education. These cases would eventually be consolidated into *Brown v. Board of Education of Topeka*.

The *Brown* case was led by NAACP attorneys Constance Motley and Thurgood Marshall. It received assistance from African American intellectuals and academics, including psychologists Kenneth and Mamie Clark who provided evidence from their infamous doll test. (The doll test was a psychological test that asked children to identify the race of four dolls and the dolls that they preferred. Their study found that the majority of the children preferred the white doll and characterized the white doll as "nice," while children labeled the Black doll as "bad." From this, the Clarks concluded that racial segregation had dangerous and damaging psychological effects on African American children.) On May 17, 1954, the Supreme Court ruled unanimously in favor of the NAACP lawyers and their clients that a classification based solely on race violated the Fourteenth Amendment.

One year after the 1954 *Brown* decision, the Supreme Court issued a second ruling, commonly known as *Brown II*, which addressed the practical process of desegregation. The Court underscored that the states in the suit should begin prompt compliance with the 1954 ruling but that this should be done with "all deliberate speed." The phrase "all deliberate speed" was interpreted differently by Blacks and whites: African Americans and their allies believed this meant immediately, while white segregationists hoped it meant gradually or never.

Two other events had a profound impact in jump-starting the civil rights movement. The first is the murder of Emmett Till in 1955. In August 1955, Till traveled from Chicago to Money, Mississippi, to visit family. On August 24, after picking cotton in the hot afternoon sun, Emmett and a group of teenagers entered Bryant's Grocery and Meat Market to buy refreshments. As Till made his purchase, Carolyn Bryant, the store's white female clerk, who was also the wife of the store owner, falsely alleged that Till whistled at, flirted with, or touched her hand. Four days later, Roy Bryant, Carolyn's husband, and his half-brother J. W. Milam kidnapped and murdered Till. Their subsequent trial, where unsurprisingly they were found not guilty by an all-white jury, was a cause célèbre.

Later that year, on December 1, Rosa Parks, the secretary of the Montgomery NAACP, refused to vacate her seat on a city bus for a white man. She had not planned to resist that day, but, as she later said, she had "decided that I would have to know once and for all what rights

I had as a human being and a citizen. . . . I was so involved with the attempt to give what I could to protest against the way I was being treated, and felt that all of our meetings, trying to negotiate, bring about petitions before the authorities . . . really hadn't done any good at all." The Women's Political Council headed by Jo Ann Robinson and the NAACP leveraged Park's actions to start the Montgomery Bus Boycott—a mass grassroots movement to end segregation on public transportation. Dr. Martin Luther King, called in from Atlanta to aid the boycott movement, quickly became its face and public voice. The boycott lasted 381 days.

The efforts of Blacks to boycott the buses were aided by the ruling in *Browder v. Gayle* (1956), a federal civil action lawsuit in the names of Claudette Colvin, Aurelia Browder, Susie McDonald, Mary Louise Smith, and Jeanette Reese, all women who had been discriminated against by drivers enforcing segregation policy in the Montgomery bus system. The Supreme Court ruled in favor of the women, ruling that the bus system had violated the Fourteenth Amendment. The Court's decision expressly overturned the 1896 *Plessy v. Ferguson* decision and ended segregation on buses and facilitated the hiring of African American bus drivers. (The *Plessy v. Ferguson* case began in 1892, when the mixed-race Homer Plessy challenged racial segregation on a Louisiana railcar. He insisted that there were stark differences between the "whites-only" car and the "colored" car in violation of a local law that required railcars to be "equal." The intent was to strike down racial segregation on the railcar and in public accommodations. After losing in the state court, the plaintiff appealed to the Supreme Court. Four years later, the Court upheld the "separate but equal" doctrine, reinforcing racial segregation in public accommodations and in nearly all aspects of life.)

In the fall of 1957, nine African American students in Little Rock, Arkansas, attempted to realize the promise of the *Brown* decision by integrating the all-white Central High School. The students became known as the Little Rock Nine. Orchestrated by local NAACP president Daisy Bates and members of the Little Rock School Board, the Little Rock Nine arrived at Central High School on September 4, 1957, to a violent mob and the Arkansas National Guard, which blocked their entrance into the school at the mandate of Arkansas governor Orval Faubus. President Dwight Eisenhower soon ordered the Arkansas National Guard to allow the students entrance to the school, in a show of federal support for school desegregation.

Federal support for school desegregation, apart from upholding federal laws, was also a strategic show of support for democracy in the context of the Cold War. Newly free nations in Africa, Asia, Latin America, and other parts of the world populated by people of color were determining their political and economic futures. The United States' ability to influence these nations to become democratic was undermined by the persistence of racial discrimination in American society. As historian Mary Dudziak argues, "Racial segregation interfered with the Cold War imperative of winning the world over to democracy, for the existence of discrimination against minority groups in the United States has an adverse effect upon our relations with other countries. Racial discrimination furnishes grist for the Communist propaganda mills, and it raises doubts even among friendly nations as to the intensity of our devotion to the democratic faith."[1] This context was not lost on civil rights activists who continued to pursue desegregation, equal access, and justice with the eyes of the world upon them.

NOTES

1. Mary Dudziak, *Cold War Civil Rights* (Princeton, NJ: Princeton University Press, 2000), 100.

Smith v. Allwright **Decision (1944)**

At the heart of *Smith v. Allwright* was the question of whether the Texas Democratic Party's policy of prohibiting Blacks from voting in primary elections constituted a violation of rights guaranteed under the Fourteenth and Fifteenth Amendments. Given the Democratic Party's dominance of southern politics and the large population of Blacks still residing in the South, this case had the potential to disrupt long-standing practices of excluding Blacks from the right to vote and engage in electoral politics.

UNITED STATES SUPREME COURT

Smith v. Allwright (1944)

Mr. Justice REED delivered the opinion of the Court.

This writ of certiorari brings here for review a claim for damages in the sum of $5,000 on the part of petitioner, a Negro citizen of the 48th precinct of Harris County, Texas, for the refusal of respondents, election and associate election judges respectively of that precinct, to give petitioner a ballot or to permit him to cast a ballot in the primary election of July 27, 1940, for the nomination of Democratic candidates for the United States Senate and House of Representatives, and Governor and other state officers. The refusal is alleged to have been solely because of the race and color of the proposed voter. . . .

The State of Texas by its Constitution and statutes provides that every person, if certain other requirements are met which are not here in issue, qualified by residence in the district or county "shall be deemed a qualified elector." . . .

The Democratic party on May 24, 1932, in a State Convention adopted the following resolution, which has not since been "amended, abrogated, annulled or avoided":

> "Be it resolved that all white citizens of the State of Texas who are qualified
> to vote under the Constitution and laws of the State shall be eligible to membership in the Democratic party and, as such, entitled to participate in its
> deliberations." It was by virtue of this resolution that the respondents refused
> to permit the petitioner to vote.

Texas is free to conduct her elections and limit her electorate as she may deem wise, save only as her action may be affected by the prohibitions of the United States Constitution or in conflict with powers delegated to and exercised by the National Government. The Fourteenth Amendment forbids a state from making or enforcing any law which abridges the privileges or immunities of citizens of the United States and the Fifteenth Amendment specifically interdicts any denial or abridgement by a state of the right of citizens to vote on account of color. Respondents appeared in the District Court and the Circuit Court of Appeals and defended on the ground that the Democratic party of Texas is a voluntary organization with members banded together for the purpose of selecting individuals of the group representing the common political beliefs as candidates in the general election. As such a voluntary organization, it was claimed, the Democratic party is free to select its own membership and limit to whites participation in the party primary. Such action, the answer asserted, does not violate the Fourteenth, Fifteenth or Seventeenth Amendment as officers of government cannot be chosen at primaries and the Amendments are applicable only to general elections where governmental officers are actually elected. Primaries, it is said, are political party affairs, handled by party not governmental officers.

. . . [T]he right to vote in such a primary for the nomination of candidates without discrimination by the State, like the right to vote in a general election, is a right secured by the Constitution. . . . By the terms of the Fifteenth Amendment that right may not be abridged by any state on account of race. Under our Constitution the great privilege of the ballot may not be denied a man by the State because of his color. . . .

The United States is a constitutional democracy. Its organic law grants to all citizens a right to participate in the choice of elected officials without restriction by any state because of race. This grant to the people of the opportunity for choice is not to be nulified [*sic*] by a state through casting its electoral process in a form which permits a private organization to practice racial discrimination in the election. Constitutional rights would be of little value if they could be thus indirectly denied.

The privilege of membership in a party may be . . . no concern of a state. But when, as here, that privilege is also the essential qualification for voting in a primary to select nominees for a general election, the state makes the action of the party the action of the state. In reaching this conclusion we are not unmindful of the desirability of continuity of decision in constitutional questions. However, when convinced of former error, this Court has never felt constrained to follow precedent. In constitutional questions, where correction depends upon amendment and not upon legislative action this Court throughout its history has freely exercised its power to reexamine the basis of its constitutional decisions. This has long been accepted practice, and this practice has continued to this day. This is particularly true when the decision believed erroneous is the application of a constitutional principle rather than an interpretation of the Constitution to extract the principle itself. Here we are applying . . . the well established principle of the Fifteenth Amendment, forbidding the abridgement by a state of a citizen's right to vote.

Judgment reversed.

Source: Stanley Forman Reed and Supreme Court of the United States, *U.S. Reports: Smith v. Allwright*, 321 U.S. 649 (1943), periodical. https://www.loc.gov/item/usrep321649/.

DOCUMENT 3.2

Shelley v. Kraemer Decision (1948)

Shelley v. Kraemer was the result of two separate cases in Missouri and Michigan that challenged the enforcement of private restrictive covenants barring African Americans, Asian Americans, and other racial, ethnic, and religious minorities from purchasing homes in particular neighborhoods. The central question in *Shelley v. Kraemer* was whether restrictive covenants violated the Equal Protection Clause of the Fourteenth Amendment and therefore deprived African Americans and others of their right to live where they pleased. The Supreme Court ultimately ruled that whereas the covenants in and of themselves constituted private agreements and actions and were thus outside of the purview of courts, the judicial or legal enforcement of such covenants constituted a violation of rights.

UNITED STATES SUPREME COURT
SHELLEY V. KRAEMER (1948)

Mr. Chief Justice VINSON delivered the opinion of the Court.

These cases present for our consideration questions relating to the validity of court enforcement of private agreements, generally described as restrictive covenants, which have as their purpose the exclusion of persons of designated race or color from the Basic constitutional issues of obvious importance have been raised.

The first of these cases comes to this Court on certiorari to the Supreme Court of Missouri. On February 16, 1911, thirty out of a total of thirty-nine owners of property . . . in the city of St. Louis, signed an agreement, which was subsequently recorded, providing in part:

> ". . . [T]he said property is hereby restricted to the use and occupancy for the term of Fifty (50) years from this date, so that it shall be a condition all the time and whether recited and referred to as (sic) not in subsequent conveyances and shall attach to the land, as a condition precedent to the sale of the same, that hereafter no part of said property or any portion thereof shall be, for said term of Fifty-years, occupied by any person not of the Caucasian race, it being intended hereby to restrict the use of said property for said period of time against the occupancy as owners or tenants of any portion of said property for resident or other purpose by people of the Negro or Mongolian Race." . . .

On August 11, 1945, pursuant to a contract of sale, petitioners Shelley, who are Negroes, for valuable consideration received from one Fitzgerald a warranty deed. . . . The trial court found that petitioners had no actual knowledge of the restrictive agreement at the time of the purchase. On October 9, 1945, respondents, as owners of other property subject to the terms of the restrictive covenant, brought suit in Circuit Court of the city of St. Louis praying [*sic*] that petitioners Shelley be restrained from taking possession of the property and that judgment be entered divesting title out of petitioners Shelley and revesting title in the immediate grantor or in such other person as the court should direct. The trial court denied the requested relief on the ground that the restrictive agreement, upon which respondents based their action, had never become final and complete because it was the intention of the parties to that agreement that it was not to become effective until signed by all property owners in the district, and signatures of all the owners had never been obtained.

The Supreme Court of Missouri sitting en banc reversed and directed the trial court to grant the relief for which respondents had prayed. That court held the agreement effective and concluded that enforcement of its provisions violated no rights guaranteed to petitioners by the Federal Constitution. . . .

The second of the cases under consideration comes to this Court from the Supreme Court of Michigan. The circumstances presented do not differ materially from the Missouri case. In June, 1934, one Ferguson and his wife, who then owned the property located in the city of Detroit which is involved in this case, executed a contract providing in part:

> "This property shall not be used or occupied by any person or persons except those of the Caucasian race.["] "It is further agreed that this restriction shall not be effective unless at least eighty percent of the property fronting on both sides of the street in the block where our land is located is subjected to this or a similar restriction." . . .

By deed dated November 30, 1944, petitioners, who were found by the trial court to be Negroes, acquired title to the property and thereupon entered into its occupancy. On January 30, 1945, respondents, as owners of property subject to the terms of the restrictive agreement, brought suit against petitioners in the Circuit Court of Wayne County. After a hearing, the court entered a decree directing petitioners to move from the property within ninety days. Petitioners were further enjoined and restrained from using or occupying the premises in the future. On appeal, the Supreme Court of Michigan affirmed, deciding adversely to petitioners' contentions that they had been denied rights protected by the Fourteenth Amendment.

Petitioners have placed primary reliance on their contentions, first raised in the state courts, that judicial enforcement of the restrictive agreements in these cases has violated rights guaranteed to petitioners by the Fourteenth Amendment of the Federal Constitution and Acts of Congress passed pursuant to that Amendment. Specifically, petitioners urge that they have been denied the equal protection of the laws, deprived of property without due process of law, and have been denied privileges and immunities of citizens of the United States.

. . .

It cannot be doubted that among the civil rights intended to be protected from discriminatory state action by the Fourteenth Amendment are the rights to acquire, enjoy, own and dispose of property. Equality in the enjoyment of property rights was regarded by the framers of that Amendment as an essential pre-condition to the realization of other basic civil rights and liberties which the Amendment was intended to guarantee. . . . [T]he Fourteenth Amendment was also under consideration, provides:

"All citizens of the United States shall have the same right, in every State and Territory, as is enjoyed by white citizens thereof to inherit, purchase, lease, sell, hold, and convey real and personal property."

. . .

. . . Here the particular patterns of discrimination and the areas in which the restrictions are to operate, are determined, in the first instance, by the terms of agreements among private individuals. Participation of the State consists in the enforcement of the restrictions so defined. The crucial issue with which we are here confronted is whether this distinction removes these cases from the operation of the prohibitory provisions of the Fourteenth Amendment. . . .

We conclude, therefore, that the restrictive agreements standing alone cannot be regarded as a violation of any rights guaranteed to [petitioners] by the Fourteenth Amendment. So long as the purposes of those agreements are effectuated by voluntary adherence to their terms, it would appear clear that there has been no action by the State and the provisions of the Amendment have not been violated.

But here there was more. These are cases in which the purposes of the agreements were secured only by judicial enforcement by state courts of the restrictive terms of the agreements. . . .

. . . .

We hold that in granting judicial enforcement of the restrictive agreements in these cases, the States have denied petitioners the equal protection of the laws and that, therefore, the action of the state courts cannot stand. We have noted that freedom from discrimination by the States in the enjoyment of property rights was among the basic objectives sought to be effectuated by the framers of the Fourteenth Amendment. That such discrimination has occurred in these cases is clear. Because of the race or color of these petitioners they have been denied rights of ownership or occupancy enjoyed as a matter of course by other citizens of different race or color. The Fourteenth Amendment declares "that all persons, whether colored or white, shall stand equal before the laws of the States, and, in regard to the colored race, for whose protection the amendment was primarily designed, that no discrimination shall be made against them by law because of their color." Only recently this Court has had occasion to declare that a state law which denied equal enjoyment of property rights to a designated class of citizens of specified race and ancestry, was not a legitimate exercise of the state's police power but violated the guaranty of the equal protect[ion] of the laws. Nor may the discriminations imposed by the state courts in these cases be justified as proper exertions of state police power. . . .

. . .

For the reasons stated, the judgment of the Supreme Court of Missouri and the judgment of the Supreme Court of Michigan must be reversed.

Reversed.

Source: Fred Moore Vinson and Supreme Court of the United States, *U.S. Reports: Shelley v. Kraemer*, 334 U.S. 1 (1947), periodical. https://www.loc.gov/item/usrep334001/.

DOCUMENT 3.3

George Hauser and Bayard Rustin, CORE, "We Challenged Jim Crow!" (1947)

This document details the Journey of Reconciliation, an initiative inspired by the Fellowship of Reconciliation (FOR) and organized by the Congress of Racial Equality to test the Supreme Court's ruling in *Morgan v. Commonwealth of Virginia* (1946) that segregation on interstate transportation was unconstitutional. George Houser, a white Methodist minister and cofounder of CORE, authored the report along with Bayard Rustin, a Black activist, FOR staff member, and organizer of the 1941 March on Washington movement. Rustin, who lived openly as a gay man, worked alongside key civil rights activists like A. Philip Randolph and later with Dr. Martin Luther King Jr. as a lead organizer of the 1963 March on Washington. The Journey of Reconciliation was a precursor to the Freedom Rides of 1961.

On June 3, 1946, the Supreme Court of the United States announced its decision in the case of Irene Morgan versus the Commonwealth of Virginia. State laws demanding segregation of interstate passengers on motor carriers are now unconstitutional, for segregation of passengers crossing state lines was declared an "undue burden on interstate commerce." Thus it was decided that state Jim Crow laws do not affect interstate travelers. In a later decision in the Court of Appeals for the District of Columbia, the Morgan decision was interpreted to apply to interstate train travel as well as bus travel.

The Executive Committee of the Congress of Racial Equality and the Racial-Industrial Committee of the Fellowship of Reconciliation decided that they should jointly sponsor a "Journey of Reconciliation" through the upper South in order to determine to how great an extent bus and train companies were recognizing the Morgan decision. They also wished to learn the reaction of bus drivers, passengers, and police to those who non-violently and persistently challenge Jim Crow in interstate travel.

During the two-week period from April 9–23, an interracial group of men, traveling as a deputation team, visited fifteen cities in Virginia, North Carolina, Tennessee, and Kentucky. More than thirty speaking engagements were met before church, N.A.A.C.P., and college groups. The Morgan decision was explained and reports made on what was happening on the buses and trains in the light of this decision. The response was most enthusiastic.

To clarify the incidents described below, it will be necessary to list the sixteen participants by race.

NEGRO: Bayard Rustin, of the Fellowship of Reconciliation and part-time worker with the American Friends Service Committee; Wallace Nelson, freelance lecturer; Conrad Lynn, New York attorney; Andrew Johnson, Cincinnati student; Dennis Banks, Chicago musician; William Worthy, of the New York Council for a Permanent FEPC; Eugene Stanley, of A. and T. College, Greensboro, North Carolina; Nathan Wright, church social worker from Cincinnati.

WHITE: George Houser, of the FOR, and Executive Secretary of the Congress of Racial Equality; Ernest Bromley, Methodist minister from North Carolina; James Peck, editor of the Workers Defense League *News Bulletin*; Igal Roodenko, New York horticulturist;

Worth Randle, Cincinnati biologist; Joseph Felmet, of the Southern Workers Defense League; Homer Jack, Executive Secretary of the Chicago Council Against Racial and Religious Discrimination; Louis Adams, Methodist minister from North Carolina.

During the two weeks of the trip, twenty-six tests of company policies were made. Arrests occurred on six occasions, with a total of twelve men arrested.

AN ACCOUNT OF THE TEST TRIPS

. . .

Petersburg, Va., to Raleigh, N. C, April 11.

Lynn was arrested on the Trailways before the bus left the station for sitting in the second seat from the front. The bus driver was courteous, but insistent. Lynn explained the Morgan decision quietly. The driver countered that he was in the employ of the bus company, not the Supreme Court, and that he followed company rules about segregation. He said aloud, so all passengers could hear: "Personally, I don't care where you sit, but I have my orders. Are you going to move?" Lynn said that he could not. The driver got the police. There were no threats, nor abusive language. It took about an hour and a half to get a warrant for Lynn's arrest. The magistrate in Petersburg would not sign the warrant until the bus company attorney in Richmond had been called, and dictated the statement of the warrant over the telephone. The warrant read that Lynn was guilty of disorderly conduct for not obeying the reasonable request of the bus driver to move to the rear in compliance with the company rules. The bus operator apologized for having to arrest Lynn. A policeman, referring to equality for Negroes said, "I'm just not Christian enough." Passengers on the bus were patient, and relatively neutral, while they waited almost two hours. A Negro porter made the only fuss when he boarded the bus, and, looking at Lynn, said, "What's the matter with him? He's crazy. Where does he think he is? We know how to deal with him. We ought to drag him off." Lynn was released on $25 bond.

. . .

Chapel Hill, N. C., to Greensboro, N. C., April 13.

Johnson and Felmet were seated in front. The driver asked them to move as soon as he boarded. They were arrested quickly, for the police station was just across the street from the bus station. Felmet did not get up to accompany the police until the officer specifically told him he was under arrest. Because he delayed rising from his seat, he was pulled up bodily, and shoved out of the bus. The bus driver distributed witness cards to occupants of the bus. One white girl said: "You don't want me to sign one of those. I'm a damn Yankee and I think this is an outrage." Rustin and Roodenko, sensing the favorable reaction on the bus, decided they would move to the seat in the front vacated by Johnson and Felmet. Their moving forward caused much discussion by passengers. The driver returned soon, and when Rustin and Roodenko refused to move, they were arrested also. A white woman at the front of the bus, a Southerner, gave her name and address to Rustin as he walked by her. They were arrested on charges of disorderly conduct for refusing to obey the order of the bus driver, and, in the case of the whites, interfering with arrest. The men were released on $50 bonds.

The bus was delayed nearly two hours. Taxi drivers standing around the bus station were becoming aroused by the events. One hit Peck a hard blow on the head, saying, "Coming down here to stir up the niggers." Peck stood quietly looking at them for several moments, but said nothing. Two persons standing by, one Negro and one white, reprimanded the cab driver for his violence. The Negro was told, "You keep out of this." In the police station, some of the men standing around could be heard saying, "They'll never get a bus out of here tonight." After the bond was placed, Rev. Charles Jones, local white Presbyterian minister, speedily drove the men to his home. They were pursued by two cabs filled with taxi men. As the interracial group got on the front porch of the Jones home, the two cabs pulled up at the curb, and men jumped out, two of them with sticks for weapons, and others picked up sizeable rocks. They started toward the house, but were called back by one of their number. In a few moments the phone rang, and an anonymous voice said to Jones, "Get those damn niggers out of town or we'll burn your house down. We'll be around to see that they go." The police were notified and they arrived in about twenty minutes. The interracial group felt it wise to leave town before nightfall. Two cars were obtained and the group was driven to Greensboro by way of Durham for an evening engagement.

. . .

Nashville, Tenn., to Louisville, Ky., April 19.

Wright and Jack had reserved seats on an all-coach reserved train of the Louisville and Nashville. There was no difficulty in getting on the train. Two conductors approached to collect the tickets. One asked Jack if Wright were his prisoner. Learning they were friends, he told Wright that company rules meant he would have to move to the Jim Crow car. "That is the way it is done down here," he concluded. When Wright refused to move, he said he would be back later. When he came back he said: "If we were in Alabama, we would throw you out of the window." He threatened to have Wright arrested in Bowling Green, Kentucky, but no arrest took place. A woman sitting the second seat behind the men approached them after the conductor left, giving them her name and address, and saying that they could call on her for help. . . .

Source: George Houser and Bayard Rustin, *We Challenged Jim Crow! A Report on the Journey of Reconciliation, April 9–23, 1947* (Newark: Congress of Racial Equality, 1947), Greensboro History Museum.

Jackie Robinson Breaks the Color Barrier (1947)

This photograph features Jackie Robinson (*far right*) in his first Major League game and his Brooklyn Dodgers teammates (*left to right*) John Jorgensen, Pee Wee Reese, and Eddie Stanky. The photograph was taken on April 15, 1947, just five days after the announcement that Robinson would became the first African American athlete to play in Major League Baseball in the modern era. As a result, all MLB baseball teams had at least one African American player by the end of the 1950s.

Source: *Jackie Robinson Breaks the Color Barrier*, April 15, 1947, photograph, National Baseball Hall of Fame Library.

Thurgood Marshall's Argument before the Supreme Court in *Brown v. Board of Education* (1954)

NAACP attorney Thurgood Marshall provided an argument before the Court in *Brown v. Board of Education of Topeka, Kansas* (1954) in which he likened segregation laws and policies to the Reconstruction-era Black Codes that the Fourteenth Amendment sought to negate. Marshall was no stranger to arguing cases that challenged segregation and provided legal arguments for plaintiffs in *Smith v. Allwright* and *Shelley v. Kraemer*. Marshall received successive judicial appointments before becoming the first Black Supreme Court justice, appointed in 1967 by President Lyndon B. Johnson.

IT FOLLOWS THAT with education, this Court has made segregation and inequality equivalent concepts. They have equal rating, equal footing, and if segregation thus necessarily imports inequality, it makes no great difference whether we say that the Negro is wronged because he is segregated, or that he is wronged because he received unequal treatment . . .

I would like to say that each lawyer on the other side has made it clear as to what the position of the state was on this, and it would be all right possibly but for the fact that this is so crucial. There is no way you can repay lost school years.

These children in these cases are guaranteed by the states some twelve years of education in varying degrees, and this idea, if I understand it, to leave it to the states until they work it out—and I think that is a most ingenious argument—you leave it to the states, they say, and then they say that the states haven't done anything about it in a hundred years, so for that reason this Court doesn't touch it.

The argument of judicial restraint has no application in this case. There is a relationship between federal and state, but there is no corollary or relationship as to the Fourteenth Amendment.

The duty of enforcing, the duty of following the Fourteenth Amendment, is placed upon the states. The duty of enforcing the Fourteenth Amendment is placed upon this Court, and the argument that they make over and over again to my mind is the same type of argument they charge us with making, the same argument Charles Sumner made. Possibly so.

And we hereby charge them with making the same argument that was made before the Civil War, the same argument that was made during the period between the ratification of the Fourteenth Amendment and the Plessy v. Ferguson case.

And I think it makes no progress for us to find out who made what argument. It is our position that whether or not you base this case solely on the Intent of Congress or whether you base it on the logical extension of the doctrine as set forth in the McLaurin case, on either basis the same conclusion is required, which is that this Court makes it clear to all of these states that in administering their governmental functions, at least those that are vital not to the life of the state alone, not to the country alone, but vital to the world in general, that little pet feelings of race, little pet feelings of custom—I got the feeling on hearing the discussion yesterday that when you put a white child in a school with a whole lot of colored children, the child would fall apart or something. Everybody knows that is not true.

Those same kids in Virginia and South Carolina—and I have seen them do it—they play in the streets together, they play on their farms together, they go down the road together, they separate to go to school, they come out of school and play ball together. They have to be separated in school.

There is some magic to it. You can have them voting together, you can have them not restricted because of law in the houses they live in. You can have them going to the same state university and the same college, but if they go to elementary and high school, the world will fall apart. And it is the exact same argument that has been made to this Court over and over again, and we submit that when they charge us with making a legislative argument, it is in truth they who are making the legislative argument.

They can't take race out of this case. From the day this case was filed until this moment, nobody has in any form or fashion, despite the fact I made it clear in the opening argument that I was relying on it, done anything to distinguish this statute from the Black Codes, which they must admit, because nobody can dispute, say anything anybody wants to say, one way or the other, the Fourteenth Amendment was intended to deprive the states of power to enforce Black Codes or anything else like it.

We charge that they are Black Codes. They obviously are Black Codes if you read them. They haven't denied that they are Black Codes, so if the Court wants to very narrowly decide this case, they can decide it on that point.

So whichever way it is done, the only way that this Court can decide this case in opposition to our position, is that there must be some reason which gives the state the right to make a classification that they can make in regard to nothing else in regard to Negroes, and we submit the only way to arrive at that decision is to find that for some reason Negroes are inferior to all other human beings.

Nobody will stand in the Court and urge that, and in order to arrive at the decision that they want us to arrive at, there would have to be some recognition of a reason why of all of the multitudinous groups of people in this country you have to single out Negroes and give them this separate treatment.

It can't be because of slavery in the past, because there are very few groups in this country that haven't had slavery some place back in history of their groups. It can't be color because there are Negroes as white as the drifted snow, with blue eyes, and they are just as segregated as the colored man.

The only thing can be is an inherent determination that the people who were formerly in slavery, regardless of anything else, shall be kept as near that stage as is possible, and now is the time, we submit, that this Court should make it clear that that is not what our Constitution stands for.

Thank you, sir.

Source: Thurgood Marshall, "Argument before the U.S. Supreme Court in *Brown v. Board of Education*" (1953). https://www.blackpast.org/african -american-history/1953-thurgood-marshall-argument-u-s-supreme-court -brown-v-board-education/.

DOCUMENT 3.6

Brown v. Board of Education **Decision (1954)**

After two years of litigation, the Supreme Court made its decision in the *Brown v. Board of Education* case. Chief Justice Earl Warren delivered the opinion. The unanimous ruling effectively overturned the *Plessy v. Ferguson* (1898) decision and provided the legal basis for challenging racial discrimination and segregation in subsequent years. Warren's ascension to chief justice marked a significant turn to a more liberal Supreme Court. Despite the *Brown* ruling, many school districts across the country failed to integrate.

U.S. SUPREME COURT

Brown v. Board of Education of Topeka, 347 U.S. 483 (1954)

Argued December 9, 1952
Reargued December 8, 1953
Decided May 17, 1954

MR. CHIEF JUSTICE WARREN delivered the opinion of the Court.

These cases come to us from the States of Kansas, South Carolina, Virginia, and Delaware. They are premised on different facts and different local conditions, but a common legal question justifies their consideration together in this consolidated opinion.

In each of the cases, minors of the Negro race, through their legal representatives, seek the aid of the courts in obtaining admission to the public schools of their community on a nonsegregated basis. In each instance, they had been denied admission to schools attended by white children under laws requiring or permitting segregation according to race. This segregation was alleged to deprive the plaintiffs of the equal protection of the laws under the Fourteenth Amendment. In each of the cases other than the Delaware case, a three-judge federal district court denied relief to the plaintiffs on the so-called "separate but equal" doctrine announced by this Court in *Plessy v. Ferguson*. Under that doctrine, equality of treatment is accorded when the races are provided substantially equal facilities, even though these facilities be separate. In the Delaware case, the Supreme Court of Delaware adhered to that doctrine, but ordered that the plaintiffs be admitted to the white schools because of their superiority to the Negro schools.

The plaintiffs contend that segregated public schools are not "equal" and cannot be made "equal," and that hence they are deprived of the equal protection of the laws. Because of the obvious importance of the question presented, the Court took jurisdiction.

. . .

In the first cases in this Court construing the Fourteenth Amendment, decided shortly after its adoption, the Court interpreted it as proscribing all state-imposed discriminations against the Negro race. The doctrine of "separate but equal" did not make its appearance in this Court until 1896 in the case of *Plessy v. Ferguson, supra,* involving not education but transportation. American courts have since labored with the doctrine for over half a century. In this Court, there have been six cases involving the "separate but equal" doctrine in the field of public education. In *Cumming v. County Board of Education,* and *Gong Lum v. Rice,* the validity of the doctrine itself was not challenged. In more recent cases, all on the graduate school level, inequality was found in that specific benefits enjoyed by white students were denied to Negro students of the same educational qualifications. In none of these cases was it necessary to reexamine the doctrine to grant relief to the Negro plaintiff. And in *Sweatt v. Painter, supra,* the Court expressly reserved decision on the question whether *Plessy v. Ferguson* should be held inapplicable to public education.

In the instant cases, that question is directly presented. Here, unlike *Sweatt v. Painter,* there are findings below that the Negro and white schools involved have been equalized, or are being equalized, with respect to buildings, curricula, qualifications and salaries of teachers, and other "tangible" factors. Our decision, therefore, cannot turn on merely a comparison of these tangible factors in the Negro and white schools involved in each of the cases. We must look instead to the effect of segregation itself on public education.

In approaching this problem, we cannot turn the clock back to 1868 when the Amendment was adopted, or even to 1896 when *Plessy v. Ferguson* was written. We must consider public education in the light of its full development and its present place in American life throughout the Nation. Only in this way can it be determined if segregation in public schools deprives these plaintiffs of the equal protection of the laws.

Today, education is perhaps the most important function of state and local governments. Compulsory school attendance laws and the great expenditures for education both demonstrate our recognition of the importance of education to our democratic society. It is required in the performance of our most basic public responsibilities, even service in the armed forces. It is the very foundation of good citizenship. Today it is a principal instrument in awakening the child to cultural values, in preparing him for later professional training, and in helping him to adjust normally to his environment. In these days, it is doubtful that any child may reasonably be expected to succeed in life if he is denied the opportunity of an education. Such an opportunity, where the state has undertaken to provide it, is a right which must be made available to all on equal terms.

We come then to the question presented: does segregation of children in public schools solely on the basis of race, even though the physical facilities and other "tangible" factors may be equal, deprive the children of the minority group of equal educational opportunities? We believe that it does.

In *Sweatt v. Painter, supra,* in finding that a segregated law school for Negroes could not provide them equal educational opportunities, this Court relied in large part on "those qualities which are incapable of objective measurement but which make for greatness in a law school." In *McLaurin v. Oklahoma State Regents, supra,* the Court, in requiring that a Negro admitted to a white graduate school be treated like all other students, again resorted to intangible considerations: ". . . his ability to study, to engage in discussions and exchange views with other students, and, in general, to learn his profession."

Such considerations apply with added force to children in grade and high schools. To separate them from others of similar age and qualifications solely because of their race generates a feeling of inferiority as to their status in the community that may affect their hearts and minds in a way unlikely ever to be undone. The effect of this separation on their educational opportunities was well stated by a finding in the Kansas case by a court which nevertheless felt compelled to rule against the Negro plaintiffs:

"Segregation of white and colored children in public schools has a detrimental effect upon the colored children. The impact is greater when it has the sanction of the law, for the policy of separating the races is usually interpreted as denoting the inferiority of the negro group. A sense of inferiority affects the motivation of a child to learn. Segregation with the sanction of law, therefore, has a tendency to [retard] the educational and mental development of negro children and to deprive them of some of the benefits they would receive in a racial[ly] integrated school system."

. . .

We conclude that, in the field of public education, the doctrine of "separate but equal" has no place. Separate educational facilities are inherently unequal. Therefore, we hold that the plaintiffs and others similarly situated for whom the actions have been brought are, by reason of the segregation complained of, deprived of the equal protection of the laws guaranteed by the Fourteenth Amendment. This disposition makes unnecessary any discussion whether such segregation also violates the Due Process Clause of the Fourteenth Amendment.

Because these are class actions, because of the wide applicability of this decision, and because of the great variety of local conditions, the formulation of decrees in these cases presents problems of considerable complexity. On reargument, the consideration of appropriate relief was necessarily subordinated to the primary question—the constitutionality of segregation in public education. We have now announced that such segregation is a denial of the equal protection of the laws. In order that we may have the full assistance of the parties in formulating decrees, the cases will be restored to the docket, and the parties are requested to present further argument on Questions 4 and 5 previously propounded by the Court for the reargument this Term. The Attorney General of the United States is again invited to participate. The Attorneys General of the states requiring or permitting segregation in public education will also be permitted to appear as amici curiae upon request to do so by September 15, 1954, and submission of briefs by October 1, 1954.

It is so ordered.

Source: *Brown v. Board of Education of Topeka,* 347 U.S. 483 (1954).
https://supreme.justia.com/cases/federal/us/347/483/.

DOCUMENT 3.7

Southern Manifesto (1956)

Southern congressmen under the leadership of North Carolina senator Sam Ervin Jr. and South Carolina senator Strom Thurmond protested the Court's ruling in *Brown v. Board of Education*. In the Southern Manifesto, white southerners vowed to fight to preserve segregation and the southern way of life. It also called the *Brown* decision an "unwarranted exercise of power by the Court, contrary to the Constitution." The only southern senators who refused to sign the "manifesto" were Albert Gore Sr. of Tennessee and Lyndon B. Johnson of Texas.

DECLARATION OF CONSTITUTIONAL PRINCIPLES

The unwarranted decision of the Supreme Court in the public school cases is now bearing the fruit always produced when men substitute naked power for established law.

The Founding Fathers gave us a Constitution of checks and balances because they realized the inescapable lesson of history that no man or group of men can be safely entrusted with unlimited power. They framed this Constitution with its provisions for change by amendment in order to secure the fundamentals of government against the dangers of temporary popular passion or the personal predilections of public officeholders.

We regard the decisions of the Supreme Court in the school cases as a clear abuse of judicial power. It climaxes a trend in the Federal Judiciary undertaking to legislate, in derogation of the authority of Congress, and to encroach upon the reserved rights of the States and the people.

The original Constitution does not mention education. Neither does the 14th Amendment nor any other amendment. The debates preceding the submission of the 14th Amendment clearly show that there was no intent that it should affect the system of education maintained by the States.

The very Congress which proposed the amendment subsequently provided for segregated schools in the District of Columbia.

. . .

Every one of the 26 States that had any substantial racial differences among its people, either approved the operation of segregated schools already in existence or subsequently established such schools by action of the same law-making body which considered the 14th Amendment.

As admitted by the Supreme Court in the public school case (Brown v. Board of Education), the doctrine of separate but equal schools "apparently originated in Roberts v. City of Boston (1849), upholding school segregation against attack as being violative of a State constitutional guarantee of equality." This constitutional doctrine began in the North, not in the South, and it was followed not only in Massachusetts, but in Connecticut, New York, Illinois, Indiana, Michigan, Minnesota, New Jersey, Ohio, Pennsylvania and other northern states until they, exercising their rights as states through the constitutional processes of local self-government, changed their school systems.

In the case of Plessy v. Ferguson in 1896 the Supreme Court expressly declared that under the 14th Amendment no person was denied any of his rights if the States provided separate but equal facilities. This decision has been followed in many other cases. It is notable that the Supreme Court, speaking through Chief Justice Taft, a former President of the United States, unanimously declared in 1927 in Lum v. Rice that the "separate but equal" principle is "within the discretion of the State in regulating its public schools and does not conflict with the 14th Amendment."

This interpretation, restated time and again, became a part of the life of the people of many of the States and confirmed their habits, traditions, and way of life. It is founded on elemental humanity and commonsense, for parents should not be deprived by Government of the right to direct the lives and education of their own children.

Though there has been no constitutional amendment or act of Congress changing this established legal principle almost a century old, the Supreme Court of the United States, with no legal basis for such action, undertook to exercise their naked judicial power and substituted their personal political and social ideas for the established law of the land.

This unwarranted exercise of power by the Court, contrary to the Constitution, is creating chaos and confusion in the States principally affected. It is destroying the amicable relations between the white and Negro races that have been created through 90 years of patient effort by the good people of both races. It has planted hatred and suspicion where there has been heretofore friendship and understanding.

Without regard to the consent of the governed, outside mediators are threatening immediate and revolutionary changes in our public schools systems. If done, this is certain to destroy the system of public education in some of the States.

With the gravest concern for the explosive and dangerous condition created by this decision and inflamed by outside meddlers:

We reaffirm our reliance on the Constitution as the fundamental law of the land.

We decry the Supreme Court's encroachment on the rights reserved to the States and to the people, contrary to established law, and to the Constitution.

We commend the motives of those States which have declared the intention to resist forced integration by any lawful means.

We appeal to the States and people who are not directly affected by these decisions to consider the constitutional principles involved against the time when they too, on issues vital to them may be the victims of judicial encroachment.

Even though we constitute a minority in the present Congress, we have full faith that a majority of the American people believe in the dual system of government which has enabled us to achieve our greatness and will in time demand that the reserved rights of the States and of the people be made secure against judicial usurpation.

We pledge ourselves to use all lawful means to bring about a reversal of this decision which is contrary to the Constitution and to prevent the use of force in its implementation.

In this trying period, as we all seek to right this wrong, we appeal to our people not to be provoked by the agitators and troublemakers invading our States and to scrupulously refrain from disorder and lawless acts.

Signed by:

Walter F. George, Richard B. Russell, John Stennis, Sam J. Elvin, Jr., Strom Thurmond, Harry F. Byrd, A. Willis Robertson, John L. McClellan, Allen J. Ellender, Russell B. Long, Lister Hill, James O. Eastland, W. Kerr Scott, John Sparkman, Olin D. Johnston, Price Daniel, J.W. Fulbright, George A. Smathers, Spessard L. Holland.

MEMBERS OF THE UNITED STATES HOUSE OF REPRESENTATIVES

ALABAMA: Frank W. Boykin, George M. Grant, George W. Andrews, Kenneth A. Roberts, Albert Rains, Armistead I. Selden, Jr., Carl Elliott, Robert E. Jones, George Huddleston, Jr.

ARKANSAS: E.C. Gathings, Wilbur D. Mills, James W. Trimble, Oren Harris, Brooks Hays, W.F. Norrell.

Florida: Charles E. Bennett, Robert L.F. Sikes, A.S. Herlong, Jr., Paul G. Rogers, James A. Haley, D.R. Matthews.

GEORGIA: Prince H. Preston, John L. Pilcher, E.L. Forrester, John James Flynt, Jr., James C. Davis, Carl Vinson, Henderson Lanham, Iris F. Blitch, Phil M. Landrum, Paul Brown.

LOUISIANA: F. Edward Hebert, Hale Boggs, Edwin E. Willis, Overton Brooks, Otto E. Passman, James H. Morrison, T. Ashton Thompson, George S. Long.

MISSISSIPPI: Thomas G. Abernathy, Jamie L. Whitten, Frank E. Smith, John Bell Williams, Arthur Winstead, William M. Colmer.

NORTH CAROLINA: Herbert C. Bonner, L.H. Fountain, Graham A. Barden, Carl T. Durham, F. Ertel Carlyle, Hugh Q. Alexander, Woodrow W. Jones, George A. Shuford.

SOUTH CAROLINA: L. Mendel Rivers, John J. Riley, W.J. Bryan Dorn, Robert T. Ashmore, James P. Richards, John L. McMillan.

TENNESSEE: James B. Frazier, Jr., Tom Murray, Jere Cooper, Clifford Davis.

Source: Howard Smith, *Declaration of Constitutional Principles,* also known as "The Southern Manifesto," House Rules Committee, 1956. http://americanradioworks.publicradio.org/features/marshall/manifesto.html.

The *Chicago Defender* on the Emmett Till Murder (1955)

In early September 1955, the murder of Chicago teenager Emmett Till while visiting family in Mississippi dominated the pages of the nation's Black and white news outlets. News papers like the *Chicago Defender* covered the murder and subsequent trial of Till's killers, J. W. Milam and Roy Bryant, who were both acquitted by an all-white jury.

Source: "Nation Shocked, Vow Action in Lynching of Chicago Youth," *Chicago Defender*,
September 10, 1955, cover. Courtesy of the *Chicago Defender*.

Emmett Till with His Mother, Mamie Till-Mobley (ca. 1950)

Taken sometime around 1950, this photograph shows a smiling Emmett Till and his mother, Mamie Till-Mobley. Till was the only child of Mamie Till, produced from a brief and volatile marriage to Emmett's father, Louis Till. After Emmett's murder, Mamie Till-Mobley fought to have her son's body relocated to Chicago and had an open-casket funeral attended by thousands. Till-Mobley testified at her son's murder trial and headlined a speaking tour with the NAACP. She later became an educator and taught for many years in the Chicago Public Schools.

Source: Emmett Till with his mother, Mamie Till-Mobley, ca. 1950, photograph, Everett Collection.
Courtesy of the Everett Collection.

DOCUMENT 3.10

Rosa Parks Recalls the Montgomery Bus Boycott (1977)

Not long after the murder of Emmett Till, Black bus riders in Montgomery, Alabama, staged a yearlong protest against segregation on city buses and police brutality of Black riders. In the following document, Rosa Parks gives her recollection of the boycott in an interview from *My Soul Is Rested: Movement Days in the Deep South Remembered* (1977). Parks had served as a secretary for the local Montgomery chapter of the NAACP since the early 1940s and was well aware of the discrimination and racial violence experienced by Blacks, especially Black women. Parks was by no means the first Black person arrested for resisting the city's discriminatory bus laws. However, her image as a respectable race woman was used to galvanize support for a boycott.

I had had problems with bus drivers over the years, because I didn't see fit to pay my money into the front and then go around to the back. Sometimes bus drivers wouldn't permit me to get on the bus, and I had been evicted from the bus. But as I say, there had been incidents over the years. One of the things that made this get so much publicity was the fact the police were called in and I was placed under arrest. See, if I had just been evicted from the bus and he hadn't placed me under arrest or had any charges brought against me, it probably could have been just another incident.

I had left my work at the men's alteration shop, a tailor shop in the Montgomery Fair department store, and as I left work, I crossed the street to a drugstore to pick up a few items instead of trying to go directly to the bus stop. And when I had finished this, I came across the street and looked for a Cleveland Avenue bus that apparently had some seats on it. At that time it was a little hard to get a seat on the bus. But when I did get to the entrance to the bus, I got in line with a number of other people who were getting on the same bus.

As I got up on the bus and walked to the seat I saw there was only one vacancy that was just back of where it was considered the white section. So this was the seat that I took, next to the aisle, and a man was sitting next to me. Across the aisle there were two women, and there were a few seats at this point in the very front of the bus that was called the white section. I went on to one stop and I didn't particularly notice who was getting on the bus, didn't particularly notice the other people getting on. And on the third stop there were some people getting on, and at this point all of the front seats were taken. Now in the beginning, at the very first stop I had got on the bus, the back of the bus was filled up with people standing in the aisle and I don't know why this one vacancy that I took was left, because there were quite a few people already standing toward the back of the bus. The third stop is when all the front seats were taken, and this one man was standing and when the driver looked around and saw he was standing, he asked the four of us, the man in the seat with me and the two women across the aisle, to let him have those front seats.

At his first request, didn't any of us move. Then he spoke again and said, "You'd better make it light on yourselves and let me have those seats." At this point, of course, the passenger who would have taken the seat hadn't said anything. In fact, he never did speak to my knowledge. When the three people, the man who was in the seat with me and the two women, stood up and moved into the aisle, I remained where I was. When the driver saw that I was still sitting there, he asked if I was going to stand up. I told him, no, I wasn't. He said, "Well, if you don't stand up, I'm going to have you arrested." I told him to go on and have me arrested.

He got off the bus and came back shortly. A few minutes later, two policemen got on the bus, and they approached me and asked if the driver had asked me to stand up, and I said yes, and they wanted to know why I didn't. I told them I didn't think I should have to stand up. After I had paid my fare and occupied a seat, I didn't think I should have to give it up. They placed me under arrest then and had me to get in the police car, and I was taken to jail and booked on suspicion, I believe. The questions were asked, the usual questions they ask a prisoner or somebody that's under arrest. They had to determine whether or not the driver wanted to press charges or swear out a warrant, which he did. Then they took me to jail and I was placed in a cell. In a little while I was taken from the cell, and my picture was made and fingerprints taken. I went back to the cell then, and a few minutes later I was called back again, and when this happened I found out that Mr. E.D. Nixon and Attorney and Mrs. Clifford Durr had come to make bond for me.

In the meantime before this, of course . . . I was given permission to make a telephone call after my picture was taken and fingerprints taken. I called my home and spoke to my mother on the telephone and told her what had happened, that I was in jail. She was quite upset and asked me had the police beaten me. I told her, no, I hadn't been physically injured, but I was being held in jail, and I wanted my husband to come and get me out. . . . He didn't have a car at that time, so he had to get someone to bring him down. At the time when he got down, Mr. Nixon and the Durrs had just made bond for me, so we all met at the jail and we went home. . . .

Source: Howell Raines, *My Soul Is Rested: Movement Days in the Deep South Remembered* (New York: Penguin Books, 1983), 40–42. Excerpt(s) from *My Soul Is Rested* by Howell Raines, copyright © 1977 by Howell Raines. Used by permission of G. P. Putnam's Sons, an imprint of Penguin Publishing Group, a division of Penguin Random House LLC.

Dr. Martin Luther King Jr.'s Speech at Holt Street Baptist Church (1955)

In the following speech, King defines the goals of the Montgomery Bus Boycott. The speech marks the beginning of King's role as a leader of the civil rights movement. King, originally from Atlanta, was pastor at Dexter Avenue Baptist Church and a relative newcomer to Montgomery. Because he was relatively unknown, local boycott leaders elected King as leader of the Montgomery Improvement Association, the organization that would lead the boycott.

My FRIENDS, we are certainly very happy to see each of you out this evening. We are here this evening for serious business. We are here in a general sense because first and foremost we are American citizens and we are determined to apply our citizenship to the fullness of its meaning. We are here also because of our love for democracy, because of our deep-seated belief that democracy transformed from thin paper to thick action is the greatest form of government on earth.

But we are here in a specific sense, because of the bus situation in Montgomery. We are here because we are determined to get the situation corrected. This situation is not at all new. The problem has existed over endless years. For many years now Negroes in Montgomery and so many other areas have been inflicted with the paralysis of crippling fears on buses in our community. On so many occasions, Negroes have been intimidated and humiliated and impressed—oppressed—because of the sheer fact that they were Negroes. . . .

Just the other day, just last Thursday to be exact, one of the finest citizens in Montgomery not one of the finest Negro citizens, but one of the finest citizens in Montgomery—was taken from a bus and carried to jail and because she refused to get up to give her seat to a white person. Now the press would have us believe that she refused to leave a reserved section for Negroes but I want you to know this evening that there is no reserved section. The law has never been clarified at that point. . . .

Mrs. Rosa Parks is a fine person. And, since it had to happen, I'm happy that it happened to a person like Mrs. Parks, for nobody can doubt the boundless outreach of her integrity. Nobody can doubt the height of her character nobody can doubt the depth of her Christian commitment and devotion to the teachings of Jesus. And I'm happy since it had to happen, it happened to a person that nobody can call a disturbing factor in the community. Mrs. Parks is a fine Christian person, unassuming, and yet there is integrity and character there. And just because she refused to get up, she was arrested.

And you know, my friends, there comes a time when people get tired of being trampled over by the iron feet of oppression. There comes a time, my friends, when people get tired of being plunged across the abyss of humiliation, where they experience the bleakness of nagging despair. There comes a time when people get tired of being pushed out of the glittering sunlight of life's July and left standing amid the piercing chill of an alpine November. There comes a time.

We are here, we are here this evening because we're tired now. And I want to say that we are not here advocating violence. We have never done that. I want it to be known throughout Montgomery and throughout this nation that we are Christian people. We believe in the Christian religion. We believe in the teachings of Jesus. The only weapon that we have in our hands this evening is the weapon of protest. That's all.

And certainly, certainly, this is the glory of America, with all of its faults. This is the glory of our democracy. If we were incarcerated behind the iron curtains of a Communistic nation we couldn't do this. If we were dropped in the dungeon of a totalitarian regime we couldn't do this. But the great glory of American democracy is the right to protest for right. My friends, don't let anybody make us feel that we are to be compared in our actions with the Ku Klux Klan or with the White Citizens Council. There will be no crosses burned at any bus stops in Montgomery. There will be no white persons pulled out of their homes and taken out on some distant road and lynched for not cooperating. There will be nobody amid, among us who will stand up and defy the Constitution of this nation. We only assemble here because of our desire to see right exist. My friends, I want it to be known that we're going to work with grim and bold determination to gain justice on the buses in this city.

And we are not wrong, we are not wrong in what we are doing. If we are wrong, the Supreme Court of this nation is wrong. If we are wrong, the Constitution of the United States is wrong. If we are wrong, God Almighty is wrong. If we are wrong, Jesus of Nazareth was merely a utopian dreamer that never came down to earth. If we are wrong, justice is a lie. Love has no meaning. And we are determined here in Montgomery to work and fight until justice runs down like water, and righteousness like a mighty stream.

I want to say that in all of our actions we must stick together. Unity is the great need of the hour, and if we are united we can get many of the things that we not only desire but which we justly deserve. And don't let anybody frighten you. We are not afraid of what we are doing because we are doing it within the law. There is never a time in our American democracy that we must ever think we're wrong when we protest. We reserve that right. When labor all over this nation came to see that it would be trampled over by capitalistic power, it was nothing wrong with labor getting together and organizing and protesting for its rights.

We, the disinherited of this land, we who have been oppressed so long, are tired of going through the long night of captivity. And now we are reaching out for the daybreak of freedom and justice and equality. May I say to you my friends, as I come to a close, and just giving some idea of why we are assembled here, that we must keep—and I want to stress this, in all of our doings, in all of our deliberations here this evening and all of the week and while—whatever we do, we must keep God in the forefront. Let us be Christian in all of our actions. But I want to tell you this evening that it is not enough for us to talk about love, love is one of the pivotal points of the Christian face, faith. There is another side called justice. And justice is really love in calculation. Justice is love correcting that which revolts against love. . . .

But just before leaving I want to say this. I want to urge you. You have voted [for this boycott], and you have done it with a great deal of enthusiasm, and I want to express my appreciation to you, on behalf of everybody here. Now let us go out to stick together and stay with this thing until the end. Now it means sacrificing, yes, it means sacrificing at points. But there are some things that we've got to learn to sacrifice for. . . .

So I'm urging you now. We have the facilities for you to get to your jobs, and we are putting, we have the cabs there at your service. Automobiles will be at your service, and don't be afraid to use up any of the gas. If you have it, if you are fortunate enough to have a little money, use it for a good cause. Now my automobile is gonna be in it, it has been in it, and I'm not concerned about how much gas I'm gonna use. I want to see this thing work. And we will not be content until oppression is wiped out of Montgomery, and really out of America. We won't be content until that is done. We are merely insisting on the dignity and worth of every human personality. And I don't stand here, I'm not arguing for any selfish person. I've never been on a bus in Montgomery. But I would be less than a Christian if I stood back and said, because I don't ride the bus, I don't have to ride a bus, that it doesn't concern me. I will not be content. I can hear a voice saying, "If you do it unto the least of these, my brother, you do it unto me." . . .

Source: Martin Luther King Jr., Speech at Holt Street Baptist Church, December 5, 1955. Reprinted by arrangement with The Heirs to the Estate of Martin Luther King Jr., c/o Writers House as agent for the proprietor New York, NY. Speech at Holt Street Baptist Church Copyright © 1955 by Dr. Martin Luther King, Jr. Renewed © 1983 by Coretta Scott King.

The Little Rock Nine and Daisy Bates (1957)

Daisy Bates (*pictured standing, second from the right*) was the local NAACP president in Little Rock and a major force behind the organization of the Little Rock Nine and the integration of Central High School. Pictured with Bates are the members of the Little Rock Nine. This photo was taken on an occasion when members of the Little Rock Nine met with New York City mayor Robert Wagner in 1958.

Seated, left to right: Thelma Mothershed, Minnijean Brown, Elizabeth Eckford, and Gloria Ray. *Standing, left to right*: Ernest Green, Melba Pattillo Beals, Terrence Roberts, Carlotta Walls, Daisy Bates, and Jefferson Thomas.

Source: Cecil Layne, *Little Rock Nine and Daisy Bates Posed in Living Room*, ca. 1957–60, photograph, Visual Materials from the NAACP Records, Prints and Photographs Division, Library of Congress, https://www.loc.gov/item/97516161/.

Melba Pattillo Beals on Integrating Central High School (1994)

In this excerpt from her memoir, *Warriors Don't Cry*, Melba Pattillo Beals describes her first day integrating Little Rock Central High School. The "integration" of Central High School led to regular attacks by white mobs, as described in this excerpt. Beals details the danger of that first day and the difficulties faced by fellow Little Rock Nine member Elizabeth Eckford, who, due to a miscommunication, approached the school and white mobs while unaccompanied.

JUDGE ORDERS INTEGRATION
—*Arkansas Gazette*, Tuesday, September 3, 1957

Dear Diary,
It's happening today. What I'm afraid of most is that they won't like
me and integration won't work. . . .

AS WE WALKED DOWN THE FRONT STEPS, MOTHER PAUSED AND turned to look back at Grandma, who was standing at the edge of the porch. In their glance I saw the fear they had never voiced in front of me. Grandma lingered for a moment and then rushed to encircle me in her arms once more. "God is always with you," she whispered as she blinked back tears.

Trailing behind Mother, I made my way down the concrete path as she climbed into the driver's seat behind the wheel of our green Pontiac. I don't know why I veered off the sidewalk, taking the shortcut through the wet grass that would make damp stains on my saddle shoes. Perhaps I wanted some reason not to go to the integration. I knew if Grandma noticed, she would force me to go back and polish my shoes all over again. But she was so preoccupied she didn't say a word. As I climbed into the passenger seat, I looked back to see her leaning against the porch column, her face weary, her eyes filled with tears.

. . . "Well, I guess we'd better get going." Mother was squinting, cupping her hands over her eyes to protect them against the glare of sunlight. A stream of white people were hurrying past us in the direction of Central High, so many that some had to walk on the grass and in the street. We stepped out of the car and into their strange parade, walking in silence in the midst of their whispers and glares.

Anxious to see the familiar faces of our friends or some of our own people, we hurried up the block lined with wood-frame houses and screened-in porches. I strained to see what lay ahead of us. In the distance, large crowds of white people were lining the curb directly across from the front of Central High. As we approached behind them, we could see only the clusters of white people that stretched for a distance of two blocks along the entire span of the school building. My mind could take in the sights and sounds only one by one: flashing cameras, voices shouting in my ears, men and women jostling each other, old people, young people, people running, uniformed police officers walking, men standing still, men and women waving their fists, and then the long line of uniformed soldiers carrying weapons just like in the war movies I had seen.

Everyone's attention seemed riveted on the center of the line of soldiers where a big commotion was taking place. At first we couldn't see what they were looking at.

People were shouting and pointing, and the noise hurt my ears and muffled the words. We couldn't understand what they were saying. As we drew near, the angry outbursts became even more intense, and we began to hear their words more clearly. "Niggers, go home! Niggers, go back where you belong!"

I stood motionless, stunned by the hurtful words. I searched for something to hang on to, something familiar that would comfort me or make sense, but there was nothing.

"Two, four, six, eight, we ain't gonna integrate!" Over and over, the words rang out. The terrifying frenzy of the crowd was building like steam in an erupting volcano.

"We have to find the others," Mama yelled in my ear. "We'll be safer with the group." She grabbed my arm to pull me forward, out of my trance. The look on her face mirrored the terror I felt. Some of the white men and women standing around us seemed to be observing anxiously. Others with angry faces and wide-open mouths were screaming their rage. Their words were becoming increasingly vile, fueled by whatever was happening directly in front of the school.

The sun beat down on our heads as we made our way through the crowd searching for our friends. Most people ignored us, jostling each other and craning their necks to see whatever was at the center of the furor. Finally, we got closer to the hub of activity. Standing on our toes, we stretched as tall as we could to see what everyone was watching.

"Oh, my Lord," Mother said.

It was my friend Elizabeth they were watching. The anger of that huge crowd was directed toward Elizabeth Eckford as she stood alone, in front of Central High, facing the long line of soldiers, with a huge crowd of white people screeching at her back. Barely five feet tall, Elizabeth cradled her books in her arms as she desperately searched for the right place to enter. Soldiers in uniforms and helmets, cradling their rifles, towered over her. Slowly, she walked first to one and then another opening in their line. Each time she approached, the soldiers closed ranks, shutting her out. As she turned toward us, her eyes hidden by dark glasses, we could see how erect and proud she stood despite the fear she must have been feeling.

As Elizabeth walked along the line of guardsmen, they did nothing to protect her from her stalkers. When a crowd of fifty or more closed in like diving vultures, the soldiers stared straight ahead, as if posing for a photograph. Once more, Elizabeth stood still, stunned, not knowing what to do. The people surrounding us shouted, stomped, and whistled as though her awful predicament were a triumph for them.

I wanted to help her, but the human wall in front of us would not be moved. We could only wedge through partway. Finally, we realized our efforts were futile; we could only pray as we watched her struggle to survive. People began to applaud and shout, "Get her, get the nigger out of there. Hang her black ass!" Not one of those white adults attempted to rescue Elizabeth. The hulking soldiers continued to observe her peril like spectators enjoying a sport.

Under siege, Elizabeth slowly made her way toward the bench at the bus stop. Looking straight ahead as she walked, she did not acknowledge the people yelping at her heels, like mad dogs. Mother and I looked at one another, suddenly conscious that we, too, were trapped by a violent mob.

Ever so slowly, we eased our way backward through the crowd, being careful not to attract attention. But a white man clawed at me, grabbing my sleeve and yelling, "We got us a nigger right here!" Just then another man tugged at his arm distracting him. Somehow I managed to scramble away. As a commotion began building around us, Mother took my arm, and we moved fast, sometimes crouching to avoid attracting more attention.

We gained some distance from the center of the crowd and made our way down the block. But when I looked back, I saw a man following us, yelling, "They're getting away! Those niggers are getting away!" Pointing to us, he enlisted others to join him. Now we were being chased by four men, and their number was growing.

We scurried down the sidewalk, bumping into people. Most of the crowd was still preoccupied watching Elizabeth. Panic-stricken, I wanted to shout for help. But I knew it would do no good. Policemen stood by watching Elizabeth being accosted. Why would they help us?

"Melba, . . . take these keys," Mother commanded as she tossed them at me. "Get to the car. Leave without me if you have to."

I plucked the car keys from the air. "No, Mama, I won't go without you." Suddenly I felt the sting of her hand as it struck the side of my face. She had never slapped me before. "Do what I say!" she shouted. Still, I knew I couldn't leave her there. I reached back to take her arm. Her pace was slowing, and I tried to pull her forward. The men were gaining on us. If we yelled for help or made any fuss, others might join our attackers. Running faster, I felt myself begin to wear out. I didn't have enough breath to keep moving so fast. My knees hurt, my calves were aching, but the car was just around the next corner.

The men chasing us were joined by another carrying a rope. At times, our pursuers were so close I could look back and see the anger in their eyes. Mama's pace slowed, and one man came close enough to touch her. He grabbed for her arm but instead tugged at her blouse. The fabric ripped, and he fell backward. Mama stepped out of her high-heeled shoes, leaving them behind, her pace quickening in stocking feet.

One of the men closest to me swung at me with a large tree branch but missed. I felt even more panic rise up in my throat. If he hit me hard enough to knock me over, I would be at his mercy. I could hear Grandma India's voice saying, God is always with you, even when things seem awful. I felt a surge of strength and a new wind. As I turned the corner, our car came into sight. I ran hard—faster than ever before—unlocked the door, and jumped in.

Mother was struggling, barely able to keep ahead of her attackers. I could see them turning the corner close on her heels, moving fast toward us. I swung open the passenger door for Mother and revved the engine. Barely waiting for her to shut the door, I shoved the gearshift into reverse and backed down the street with more speed than I'd ever driven forward. I slowed to back around the corner. One of the men caught up and pounded his fists on the hood of our car, while another threw a brick at the windshield.

Turning left, we gained speed as we drove through a hail of shouts and stones and glaring faces. But I knew I would make it because the car was moving fast and Mama was with me.

Source: Melba Pattillo Beals, *Warriors Don't Cry: A Searing Memoir of the Battle to Integrate Little Rock's Central High* (New York: Pocket Books, 1994), 46–51. Copyright © 1994, 1995 by Melba Beals. Reprinted with the permission of Atria Books, a division of Simon & Schuster, Inc. All rights reserved.

FURTHER READING

Bates, Daisy. *The Long Shadow of Little Rock: A Memoir*. Fayetteville: University of Arkansas Press, 2007.

Chappell, Marissa, Jenny Hutchinson, and Brian Ward. "'Dress Modestly, Neatly ... as If You Were Going to Church': Respectability, Class and Gender in the Montgomery Bus Boycott and the Early Civil Rights Movement." In *Gender and the Civil Rights Movement*, edited by Peter Ling and Sharon Monteith, 69–100. New Brunswick, NJ: Rutgers University Press, 1999.

D'Emilio, John. *Lost Prophet: The Life and Times of Bayard Rustin*. Chicago: University of Chicago Press, 2003.

Dudziak, Mary. *Cold War Civil Rights*. Princeton, NJ: Princeton University Press, 2000.

Feldstein, Ruth. "'I Wanted the Whole World to See': Race, Gender, and Constructions of Motherhood in the Death of Emmett Till." In *Not June Cleaver: Women and Gender in Postwar America, 1945–1960*, edited by Joanne Meyerowitz, 263–303. Philadelphia: Temple University Press, 1994.

Gonda, Jeffrey. *Unjust Deeds: The Restrictive Covenant Cases and the Making of the Civil Rights Movement*. Chapel Hill: University of North Carolina Press, 2015.

James, Rawn, Jr. *Root and Branch: Charles Hamilton Houston, Thurgood Marshall, and the Struggle to End Segregation*. London: Bloomsbury Press, 2010.

Klarman, Michael J. *"Brown vs. Board of Education" and the Civil Rights Movement*. Oxford: Oxford University Press, 2007.

Long, Michael G., ed. *First Class Citizenship: The Civil Rights Letters of Jackie Robinson*. New York: Times Books, 2007.

———. *I Must Resist: Bayard Rustin's Life in Letters*. San Francisco: City Lights, 2012.

Margolick, David. *Elizabeth and Hazel: Two Women of Little Rock*. New Haven, CT: Yale University Press, 2012.

McGuire, Danielle. *At the Dark End of the Street: Black Women, Rape and Resistance—a New History of the Civil Rights Movement from Rosa Parks to the Rise of Black Power*. New York: Vintage Press, 2011.

Meier, August, and Elliott Rudwick. *CORE: A Study in the Civil Rights Movement, 1942–1968*. Oxford: Oxford University Press, 1973.

Michaeli, Ethan. *The Defender: How the Legendary Black Newspaper Changed America*. Boston: Houghton Mifflin Harcourt, 2016.

Robinson, Jo Ann. *The Montgomery Bus Boycott and the Women Who Made It: The Memoir of Jo Ann Gibson Robinson*. Knoxville: University of Tennessee Press, 1987.

Theoharis, Jeanne. *The Rebellious Life of Rosa Parks*. Boston: Beacon Press, 2015.

Till-Mobley, Mamie, and Christopher Bennett. *Death of Innocence: The Story of the Hate Crime That Changed America*. London: Oneworld, 2004.

Tushnet, Mark V. *Making Civil Rights: Thurgood Marshall and the Supreme Court, 1936–1961*. Oxford: Oxford University Press, 1994.

Tyson, Timothy. *The Blood of Emmett Till*. New York: Simon and Schuster, 2017.

Walls Lanier, Carlotta, and Lisa Frazier Page. *A Mighty Long Walk: My Journey to Justice at Little Rock Central High School*. London: Oneworld, 2010.

Zeiler, Thomas. *Jackie Robinson and Race in America*. Boston: Bedford/St. Martin's, 2013.

Zelden, Charles. *The Battle for the Black Ballot: "Smith v. Allwright" and the Defeat of the Texas All-White Primary*. Lawrence: University Press of Kansas, 2004.

4

Youth Activism in the Early 1960s

How did young African Americans build on traditional forms of Black protest and radical ideologies to jump-start the civil rights movement? How did they leverage their position as college students—participants in higher-education institutions—to disrupt long-standing patterns of segregation?

Coming of age during the Emmett Till murder and the activism of the Little Rock Nine, a new generation of activists—African American youth—had experienced both the horrors of Jim Crow as well as the possibilities of realizing true democracy, one not grounded in racial exclusion. These young adults were of the Emmett Till cohort in that they were of his age group and were now enrolled in high school and colleges. Many of them were frustrated by the slow process of civil rights and as a result acted on their own terms. Drawing on an arsenal of nonviolent tactics historically used by labor, civil rights, and religious groups, these students staged sit-in demonstrations to desegregate public accommodations and demand that they were treated as and granted the rights of first-class citizens. These protests also made demands on behalf of African American workers, helping to open sales and office jobs (positions historically held by whites) in public accommodations.

Students rightly understood that these places most visibly highlighted the contradictions of American democracy and that African Americans' rapidly increasing purchasing power—which swelled from $8–9 billion in 1947 to $30 billion by 1969—could be leveraged (using them in businesses that treated them well or withholding them from those that discriminated against them) to enact change. In department stores, five-and-dimes, and other sites of consumption, racial discrimination and segregation were glaringly obvious. African Americans were not permitted to try on and return clothes, they had to drink from separate drinking fountains, they were forbidden from eating at store restaurants, and if they were allowed to eat at store restaurants they were forced to do so in segregated and unequal sections.

The Greensboro sit-in in 1960 at Woolworth's lunch counter not only exemplified these efforts but also kick-started a new phase in the civil rights movement: the Student Movement. The sit-in was the brainchild of four college students at North Carolina Agricultural and Technical College, a local historically Black college. The students were part of an NAACP student chapter that met at Bennett College, a local historically Black college for women. The women of Bennett College served as the movement's "foot soldiers," picketing storefronts, marching, and canvassing the community; they coordinated carpools and served as replacement protesters; and, during the sit-in, "as much as 40 percent of Bennett College's student body was in the local jail," having been arrested for their participation in the movement.[1]

The Greensboro protest was not the first sit-in, but it did serve as a catalyst for a series of sit-ins across the South in the early 1960s. Local college students were often at the helm of these sit-ins and galvanized the surrounding community to participate. Soon, young activists like John Lewis, Diane Nash, Julian Bond, Marion Barry, and many others were leading a new phase of the civil rights movement.

Civil rights organizations like CORE, the NAACP, and the Southern Christian Leadership Conference (SCLC) were active in the movement, but youth activists sought to establish an organization that would speak to their concerns and would be led by students. Guided by veteran civil rights activist Ella Baker, who recognized the significance of this region-wide effort, youths active in the sit-ins and other civil rights protests met at a conference at Shaw University in 1960. The result of the conference was the creation of the Student Nonviolent Coordinating Committee. SNCC would become one of the major civil rights organizations promoting the use of participatory democracy. SNCC organized in local communities across the South to desegregate public spaces as well as procure voting rights and improve economic conditions for African Americans.

One year after the founding of SNCC, in early May 1960, African American youths initiated the Freedom Rides. The Freedom Rides sought to force the South to adhere to the Supreme Court's ruling in *Boynton v. Virginia* (1960), where it extended its 1946 ruling in *Irene Morgan v. Commonwealth of Virginia* and added bus terminals used in interstate bus travel as a site where segregation was illegal. Despite this ruling, the South continued to force African Americans to ride at the back of the bus and prohibited them from sitting in whites-only waiting rooms. Beginning in Washington, D.C., and ending in Mississippi, the Freedom Rides had whites and Blacks ride together on interstate buses, with whites sitting in the back and Blacks sitting in the front of the buses. When they stopped at terminals, whites went to the Black waiting room, while African Americans went to the white waiting room.

Mass demonstrations, however, were not the only form of African American youth protest in the early 1960s. In 1960, after applying and being denied admission to the University of Georgia, Charlayne Hunter-Gault and Hamilton Holmes filed suit against the university, alleging racial discrimination. Their case went to court in 1960. A year later, the judge issued his ruling, stating that Hunter and Holmes "would have already been admitted had it not been for their race and color" and ordered the University of Georgia to immediately admit them. Three days later, they became the first African Americans to attend this university.

That same year, with the assistance of the NAACP, James Meredith filed a similar suit against the all-white University of Mississippi. Once again, a southern university had refused to admit a qualified Black applicant because of their race. The case was eventually settled on appeal by the Supreme Court in Meredith's favor in September 1962. On October 1, 1962, Meredith became the first African American to enroll at the University of Mississippi.

NOTES

1. William H. Chafe, *Civilities and Civil Rights: Greensboro, North Carolina, and the Black Struggle for Freedom* (Oxford: Oxford University Press, 1980), 99, 137; Linda Beatrice Brown, *The Long Walk: The Story of Willa B. Player at Bennett College* (Danville, VA: Bennett College, 1998), 169; Deidre Flowers, "The Launching of the Student Sit-in Movement: The Role of Black Women at Bennett College," *Journal of African American History* 90 (Winter 2005): 52–63.

DOCUMENT 4.1

David Richmond, Franklin McCain, Ezell Blair, and Joseph McNeil Are Seen Leaving the Woolworth Store (1960)

The four college students—Joseph McNeil, Franklin McCain, Ezell Blair Jr. (now Jibreel Khazan), and David Richmond—who started the Greensboro sit-in movement on February 1, 1960, are shown here. These men were in their freshman year at North Carolina Agricultural and Technical State University when they launched the Greensboro sit-ins, a series of nonviolent direct-action protests to integrate lunch counters and eating establishments. Their first target was the F. W. Woolworth, a discount department store in downtown Greensboro. Soon thereafter, protests spread to other eating and retail establishments in Greensboro and the American South.

Source: Jack Moebes, *David Richmond, Franklin McCain, Ezell Blair, and Joseph McNeil Are Seen Leaving the Woolworth Store on February 1, 1960*, 1960, photograph, *Greensboro Daily News*. Used with permission of the Jack Moebes Photo Archive.

DOCUMENT 4.2

Anne Moody's Involvement in Student Demonstrations in Jackson, Mississippi (1963)

In this document, Anne Moody recounts her experience participating in the Woolworth sit-in in Jackson, Mississippi. On May 28, 1963, Moody alongside other students and faculty from Tougaloo College staged a sit-in demonstration to protest segregated lunch-counter seating at the F. W. Woolworth department store in downtown Jackson. Moody details that this protest was one of the most violently attacked demonstrations to end racial discrimination and segregation in public accommodations. Protesters were verbally and physically assaulted, including being spat upon and having scalding hot coffee and food poured on them, until the police (who watched for much of the time) finally intervened. The Jackson sit-in galvanized the local Black community to participate in the movement to dismantle Jim Crow in every facet of life. Jackson's eating facilities, however, remained segregated until the passage of the Civil Rights Act of 1964.

. . . . I had become very friendly with my social science professor [at Tougaloo College], John Salter, who was in charge of NAACP activities on campus. All during the year, while the NAACP conducted a boycott of the downtown stores in Jackson, I had been one of Salter's most faithful canvassers and church speakers. During the last week of school, he told me that sit-in demonstrations were about to start in Jackson and that he wanted me to be the spokesman for a team that would sit-in at Woolworth's lunch counter. The two other demonstrators would be classmates of mine, Memphis [Norman] and Pearlena [Lewis]. Pearlena was a dedicated NAACP worker, but Memphis had not been very involved in the Movement on campus. It seemed that the organization had had a rough time finding students who were in a position to go to jail. I had nothing to lose one way or the other. Around ten o'clock the morning of the demonstrations, NAACP headquarters alerted the news services. As a result, the police department was also informed, but neither the policemen nor the newsmen knew exactly where or when the demonstrations would start. They stationed themselves along Capitol Street and waited.

To divert attention from the sit-in at Woolworth's, the picketing started at JCPenney's a good fifteen minutes before. The pickets were allowed to walk up and down in front of the store three or four times before they were arrested. At exactly 11 A.M., Pearlena, Memphis, and I entered Woolworth's from the rear entrance. We separated as soon as we stepped into the store, and made small purchases from various counters. Pearlena had given Memphis her watch. He was to let us know when it was 11:14. At 11:14 we were to join him near the lunch counter and at exactly 11:15 we were to take seats at it.

Seconds before 11:15 we were occupying three seats at the previously segregated Woolworth's lunch counter. In the beginning the waitresses seemed to ignore us, as if they really didn't know what was going on. Our waitress walked past us a couple of times before she noticed we had started to write our own orders down and realized we wanted service. She asked us what we wanted. We began to read to her from our order slips. She told us that we would be served at the back counter, which was for Negroes.

"We would like to be served here," I said.

The waitress started to repeat what she had said, then stopped in the middle of the sentence. She turned the lights out behind the counter, and she and the other waitresses almost ran to the back of the store, deserting all their white customers. I guess they thought that violence would start immediately after the whites at the counter realized what was going on. There were five or six other people at the counter. A couple of them just got up and walked away. A girl sitting next to me finished her banana split before leaving. A middle-aged white woman who had not yet been served rose from her seat and came over to us. "I'd like to stay here with you," she said, "but my husband is waiting."

The newsmen came in just as she was leaving. They must have discovered what was going on shortly after some of the people began to leave the store. One of the newsmen ran behind the woman who spoke to us and asked her to identify herself. She refused to give her name, but said she was a native of Vicksburg and a former resident of California. When asked why she had said what she had said to us, she replied, "I am in sympathy with the Negro movement." By this time a crowd of cameramen and reporters had gathered around us taking pictures and asking questions, such as Where were we from? Why did we sit-in? What organization sponsored it? Were we students? From what school? How were we classified?

I told them that we were all students at Tougaloo College, that we were represented by no particular organization, and that we planned to stay there even after the store closed. "All we want is service," was my reply to one of them. After they had finished probing for about twenty minutes, they were almost ready to leave.

At noon, students from a nearby white high school started pouring in to Woolworth's. When they first saw us they were sort of surprised. They didn't know how to react. A few started to heckle and the newsmen became interested again. Then the white students started chanting all kinds of anti-Negro slogans. We were called a little bit of everything. The rest of the seats except the three we were occupying had been roped off to prevent others from sitting down. A couple of the boys took one end of the rope and made it into a hangman's noose. Several attempts were made to put it around our necks. The crowds grew as more students and adults came in for lunch.

We kept our eyes straight forward and did not look at the crowd except for occasional glances to see what was going on. All of a sudden I saw a face I remembered—the drunkard from the bus station sit-in. My eyes lingered on him just long enough for us to recognize each other. Today he was drunk too, so I don't think he remembered where he had seen me before. He took out a knife, opened it, put it in his pocket, and then began to pace the floor. At this point, I told Memphis and Pearlena what was going on. Memphis suggested that we pray. We bowed our heads, and all hell broke loose. A man rushed forward, threw Memphis from his seat, and slapped my face. Then another man who worked in the store threw me against an adjoining counter.

Down on my knees on the floor, I saw Memphis lying near the lunch counter with blood running out of the corners of his mouth. As he tried to protect his face, the man who'd thrown him down kept kicking him against the head. If he had worn hard-soled shoes instead of sneakers, the first kick probably would have killed Memphis. Finally a man dressed in plain clothes identified himself as a police officer and arrested Memphis and his attacker.

Pearlena had been thrown to the floor. She and I got back on our stools after Memphis was arrested. There were some white Tougaloo teachers in the crowd. They asked Pearlena and me if we wanted to leave. They said that things were getting too rough. We didn't know what to do. While we were trying to make up our minds, we were joined by Joan Trumpauer. Now there were three of us and we were integrated. The crowd began to chant, "Communists, Communists, Communists." Some old man in the crowd ordered the students to take us off the stools.

"Which one should I get first?" a big husky boy said.

"That white nigger," the old man said.

The boy lifted Joan from the counter by her waist and carried her out of the store. Simultaneously, I was snatched from my stool by two high school students. I was dragged about thirty feet toward the door by my hair when someone made them turn me loose. As I was getting up off the floor, I saw Joan coming back inside. We started back to the center of the counter to join Pearlena. Lois Chaffee, a white Tougaloo faculty member, was now sitting next to her. So Joan and I just climbed across the rope at the front end of the counter and sat down. There were now four of us, two whites and two Negroes, all women. The mob started smearing us with ketchup, mustard, sugar, pies, and everything on the counter. Soon Joan and I were joined by John Salter, but the moment he sat down he was hit on the jaw with what appeared to be brass knuckles. Blood gushed from his face and someone threw salt into the open wound. Ed King, Tougaloo's chaplain, rushed to him.

At the other end of the counter, Lois and Pearlena were joined by George Raymond, a CORE [Congress of Racial Equality] field worker and a student from Jackson State College. Then a Negro high school boy sat down next to me. The mob took spray paint from the counter and sprayed it on the new demonstrators. The high school student had on a white shirt; the word "nigger" was written on his back with red spray paint.

We sat there for three hours taking a beating when the manager decided to close the store because the mob had begun to go wild with stuff from other counters. He begged and begged everyone to leave. But even after fifteen minutes of begging, no one budged. They would not leave until we did. Then Dr. [A. Daniel] Beittel, the president of Tougaloo College, came running in. He said he had just heard what was happening.

About ninety policemen were standing outside the store; they had been watching the whole thing through the windows, but had not come in to stop the mob or do anything. President Beittel went outside and asked Captain Ray to come and escort us out. The captain refused, stating the manager had to invite him in before he could enter the premises, so Dr. Beittel himself brought us out. He had told the police that they had better protect us after we were outside the store. When we got outside, the policemen formed a single line that blocked the mob from us. However, they were allowed to throw at us everything they had collected. Within ten minutes, we were picked up by Reverend [Edwin] King in his station wagon and taken to the NAACP headquarters on Lynch Street.

After the sit-in, all I could think of was how sick Mississippi whites were. They believed so much in the segregated Southern way of life, they would kill to preserve it. I sat there in the NAACP office and thought of how many times they had killed when this way of life was threatened. I knew that the killing had just begun. "Many more will die before it is over with," I thought. Before the sit-in, I had always hated the whites in Mississippi. Now I knew it was impossible for me to hate sickness. The whites had a disease, an incurable disease in its final stage. What were our chances against such a disease? . . .

DOCUMENT 4.3

Anne Moody, Joan Trumpauer, and John Salter Sit in at a Jackson Restaurant (1963)

Civil rights sit-in demonstrators John Salter, Joan Trumpauer, and Anne Moody photographed at Woolworth's lunch counter on May 28, 1963. As Anne Moody described in her autobiography (see previous document), a white mob surrounded the protesters and assailed them with hot coffee, sugar, ketchup, and mustard. Looking on as part of the crowd are Red Hydrick, seen in the upper left wearing a hat and eyeglasses, and teenager D. C. Sullivan, who is in the middle of the crowd smoking a cigarette.

Source: Fred Blackwell, *John Salter, Joan Trumpauer, and Anne Moody Sit in at the Downtown Woolworth's in Jackson, Mississippi, on May 28, 1963*, 1963, photograph, Hunter Gray (John R. Salter) Papers, 1889–1992, 1996–2000, Wisconsin Historical Society, https://www.wisconsinhistory.org/Records/Image/IM2381. Courtesy of Fred and Phyllis Blackwell.

Diane Nash, "Speech at National Catholic Conference for Interracial Justice" (1961)

On August 25, 1961, civil rights activist Diane Nash addressed the National Catholic Conference for Interracial Justice in Detroit, Michigan. Nash became involved in the civil rights movement in 1960, while attending Fisk University in Nashville, Tennessee. She attended the Reverend James Lawson's nonviolent civil disobedience workshops in Nashville and began organizing sit-ins. Later, Nash participated in the Freedom Rides—a protest movement whereby activists rode interstate buses through the segregated South in 1961. She was a founding member of the Student Nonviolent Coordinating Committee and an organizer in the Southern Christian Leadership Conference. In her speech to the National Catholic Conference for Interracial Justice, Nash argues that the woes of the world are the result of a lack of respect for human dignity and insists that direct-action protests, namely, boycotts and Freedom Rides, are the most effective tools for realizing true democracy and freedom.

. . . My participation in the movement began in February 1960, with the lunch counter "sit-ins." I was then a student at Fisk University, but several months ago I interrupted my schoolwork for a year in order to work full time with the movement. My occupation at present is coordinating secretary for the Nashville Nonviolent Movement. . . .

I submit, then, that the nonviolent movement in that city:

1. is based upon and motivated by love;
2. attempts to serve God and mankind;
3. strives toward what we call the beloved community.

This is religion. This is applied religion. I think it has worked for me and I think it has worked for you and I think it is the work of our Church.

. . . [T]he problems lie not so much in our action as in our inaction. We have upon ourselves as individuals in a democracy the political, economic, sociological, and spiritual responsibilities of our country. I'm wondering now if we in the United States are really remembering that this must be a government "of the people" and "by the people" as well as "for the people." Are we really appreciating the fact that if you and I do not meet these responsibilities then our government *cannot* survive as a democracy?

The problems in Berlin, Cuba, or South Africa are, I think, identical with the problem in Jackson, Mississippi, or Nashville, Tennessee. I believe that when men come to believe in their own dignity and in the worth of their own freedom, and when they can acknowledge the God and the dignity that is within every man, then Berlin and Jackson will not be problems. . . .

The purpose of the movement and of the sit-ins and the Freedom Rides and any other such actions, as I see it, is to bring about a climate in which all men are respected as men, in which there is appreciation of the dignity of man and in which each individual is free to grow and produce to his fullest capacity. We of the movement often refer to this goal as the concept of the redeemed or the "beloved" community.

In September 1959, I came to Nashville as a student at Fisk University. This was the first time that I had been as far south as Tennessee; therefore, it was the first time that I had encountered the blatant segregation that exists in the South. I came then to see the community in sin. Seeing signs designating "white" or "colored," being told, "We don't serve niggers in here," and, as happened in one restaurant, being looked in the eye and told, "Go around to the back door where you belong," had a tremendous psychological impact on me. To begin with, I didn't agree with the premise that I was inferior, and I had a difficult time complying with it. Also, I felt stifled and boxed in since so many areas of living were restricted. The Negro in the South is told constantly, "You can't sit here." "You can't work there." "You can't live here, or send your children to school there." "You can't use this park, or that swimming pool," and on and on and on. Restrictions extend into housing, schools, jobs (Negroes, who provide a built-in lower economic class, are employed in the most menial capacities and are paid the lowest wages). Segregation encompasses city parks, swimming pools, and recreational facilities, lunch counters, restaurants, movies, drive-in movies, drive-in restaurants, restrooms, water fountains, bus terminals, train stations, hotels, motels, auditoriums (Negro college students usually attend the most important formal dances of the year in the school gymnasium), amusement parks, legitimate theaters, bowling alleys, skating rinks—all of these areas are segregated. Oppression extends to every area of life. . . .

Segregation has its destructive effect upon the segregator also. The most outstanding of these effects perhaps is fear. I can't forget how openly this fear was displayed in Nashville on the very first day that students there sat-in. Here were Negro students, quiet, in good discipline, who were consciously attempting to show no ill will, even to the point of making sure that they had pleasant and calm facial expressions. The demonstrators did nothing more than sit on the stools at the lunch counter. Yet, from the reaction of the white employees of the variety stores and from the onlookers, some dreadful monster might just as well have been about to devour them all. Waitresses dropped things. Store managers and personnel perspired. Several cashiers were led off in tears. One of the best remembered incidents of that day took place in a ladies restroom of a department store. Two Negro students, who had sat-in at the lunch counter, went into the ladies restroom which was marked "white" and were there as a heavy-set, older white lady, who might have been seeking refuge from the scene taking place at the lunch counter, entered. Upon opening the door and finding the two Negro girls inside, the woman threw up her hands and, nearly in tears, exclaimed, "Oh! Nigras everywhere!"

So segregation engenders fear in the segregator, especially needless fear of what will happen if integration comes; in short, fear of the unknown. Then Jim Crow fosters ignorance. The white person is denied the educational opportunities of exchange with people of a race other than his own. Bias makes for the hatred which we've all seen stamped upon the faces of whites in newspaper pictures of the mob. The white hoodlum element is often provoked and egged on by the management or by onlookers; this is a type of degradation into which the segregator unfortunately slips.

Police departments can also sink to a sorry state. Bias lets the police turn their heads and not see the attacks made against demonstrators. In Nashville, police permissiveness has served to make the hoodlum element more and more bold, with incidents of real seriousness resulting, even a real tragedy, as was the case in the bombing of a Negro attorney's home last year during the sit-ins.

An unhappy result of segregation is that communications between the races become so limited as to be virtually nonexistent. The "good race relations" to which segregators in the South often refer is nothing more than a complete breakdown in communication so that one race is not aware of any of the other race's objections or of interracial problems. This has been clearly exemplified in cities where race relations have been called "good" and where the masses of Negroes have rallied behind students in boycotts of downtown areas that have been, reportedly, up to 98 percent effective among the Negro population.

By not allowing all its citizens to produce and contribute to the limit of their capacities, the entire city, or region, or country, will suffer, as can be seen in the South's slow progress in industrial, political, and other areas today and in the weakening of American influence abroad as a result of race hatred.

Segregation, moreover, fosters dishonesty between the races. It makes people lie to each other. It allows white merchants to accept the customers' money, but to give them unequal service, as at the Greyhound and Trailways Bus Lines, where all customers pay the same fares but some are not free to use all the facilities in the terminals and at restaurants where rest stops are made. Fares are equal, but service is not. The system forces the Negro maid to tell her employer that everything is all right and that she's satisfied, but when she is among her friends she talks about the injustice of the system.

Worst of all, however, is the stagnancy of thought and character—of both whites and Negroes—which is the result of the rationalization that is necessary in order that the oppressed and oppressor may live with a system of slavery and human abasement.

. . .

It interests me that the Freedom Riders have been called "troublemakers," "seekers of violence," and "seekers of publicity." Few people have seen the point: here are people acting within their constitutional and moral rights; they have done nothing more than ride a bus or use a facility that anyone else would normally expect to use any day of the year, but they have been confined and imprisoned for it. And somehow the attorney general and the president of the United States and the Justice Department of the United States can do nothing about such a gross injustice. As far as being seekers of violence and publicity, the students have, at all times, remained nonviolent. Are not the committers of violence responsible for their own actions? . . .

Now I think that this is a serious question for the American public to consider. Is this really the country in which we live? This is a serious moment, I think, for those who take democracy and freedom seriously. Remember now that these Freedom Riders are citizens of the United States who can be called on to go to war and who are receiving treatment of this type.

If so harsh a treatment is involved for an action as right as riding a bus, perhaps one as unimportant as riding a bus, can we not draw from that an inference of what life in the South for the Negro must really be like? . . .

The Negro must be represented by those who govern. Without this representation, there is moral slavery, if not physical. No person or country can have a clear conscience and a noble mien with such a sin on its conscience. I'm interested now in the people who call for gradualism. The answer, it seems to me, is to stop sinning and stop now! How long must we wait? It's been a century. How gradual can you get? . . .

The Negro is seeking to take advantage of the opportunities that society offers; the same opportunities that others take for granted, such as a cup of coffee at Woolworth's, a good job, an evening at the movies, and dignity. Persons favoring segregation often refer to the rights of man, but they never mention the rights of Negro men. . . .

From those who say they approve the ends, not the means, I would be interested in suggestions for a means which would yield freedom without delay. Let us look at the means. The students have chosen nonviolence as a technique; there is no reason why they couldn't have taken up guns. It was a responsible choice, I think. We have decided that if there is to be suffering in this revolution (which is really what the movement is—a revolution), we will take the suffering upon ourselves and never inflict it upon our fellow man, because we respect him and recognize the God within him. . . .

Finally, this movement has been called one of passive resistance. But it is not that at all. Rather it might be called one of active insistence. In regard to our own roles and the role of our Church, I think we need to understand that this is a question of *real* love of man and love of God. Is there such a thing as moderate love of God or moderate disdain for sin? I think we need radical good to combat radical evil. Consider the South. It can be the answer for the free world; it can be the pivot. The problem there is a vital challenge for truth; for respect for man. In a word, it is a question of dignity.

Source: Diane Nash, "Speech at National Catholic Conference for Interracial Justice," in *Women and the Civil Rights Movement, 1954–1965,* edited by Davis W. Houck and David E. Dixon (Jackson: University Press of Mississippi, 2009), 155–68. Courtesy of Diane Nash.

DOCUMENT 4.5

Student Nonviolent Coordinating Committee, "Statement of Purpose" (1960)

The Student Nonviolent Coordinating Committee, an independent student-led civil rights organization, was founded at a meeting of sit-in movement leaders at Shaw University in Raleigh, North Carolina, in April 1960—just two and a half months after the Greensboro sit-ins. It was here that the organization's statement of purpose was adopted.

CONSTITUTION OF THE STUDENT NONVIOLENT COORDINATING COMMITTEE
Originally adopted spring 1960, Raleigh, North Carolina
As revised 29 April 1962

We affirm the philosophical or religious ideal of nonviolence as the foundation of our purpose, the presupposition of our faith, and the manner of our action. Nonviolence as it grows from the Judaeo-Christian tradition seeks a social order of justice permeated by love. Integration of human endeavor represents the crucial first step towards such a society.

Through nonviolence, courage displaces fear; love transforms hate. Acceptance dissipates prejudice; hopes [sic] ends despair. Peace dominates war; faith reconciles doubt. Mutual regard cancels enmity. Justice for all overcomes injustice. The redemptive community supersedes systems of gross social immorality.

Love is the central motif of nonviolence. Love is the force by which God binds man to himself and man to man. Such love goes to the extreme; it remains loving and forgiving even in the midst of hostility. It matches the capacity of evil to inflict suffering with an even more enduring capacity to absorb evil, all the while persisting in love.

By appealing to conscience and standing on the moral nature of human existence, nonviolence nurtures the atmosphere in which reconciliation and justice become actual possibilities.

Source: SNCC, "Statement of Purpose," 1960, in *Nonviolence in America: A Documentary History*, edited by Staughton Lynd (New York: Bobbs-Merrill, 1966), 398–99, http://nationalhumanitiescenter.org/pds/maai3/protest/text2/snccstatementofpurpose.pdf.

Ella Baker, "Bigger than a Hamburger" (1960)

Ella Baker's "Bigger than a Hamburger" was published in the *Southern Patriot* in May 1960. Baker was a veteran civil rights activist who played an instrumental role in the founding and direction of Student Nonviolent Coordinating Committee. For many years prior to SNCC, Baker worked as a field secretary and branch director in the NAACP and was an executive secretary for the Southern Christian Leadership Conference, where her philosophies on group-centered leadership and focus on grassroots organizing at times clashed with the charismatic leadership of Dr. King and the SCLC's male leadership. Her article is a summary of the address she gave at the organization founding conference held at Shaw University in Raleigh, North Carolina, one month prior.

Raleigh, NC—The Student Leadership Conference made it crystal clear that current sit-ins and other demonstrations are concerned with something much bigger than a hamburger or even a giant-sized Coke.

Whatever may be the difference in approach to their goal, the Negro and white students, North and South, are seeking to rid America of the scourge of racial segregation and discrimination—not only at lunch counters, but in every aspect of life.

In reports, casual conversations, discussion groups, and speeches, the sense and the spirit of the following statement that appeared in the initial newsletter of the students at Barber-Scotia College, Concord, N.C., were re-echoed time and again:

> We want the world to know that we no longer accept the inferior position
> of second-class citizenship. We are willing to go to jail, be ridiculed, spat
> upon and even suffer physical violence to obtain First Class Citizenship.

By and large, this feeling that they have a destined date with freedom, was not limited to a drive for personal freedom, or even freedom for the Negro in the South.

Repeatedly it was emphasized that the movement was concerned with the moral implications of racial discrimination for the "whole world" and the "Human Race."

This universality of approach was linked with a perceptive recognition that "it is important to keep the movement democratic and to avoid struggles for personal leadership."

It was further evident that desire for supportive cooperation from adult leaders and the adult community was also tempered by apprehension that adults might try to "capture" the student movement. The students showed willingness to be met on the basis of equality, but were intolerant of anything that smacked of manipulation or domination.

This inclination toward *group-centered leadership*, rather than toward a *leader-centered group pattern of organization*, was refreshing indeed to those of the older group who bear the scars of the battle, the frustrations and the disillusionment that come when the prophetic leader turns out to have heavy feet of clay.

However hopeful might be the signs in the direction of group-centeredness, the fact that many schools and communities, especially in the South, have not provided adequate experience for young Negroes to assume initiative and think and act independently accentuated the need for guarding the student movement against well-meaning, but nevertheless unhealthy, over-protectiveness.

Here is an opportunity for adult and youth to work together and provide genuine leadership—the development of the individual to his highest potential for the benefit of the group.

Many adults and youth characterized the Raleigh meeting as the greatest or most significant conference of our period.

Whether it lives up to this high evaluation or not will, in a large measure, be determined by the extent to which there is more effective training in and understanding of non-violent principles and practices, in group dynamics, and in the re-direction into creative channels of the normal frustrations and hostilities that result from second-class citizenship.

Source: Ella Baker, "Bigger than a Hamburger," *Southern Patriot*, June 18, 1960.

Mug Shots of Freedom Riders C. T. Vivian, Mary Hamilton, and Jean Thompson (1961)

Below are mug shots of activists the Reverend C. T. Vivian, Mary Hamilton, and Jean Thompson who were arrested during the Freedom Rides in 1961.

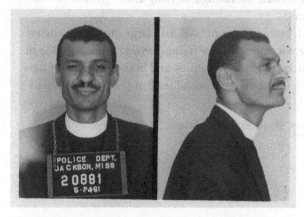

Source: *Mississippi State Sovereignty Commission Photograph*, photograph, May 24, 1961, Mississippi State Sovereignty Commission Records Online, 1994–2006, Mississippi Department of Archives and History, https://da.mdah .ms.gov/sovcom/photo.php?display= item&oid=76. Courtesy of the Archives and Records Services Division, Mississippi Department of Archives and History.

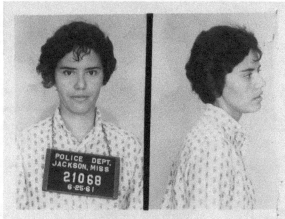

Source: *Mississippi State Sovereignty Commission Photograph*, June 25, 1961, Mississippi State Sovereignty Commission Records Online, 1994–2006, Mississippi Department of Archives and History, https://da.mdah .ms.gov/sovcom/photo .php?display =item&oid=303. Courtesy of the Archives and Records Services Division, Mississippi Department of Archives and History.

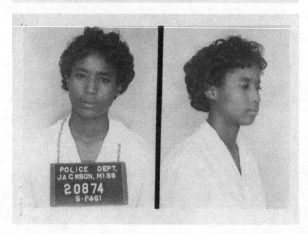

Mississippi State Sovereignty Commission Photograph, photograph, May 24, 1961, Mississippi State Sovereignty Commission Records Online, 1994–2006, Mississippi Department of Archives and History, https://da.mdah .ms.gov/sovcom/photo.php?display =item&oid=79. Courtesy of the Archives and Records Services Division, Mississippi Department of Archives and History.

James Meredith, "I Can't Fight Alone" (1963)

James Meredith was the first African American student admitted to the University of Mississippi, also known as Ole Miss, in 1962. Meredith decided to submit his application to the university in January 1961, the day after President John F. Kennedy's inauguration. Twice rejected, Meredith eventually received support from the National Association for the Advancement of Colored People and legally challenged the university's segregation policy. On October 1, 1962, after a lengthy court battle, Meredith was admitted to the university. This was only the beginning of his struggle, however. In this document, Meredith details his experiences integrating the university and ongoing racism and alienation at the institution.

People are always saying to me, "You are in the University of Mississippi, and that's the important fact." But so many unusual unique things have been a part of my stay here that I seriously doubt that I am in a true sense a student of the university. I'm inclined to go along with the diehard segregationists on this point. Just having a Negro in residence does not mean that the university has been integrated. Most of the time, I am perhaps the most segregated Negro in the world.

. . . . Though no price is too high to pay for liberation, I am convinced that you can pay a price for one piece of freedom that is greater than the benefits you get.

. . . . The political leadership of our state was, in my opinion, most responsible for what has gone on in Mississippi. . . . That these leaders chose to make a showdown fight over integration at the college level seemed to me to be completely illogical.

With the state government taking the position that it did, the students had no choice but to act as they did. . . . Just as a matter of maintaining their pride, and backing up their families who are the leaders of the state, they had to take a position similar to the one taken by the State of Mississippi.

Through it all, the most intolerable thing has been the campaign of ostracizing me. It does not harm me directly. If anyone doesn't want to associate with me, I'm sure that the feeling is at least mutual. . . . However, the ostracizers not only don't associate with me, but assume the right to see that no one else associates with me.

If a white student sits down and drinks a cup of coffee with me, or walks with me across the campus, he is subjected to unhampered intimidation and harassment. I have been denied my privileges all along, but these whites have not been. Now they have lost a simple freedom. This sets back the Negro, because anytime you move backward, the person already down suffers more. This campaign, which apparently has been permitted to go on, really results in a reduction of everybody's rights. . . .

The real question we are facing is whether Negroes, including Negroes in Mississippi, are able to obtain the education that their states offer. This is the basic issue—the right of access. The right to fail is just as important as the right to succeed.

The great purpose I have is to make way for the average Negro. Negro progress up to now has been on the basis of selection. Great efforts have always been made to get the superior, the above average Negro the right to certain things. This is a position I've always been cautious about. It's very dangerous. To make way for the above average can, of course, be only token progress. But if we can make way for the average, the above average will always find his place. If getting a degree from the University of Mississippi were all I ever did with my life, I would have done very little.

Throughout the first semester I received about 200 letters a day. Most of the people who wrote, particularly the Negroes, said that they had great admiration for me. They were praying and hoping that I would make it. Their basic attitude alarmed me. The letter that alarmed me most came from students at Alabama State College, a Negro school. The major message conveyed in this letter was that they had committed themselves to God and to me, to prove to the world that Negroes are somebody. The letter was alarming, because they had relieved themselves of all responsibility. They thought there was nothing more that they had to do. I feel that every young Negro must make his personal contribution toward the accomplishment of his freedom. No one man can fight alone. You can't confine the struggle for human freedom and dignity to one place or to one man.

. . . I have the problem of resolving whether my staying at the university is worth the intimidation and harassment that my family has to endure. My father is 71 years old, worked hard all his life, lived a good life, paid all his debts, never was in trouble, was a good citizen—but he can't sleep in peace without the danger of someone attacking him violently. He had not gone to the University of Mississippi, or done any of the other things that the opposition might have been fighting about. Yet, one night, they fired into his house with shotguns. Our system of laws allowed such a thing to happen, and it is tragic that the opposition has degenerated to this level.

. . . [T]he letters from this country, especially from Negroes, often did not even acknowledge that I have any right to be concerned about the welfare of my family. For a long time, not one in a hundred seemed to have understood at all. This pointed out to me the unrealistic hopes that the Negroes hold about the future. In their failure to conceive of all the costs, both physical and mental, they showed that they were failing to realize the real price that they would themselves someday have to pay if they were to do their part. . . .

The reports that I might not stay produced a most heartening change in the mail that came to me. The president of the student body in a Negro school out in Texas wrote a letter signed by a number of the students. Of course, they hoped that I would find my way clear to remain at the University of Mississippi. But this was a minor point. The main point was that they realized their obligation to move forward and were prepared to work hard for their aims, regardless of what happened in Mississippi. This was a manifestation that I had long looked for, and the same general trend soon began to appear in a strong majority of the letters from Negroes, especially those under 35. . . .

I have spent the biggest portion of my life trying to settle on some method—some simple, effective method—of bringing about the uplift of the Negro in general and Mississippi Negroes in particular. As I see it, we have to start making long-range plans and work together for predetermined goals. The first thing we've got to do in Mississippi, if the Negro is to improve his lot, is to get Negro doctors, lawyers, businessmen and professional men into our community. Not just teachers. Today, there are only four Negro lawyers in the whole state, and they all have offices in Jackson. Through a cooperative effort, we could in five years have a doctor and a lawyer in every major town in the state. In ten years, we could have a lawyer in every county and a doctor in every town, small as well as large. Within fifteen years, by this community system, the Negro can obtain his rights—including the right to vote—and help decide his own destiny and the destiny of his people. In twenty years, the Negro in Mississippi, working diligently, cooperatively, quietly, can lift himself up to a complete position of respect and decency.

I think that the Negro has been widely misled about the realities of the political structure of the South. . . . We all speak of our constitutional rights. But when a Negro speaks of constitutional rights, he speaks only of the Constitution of the United States. . . . However, the things that affect the daily lives and welfare of the people most are the provisions written into the state constitutions and statutes. This is a fact of life. I have been accused of being a states' righter because I have consistently refused to condemn or otherwise talk too unfavorably about the white Southern leadership and the leadership in Mississippi. As I see it, to solve our problem is going to call for full effort on the part of everyone affected by it. This includes the Negro, the segregationist, the government at both state and local levels, the churches and all other institutions. We must have more communication and coordination within the community. And of course it is of utmost importance that the Negro, the one who is actually suffering, do far more in the future than he has done in the past. I feel that, whereas the Negro certainly needs organization and planning on the national level, the real solution to our problem must come on the other levels—regional, state and local. I have great hope.

The best way to start is to find some common ground for communication, and being together in an institution of learning puts you on common ground. . . .

I must honestly admit that it has become more and more difficult for me to place too much hope in the idea of mutual understanding and the changing of hearts. Hearts have now shown that they don't intend to change. So the law has to come in. If the law of the land gives certain rights and privileges to its citizens, then it must be enforced.

In this situation, each Negro has no choice but to give his best attention and deepest effort to the solution of our problem. He must feel proud of himself. Whether he's illegitimate, or comes from a broken home, no matter where he lodges, be he illiterate, poor, a butler or a maid, no matter what his past, he looks to the future and the changes he will help bring about. He feels that, whatever I was tomorrow, I can be what I want to be. The great principles upon which America establishes herself will be made a reality for all. No matter what is the outcome of my endeavors at the University of Mississippi, the objective for all of us is clear: complete freedom, complete rights and privileges for each citizen in this democracy.

Source: James H. Meredith, "I Can't Fight Alone," *Look*, April 19, 1963, 70–78, http://historymatters.gmu.edu/d/6326/. Courtesy of James H. Meredith.

FURTHER READING

Arsenault, Ray. *Freedom Riders: 1961 and the Struggle for Racial Justice.* Oxford: Oxford University Press, 2006.

Carson, Clayborne. *In Struggle: SNCC and the Black Awakening of the 1960s.* Cambridge, MA: Harvard University Press, 1981.

Catsam, Derek Charles. *Freedom's Line: The Journey of Reconciliation and the Freedom Rides.* Lexington: University Press of Kentucky, 2009.

Cohen, Robert. *Rebellion in Black and White: Southern Student Activism in the 1960s.* Baltimore: Johns Hopkins University Press, 2013.

Garrow, David. *Bearing the Cross: Martin Luther King, Jr., and the Southern Christian Leadership Conference.* New York: William Morrow, 1986.

Greenberg, Cheryl Lynn. *A Circle of Trust: Remembering SNCC.* Newark, NJ: Rutgers University Press, 1998.

Halberstam, David. *The Children.* New York: Fawcett Books, 1999.

Hamlin, Francoise. *Crossroads at Clarksdale: The Black Freedom Struggle in Mississippi Delta after World War II.* Chapel Hill: University of North Carolina Press, 2012.

Hogan, Wesley. *Many Minds, One Heart: SNCC's Dream for a New America.* Chapel Hill: University of North Carolina Press, 2007.

Holsaert, Faith S., et al. *Hands on the Freedom Plow: Personal Accounts by Women in SNCC.* Urbana: University of Illinois Press, 2012.

Houston, Benjamin. *The Nashville Way: The Racial Etiquette and the Struggle for Social Justice in Southern City.* Athens: University of Georgia Press, 2012.

Lewis, Andrew. *The Shadow of Youth: The Remarkable Journey of the Civil Rights Generation.* New York: Hill & Wang, 2010.

Lewis, John, and Mike D'Orso. *Walking with the Wind: A Memoir of the Movement.* San Diego: Harcourt Brace, 1998.

Meredith, James. *Three Years in Mississippi.* Bloomington: Indiana University Press, 1966.

Monteith, Sharon. *SNCC's Stories: The African American Freedom Movement in the Civil Rights South.* Athens: University of Georgia Press, 2020.

Morgan, Iwan, and Philip Davies. *From Sit-ins to SNCC: The Student Civil Rights Movement in the 1960s.* Gainesville: University Press of Florida, 2012.

Moye, J. Todd. *Ella Baker: Community Organizer of the Civil Rights Movement.* Lanham, MD: Rowman & Littlefield, 2013.

Mullins, Lisa. *Diane Nash: The Fire of the Civil Rights Movement, a Biography.* Miami: Barnhardt & Ashe, 2007.

Olson, Lynne. *Freedom's Daughter: The Unsung Heroines of the Civil Rights Movement from 1830 to 1970.* New York: Scribner, 2001.

Parker, Traci. *Department Stores and the Black Freedom Movement: Workers, Consumers, and Civil Rights from the 1930s to the 1980s.* Chapel Hill: University of North Carolina Press, 2019.

———. "Southern Retail Campaigns and the Struggle for Black Economic Freedom in the 1950s and 1960s." In *Race and Retail: Consumption across the Color Line,* edited by Mia Bay and Ann Fabian, 87–108. New Brunswick, NJ: Rutgers University Press, 2015.

Peck, James. *Freedom Ride.* New York: Simon & Schuster, 1962.

Ransby, Barbara. *Ella Baker and the Black Freedom Movement.* Chapel Hill: University of North Carolina Press, 2003.

Weems, Robert. *Desegregating the Dollar: African American Consumerism in the Twentieth Century.* New York: New York University Press, 1998.

Zinn, Howard. *SNCC: The New Abolitionists.* Boston: South End Press, 2002.

5

Local Struggles

How did activists on the local level fight for civil rights? What were their connections to the national movement? To what extent did local activists push for civil rights strategies beyond nonviolent direct action such as self-defense? How did the debate between proponents of nonviolence versus those of self-defense play out at the local level? When and where did calls for violence, or rather self-defense, originate and prove to be more effective in galvanizing African American support and engagement in the movement? When did violence make more sense as a strategy?

The philosophy of nonviolence dominated mainstream civil rights. This was apparent even at the local level, where activists like Septima Clark sought to remedy African Americans' political disenfranchisement through literacy and voter education. Not everyone, however, believed that nonviolence was always the best and most effective strategy. A number of African Americans, including World War II veterans like Robert F. Williams, believed that self-defense was the best, and perhaps only, strategy to respond to the terror of Jim Crow and the near-daily violence African Americans faced at the hands of white supremacists. Calls for self-defense also originated from Maryland activist Gloria Richardson, the Deacons for Defense in Louisiana, and many others. The stakes of the debate between nonviolent direct-action proponents and self-defense proponents were high. On the one hand, nonviolence proponents like Dr. Martin Luther King Jr. feared that armed African Americans would provoke even more violence from white supremacists or the state, while dampening support from more moderate whites and civil rights supporters. Self-defense advocates argued that African Americans could count only on themselves to defend their families and communities and believed that self-defense might deter further attacks.

As the philosophical debate over nonviolence versus violence ensued, two major civil rights campaigns were afoot: the Albany Movement and the Birmingham Campaign. The Albany Movement began in the summer of 1961, when members of the Student Nonviolent Coordinating Committee moved to the city to conduct a voter registration project.

Seeing how dire the situation was in Albany, Georgia, activists moved to desegregate the entire town. Activists, however, faced a major obstacle in Sheriff Laurie Pritchett. Pritchett had studied the past tactics of SNCC and King and took measures to avoid negative media attention and intervention from the federal government. This, coupled with factions within the movement and lack of planning, caused the Albany Movement to fail.

Reflecting on Albany, King said

> The mistake I made there was to protest against segregation generally rather than against a single and distinct facet of it. Our protest was so vague that we got nothing, and the people were left very depressed and in despair. It would have been much better to have concentrated upon integrating the buses or the lunch counters. One victory of this kind would have been symbolic, would have galvanized support and boosted morale. . . . When we planned our strategy for Birmingham months later, we spent many hours assessing Albany and trying to learn from its errors. Our appraisals not only helped to make our subsequent tactics more effective, but revealed that Albany was far from an unqualified failure.

In Birmingham, Dr. King, the Southern Christian Leadership Conference, and local activists sought to take on "the most segregated city in America." The Birmingham Campaign was organized around Project C, the most intensive civil rights program up until this point. Project C demanded the integration of public accommodations, guarantees of employment opportunities for African American workers in downtown facilities, the desegregation of schools, the improvement of services in Black neighborhoods, and the provision of low-income housing. To meet this end, the campaign involved three major sets of demonstrations intended to desegregate lunch counters, water fountains, and the downtown business district; a march on city hall culminating in a kneel of prayer; and the infamous Children's March. The involvement of children in Project C was controversial given the anticipated violence the marchers would be subjected to by the city's segregationist police force, led by Eugene "Bull" Connor. Indeed, children in the march were subject to high-power water hoses, police dogs, and beatings that were captured on national and international news media. At the time of the Children's March, King was already in jail, having been arrested in a previous demonstration. It was during his imprisonment that he wrote "Letter from Birmingham Jail." The Birmingham Campaign did not win every demand, but it was still a major triumph and turning point in the civil rights movement. This campaign inspired a massive upsurge of protests throughout the South and compelled President John F. Kennedy to propose what would become the Civil Rights Act of 1964.

DOCUMENT 5.1

Robert F. Williams, "Can Negroes Afford to Be Pacifists?" (1959)

Born in Monroe, North Carolina, in 1925, Robert F. Williams became one of the foremost proponents of armed self-defense as a response to the murders, beatings, and other forms of unprovoked violence that African Americans faced across the South. Williams and other

Black veterans revived a local chapter of the NAACP and quickly set about challenging segregation in public spaces and protecting prominent Blacks and Black activists from white racial violence. Williams gained particular notoriety during the 1958 Kissing Case in which his media campaign and organizing efforts helped save two young Black boys from imprisonment for receiving a kiss on the cheek by a young white girl. Williams's vocal criticism of high-profile civil rights activists and support for armed self-defense eventually led to his suspension from the NAACP.

In 1954 I was an enlisted man in the United States Marine Corps. As a Negro in an integrated unit that was overwhelmingly white, I shall never forget the evening we were lounging in the recreation room watching television as a news bulletin flashed on the screen. This was the historic Supreme Court decision that segregation in the public schools is unconstitutional. Because of the interracial atmosphere, there was no vocal comment. . . . [M]y inner emotions must have been approximate to the Negro slaves when they first heard about the Emancipation Proclamation. Elation took hold of me so strongly that I found it very difficult to refrain from yielding to an urge of jubilation. I learned later that night that other Negroes in my outfit had felt the same surge of elation.

On this momentous night of May 17, 1954, I felt that at last the government was willing to assert itself on behalf of first-class citizenship, even for Negroes. I experienced a sense of loyalty that I had never felt before. I was sure that this was the beginning of a new era of American democracy. At last I felt that I was a part of America and that I belonged. . . .

I returned to civilian life in 1955 and the hope I had for Negro liberation faltered. I had returned to a South that was determined to stay the hand of progress at all cost. . . .

NEWS BLACKOUT

Since my release from the Marine Corps I could cite many cases of unprovoked violence that have been visited upon my people. Some, like the Emmett Till case, the Asbury Howard case and the Mack Parker incident, have been widely publicized. There are more, many many more, occurring daily in the South that never come to the light of the press because of a news blackout sponsored by local racist officials.

. . . Only highly civilized and moral individuals respect the rights of others. The low-mentality bigots of the South have shown a wanton disregard for the wellbeing and rights of their fellowmen of color, but there is one thing that even the most savage beast respects, and that is force. . . . The Southern brute respects only force. Nonviolence is a very potent weapon when the opponent is civilized, but nonviolence is no match or repellent for a sadist.

"TURN-THE-OTHER-CHEEKISM"

Rev. Martin Luther King is a great and successful leader of our race. The Montgomery bus boycott was a great victory for American democracy. However, most people have confused the issues facing the race. In Montgomery the issue was a matter of struggle for human dignity. Nonviolence is made to order for that type of conflict. . . . In a great many localities in the South Negroes are faced with the necessity of combating savage violence. The struggle is for mere existence. The Negro is in a position of begging for life. There is no lawful deterrent against those who would do him violence. An open declaration of nonviolence, or turn-the-other-cheekism is an invitation that the white racist brutes will certainly honor by brutal attack on cringing, submissive Negroes. . . .

In 1957 the Klan moved into Monroe and Union County. In the beginning we did not notice them much. Their numbers steadily increased to the point wherein the local press reported as many as seventy-five hundred racists massed at one rally. They became so brazen that mile-long motorcades started invading the Negro community. These hooded thugs fired pistols from car windows, screamed, and incessantly blew their automobile horns. On one occasion they caught a Negro woman on the street and tried to force her to dance for them at gun point. She escaped into the night, screaming and hysterical. They forced a Negro merchant to close down his business on direct orders from the Klan. Drivers of cars tried to run Negroes down when seen walking on the streets at night. Negro women were struck with missiles thrown from passing vehicles. Lawlessness was rampant. A Negro doctor was framed to jail on a charge of performing an abortion on a white woman. This doctor, who was vice-president of the N.A.A.C.P., was placed in a lonely cell in the basement of a jail, although men prisoners are usually confined upstairs. A crowd of white men started congregating around the jail. It is common knowledge that a lynching was averted. We have had the usual threats of the Klan here, but instead of cowing, we organized an armed guard and set up a defense force around the doctor's house. On one occasion, we had to exchange gunfire with the Klan. Each time the Klan came on a raid they were led by police cars. . . . We appealed to Governor Luther Hodges. All our appeals to constituted law were in vain. Governor Hodges, in an underhanded way, defended the Klan. . . .

CRINGING NEGRO MINISTERS

A group of nonviolent ministers met the city Board of Alderman and pleaded with them to restrict the Klan from the colored community. The city fathers advised these cringing, begging Negro ministers that the Klan had constitutional rights to meet and organize in the same way as the N.A.A.C.P. Not having been infected by turn-the-other-cheekism, a group of Negroes who showed a willingness to fight caused the city officials to deprive the Klan of its constitutional rights after local papers told of dangerous incidents between Klansmen and armed Negroes. Klan motorcades have been legally banned from the City of Monroe.

The possibility of tragedy's striking both sides of the tracks has caused a mutual desire to have a peaceful coexistence. The fact that any racial brutality may cause white blood to flow as well as Negro is lessening racial tension. The white bigots are sparing Negroes from brutal attack, not because of a new sense of morality, but because Negroes have adopted a policy of meeting violence with violence.

THE SCREAMS OF THE INNOCENT

I think there is enough latitude in the struggle for Negro liberation for the acceptance of diverse tactics and philosophies. There is need for pacifists and nonpacifists. I think each freedom fighter must unselfishly contribute what he has to offer. I have been a soldier and a Marine. I have been trained in the way of violence. I have been trained to defend myself. Self-defense to a Marine is a reflex action. People like Rev. Martin Luther King have been trained for the pulpit. I think they would be as out of place in a conflict that demanded real violent action as I would in a pulpit praying for an indifferent God to come down from Heaven and rescue a screaming Mack Parker or Emmett Till from an ungodly howling mob. . . .

STOP LYNCHING WITH VIOLENCE

On May 5, 1959, while president of the Union County branch of the National Association for the Advancement of Colored People, I made a statement to the United Press International after a trial wherein a white man was supposed to have been tried for kicking a Negro maid down a flight of stairs in a local white hotel. In spite of the fact that there was an eyewitness, the defendant failed to show up for his trial, and was completely exonerated. Another case in the same court involved a white man who had come to a pregnant Negro mother's home and attempted to rape her. In recorder's court the only defense offered for the defendant was that "he's not guilty. He was just drunk and having a little fun." Despite the fact that this pregnant Negro mother was brutally beaten and driven from her home because she refused to submit, and a white woman neighbor testified that the woman had come to her house excited, her clothes torn, her feet bare, and begging her for assistance, the court was unmoved. The defendant's wife was allowed to sit with him throughout the trial, and his attorney asked the jury if they thought this white man would leave "this beautiful white woman, the flower of life for this Negro woman." Some of the jurymen laughed and the defendant went free. This great miscarriage of justice left me sick inside, and I said then what I say now. I believe that Negroes must be willing to defend themselves, their women, their children and their homes. They must be willing to die and to kill in repelling their assailants. There is no Fourteenth Amendment, no equal protection under the law. Negroes *must* protect themselves, it is obvious that the federal government will not put an end to lynching; therefore it becomes necessary for us to stop lynching with violence. We must defend ourselves. . . .

KING CASHES IN ON WAR

It is obvious that the Negro leadership is caught in a terrible dilemma. It is trying to appease both white liberals who want to see Negro liberation given to us in eye-dropper doses and the Negro masses, who are growing impatient and restive under brutal oppression. There is a new Negro coming into manhood on the American scene and an indifferent government must take cognizance of this fact. The Negro is becoming more militant, and pacifism will never be accepted wholeheartedly by the masses of Negroes so long as violence is rampant in Dixie. . . .

Some Negro leaders have cautioned me that if Negroes fight back, the racist will have cause to exterminate the race. How asinine can one get? This government is in no position to allow mass violence to erupt, let alone allow twenty million Negroes to be exterminated. I am not half so worried about being exterminated as I am about my children's growing up under oppression and being mentally twisted out of human proportions.

We live in perilous times in America, and especially in the South. Segregation is an expensive commodity, but liberty and democracy too, have their price. So often the purchase check of democracy must be signed in blood. Someone must be willing to pay the price, despite the scoffs from the Uncle Toms. I am told that patience is commendable and that we must never tire of waiting, yet it is instilled at an early age that men who violently and swiftly rise to oppose tyranny are virtuous examples to emulate. I have been taught by my government to fight, and if I find it necessary I shall do just that. All Negroes must learn to fight back, for nowhere in the annals of history does the record show a people delivered from bondage by patience alone.

Source: Robert F. Williams, "Can Negroes Afford to Be Pacifists?," *Liberation* (1959): 4–7.

DOCUMENT 5.2

Septima Poinsette Clark on Organizing Citizenship Schools (1976)

Septima Poinsette Clark, an educator from South Carolina, was a driving force behind the Citizenship Schools—a massive effort to increase Black literacy and political engagement across the South. In the following interview, Clark discusses Highlander Folk School in Monteagle, Tennessee, which offered leadership training to civil rights activists in an integrated setting. At Highlander, Clark, Bernice Robinson, and Esau Jenkins developed the first Citizenship Schools. In the interview excerpt below, Clark discusses how the Citizenship Schools were picked up by the Southern Christian Leadership Council and implemented across the South. In addition to helping Blacks gain the literacy skills needed to pass literacy tests often administered to exclude them from voting, the Citizenship Schools inspired the development of community-based leaders.

EUGENE WALKER: I should like to begin by asking Ms. Clark if she would please state her name and her present residence.

SEPTIMA POINSETTE CLARK: My name is Septima P. Clark, and I live in Charleston, South Carolina. I started working at the Highlander Folk School in 1954, and we had a court case in 1959. I was arrested, and padlocks were put on the doors at Highlander Folk School. And Dr. King said that he would like to have the program that we started at Highlander come to Atlanta. So I was sent to Atlanta to carry out the citizenship education program, a program designed to eliminate illiteracy and get people ready to register and vote. When Dr. King took it over, we worked at a center in Liberty County, Georgia, a center that was owned by the American Missionary Association.

. . .

EUGENE WALKER: What kind of people were you looking for?

SEPTIMA POINSETTE CLARK: We were looking for those who could read well aloud and who could write legibly to come and be trained and go back into their communities and work with the illiterate. We didn't need anyone with a high school education, nor did we need anyone with a college education. We just wanted to have a community person, so that the illiterates would feel comfortable and happy with . . .

EUGENE WALKER: Did you encounter difficulty recruiting individuals to be trained to go back to their community and teach?

SEPTIMA POINSETTE CLARK: We did encounter difficulty, because under the name of Highlander, there were too many people in the South who were afraid of Highlander Folk School. It was really a school for problems, but it was designated as a communist outfit, and so that gave us a good bit of trouble in the communities. And until we could go around and have some lectures and explain to the people what we were doing, we couldn't get them at first.

EUGENE WALKER: Why did Highlander have this communist designation?

SEPTIMA POINSETTE CLARK: Because blacks and whites were able to live together and to work together at Highlander, the people of the South had a feeling—in fact, that came out in the McCarthy era—that if blacks and whites mixed, they're bound to have been communists. I had a wonderful experience in the Atlanta airport. A white woman came over to me and was talking about coming from Lake Junaluska. She was really one of the Methodist women that I knew. And another white woman was sitting to the end of the seat didn't know what we were talking about. As soon as this white woman left to go on her plane, she came over to me and said, "What is she talking to you about? Is she telling you about communism?" And I said, "Oh, no. We're church sisters, and we were talking about our churches."

EUGENE WALKER: So when you all went out and recruited people to bring them in, to go back into their various communities, was there any particular section of Georgia or the South you concentrated in?

SEPTIMA POINSETTE CLARK: The first part of Georgia that we worked through was Savannah, Georgia, and we worked with Savannah because Hosea Williams was there trying to get people to register to vote and didn't know that he had to teach them to read and write so they could answer the thirty questions that Georgia had for them to answer. When we were successful in Savannah, then Hosea found eighteen counties in the southeastern part of Georgia, and we started schools in those eighteen counties. That's when we brought in people to the center and trained them.

EUGENE WALKER: What happened in Savannah?

SEPTIMA POINSETTE CLARK: In Savannah the success was great. We got these people registered to vote, and in three weeks' time we were able, with the help of the SNCC boys and Southern Christian Leadership Conference's staff, we put 9,000 black registered voters on the books.

. . .

EUGENE WALKER: So when you recruited someone, what was their responsibility other than agreeing to be one of the participants, in terms of their upkeep?

SEPTIMA POINSETTE CLARK: They had to also promise that they would go back to the community and open up a school, and they were supposed to teach two nights a week, two hours each night. We had all of the books mimeographed that we wanted them to use in teaching.

EUGENE WALKER: Could you demonstrate for me, not in detail, but generally what it was that you taught these people and what it was they were expected to take back to their communities?

SEPTIMA POINSETTE CLARK: We used the election laws of that particular state to teach the reading. We used the amount of fertilizer and the amount of seeds to teach the arithmetic, how much they would pay for it and the like. We did some political work by having them to find out about the kind of government that they had in their particular community. And these were the things that we taught them when they went back home. Each state had to have its own particular reading, because each state had different requirements for the election laws.

EUGENE WALKER: Aside from Tallahassee, can you recall any other area of the South whereby you encountered great difficulty in trying to recruit or establish schools?

SEPTIMA POINSETTE CLARK: In Natchez, Mississippi, I went down there to recruit and to establish schools. And while I was down there, one night in a Baptist church the Ku Klux Klan surrounded us and had planned to come into the church. The Deacons of Defense from Louisiana had come over that night for the program.

EUGENE WALKER: Do you recall the year?

SEPTIMA POINSETTE CLARK: That was in the early part of '65, because in '64 we went to Europe and we had just come back. Anyway, at that place we were really having a lot of trouble, but the Chief of Police came out and asked the Ku Klux Klan to go back into their home and asked the colored people would they go to their homes. The reason why I think the Klansmen surrounded us that night at the church was because that day we had carried a large number of people up to the courthouse to register to vote. And while there, one of the white men of the White Citizens' Council kicked a white boy who was working along with me. And when he did that, I called Washington to get the Attorney General to see if we could peacefully work at that courthouse. That's where we had to register. In a few minutes, he called the Chief of Police of Natchez, and when he did that we got protection at the registration office. . . .

EUGENE WALKER: Good. Did any of the leaders of SCLC, like Wyatt T. Walker, Dorothy King, Abernathy, [unknown], did any of these individuals ever seek your counsel in regard to what should be done in the Citizenship Education Program or in regard to the direction SCLC should be going?

SEPTIMA POINSETTE CLARK: I wrote out a citizenship program, but I had to write a proposal to get the money, and I wrote out the day-by-day program that I took with me to the Southern Christian Leadership Conference. I can remember Reverend Abernathy asking many times, why was Septima Clark on the Executive Board of the Southern Christian Leadership Conference? And Dr. King would always say, "She was the one who proposed this citizenship education which is bringing to us not only money but a lot of people who will register and vote." And he asked that many times. It was hard for him to see a woman on that executive body.

EUGENE WALKER: How can you interpret that? What was he concerned about? Do you have any idea?

SEPTIMA POINSETTE CLARK: Well, I think that we live in a man-made world, and because of that, as a man, he didn't feel as if women had really enough intelligence to do a thing like what I was doing.

EUGENE WALKER: This was never expressed, but this is the way you interpret.

SEPTIMA POINSETTE CLARK: This is the way I interpreted it, because he kept asking the question. Many times we'd go into the meeting, and he'd always want to know why was I a member of that trustee board? . . .

Source: Septima Poinsette Clark, interview with Eugene Walker, July 30, 1976 (G-0017), in Southern Oral History Program Collection (#4007), Southern Historical Collection, Louis Round Wilson Special Collections Library, The University of North Carolina at Chapel Hill.

DOCUMENT 5.3

Charles Sherrod on the Albany Movement (2011)

Charles Sherrod, born in 1937 in Virginia, became active in the civil rights movement as a young person and later joined SNCC. In 1961, he became SNCC's first national field secretary and led the organization's Albany Project in Georgia that would focus on grassroots voter registration and community-based organizing. SNCC's efforts, combined with the demonstrations of local student activists as well as civic and civil rights organizations, came to be known as the Albany Movement. In the following interview, Sherrod discusses the Albany Movement and how SNCC organizers used local elders' religiosity and concern for local student activists to galvanize greater African American support for organizing to protest segregation in the city's public accommodations. Sherrod, who became a minister, met his future wife and fellow civil rights activist, Shirley Sherrod, in Albany.

. . . .

JOE MOSNIER: Reverend Sherrod, um, we mentioned before we started today that we'd focus right in on the work you did when you arrived here to build the Albany Movement.

CHARLES SHERROD: Yes, I came in about October, 1961, when, uh, just the experiences behind me were the jail-in in Rock Hill, South Carolina, where I spent a month or so there. . . . The Scripture, the eighth chapter of Romans, I carried with me the rest of the way until now in the movement. It had very important meaning to me while in the Rock Hill jail and chain gang, and I brought that with me to Albany. Uh, I'm persuaded that "nothing can separate me from the love of God in Christ Jesus, our Lord," a simple verse, but very meaningful to me. What it meant was that nothing but death could stop me from the mission that I had of developing our people. . . .

But it took me time to understand how to get an old fellow who says, "Yassuh," "Nawsuh," while looking down straight at the ground, he's talking to a white man or woman in front of him, um, I never understood—or it took me a long time to understand how to touch a man like that. And the indignity that women had when they went into stores to buy a hat, for example, to try on a hat. They could look at other white women trying on hats, but knowing that when they tried on a hat, they had to put a stocking cap over their head and then try on the hat. And they would then pay their money and say, "Yes, ma'am," "No, ma'am," paying their money. How to break them away from fearing the giant in the county, the sheriff, and to go down to the courthouse was to go down to the courthouse and face the sheriff.

It took us all of a month, because, after getting permission from the elders—you know, it wasn't as if the movement wasn't doing anything, the people weren't doing anything—they had, uh, voter registration drives, uh, trying to get people registered to vote, uh, the Criteria Club in Albany, Georgia, went to the City Commission and asked for paved streets and better lighting in their neighborhoods. They didn't get anything, but there was activity, I'm saying. So, there was leadership, there was some leadership in Albany before I even came. But when Charles Jones and Cordell Reagon and myself got the permission from the adults in the community to bring the movement into Albany, Georgia, we felt good.

We talked—first we talked to people who were just natural for us to talk to. At nineteen and twenty and twenty-one years old, we had to be talking to young people, so we talked to the young people first. And we got, uh, small numbers of young people—uh, ten, twenty, thirty, forty young people to come to meetings in the small churches where we were allowed to come. And the first church was a Presbyterian Church in the city. The other churches took a little time to think about it, because the word was that wherever the meetings were going to be held, the churches were going to be burned down to the ground. And that word spread all over the area. And some churches *were* burned down to the ground; they made good their promise.

But how do you get the fear that our people had out of them to stand up to the sheriff, stand up to the police, stand up to the Chief [Laurie] Pritchett? And the answer was our children, because the children had not been persecuted. They had not known any Pharaoh. They weren't afraid of their mama and their daddy [laughs] half of the time.

So, uh, after talking with them, week after week, and talking about nonviolence, because we were going up against, uh, a group of people who could deal with violence. They were looking for violence. If they could promote violence among us, then they could break us. But these young people they could not break, uh, if we confronted them with love. That's what we were talking about, confronting them with peace and confronting—and *expecting* peace from it, and confronting them with love and *expecting* love from it.

And so, although I can't remember a time that we lined up in the church before marching that we didn't find at least one switchblade knife, we had gangs that we recruited to march with us nonviolently and we were successful at that. We had four gangs: the Eastside gang, the Westside gang, uh, Northside gang, all of them. We had four gangs, and we had representation from all four of those gangs among, among the young people. Then we had high school kids, and we had Albany State College kids. And when the time came, they were ready to march. They were ready to—I think our first project was the integration of the bus station, the local bus station. And Charles Jones and I and Cordell tried it out first to see if they really were going to arrest, and we found out that they were going to arrest.

But one of the first things that came out of this was the feeling of strength that the people felt and the showing of strength that the people showed after they arrested their children. Because after that first march we had, when about two hundred and fifty-some people marched with us, we came and we filled two churches. Two churches were right in front of each other, Shiloh Baptist Church and Mount Zion Baptist Church. They were filled, and there were large numbers of people milling around in the streets outside of both churches, as well. So, I dare say there were two to three thousand people at, uh, at that particular meeting that we had. . . .

. . . [H]undreds of more people went to, uh, demonstrate after we had taken the first groups in, and that was the plan: to keep on until we filled the whole jail system. And they had to take us—we filled the Albany jail, then they took us to the jails in Americus and Sumter County, Terrell County, Baker County, Mitchell County, all the same counties that we would eventually go back to and organize. And, uh, it was just a great joy to find the same old people, bent over, talking with their heads down, were now talking with their heads up, and speaking to white people without fear, and demonstrating, you know, going in the store and taking, trying on a hat, and picketing stores who would not change, uh, in their morals. Uh, it was a great day for Albany, and, uh, the strength that we showed by marching together, but still loving.

. . . .

JOE MOSNIER: How did you, how did you chart your course? What were your best ways to make your decisions about how to press ahead?

CHARLES SHERROD: Okay, first of all, I didn't make all the decisions and the SNCC guys didn't make all the decisions.

JOE MOSNIER: Of course.

CHARLES SHERROD: We made decisions together. We had a steering committee, uh, Albany Movement Steering Committee, and most of our strategy came out of the steering committee. But we—our first effort was to desegregate all public accommodations. And we did that by, uh, picketing—well, first going and talking with the people who owned their businesses, asking would they please, uh, change their policies. Then, when they would not change their policies, then we would picket them. . . .

Source: Charles Sherrod, interview with Joseph Mosnier, June 4, 2011. U.S. Civil Rights History Project, American Folklife Center, Library of Congress, https://www.loc.gov/item/2015669121/.
Courtesy of Shirley Sherrod.

DOCUMENT 5.4

"Letter from the Albany Movement to the Albany City Commission" (1962)

The Albany Movement galvanized Blacks in the city, as evidenced by their first mass meeting in history at the local Mount Zion Baptist Church, which featured powerful testimony and song. Perhaps it was this level of visible frustration and organizing, along with protests in December 1961 against segregation and discrimination, that prompted the Albany City Commission to verbally agree to a list of demands by Blacks to improve city services, desegregate polling places and transportation, and address discrimination in employment. When the commission failed to act, leaders of the Albany Movement presented the following letter to the commission. City officials rejected the letter, which prompted renewed protests.

Gentlemen:

The Albany Movement came into being as a result of repeated denials of redress for inadequacies and wrongs, and finally, for the refusal to even consider petitions which have been presented to your group from as far back as 1957.

The first request was for sewage and paving relief in the Lincoln Heights area—nothing done. Next, the stoning of Negro ministers' houses, following an inflamatory [sic] editorial in the local press, caused a request to be sent by registered mail to the Mayor that a joint group try to stop the worsening conditions—no official acknowledgement of this request has ever been received by us. Again, a request that segregated polling places, which we felt were used to counteract the effect of our vote, was made from the top to the bottom—the refusal to attempt any kind of redress necessitated a successful suti [sic] to be waged in the Federal Court by us. Finally, it was the refusal of Albany officials, through its police department, to comply with the ICC regulation which became effective last November 1, that made the creation of this body a necessity. Test rides were conducted throughout the entire state of Georgia. Atlanta,

Savannah, Augusta, Macon, Columbus, Valdosta and Waycross all complied. Only Albany resisted.

Accordingly we staged further tests on November 22, which resulted in the initial arrests, trials, convictions and appeals. The cases were headed for higher courts and things would have proceeded in an orderly fashion to its conclusion, but for the arrests of the so-called "Freedom Riders."

This testing of the railroad's compliance with another ICC directive has been laid at our doors. Actually, we had absolutely nothing to do with this. It was the elaborately staged "infraction" and arrests of those people that caused us to rush to their defense. They were fighting for the same purpose as we and we could not abandon them to the wolves.

The mockery of fair play and justice which followed, in turn, caused the first planned "Marching Protest." The harsh, repressive measures employed caused further protests and further arrests. By now, the whole country, and the world for that matter, were aware of the unyielding, cruelly repressive measures used to combat our use of that First Amendment to the United States Constitution, "Freedom of Speech" through peaceful protest.

When an agreement was reached on December 18, one of the cardinal points was the privilege of substituting signature bonds in lieu of cash bonds. This agreement has not been kept by the city of Albany. Another agreement was that the police department would not interfere with the compliance of the bus company to the ICC order. This agreement has been only partly kept by the city of Albany.

The Albany Movement wishes to go on record, without reservation, of requesting the city of Albany to keep the faith by honoring its commitments.

We the members of the Albany Movement, wit the realization that ultimately the people of Albany, Negro and white, will have to solve our difficulties; realizing fulll [sic] well that racial hostility can be the downfall of our city; realizing that what happens in Albany, as well as what does NOT happen in Albany, affects the whole free world, call upon you tonight to hear our position.

It is our belief that discrimination based on race, color or religion is fundamentally wrong and contrary to the letter and intent of the Constitution of the United States. It is our aim in the Albany Movement to seek means of ending discriminatory practices in public facilities, both in employment and in use. Further, it is our aim to encourage private businesses to offer equal opportunity for all persons in employment and in service.

Some of these ideals which are inherent in the Constitution of the United States of America are:

1. Equal opportunity to improve one's self by good education.
2. Equal opportunity to exercise freedom and responsibility through the vote and participation in governmental processes.
3. Equal opportunity to work and advance economically.
4. Equal protection under the law.
5. The creation of a climate in which the talents and abilities of the entire community may be used for the good of all, unfettered by consideration of race of [sic] class.

Before going into plans for implementation of these goals, we wish to ask of you, gentlemen, tonight to reaffirm in writing your oral agreement of December 18, 1961, that, (1) the bus and train station will be open at all times without interference from the police; (2) the cash bonds will be refunded in exchange for security bonds, at an early date, the date to be set tonight.

We submit as the next step the creation of a biracial planning committee . . . [to] be composed of 6 members, 3 of which shall be appointed by the Albany Movement and 3 by the City Commission. Because of the tremendous responsibilities that will be invested in this committee, we pledge ourselves, as we also urge the commission, to choose men of the highest integrity, good will and security.

It is our hope that through negotiations and arbitrations, through listening and learning from each other, that we can achieve the purposes that will benefit the total community.

The problem of human rights belongs to us all, therefore, let us not falter in seizing the opportunity which almighty God has given to create a new order of freedom and human dignity. What is your pleasure, gentlemen, in proceeding with negotiations?

Respectfully Submitted,
For the Albany Movement
W.G. Anderson, President
M.S. Page, Executive
Secretary

Source: "Letter from the Albany Movement to the Albany City Commission, January 23, 1962," in *The Eyes on the Prize Civil Rights Reader*, edited by Clayborne Carson et al. (New York: Penguin Books, 1991), 140–42. Reprinted by arrangement with The Heirs to the Estate of Martin Luther King Jr., c/o Writers House as agent for the proprietor New York, NY. Copyright © 1962 by Dr. Martin Luther King, Jr. Renewed © 1990 by Coretta Scott King.

DOCUMENT 5.5

Gloria Richardson, "Focus on Cambridge" (1964)

Gloria St. Clair Hayes Richardson was born in Baltimore, Maryland, in 1922, though the family eventually relocated to Cambridge, Maryland. Richardson came from a prominent Black middle-class family of entrepreneurs, activists, and politicians, and she graduated from Howard University in 1942 with a degree in sociology. Segregation in Cambridge and a lack of economic opportunities for Blacks led young SNCC activists and local adults, including Richardson, to form the Cambridge Nonviolent Action Committee. Richardson became the head of CNAC and was unafraid to direct the organization in ways that departed from more mainstream civil rights organizations like the SCLC, including the use of armed self-defense and political boycotts. In the passage below, Richardson documents the formation of CNAC and its demands.

Originally published in *Freedomways,* 1st Quarter

. . . Two years ago the Student Nonviolent Coordinating Committee formed what has now become known as the Cambridge Nonviolent Action Committee. This was the year that active change began in this city. Prior to this time individual Negroes had continuously voiced to their friends, and in social or religious gatherings, discontent with their life. Although these people were disgruntled, there was no actual coming together to bring into focus their inherited frustrations. . . .

Then came the "Freedom Rides" of 1962 that suddenly catapulted all the things that we had previously considered as descriptive of the Alabamas, Mississippis, and Georgias, into the Eastern Shore of Maryland. Cambridge has always been considered the town on the shore with "good race relations." . . .

With these "Rides" the change was begun that will never stop until full equality and opportunity are won. In the beginning Negro participation in demonstrations was good. The boycott that had been set was successful. Students from the high school picketed nightly in freezing weather; some adults joined them.

It was at this precise point, two months after the beginning, trouble started. This was the problem of the "well-thinking Negro moderate." These were the people that the white power structure patted on the back, smiled at, told them how intelligent and, heaven forbid, how cultured they were. True leaders of their people ". . . who could tell your people what to do." And these people who had never faced jail or insult or beatings on the picket line swelled up with pride and agreed to settle down for peace. With what? Promises from and faith in their white brethren. . . .

STUDENTS GIVE LEADERSHIP

The students who had suffered so when the campaign was begun knew what they wanted and must have. These same students knew when they had been betrayed by the then "recognized" Negro leadership. This attitude fortunately, did not stop with the students, but included some parents also, even though some were unable to demonstrate because of job reprisals and various other economic fears.

There followed for those still working a period when we sought to prove that we would not follow this same pattern of giving in too quickly for too little. The people who are most involved and most concerned are those hundreds and thousands who for generations have been consigned to the job, school and housing ghettos no matter what their strivings, yearnings, desires or intelligence may be. These are the people to whom those of us who are fighting against terrific odds are then accountable.

To them the student movement has brought hope; that one thing that few of us had before. These students are not subject to political pressures. . . . [S]ome of them have not yet voted; they are not subject to economic pressures. . . . [T]hey have not yet had jobs and have not become used to soft living; their egos are immune to bad press or condemnation from the white power structure; they would fly into the face of hell rather than give up and when they have been temporarily slowed down, their minds are capable of the type of creative thinking that finds a new method of nonviolent attack. . . .

. . . The "new Negro" does not tell the people involved what to do. He listens to the rumblings and the discontent. He creatively fashions this discontent into protest.

Although many roadblocks are thrown in his path he is committed as part of his own faith not to give up, not to settle for tokenism, to continuously work for freedom, for himself, for his people and for the salvation of America. . . .

THE OCTOBER 2ND REFERENDUM

On October 2, 1963, Negro voters in Cambridge rejected the proposed Charter Amendment which would have made discrimination on the basis of race, illegal in restaurants, hotels and motels in this city. This plebiscite followed a period of violence and tension initiated and perpetuated by white mobs in retaliation to nonviolent street demonstrations—directed by the Cambridge Nonviolent Action Committee. This fight, which intensified last summer, had been going on for two years with the support of the overwhelming majority of the Negro people here, who believed in, or were persuaded to believe in, the tactics of nonviolence.

When the October 2nd referendum was called, CNAC took the position that the referendum was unconstitutional, illegal and immoral. We called for Negroes to boycott the polls in an expression of passive resistance in the face of an illegal hoax being perpetrated against the people. At that time I was generally credited with irresponsible leadership, although since that time much of the press and people have begun to agree with our position.

There were several facts to be considered here, and who is to say which is the most important. In the first place those Negroes who have fought for America, who have paid direct and indirect taxes, were not inclined to vote on something which no other citizen or alien in America had to vote upon. These same Negro citizens were not permitted to vote as to whether they should fight for this country or pay taxes or any of the other responsibilities imposed on United States citizens. We were being asked to tuck our dignity in our pockets and crawl to the polls to prove in a stacked vote that once again we were going to let the whites in control say what we would be permitted to do in a "free, democratic country."

. . .

In the name of all the black and white people in America this type of precedent would have laid people bare to the whims of dishonest, big business politicians who would piously use "the referendum" as a tool to shove down the throats of an unsuspecting and unwary racial or economic minority any type of racially punitive or economically punitive legislation, on a local, state or federal level. (As a matter of fact it is now used against voters not exposed to a voter education program.)

Finally, and specifically, in reference to this referendum, it was clearly unconstitutional. Equal accommodations in public places is a right inherent to citizens, and should not be subject to the wishes and prejudices of any individual or group. Two years ago the Supreme Court of the United States, in reversing the convictions of Negro students arrested for "sitting-in" made this quite clear. In its decision the Court stated unequivocally that any facility or establishment that is public, that is to say, that operates on the basis of a franchise or license to "serve the public" granted by any unit of government, be it local, state or federal, is operating in contract with that government, and consequently with its constituents, the people. . . .

The referendum was an attempt to make the constitutional rights of the Negro people, as citizens of Cambridge, subject to the possible prejudices of the white majority. . . . Equal accommodation in public places is a right to which we are entitled, and it is as important as any other human right. But it is not the most pressing problem facing Cambridge Negroes. Here Negroes are faced with chronic and widespread unemployment and underemployment, inadequate and substandard housing and living conditions, discrimination in every area of endeavor and what is worse, in the absence of any indication that the power structure of Cambridge is prepared to reform the system, or to effect any real improvement in the foreseeable future.

Today the revolt is now ready to go into a new phase. No longer are we primarily interested in public accommodations. The "bread and butter" issues have come to the fore. . . . The attack now has to be directed toward the economic and political structure of a community if any real progress is to be made and if tokenism is to be eliminated. The leadership within the movement is moving toward this and the people are moving with them. . . . If the leadership ever defaults I am sure that the people for whom we are fighting will continue their own battle. . . .

IMPORTANT TO EDUCATE THE COMMUNITY

This brings me to another facet of the Negro revolt: it is incumbent on every civil rights worker to educate the community as well as to articulate its desires. This does not mean educate in terms of books or schools. Many so-called educated people today do not understand what we mean when we say the first step is to educate the people, and a serious mistake can be made here. Education in this context simply means that a community has to become familiar with what it wants to achieve, how it can be achieved and how to apply techniques so that they become second nature, a part of one's way of life.

To learn and believe that they can overcome, to learn that the fight will be hard, that great sacrifices will be demanded but that it will not take another hundred years or even ten to gain the victory. To learn that what happens in Danville, Selma, Birmingham, Jackson, Albany happens to us too, in Cambridge, Baltimore, and Washington: to feel the rapport with other Negroes in other parts of the country and to become slowly and surely aware that as long as one of us has a segregationist breathing down our necks all of us are enslaved; that even though we have partial progress within our own locale, we will have to continue to stage sympathy demonstrations or acts of civil disobedience until discrimination and segregation are erased, everywhere. . . .

Source: Gloria Richardson, "Focus on Cambridge," *Freedomways* 4, no. 1 (1964), Freedomways Associates, New York. Courtesy of the estate of Gloria Richardson. CC BY-NC 4.0 (https://creativecommons.org/licenses/by-nc/4.0/).

DOCUMENT 5.6

"Birmingham Manifesto" (1963)

Over the course of April and early May 1963, the SCLC joined the Alabama Christian Movement for Human Rights in coordinated efforts to challenge entrenched segregation and racial discrimination in Birmingham. Despite tensions between local ACMHR leadership and Dr. King and the SCLC, the Birmingham Campaign focused on nonviolent direct action in the form of sit-ins, marches, boycotts, and mass meetings to press for fair and equitable treatment as well as equal access to public accommodations and economic opportunities. In the following manifesto, Fred Shuttlesworth, the local leader of the ACMHR, discusses the reasons for the mass protests.

The patience of an oppressed people cannot endure forever. The Negro citizens of Birmingham for the last several years have hoped in vain for some evidence of good faith resolution of our just grievances.

Birmingham is part of the United States and we are *bona fide* citizens. Yet the history of Birmingham reveals that very little of the democratic process touches the life of the Negro in Birmingham. We have been segregated racially, exploited economically, and dominated politically. Under the leadership of the Alabama Christian Movement for Human Rights, we sought relief by petition for the repeal of city ordinances requiring segregation and the institution of a merit hiring policy in city employment. We were rebuffed. We then turned to the system of the courts. We weathered set-back after set-back, with all of its costliness, finally winning the terminal, bus, parks and airport cases. The bus decision has been implemented . . . begrudgingly and the parks decision prompted the closing of all municipally-owned recreational facilities with the exception of the zoo and Legion Field. The airport case has been a slightly better experience with the experience of hotel accommodations and the subtle discrimination that continues in the limousine service.

We have always been a peaceful people, bearing our oppression with super-human effort. Yet we have been the victims of repeated violence, not only that inflicted by the hoodlum element but also that inflicted by the blatant misuse of police power. Our memories are seared with painful mob experience of Mother's Day 1961 during the Freedom Rides. For years, while our homes and churches were being bombed, we heard nothing but the rantings and ravings of racist city officials.

The Negro protest for equality and justice has been a voice crying in the wilderness. Most of Birmingham has remained silent, probably, out of fear. In the meanwhile, our city has acquired the dubious reputation of being the worst big city in race relations in the United States. Last fall, for a flickering moment, it appeared that sincere community leaders from religion, business and industry discerned the inevitable Confrontation in race relations approaching. Their Concern for the city's image and Commonweal of all its citizens did not run deep enough. Solemn promises were made, pending a postponement of direct action, that we would be joined in a suit seeking the relief of segregation ordinances. Some merchants agreed to desegregate their rest-rooms as a good-faith start, some actually complying, only to retreat shortly thereafter. We hold in our hands now, broken faith and broken promises.

We believe in the American Dream of democracy, in the Jeffersonian doctrine that "all men are created equal and are endowed by their Creator with certain inalienable rights, among these being life, liberty and the pursuit of happiness."

Twice since September we have deferred our direct action thrust in order that a change in city government would not be made in the hysteria of community crisis. We act today in full Concert with our Hebraic-Christian tradition, the law of morality and the Constitution of our nation. The absence of justice and progress in Birmingham demands that we make a moral witness to give our community a chance to survive. We demonstrate our faith that we believe that The Beloved Community can come to Birmingham.

We appeal to the citizenry of Birmingham, Negro and white, to join us in this witness for decency, morality, self-respect and human dignity. Your individual and corporate support can hasten the day of "liberty and justice for all." This is Birmingham's moment of truth in which every citizen can play his part in her larger destiny. The Alabama Christian Movement for Human Rights, in behalf of the Negro community of Birmingham.

F. L. Shuttlesworth, President

N. H. Smith, Secretary

Source: F. L. Shuttlesworth and L. H. Smith, "Birmingham Manifesto," Alabama Christian Movement for Human Rights, April 3, 1963, Bhamwiki, https://www.bhamwiki.com/w/Birmingham_Manifesto. CC BY-SA 3.0 (https://creativecommons.org/licenses/by-sa/3.0/).

DOCUMENT 5.7

Martin Luther King Jr., "Letter from Birmingham Jail" (1963)

In response to the first wave of demonstrations in Birmingham, city officials procured an injunction against protests that leaders of the Birmingham Campaign decided to disobey. On April 12, 1963, Dr. King was arrested for participating in a protest. While in jail, King authored "Letter from Birmingham Jail" in response to local white clergy who criticized the Birmingham Campaign.

April 16, 1963

My Dear Fellow Clergymen:

While confined here in the Birmingham city jail, I came across your recent statement calling my present activities "unwise and untimely." Seldom do I pause to answer criticism of my work and ideas. . . . But since I feel that you are men of genuine good will and that your criticisms are sincerely set forth, I want to try to answer your statement in what I hope will be patient and reasonable terms.

. . . I am in Birmingham because injustice is here. Just as the prophets of the eighth century B.C. left their villages and carried their "thus saith the Lord" far beyond the boundaries of their home towns, and just as the Apostle Paul left his village of Tarsus and carried the gospel of Jesus Christ to the far corners of the Greco-Roman world, so am I compelled to carry the gospel of freedom beyond my own home town. . . .

Moreover, I am cognizant of the interrelatedness of all communities and states. I cannot sit idly by in Atlanta and not be concerned about what happens in Birmingham. Injustice anywhere is a threat to justice everywhere. We are caught in an inescapable network of mutuality, tied in a single garment of destiny. Whatever affects one directly, affects all indirectly. Never again can we afford to live with the narrow, provincial "outside agitator" idea. . . .

You deplore the demonstrations taking place in Birmingham. But your statement, I am sorry to say, fails to express a similar concern for the conditions that brought about the demonstrations. . . . It is unfortunate that demonstrations are taking place in Birmingham, but it is even more unfortunate that the city's white power structure left the Negro community with no alternative.

In any nonviolent campaign there are four basic steps: collection of the facts to determine whether injustices exist; negotiation; self-purification; and direct action. We have gone through all these steps in Birmingham. There can be no gainsaying the fact that racial injustice engulfs this community. Birmingham is probably the most thoroughly segregated city in the United States. Its ugly record of brutality is widely known. Negroes have experienced grossly unjust treatment in the courts. There have been more unsolved bombings of Negro homes and churches in Birmingham than in any other city in the nation. These are the hard, brutal facts of the case. On the basis of these conditions, Negro leaders sought to negotiate with the city fathers. But the latter consistently refused to engage in good-faith negotiation.

Then, last September, came the opportunity to talk with leaders of Birmingham's economic community. In the course of the negotiations, certain promises were made by the merchants—for example, to remove the stores' humiliating racial signs. On the basis of these promises, the Reverend Fred Shuttlesworth and the leaders of the Alabama Christian Movement for Human Rights agreed to a moratorium on all demonstrations. As the weeks and months went by, we realized that we were the victims of a broken promise. . . . We had no alternative except to prepare for direct action, whereby we would present our very bodies as a means of laying our case before the conscience of the local and the national community. . . .

. . .

You may well ask: "Why direct action? Why sit-ins, marches and so forth? Isn't negotiation a better path?" You are quite right in calling for negotiation. Indeed, this is the very purpose of direct action. Nonviolent direct action seeks to create such a crisis and foster such a tension that a community which has constantly refused to negotiate is forced to confront the issue. . . . I have earnestly opposed violent tension, but there is a type of constructive, nonviolent tension which is necessary for growth. . . . The purpose of our direct-action program is to create a situation so crisis-packed that it will inevitably open the door to negotiation. . . .

We know through painful experience that freedom is never voluntarily given by the oppressor; it must be demanded by the oppressed. Frankly, I have yet to engage in a direct-action campaign that was "well timed" in the view of those who have not suffered unduly from the disease of segregation. For years now I have heard the word "Wait!" It rings in the ear of every Negro with piercing familiarity. This "Wait" has almost always meant "Never." We must come to see, with one of our distinguished jurists, that "justice too long delayed is justice denied."

. . . Perhaps it is easy for those who have never felt the stinging darts of segregation to say, "Wait." But when you have seen vicious mobs lynch your mothers and fathers at will and drown your sisters and brothers at whim; when you have seen hate-filled policemen curse, kick and even kill your black brothers and sisters; when you see the vast majority of your twenty million Negro brothers smothering in an airtight cage of poverty in the midst of an affluent society; when you suddenly find your tongue twisted and your speech stammering as you seek to explain to your six-year-old daughter why she can't go to the public amusement park that has just been advertised on television, and see tears welling up in her eyes when she is told that Funtown is closed to colored children, and see ominous clouds of inferiority beginning to form in her little mental sky, and see her beginning to distort her personality by developing an unconscious bitterness toward white people; when you have to concoct an answer for a five-year-old son who is asking: "Daddy, why do white people treat colored people so mean?"; when you take a cross-county drive and find it necessary to sleep night after night in the uncomfortable corners of your automobile because no motel will accept you; when you are humiliated day in and day out by nagging signs reading "white" and "colored"; when your first name becomes "nigger," your middle name becomes "boy" (however old you are) and your last name becomes "John," and your wife and mother are never given the respected title "Mrs."; when you are harried by day and haunted by night by the fact that you are a Negro, living constantly at tiptoe stance, never quite knowing what to expect next, and are plagued with inner fears and outer resentments; when you are forever fighting a degenerating sense of "nobodiness"—then you will understand why we find it difficult to wait. There comes a time when the cup of endurance runs over, and men are no longer willing to be plunged into the abyss of despair. I hope, sirs, you can understand our legitimate and unavoidable impatience.

You express a great deal of anxiety over our willingness to break laws. This is certainly a legitimate concern. . . . One may well ask: "How can you advocate breaking some laws and obeying others?" The answer lies in the fact that there are two types of laws: just and unjust. I would be the first to advocate obeying just laws. One has not only a legal but a moral responsibility to obey just laws. Conversely, one has a moral responsibility to disobey unjust laws. I would agree with St. Augustine that "an unjust law is no law at all."

Now, what is the difference between the two? How does one determine whether a law is just or unjust? A just law is a man-made code that squares with the moral law or the law of God. An unjust law is a code that is out of harmony with the moral law. . . . Any law that uplifts human personality is just. Any law that degrades human personality is unjust. All segregation statutes are unjust because segregation distorts the soul and damages the personality. It gives the segregator a false sense of superiority and the segregated a false sense of inferiority. . . . Hence segregation is not only politically, economically and sociologically unsound, it is morally wrong and sinful. . . .

. . . In no sense do I advocate evading or defying the law, as would the rabid segregationist. That would lead to anarchy. One who breaks an unjust law must do so openly, lovingly, and with a willingness to accept the penalty. I submit that an individual who breaks a law that conscience tells him is unjust, and who willingly accepts the penalty of imprisonment in order to arouse the conscience of the community over its injustice, is in reality expressing the highest respect for law.

. . .

I must make two honest confessions to you, my Christian and Jewish brothers. First, I must confess that over the past few years I have been gravely disappointed with the white moderate. I have almost reached the regrettable conclusion that the Negro's great stumbling block in his stride toward freedom is not the White Citizens' Counciler or the Ku Klux Klanner, but the white moderate, who is more devoted to "order" than to justice; who prefers a negative peace which is the absence of tension to a positive peace which is the presence of justice; who constantly says: "I agree with you in the goal you seek, but I cannot agree with your methods of direct action"; who paternalistically believes he can set the timetable for another man's freedom; who lives by a mythical concept of time and who constantly advises the Negro to wait for a "more convenient season." . . .

. . . We will have to repent in this generation not merely for the hateful words and actions of the bad people but for the appalling silence of the good people. Human progress never rolls in on wheels of inevitability; it comes through the tireless efforts of men willing to be coworkers with God, and without this hard work, time itself becomes an ally of the forces of social stagnation. . . .

You speak of our activity in Birmingham as extreme. At first I was rather disappointed that fellow clergymen would see my nonviolent efforts as those of an extremist. I began thinking about the fact that I stand in the middle of two opposing forces in the Negro community. One is a force of complacency, made up in part of Negroes who, as a result of long years of oppression, are so drained of self-respect and a sense of "somebodiness" that they have adjusted to segregation; and in part of a few middle-class Negroes who, because of a degree of academic and economic security and because in some ways they profit by segregation, have become insensitive to the problems of the masses. The other force is one of bitterness and hatred, and it comes perilously close to advocating violence. It is expressed in the various black nationalist groups that are springing up across the nation, the largest and best known being Elijah Muhammad's Muslim movement. Nourished by the Negro's frustration over the continued existence of racial discrimination, this movement is made up of people who have lost faith in America, who have absolutely repudiated Christianity, and who have concluded that the white man is an incorrigible "devil."

I have tried to stand between these two forces, saying that we need emulate neither the " do-nothingism" of the complacent nor the hatred and despair of the black nationalist. For there is the more excellent way of love and nonviolent protest. I am grateful to God that, through the influence of the Negro church, the way of nonviolence became an integral part of our struggle.

If this philosophy had not emerged, by now many streets of the South would, I am convinced, be flowing with blood. And I am further convinced that if our white brothers dismiss as " rabble-rousers" and "outside agitators" those of us who employ nonviolent direct action, and if they refuse to support our nonviolent efforts, millions of Negroes will, out of frustration and despair, seek solace and security in black-nationalist ideologies—a development that would inevitably lead to a frightening racial nightmare.

Oppressed people cannot remain oppressed forever. The yearning for freedom eventually manifests itself, and that is what has happened to the American Negro. Something within has reminded him of his birthright of freedom, and something without has reminded him that it can be gained. . . .

When I was suddenly catapulted into the leadership of the bus protest in Montgomery, Alabama, a few years ago, I felt we would be supported by the white church. I felt that the white ministers, priests and rabbis of the South would be among our strongest allies. Instead, some have been outright opponents, refusing to understand the freedom movement and misrepresenting its leaders; all too many others have been more cautious than courageous and have remained silent behind the anesthetizing security of stained-glass windows.

. . .

I have heard numerous southern religious leaders admonish their worshipers to comply with a desegregation decision because it is the law, but I have longed to hear white ministers declare: "Follow this decree because integration is morally right and because the Negro is your brother." In the midst of blatant injustices inflicted upon the Negro, I have watched white churchmen stand on the sideline and mouth pious irrelevancies and sanctimonious trivialities. In the midst of a mighty struggle to rid our nation of racial and economic injustice, I have heard many ministers say: "Those are social issues, with which the gospel has no real concern." And I have watched many churches commit themselves to a completely otherworldly religion which makes a strange, un-Biblical distinction between body and soul, between the sacred and the secular.

. . . We will win our freedom because the sacred heritage of our nation and the eternal will of God are embodied in our echoing demands.

Before closing I feel impelled to mention one other point in your statement that has troubled me profoundly. You warmly commended the Birmingham police force for keeping "order" and "preventing violence." I doubt that you would have so warmly commended the police force if you had seen its dogs sinking their teeth into unarmed, nonviolent Negroes. I doubt that you would so quickly commend the policemen if you were to observe their ugly and inhumane treatment of Negroes here in the city jail; if you were to watch them push and curse old Negro women and young Negro girls; if you were to see them slap and kick old Negro men and young boys; if you were to observe them, as they did on two occasions, refuse to give us food because we wanted to sing our grace together. I cannot join you in your praise of the Birmingham police department.

It is true that the police have exercised a degree of discipline in handling the demonstrators. In this sense they have conducted themselves rather "nonviolently" in public. But for what purpose? To preserve the evil system of segregation. Over the past few years I have consistently preached that nonviolence demands that the means we use must be as pure as the ends we seek. I have tried to make clear that it is wrong to use immoral means to attain moral ends. But now I must affirm that it is just as wrong, or perhaps even more so, to use moral means to preserve immoral ends. Perhaps Mr. Connor and his policemen have been rather nonviolent in public, as was Chief Pritchett in Albany, Georgia, but they have used the moral means of non-violence to maintain the immoral end of racial injustice. . . .

I wish you had commended the Negro sit-inners and demonstrators of Birmingham for their sublime courage, their willingness to suffer and their amazing discipline in the midst of great provocation. One day the South will recognize its real heroes. They will be the James Merediths, with the noble sense of purpose that enables them to face jeering and hostile mobs, and with the agonizing loneliness that characterizes the life of the pioneer. They will be old, oppressed, battered Negro women, symbolized in a seventy-two-year-old woman in Montgomery, Alabama, who rose up with a sense of dignity and with her people decided not to ride segregated buses, and who responded with ungrammatical profundity to one who inquired about her weariness: "My feets is tired, but my soul is at rest." They will be the young high school and college students, the young ministers of the gospel and a host of their elders, courageously and nonviolently sitting in at lunch counters and willingly going to jail for conscience sake. . . .

I hope this letter finds you strong in the faith. I also hope that circumstances will soon make it possible for me to meet each of you, not as an integrationist or a civil-rights leader but as a fellow clergyman and a Christian brother. Let us all hope that the dark clouds of racial prejudice will soon pass away and the deep fog of misunderstanding will be lifted from our fear-drenched communities, and in some not too distant tomorrow the radiant stars of love and brotherhood will shine over our great nation with all their scintillating beauty.

Yours for the cause of Peace and Brotherhood,
Martin Luther King, Jr.

Source: Martin Luther King Jr., "Letter from Birmingham Jail," originally published as "The Negro Is Your Brother," *Atlantic,* August 1963. Reprinted by arrangement with The Heirs to the Estate of Martin Luther King Jr., c/o Writers House as agent for the proprietor New York, NY. "Letter From a Birmingham Jail" Copyright © 1963 by Dr. Martin Luther King, Jr. Renewed © 1991 by Coretta Scott King.

DOCUMENT 5.8

Police in Birmingham, Ala., Take a Group of Black Schoolchildren to Jail (1963)

One of the most controversial components of the Birmingham Campaign was its involvement of children. In the aftermath of the city injunction against protests and Dr. King's arrest, the Birmingham Campaign organized children's marches, known as the Children's Crusade. National and international news media captured images of children marching peacefully and their subsequent arrests. The media also captured even more disturbing images of children under attack by police dogs and fire hoses. A combination of effective protests, suffering local businesses, media attention, and federal intervention led to a compromise and tentative agreement to remove some of Birmingham's most visible forms of segregation. In retaliation, local segregationists and Ku Klux Klan members attacked Black civil rights activists and residents, most notably the bombing of Birmingham's Sixteenth Street Baptist Church that resulted in the murder of four Black girls.

Source: Bill Hudson, *Police in Birmingham, Ala., Take a Group of Black Schoolchildren to Jail on May 4, 1963, after Their Arrest for Protesting against Segregation*, May 4, 1963, photograph, Associated Press, http://www.apimages.com/metadata/Index /Associated-Press-Domestic-News-Alabama-United-S-/3276bdfadfe6da11af9f0014c2589dfb/230. AP Photo/Bill Hudson.

Charles Sims on the Deacons for Defense (1965)

The Deacons for Defense and Justice were founded in Jonesboro, Louisiana, in July 1964 to protect CORE activists from local Ku Klux Klan members. Charles Sims, president of the Bogalusa, Louisiana, chapter of the Deacons for Defense and Justice, explains the origins of the Deacons for Defense and Justice and their circumstances under which they exercised self-defense and protected the rights of Blacks to vote, protest peacefully, and engage in other civil rights activities. Most members of the Deacons for Defense were Black veterans who served in World War II and the Korean War.

ARMED DEFENSE ~ CHARLES R. SIMS (1965)

[Interview with Charles R. Sims, President, Bogalusa chapter, Deacons for Defense and Justice, conducted by William Price, reporter for the *National Guardian* newsweekly, on August 20, 1965, in Bogalusa, Louisiana. As reprinted from *Black Protest: 350 Years of History, Documents, and Analyses*, by Joanne Grant.]

PRICE: Mr. Sims, why do you feel there is need for the Deacons in the civil rights movement and in Bogalusa?

SIMS: First of all, the reason why we had to organize the Deacons in the city of Bogalusa was the Negro people and civil rights workers didn't have no adequate police protection.

PRICE: Can you tell us what difference it may have made in Bogalusa to have the Deacons here?

SIMS: Well, when the white power structure found out that they had mens, Negro mens that had made up their minds to stand up for their people and to give no ground, would not tolerate with no more police brutality, it had a tendency to keep the night-riders out of the neighborhood.

. . .

PRICE: Can you tell me how the Deacons view the use of weapons?

SIMS: Self-protection.

. . .

PRICE: Do the local authorities object to your carrying weapons?

SIMS: Oh yeah, the local, the federal, the state, everybody object to us carrying weapons, they don't want us armed, but we had to arm ourselves because we got tired of the women, the children being harassed by the white night-riders.

PRICE: Have they done anything to try to get the weapons away from you?

SIMS: Well, they threatened several times. The governor even said he was going to have all the weapons confiscated, all that the state troopers could find. But on the other hand, the governor forgot one thing—in an organization as large as the Deacons, we also have lawyers and we know about what the government can do. That would be unconstitutional for him just to walk up and start searching cars and taking people's stuff without cause.

PRICE: The Second Amendment to the United States Constitution guarantees the right of the people to carry weapons, is that the way you feel about it, that the people have a right to carry weapons in their own self-defense?

SIMS: I think a person should have the right to carry a weapon in self-defense, and I think the Louisiana state law says a man can carry a weapon in his car as long as it is not concealed. We found out in Bogalusa that that law meant for the white man, it didn't mean for the colored. Any time a colored man was caught with a weapon in his car, they jailed him for carrying a concealed weapon. So we carried them to court.

. . .

PRICE: Can you tell me what difference it has made with the white community, the fact that there are the Deacons here in Bogalusa and that they are prepared to use arms even if they may not?

SIMS: For one thing that made a difference, there were a lot of night-riders riding through the neighborhood; we stopped them. We put them out and gave them fair warning. A couple of incidents happened when people were fired on. So the white man right away found out that a brand new Negro was born. We definitely couldn't swim and we was as close to the river as we could get so there was but one way to go.

PRICE: So you think there has been a difference in the attitude of the white people towards the civil rights movement in Bogalusa because you have been here to protect it?

SIMS: Yes, I do believe that. I believe that if the Deacons had been organized in 1964, the three civil rights workers that was murdered in Philadelphia, Mississippi, might have been living today because we'd have been around to stop it.

. . .

PRICE: Is there anything you can say about the pledge that a Deacon takes, or the oath?

SIMS: He pledges his life for the defense of justice, that's one thing he do, for the defense of the Negro people, and the civil rights workers in this area. When I say this area, that doesn't necessarily mean Bogalusa, that's anywhere we're needed in this vicinity.

. . .

PRICE: What has been the response to the existence of the Deacons from the civil rights movement, from the Congress of Racial Equality, other civil rights organizations or from unaffiliated whites that come in like we might come in?

SIMS: They're most glad we have the Deacons organized. See, right now it's rather quiet. Two months ago a white civil rights worker or even a colored civil rights worker, he couldn't come into Bogalusa unless we brought him in. The whites would be on the road trying to stop cars. We've taken on the job of transportation in and out of Bogalusa, bringing people backwards and forwards, making sure that they get here safe.

. . .

PRICE: The mere showing of a weapon, does that sometimes take care of a situation?

SIMS: The showing of a weapon stops many things. Everybody want to live and nobody want to die. But here in Bogalusa, I'm one of the few peoples who is really known as a Deacon and anybody that I associate with, they just take for granted they are Deacons. I show up then ten, twelve more mens show up, whether they Deacons or not, they branded, you know. That make the white man respect us even more, because nine out of ten he be right.

. . .

PRICE: Could you say how many Deacons there are in Bogalusa and throughout the South?

SIMS: No, but I'll tell you this, we have throughout the South at this time somewhere between 50 and 60 chapters.

PRICE: Roughly how many people in each chapter?

SIMS: I won't tell you that.

PRICE: Could tell us what areas they cover?

SIMS: Alabama, Mississippi, Arkansas, Louisiana, Texas.

PRICE: Georgia?

SIMS: No. We have Georgia and North Carolina in mind. As a matter of fact I was supposed to go to North Carolina and organize the people there, and in Florida, but I don't have time right now to do it.

PRICE: Have you been making trips outside of Louisiana to see these other groups, to help them organize?

SIMS: No, I send mens. And the headquarters in Jonesboro sends mens out.

PRICE: The headquarters is in Jonesboro, Louisiana?

SIMS: Yes.

. . .

PRICE: Could you tell us what views you might have on the civil rights tactic of nonviolence?

SIMS: The nonviolent act is a good act—providing the police mens do their job. But in the Southern states, not just Louisiana, but in the Southern states, the police have never done their job when the white and the Negro are involved—unless the Negro's getting the best of the white man.

PRICE: How do you think the movement could best be advanced or get its aims the quickest if it didn't use nonviolence?

SIMS: I believe nonviolence is the only way. Negotiations are going to be the main point in this fight.

PRICE: Would it be correct to put it this way, that you feel nonviolence is the correct way to get political and economic things done. . . .

SIMS: Sure.

PRICE: But that behind that, behind the nonviolence, the Deacons or organizations like the Deacons are necessary to protect the rights of this nonviolent movement?

SIMS: That's right.

. . .

PRICE: Mr. Sims, just one last question, how long do you think the Deacons will be needed in the civil rights movement?

SIMS: First of all, this is a long fight. In 1965 there will be a great change made. But after this change is made, the biggest fight is to keep it. My son, his son might have to fight this fight and that's one reason why we won't be able to disband the Deacons for a long time. How long, Heaven only knows. But it will be a long time.

Source: Charles R. Sims (president of the Deacons for Defense and Justice's Bogalusa, LA Chapter), interview with William Price, August 20, 1965, reprinted from *Black Protest: 350 Years of History, Documents, and Analyses,* by Joanne Grant (Greenwich, CT: Fawcett, 1986), https://www.crmvet.org/nars/sims65.htm.

FURTHER READING

Carson, Clayborne. *The Autobiography of Martin Luther King, Jr.* New York: Warner Books, 2001.

Charron, Katherine Mellen. *Freedom's Teacher: The Life of Septima Clark.* Chapel Hill: University of North Carolina Press, 2012.

Clark, Septima, and Cynthia Stokes Brown. *Ready from Within: Septima Clark and the Civil Rights Movement, a First Person Narrative.* Trenton, NJ: Africa World Press, 1990.

Cobb, Charles E., Jr. *This Nonviolent Stuff'll Get You Killed: How Guns Made the Civil Rights Movement Possible.* Durham, NC: Duke University Press, 2015.

Crosby, Emilye. *Civil Rights History from the Ground Up: Local History, National Struggle.* Athens: University of Georgia Press, 2011.

Fitzgerald, Joseph R. *The Struggle Is Eternal: Gloria Richardson and Black Liberation.* Lexington: University Press of Kentucky, 2019.

Garrow, David. *Bearing the Cross: Martin Luther King, Jr., and the Southern Christian Leadership Conference.* New York: William Morrow Paperbacks, 2004.

Hill, Lance. *The Deacons for Defense: Armed Resistance and the Civil Rights Movement.* Chapel Hill: University of North Carolina Press, 2006.

Honigsberd, Peter Jan. *Crossing Border Street: A Civil Rights Memoir.* Berkeley: University of California Press, 2002.

King, Martin Luther, Jr. *Why We Can't Wait.* New York: Harper & Row, 1964.

Levy, Peter B. *Civil War on Race Street: The Civil Rights Movement in Cambridge, Maryland.* Gainesville: University Press of Florida, 2003.

Richardson Dandridge, Gloria. "The Energy of the People Passing through Me." In *Hands on the Freedom Plow: Personal Accounts by Women in SNCC*, edited by Faith S. Holsaert et al., 273–97. Urbana: University of Illinois Press, 2012.

Rouse, Jacqueline. "We Seek to Know . . . in Order to Speak the Truth." In *Sisters in the Struggle: African American Women in the Civil Rights–Black Power Movement*, edited by Bettye Collier-Thomas and V. P. Franklin, 95–119. New York: New York University Press, 2001.

Strain, Christopher. *Pure Fire: Self Defense as Activism in the Civil Rights Era.* Athens: University of Georgia Press, 2005.

Street, Joe. "Singing for Freedom." In *The Culture War in the Civil Rights Movement*, by Joe Street, 22–40. Gainesville: University Press of Florida, 2007.

Theoharis, Jeanne, and Komozi Woodard. *Groundwork: Local Black Freedom Movements in America.* New York: New York University Press, 2005.

Umoja, Akinyele Omowale. *We Will Shoot Back: Armed Resistance in the Mississippi Freedom Movement.* New York: New York University Press, 2014.

Williams, Robert F. "Black Power, and the Roots of the African American Freedom Struggle." *Journal of American History* 85, no. 2 (1998): 540–70.

———. *Negroes with Guns.* New York: Marzani and Mansell, 1962.

6

The Struggles for Voting and Political Power in Mississippi and Alabama

How did the shift toward voting rights and political representation illustrate local and regional struggles in the civil rights movement? How did the efforts of these local struggles facilitate the passage of federal acts and laws that would benefit African Americans throughout the country? To what degree did this new legislation facilitate African Americans' realization of first-class citizenship? At the same time, what barriers to voting rights and political representation remained?

Though the struggle for equal access to public accommodations tends to dominate coverage of the civil rights movement in the 1950s, the movement in the 1960s moved toward concerns over voting rights and political representation. Integration, activists concluded, *must* include the ballot. This shift is most visible when focusing on the movement in Mississippi and Alabama.

The Civil Rights Act of 1957 created the U.S. Commission for Civil Rights, which was tasked to monitor Black civil rights violations and propose remedies for infringements on Black voting. Unfortunately, however, the act was weak. It was more symbolic than anything else. Nevertheless, it was a step in the right direction and encouraged southern activists to seize upon voting rights abuses.

Mississippi subsequently became a major site for challenging voting rights violations by organizing greater numbers of African Americans to register to vote, despite fears of retaliation. Long seen as a segregationist stronghold, the state of Mississippi also produced some of the most outspoken civil rights activists, such as Medgar Evers, Fannie Lou Hamer, and Amzie Moore. Recall, Mississippi was also the state where Emmett Till was murdered and a stop and major site of protest during the Freedom Rides in 1961.

A major campaign of the Mississippi movement was Freedom Summer. Freedom Summer was a massive voter registration project that relied on the leadership of local grassroots activists, volunteers from throughout the nation, the Student Nonviolent Coordinating Committee, and the Council of Federated Organization (COFO) members. Additionally, Freedom Summer established dozens of Freedom Schools and community centers throughout the state.

The efforts of activists in Mississippi ensured the ratification of the Civil Rights Act of 1964. The Civil Rights Act of 1964 was one of the landmark pieces of legislation that came into fruition because of the civil rights movement. President John F. Kennedy first advocated for a civil rights bill following the March on Washington in August 1963. He would be assassinated before its passage, however. His successor, Lyndon B. Johnson, lobbied hard for its ratification. Finally, on July 2, 1964, the Civil Rights Act of 1964 was signed into law. The act banned civil rights and labor discrimination based on race, sex, color, religion, and national origin; allowed government agencies to withhold federal funds from programs permitting or practicing discrimination; established the Equal Employment Opportunities Commission to monitor employment discrimination; and gave the U.S. attorney general the power to initiate proceedings against segregated facilities and schools that refuse to obey the act.

Though the Civil Rights Act of 1964 opened up opportunities for civil rights activists to challenge voting rights violations, white southerners remained resistant to Black enfranchisement. As a result, activists challenged the impact of voting rights discrimination in the lily-white Mississippi Democratic Party—arguably the most visible and hostile political sect to Black political power. Fannie Lou Hamer, Aaron Henry, Bob Moses, Ella Baker, Lawrence Guyot, Annie Devine, Victoria Gray, and others formed the Mississippi Freedom Democratic Party in the spring of 1964. The MFDP challenged the state Democratic Party for leadership and credentials at the 1964 Democratic National Convention (DNC) in New Jersey. In short, African Americans sought a seat at the political table.

After Fannie Lou Hamer's moving testimony, President Lyndon B. Johnson asked his vice president, Hubert Humphrey, and Senator Walter Mondale to coordinate a resolution and save his reelection. Humphrey and Mondale proposed the seating of Mississippi regulars who pledged their loyalty to the national party and their votes to Johnson. Their proposal also provided for the creation of two delegate seats to be filled by MFDP members Aaron Henry and Ed King. The rest of the MFDP could attend the convention as nonvoting guests. Black civil rights leaders Martin Luther King Jr., Bayard Rustin, and others counseled acceptance of the proposal, insisting that the reelection of Johnson and the Democrats—considered "friends" of the movement—would advance the plight of African Americans. The MFDP, however, was unwilling to settle for token representation and rejected the offer.

Along with the MFDP, sharecropper Fannie Lou Hamer joined the Mississippi Freedom Labor Union, a union composed of Black domestic, farm, and day laborers. The MFLU sought to reduce the economic exploitation of Black workers and increase Black ownership of homes, lands, and businesses. While the MFDP tackled political representation, the MFLU sought to reduce Black poverty and increase Black economic self-sufficiency.

Several months after the DNC, in January 1965, Martin Luther King Jr. returned from Oslo, Norway, where he had just been awarded the Nobel Peace Prize, and joined the ongoing movement for Black voter rights in Selma, Alabama. In Dallas County, where Selma is located, out of 15,000 registered votes, only 355 were African American. In Alabama, as a whole, an estimated 77 percent of Black citizens were excluded from the voting rolls—a much higher percentage than other places in the South.

The first Selma voting rights march took place on Sunday, March 7, 1965. Approximately 600 protesters, with SNCC chairman John Lewis at the lead, approached the Edmund Pettus Bridge. As they did so, Alabama state troopers and county police officers beat and teargassed the marchers, while horses trampled those who had fallen as they tried to retreat. The brutality of the state—in what would become known as "Bloody Sunday"—was photographed and captured on film and disseminated throughout the nation and the world.

Two days later, activists attempted a second march to Montgomery. This time, however, when King, leading the march, reached the end of the bridge, he prayed and turned the march around. Because of this, SNCC felt betrayed and King's leadership suffered.

The third march began on March 21, 1965. Under the protection of the federalized Alabama National Guard, U.S. Army, FBI agents, and federal marshals, activists successfully arrived in Montgomery on March 24 and to Alabama's state capital on March 25.

The Selma campaign—most notably Bloody Sunday and the beating of white Unitarian minister James Reeb after the second march—spurred the U.S. Congress to pass the Voting Rights Act on August 6, 1965. The act outlawed discriminatory practices in voting such as literacy tests, poll taxes, and intimidation and empowered the federal government to supersede local affairs and assign federal registrars to enroll voters and protect the right to vote. The Voting Rights Act had an astonishing effect—within four years, three-fifths of adult African Americans were now registered to vote, and by the late 1970s African Americans were elected to public office in growing numbers at every level of government.

DOCUMENT 6.1

Medgar Evers, Address at Mount Heron Baptist Church (1957)

Mississippi civil rights leader Medgar Evers addressed the congregation at Mount Heron Baptist Church in Vicksburg, Mississippi, in 1957. In his speech, Evers encourages church parishioners to join their local National Association for the Advancement of Colored People. Evers's involvement in the civil rights movement began to intensify in February 1954, after the Supreme Court's decision in *Brown v. Board of Education*, when he applied to the University of Mississippi Law School, but was rejected based on his race. After the rejection, Evers worked with the NAACP to integrate the university via the legal system. Later that year, Evers became the first field secretary for the NAACP in the state of Mississippi. In this position, he organized boycotts and protests against racial segregation and discrimination in downtown stores, restaurants, public beaches and parks, and schools; organized voter registration drives; established new local chapters of the organization; and participated in James Meredith's efforts to integrate the University of Mississippi. Evers also called for a new investigation into the 1955 murder of Emmett Till. Because of his efforts to dismantle Jim Crow, white supremacists assassinated Evers on June 12, 1963, as he was getting out of his car at the end of a long day of work and activism.

Christian friends, brothers and sisters, ladies and gentlemen. I consider it a blessing from almighty God to have this very spiritual pleasure to fellowship with you on this men's day program and to be able to acknowledge the very presence of God within me. . . .

My topic for today is "Man's obligation to God and to man." *Obligation to God.* You know we are not as grateful and obliging to God as He would have us to be. We men often take our being too much for granted. We often feel that our responsibility and obligation to God ends when we make a liberal church contribution and attend services regularly. Granted, both are essential in our daily Christian lives but one equally important factor is often expressed in the "negative" by the following quotation: "Man's inhumanity to man makes countless thousands mourn." As I remember from my youth being taught the Golden Rule of "Do unto others as you would have them do unto you." That part of the Golden Rule is now in many instances being shelved as being obsolete or outdated and therefore no longer usable in this day and time which is possibly the saddest mistake we find ourselves making.

Man is, I would say, God's chosen creature on the face of the earth so much so until in the creation God said, "Let us make man in our image, after our likeness, and let them have dominion over the fish of the sea and the fowl of the air, and over the cattle, and over all the earth, and over every creeping thing that creepeth upon the earth." So God created man in his own image, in the image of God, created He Him: male and female, created He them.

If we note with care the word image which means likeness or an imitation of any person or thing one is immediately impressed with the fact that we are God's children who possess his likeness and who consequently should do His will. That is unquestionably the obligation man owes to God—do His will.

Now we come to the other part of our topic, "man's obligation to man." Certainly we cannot do the will of God without treating our fellow man as we would have him treat us. It is a biblical axiom that to say you love God and hate your fellow man is hypocrisy of possibly the greatest magnitude. So many of us fall into this category either consciously or unconsciously until it behooves each of us to check ourselves closely so as to avoid becoming a party to hate or misunderstanding.

While we must not hate our fellow man, black, white, yellow or what have you, we must nevertheless, stand firmly on those principles we know are right which brings us to the point of being reminded of the courage of Joshua and Caleb when after 400 years of bondage under the Egyptians and 40 years of freedom, there were many among the Israelites who wanted to go back into Egypt and slavery, because they were not willing to suffer for a cause and for a principle. So it is today many people are not willing to stand up for a cause and a principle. Many persons are willing to sacrifice their birthright, go back into slavery and maintain segregation, and take the easy way out, rather than to suffer a little and gain what is rightfully theirs. In this instance, we find history repeating itself.

We, as men, owe it to our fellow man and to our children to stand firm and stand out for those things that we are entitled to. I count it a blessing from God that I am able to withstand ridicule and abuse because I am willing to stand for my fellow man though many show no appreciation for the work that we are trying to do in their behalf. But let it not be said in the final analysis when history will only record these glorious moments and when your grandchildren will invariably ask: "Granddaddy, what role did you play in helping to make us free men and free women?" Did you actively participate in the struggle or was your support only a moral one? Certainly each person here, and man in particular, should be in a position to say "I was active in the struggle from all phases for your unrestrictive privileges as an American citizen."

Christian friends, we are in a righteous struggle. We are living in a great day, a momentous day, a glorious day, a day that will be forever inscribed in the annals of history and in the minds of men.

Now, my friends, I have one or two requests to make and I feel that these requests should be the paramount objective of each person here today. Number one: let us vow to treat our fellow man as we would like him to treat us. Two, let us be in a spirit of cooperativeness. For example, the Reverend Dr. Martin Luther King and others in Montgomery, Alabama, have to me set an example of cooperation that has been unexcelled in my lifetime and possibly yours.

Those Christian people in Montgomery have really demonstrated cooperation, and how effective it can be in a community. Certainly Reverend King and others demonstrating through actual practice that that [sic] they preach from the pulpit can be used in other forms of protest, such as registering and voting, which is my third request: that you select a committee in your community to teach the importance and use of the ballot, so that every person twenty-one years and above is provided with transportation to go down and register and also collect two dollars from everyone twenty-two through fifty-nine years and pay their poll tax.

My last request is that you support more earnestly the *National Association for the Advancement of Colored People*, an organization that has contributed possibly more than any other in our struggle for first class citizenship. Just think where we would have been today had it not been for the work of the *National Association for the Advancement of Colored People*. Many of the achievements of the organization have been forgotten or ignored. For example, the grandfather clause and the white primaries were declared unconstitutional through the legal maneuvering of the organization. Restrictive covenants, discrimination in public education, and the separate but equal doctrine have all been declared contrary to the U.S. Constitution and the American way of life. And even here in our state where sickness knows no color, veterans' hospitals have been integrated, and in Army, Navy, and Air installations the work of the NAACP has made the brotherhood of man a workable thing in Mississippi. . . .

As men living in as highly a diversified and complex society as ours, it is our duty and responsibility to our fellow men and our children to tackle the problems that lie ahead with faith and courage. Faith that is spoken of in the Bible, which in paraphrase says "Only possess the faith of a small mustard seed and you will be able to move mountains and then the courage to withstand the greatest onslaught the enemy can muster, and you are bound to succeed." No, it will not be easy, but neither does one find it altogether easy to be a Christian in this very sin sick world.

I am reminded here of a secular song, the lyrics of which are as follows: "Give me some men who are stout-hearted men, who will fight for the rights they adore. Start me with ten who are stout-hearted men, and I will soon give you ten thousand more.

Oh, shoulder to shoulder, and bolder and bolder, they grow as they go to meet the foe. Then there is nothing in this world that can halt or mar a plan when we stick together man to man." There is no doubt in my mind that the lyrics to that song have a very appropriate meaning in this day and time.

Then it was Samuel Garth who said: "When honor is lost, it is a treat to die; death's but a sure retreat from infamy."

There is an urgent need for dedicated and courageous leadership. If we are to solve the problems ahead and make social justice a reality, this leadership must be four-fold in our various communities. Men and women in every possible community endeavor should busy themselves in an effort to work out our problem on a mutual respectful basis with our fellow men. This is no time for faint-hearted men, but rather a time when our true faith in God should emerge and take over our complete self. It is spoke of in one passage of the scripture, that man should not fear men who can only destroy the body but rather God, who can destroy both body and soul.

In closing, I am reminded of the writings of James Weldon Johnson, who wrote: "God of our weary years, God of our silent tears, Thou who hast brought us this far on the way; Thou who hast by thy might, led us into the light, keep us forever in Thy path, we pray. Lest our feet stray from the places, our God, where we met Thee. Lest our hearts, drunk with the wine of the world, we forget Thee; shadowed beneath Thy hand, may we forever stand true to our God, true to our native land."

Source: Myrlie Evers-Williams and Manning Marable, eds., *The Autobiography of Medgar Evers: A Hero's Life and Legacy Revealed through His Writings, Letters, and Speeches* (New York: Basic Books, 2005). Copyright © 2005. Reprinted by permission of Civitas Books, an imprint of Hachette Book Group, Inc.

DOCUMENT 6.2

Missing Poster of Andrew Goodman, James Chaney, and Michael Schwerner (1964)

In June 1964, Andrew Goodman, James Chaney, and Michael Schwerner—three Freedom Summer activists aged twenty, twenty-one, and twenty-four years old, respectively—were abducted and murdered by local members of the Ku Klux Klan in Mississippi, while registering African Americans to vote. Goodman, Chaney, and Schwerner were arrested and jailed on trumped-up speeding charges in Philadelphia, Mississippi. The police eventually released and deposited the three young men on a deserted road, where three carloads of Klansmen waited. The Klansmen shot Schwerner and Goodman and beat Chaney with chains before shooting him. Their bodies were buried in an earthen dam. The disappearance of the Freedom Summer activists drew national attention and a federal investigation. The Federal Bureau of Investigation released a missing poster to entice informers with a $30,000 reward. As a result, Klan informers eventually came forward, revealed details of the crime, and led investigators to the men's burial site.

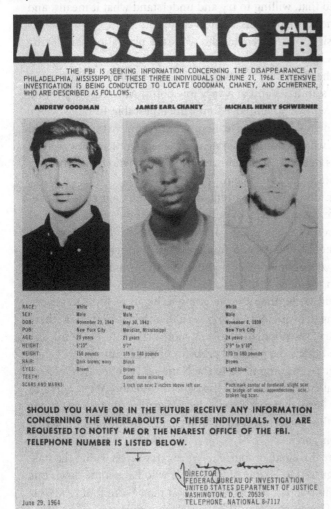

Source: Federal Bureau of Investigation, *Poster of Missing Civil Rights Workers*, June 29, 1964, https://www.fbi.gov/image-repository/fbi_poster_of_missing_civil_rights_workers.jpg.

Bob Moses, "Speech on Freedom Summer at Stanford University" (1964)

On April 24, 1964, Student Nonviolent Coordinating Committee activist Robert "Bob" Moses addressed students at Stanford University's Cubberly Auditorium in Palo Alto, California. In his address, he outlined the goals, strategies, and difficulties activists faced during Freedom Summer. Moses was a central figure in the Mississippi Freedom Summer, an interracial political and community initiative whereby Black and white college students flooded Mississippi to end African American voter disenfranchisement.

... The feeling that we have is that the vital changes which are needed cannot be gotten unless there is some political change. In Mississippi, you have to have political changes to get any real change in that state. In this country, we're going to have to have political changes to get any real change across the board. The question is whether the American people are willing to listen to that, willing to try and understand what it means, and willing to try and do what they have to do in order to change it? ...

In the Delta area of Mississippi, the people who work the plantations are facing the fact that, every year, there are 10 percent fewer jobs for them. In probably five years ... the automation of the plantation will be completed. The labor market on the plantation will be very well stabilized and at a very low point. And the people who come off those plantations will be unemployed and unemployable in our society. They will be permanently unemployed because, first, they don't have the skills. And there isn't anywhere, in our whole country, a system for teaching them how to read and write. Because, that was nobody's problem who had power, who had resources, who had money, who could tackle that problem.

It's only since we've been down in Mississippi, and since the civil rights movement has begun in the last few years, that you've begun to get some concerted effort with very minimum resources. We got a grant—an anonymous grant, mind you—of $80,000 to tackle the problem of literacy at a fundamental, bedrock level. And the person who gave it had to give it anonymously because the problem of literacy in the Delta, and in Mississippi, in the deep South, is a political problem. Because, if you teach people how to read and write, then they're going to begin to want to govern themselves. And they're going to begin to want to govern themselves in an area where they form the predominance of the population, over a more articulate, economically controlling white group. And that's the political problem in our country. ...

For our part, this summer we're going to go to the National Democratic Convention in Atlantic City and challenge the regular Mississippi delegation. We're going to ask the national Democratic Party that they unseat that delegation, that they seat our people in its place, and that they make a real structural change, or the beginning of a structural change within their party.

Our basis for doing that are threefold, or fourfold. We're carrying on within the state what we call a "Freedom Registration." Some of the people who have come down this summer, who are interested in politics, will be working on that. We're setting up our own registrars in every one of the 82 counties. They have deputy registrars, we have our own forms. We're challenging the whole basis of the registration in Mississippi. We don't have any questions which will make people interpret some section of the Constitution. We're making it as simple as we possibly can. We want to register upwards of 300,000 to 400,000 Negroes around the state of Mississippi. To dispel, at least, once and for all, the argument that the reason Negroes don't register is because they're apathetic. Because there are these 400,000 people to be registered. But for one thing, people don't even know that they're there. And if they are, or if they do know, they say, "Well, if so many people are not registering, part of the reason, and probably a large part of the reason, must be their apathy."

With the freedom registration, we also have freedom candidates. We have three people who are running for Congress. One from the 2nd Congressional District, one from the Third, and one from the Fifth. And then a person who's running against Sen. Stennis. They have all filed, met all the qualifications, and their names should appear on the Democratic primary June 2. The idea is to begin to develop again, within the people, the Negro people and some white people in the state, a different conception of their politics, and to begin to see if we can evolve a political organization in Mississippi.

We also are going to attend the precinct meetings that the regular Democratic delegates will be holding around the state. We figure that many of our people will be thrown out of these meetings because they're segregated. And we're going to use this as part of the documentation as [to] why that delegation should not be seated. We also are going to elect our own delegates, paralleling their procedures right from the start. Precinct meetings, county conventions, district caucuses, the state convention. A total of 68 delegates representing 24 votes, two whole votes and 22 half votes. We're going to send them to Atlantic City. We're going to ask that they be seated. We're going to demand that they be seated. . . .

. . . The staff in Mississippi were violently opposed to the summer project when it was first announced. They were opposed to an invasion of white people coming in to do good, and to work for a summer, and to essentially run projects, they thought, without having any experience and basis for doing that. . . .

Now, on other hand, the people in Mississippi did not have the reaction of the staff at all. The farmers, and the people who live and work there, welcomed the whole idea. Because they feel that anybody who comes down to help is good. . . . [They feel] that they're isolated, that they're alone, that they have no real tools, that they face an overwhelming enemy, that any kind of help that they can get is welcome. . . .

. . . [I]n the Freedom Schools we have one track, which is basically just a set of questions which is devised to draw out of the Negro youngsters some ideas about themselves and the lives they lead. . . . Questions which can be handled by people who have some sensitivity to other people, who have some concern about them, who are not so interested in projecting themselves, but are able to try and reach out and really cross what is a really very wide gap, between white people from middle-class backgrounds in the North, and Negro youngsters who've grown up in slums, rural or urban, in the South. So that one of the things we hoped to do was, working across the summer, if we touched in 20 Freedom Schools 1,000 kids, and began to draw some things like that out of them, then we felt that we'd have another layer, another stage, another base that we would have to operate from and on.

On the question of voting, we decided that we would like to try to establish, across the summer, the right to picket at the courthouses in the downtown urban areas. . . .

If it's possible this summer to have interracial teams living and working in Mississippi in the Negro communities, it might change the whole conception around the country of how it might be possible to get at some of these problems in the deep South. The federal government cannot have a real, domestic Peace Corps. It's possible for our country to organize youth all over the country, to give them elaborate training, to spend millions and millions of dollars. Very worthwhile to train them and send them abroad to work in under-developed countries all across the world. It would be impossible for them to mount anywhere near that kind of program in this country. They could not send segregated teams into the South. The country wouldn't have it. They couldn't send integrated teams into the South—they couldn't guarantee their protection.

     . . .

The question comes up all the time about nonviolence and what it means. And they're really deep, moral problems, which are connected, already, with the summer project. I realized one type of problem two-and-a-half years ago when we first went down to Amite County because Herbert Lee was killed that summer. Was killed just as surely because we went in there to organize, as rain comes because of clouds. If we hadn't gone in there, he wouldn't have been killed. The action which was started in that county wouldn't have happened. The chain of events leading up to his death wouldn't have happened. So, in some sense, if you're concerned about people and concerned about these kind of questions, you have to dig into yourself to find out, in what sense do you share responsibility? What does it mean to be involved in that kind of action which might precipitate that kind of death? . . .

Source: Robert P. Moses, "Speech on Freedom Summer at Stanford University" (speech, April 24, 1964), American Radio Works, http://americanradioworks.publicradio.org/features/blackspeech/bmoses.html. Courtesy of Janet Moses.

DOCUMENT 6.4

Freedom School Lecture (1964)

Freedom Summer did more than organize voter registration drives. It also established Freedom Schools and community centers that provided instruction to children, teens, and adults about Black history, leadership, and community empowerment. Below is a photograph of a Freedom School in True Light Baptist Church. Specifically, it captures the audience at a Mississippi Freedom Democratic Party at a lecture given by SNCC field secretary Sandy Leigh, a New York native and director of the Hattiesburg Project. Some of the Freedom School students are Sandra Blalock, Ann Conner, Rena Corley, Audrey "Pee Wee" Easterling, Myrtis Easterling, Beverly Harris, James Townes, Alma Travis, Janice Walter, Shirley White, and Jerry Wilson. Three volunteers who taught in the Freedom School at True Light are William D. Jones (a native of Birmingham, Alabama, and a teacher in the Long Island, New York, public schools), who is standing gesturing from a rear pew; Nancy Ellin (from Kalamazoo, Michigan), sitting next to him; and Peter Werner (from Flint, Michigan, and a graduate student at the University of Michigan), the white male seated in the fourth pew from the camera.

Source: Herbert Randall, *View of the Audience at an MFDP Lecture*, 1964, M351.0296, Herbert Randall Freedom Summer Photographs, Historical Manuscripts, The University of Southern Mississippi.

"Challenge of the Mississippi Freedom Democratic Party" (1964)

The "Challenge of the Mississippi Freedom Democratic Party" details the origins of this political party and its plans to challenge the seating of the delegation of the regular Mississippi Democratic Party at the 1964 Democratic National Convention in Atlantic City, New Jersey. SNCC formed the MFDP to expand Black voter registration, increase Black political presence and power, and displace the state's all-white Democratic Party. Veteran civil rights activists Fannie Lou Hamer, Victoria Gray, Annie Divine, and Aaron Henry led the party.

I. DEVELOPMENT OF THE MISSISSIPPI FREEDOM DEMOCRATIC PARTY

Three basic considerations underlie the development of the Mississippi Freedom Democratic Party and its plans to challenge the seating of the delegation of the Mississippi Democratic Party at the 1964 National Democratic Convention. They are:

1. The long history of systematic and studied exclusion of Negro citizens from equal participation in the political processes of the state grows more flagrant and intensified daily.
2. The Mississippi Democratic Party has conclusively demonstrated its lack of loyalty to the National Democratic Party, in the past, and currently indicates no intention of supporting the platform of the 1964 National Democratic Convention.
3. The intransigent and fanatical determination of the State's political power-structure to maintain status-quo, clearly demonstrates that the "Mississippi closed society," as Professor James W Silver of the University of Mississippi asserts, is without leadership or moral resources to reform itself, and hence can only be brought into the mainstream of the twentieth century by forces outside of itself.

. . .

II. ORGANIZATIONAL STRUCTURE OF THE FREEDOM DEMOCRATIC PARTY

To give Negro citizens of Mississippi an experience in political democracy and to establish a channel through which all citizens, Negro and white, can actively support the principles and programs of the National Democratic Party, the Mississippi Freedom Democratic Party was conceived. The Council of Federated Organizations (COFO), a confederation of all the national and local civil rights and citizenship education groups in Mississippi is assisting local citizens to develop the Mississippi Freedom Democratic Party. This party is open to all citizens regardless of race. It was officially established at a meeting in Jackson, Mississippi on April 26th; and the approximately 200 delegates present elected a temporary state executive committee, which will be responsible for setting precinct and other state meetings. These meetings will parallel those of the Mississippi Democratic Party, and every effort will be made to comply with all state laws which apply to the formation of political parties. Registered voters in the Freedom Democratic Party will attempt to attend precinct and county meetings of the Mississippi Democratic Party.

The Mississippi Freedom Democratic Party is presently engaged in three major efforts: (1) Freedom Registration; (2) Freedom Candidates; and (3) Convention Challenge.

1. Freedom Registration:

Official registration figures show that only some 20,000 Negroes are registered in Mississippi as compared to 500,000 whites. This represents less than 7% of the 435,000 Negroes 21 years of age in the state. The Freedom Registration is designed to show that thousands of Negroes want to become registered voters. By setting up registrars and deputy registrars in each of the 82 counties of the state, 300,000 persons may be registered in the Freedom Registration. Last November some 83,000 Negroes were registered in a mock gubernatorial race. In the present drive, 75,000 are reported registered, and this will be greatly stepped up when the summer program officially begins at the end of June. This registration will use simplified registration forms based on voting applications used in several Northern States. Any person who registers in the Freedom Registration will be eligible to vote in the Freedom Democratic Party Convention and participate in party work.

2. Freedom Candidates:

The four (4) candidates who qualified to run in the June 2 primary in Mississippi were nominees of the Freedom Democratic Party and in addition to their bid in the regular Democratic primary, they will also run in a mock election under the Mississippi Freedom Democratic Party in November. This will help to establish the fact that thousands of Negroes are deprived of citizenship participation because of the racist character of Mississippi's voter registration procedures.

The four candidates are, Mrs. Victoria Gray, opposing Sen. John Stennis; Mrs. Fannie Lou Hamer, opposing Rep. Jamie L. Whitten; the Rev. John Cameron, opposing Rep. William M. Colmer, and Mr. James Houston, opposing Rep. John Bell Williams.

The Platforms of the candidates of the Freedom Democratic Party articulate the needs of all the people of Mississippi, such as anti-poverty programs, medicare, aid to education, rural development, urban renewal, and the guarantee of constitutional rights to all. This is in sharp contrast to the lack of real issues in the campaigns of the candidates who won in the primary. Senator Stennis did not even bother to campaign in the state.

3. The Challenge to the Democratic National Convention:

Delegates from the Freedom Democratic Party will challenge the seating of the "old-line" Mississippi delegation at the Democratic National Convention this August in Atlantic City, N.J. These delegates will have been chosen through precinct meetings, county conventions, caucuses in congressional districts, and at a state wide convention of the Freedom Democratic Party. The State Executive Committee will be ratified and the national Committeeman and Committeewoman will be chosen at this state wide convention. . . .

Source: Mississippi Freedom Democratic Party, "Challenge of the Mississippi Freedom Democratic Party," 1964, box 1, folder 9, Matthew Zwerling Freedom Summer Collection, University of Southern Mississippi.

DOCUMENT 6.6

Fannie Lou Hamer Testimony before DNC Credentials Committee (1964)

Fannie Lou's testimony before the 1964 Democratic National Convention's Credentials Committee follows. Hamer was the vice president of the MFDP. In her testimony, she details her efforts to organize people to exercise their full civil and voting rights and describes what citizenship meant for Black Mississippians. While Hamer was giving her testimony to the committee, President Lyndon B. Johnson—who did not support the MFDP because he feared that it would ruin his reelection chances—immediately called a press conference, hoping to distract the country's attention from the charismatic and moving Hamer. But to his dismay, Hamer's message not only reached but also moved Americans.

Mr. Chairman, and the Credentials Committee, my name is Mrs. Fannie Lou Hamer, and I live at 626 East Lafayette Street, Ruleville, Mississippi, Sunflower County, the home of Senator James O. Eastland, and Senator Stennis.

It was the 31st of August in 1962 that 18 of us traveled 26 miles to the country courthouse in Indianola to try to register to try to become first-class citizens. We was met in Indianola by policemen, Highway Patrolmens, and they only allowed two of us in to take the literacy test at the time.

After we had taken this test and started back to Ruleville, we was held up by the City Police and the State Highway Patrolmen and carried back to Indianola where the bus driver was charged that day with driving a bus the wrong color.

After we paid the fine among us, we continued on to Ruleville, and Reverend Jeff Sunny carried me four miles in the rural area to where I had worked as a timekeeper and sharecropper for 18 years. I was met there by my children, who told me that the plantation owner was angry because I had gone down to try to register. After they told me, my husband came, and said that the plantation owner was raising cain because I had tried to register, and before he quit talking the plantation owner came, and said, "*Fannie Lou, do you know—did Pap tell you what I said?*"

And I said, "*Yes, sir.*"

He said, "*I mean that.*" He said, "*If you don't go down and withdraw your registration, you will have to leave.*" [He] said, "Then if you go down and withdraw," he said, "*you still might have to go because we are not ready for that in Mississippi.*"

And I addressed him and told him and said, "*I didn't try to register for you. I tried to register for myself.*"

I had to leave that same night.

On the 10th of September 1962, 16 bullets was fired into the home of Mr. and Mrs. Robert Tucker for me. That same night two girls were shot in Ruleville, Mississippi. Also Mr. Joe McDonald's house was shot in.

And June the 9th, 1963, I had attended a voter registration workshop; was returning back to Mississippi. Ten of us was traveling by the Continental Trailway bus. When we got to Winona, Mississippi, which is Montgomery County, four of the people got off to use the washroom, and two of the people—to use the restaurant—two of the people wanted to use the washroom.

The four people that had gone in to use the restaurant was ordered out. During this time I was on the bus. But when I looked through the window and saw they had rushed out I got off of the bus to see what had happened. And one of the ladies said, "*It was a State Highway Patrolman and a Chief of Police ordered us out.*"

I got back on the bus and one of the persons had used the washroom got back on the bus, too. As soon as I was seated on the bus, I saw when they began to get the five people in a Highway Patrolman's car. I stepped off of the bus to see what was happening and somebody screamed from the car that the five workers was in, and said, "*Get that one there.*" When I went to get in the car, when the man told me I was under arrest, he kicked me.

I was carried to the county jail and put in the booking room. They left some of the people in the booking room and began to place us in cells. I was placed in a cell with a young woman called Miss Euvester Simpson. After I was placed in the cell I began to hear sounds of licks and screams, I could hear the sounds of licks and horrible screams. And I could hear somebody say, "*Can you say, 'yes, sir,' nigger? Can you say 'yes, sir'?*" And they would say other horrible names.

She would say, "*Yes, I can say 'yes, sir.'*"

"*So, well, say it.*"

She said, "*I don't know you well enough.*"

They beat her, I don't know how long. And after a while she began to pray, and asked God to have mercy on those people.

And it wasn't too long before three white men came to my cell. One of these men was a State Highway Patrolman and he asked me where I was from. I told him Ruleville and he said, "*We are going to check this.*"

They left my cell and it wasn't too long before they came back. He said, "*You are from Ruleville all right,*" and he used a curse word. And he said, "*We are going to make you wish you was dead.*"

I was carried out of that cell into another cell where they had two Negro prisoners. The State Highway Patrolmen ordered the first Negro to take the blackjack. The first Negro prisoner ordered me, by orders from the State Highway Patrolman, for me to lay down on a bunk bed on my face. I laid on my face and the first Negro began to beat. I was beat by the first Negro until he was exhausted. I was holding my hands behind me at that time on my left side, because I suffered from polio when I was six years old.

After the first Negro had beat until he was exhausted, the State Highway Patrolman ordered the second Negro to take the blackjack.

The second Negro began to beat and I began to work my feet, and the State Highway Patrolman ordered the first Negro who had beat me to sit on my feet—to keep me from working my feet. I began to scream and one white man got up and began to beat me in my head and tell me to hush.

One white man—my dress had worked up high—he walked over and pulled my dress—I pulled my dress down and he pulled my dress back up.

I was in jail when Medgar Evers was murdered.

All of this is on account of we want to register, to become first-class citizens. And if the Freedom Democratic Party is not seated now, I question America. Is this America, the land of the free and the home of the brave, where we have to sleep with our telephones off the hooks because our lives be threatened daily, because we want to live as decent human beings, in America?

Thank you.

Source: Fannie Lou Hamer, "Testimony before Democratic National Convention Credentials Committee" (speech, Atlantic City, New Jersey, August 22, 1964), American Radio Works, http://americanradioworks.publicradio.org/features/sayitplain/flhamer.html. Courtesy of Jacqueline Hamer Flakes.

DOCUMENT 6.7

"Mississippi Freedom Labor Union Pledge" (1965)

In 1965, African American cotton workers troubled by low wages and poor conditions and working with the Congress of Federated Organizations formed the Mississippi Freedom Labor Union. The MFLU sought to increase wages to $1.25 per hour and help workers bargain with their employers at a time when Jim Crow remained the law of the land. Its membership eventually grew to nearly one thousand workers in ten Delta counties. Many of these workers were fired or evicted (or both) for joining the union. The MFLU organized labor strikes against Senator James Eastland's plantation in Sunflower County and the Andrews Plantation in Washington County, among others. The union was short-lived, however. According to the historian John Dittmer, the "MFLU was a bold and romantic venture, but it was anachronistic, and activists began to explore other initiatives to deal with the changing agricultural economy."[1]

I AM A MEMBER OF THE MISSISSIPPI FREEDOM LABOR UNION.

I believe that everyone should receive at least $1.25 an hour for their work

I believe that children under the age of 16 should not have to work.

I believe that people should not have to work for more than 8 hours a day unless they get time and a half for overtime.

I believe that people over 60 should not have to work.

I believe that people who are sick should not have to work, and should receive free medical care.

I believe that all people who cannot get full-time jobs should get full compensation from the Government.

I believe that all work should carry social security and accident insurance.

I believe that all people should be treated equally in hiring, wages, and working conditions whatever their race or color.

I pledge to work together with other members of the MISSISSIPPI FREEDOM LABOR UNION to win these rights.

I believe that we should use strikes, picketing, boycotts, collective bargaining, and non-violent direct action to make the people we work for meet our demands.

Source: Mississippi Freedom Labor Union, "Mississippi Freedom Labor Union Pledge," 1965, Civil Rights Movement Archive, http://www.crmvet.org/docs/flu_pledge.pdf.

NOTES

1. John Dittmer, *Local People: The Struggle for Civil Rights in Mississippi* (Urbana: University of Illinois Press, 1995), 365.

DOCUMENT 6.8

James Forman on SNCC, SCLC, and Selma (1985)

James Forman remembers Turnaround Tuesday and the tension between SNCC and SCLC in Selma. The Selma movement consisted of three marches. The first march—better known as Bloody Sunday—occurred on Sunday, March 7, 1965. Approximately six hundred protesters began their walk to Montgomery, the state capital of Alabama; however, as they approached the Edmund Pettus Bridge, state troopers and local police brutally attacked marchers. Two days later, now with more protesters (as thousands flocked to Selma to participate after viewing the carnage on television), a second march took place despite an injunction and President Lyndon B. Johnson's disapproval and refusal to intervene. Led by Dr. Martin Luther King Jr., protesters crossed the bridge singing "Ain't Gonna Let Nobody Turn Me 'Round" and other freedom songs. To their surprise, once King reached the end of the bridge, rather than continue, he stopped, prayed, and turned around. They later learned that King had made a face-saving compromise with federal authorities. King's leadership suffered as a result.

. . .

James Forman: Well, the, the basic disagreement that the Student Nonviolent Coordinating Committee had with the Southern Christian Leadership Conference was over the question of leadership. And we felt that there should be a projection and an organization of indigenous leadership, I mean leadership from the community, whereas the Southern Christian Leadership Conference took the position that Martin was a charismatic leader who was mainly responsible for, for raising money, and they raised most of the money off of his leadership. But this differences in leadership then led to differences in style or work. . . . In Albany, Georgia for instances we went in with the express purpose of developing a people's movement, an indigenous people's movement and we did that. And that at the time of the uh uh ride from Atlanta to Albany uh, that everything was in place for this type of projection including press, press from all over the United States was already in place in in in Albany, Georgia, and that as a result of the demonstrations, then Dr. King, who heard about them, felt that he should come in as the charismatic leader, and that there were some even tensions, but I mean people wanted that to happen and so you know we agreed to it. But at the same time, oh, well this, this difference in the leadership carried over into Birmingham and it also carried over into Selma.

INTERVIEWER: TELL ME HOW IT CARRIED OVER INTO SELMA.

JAMES FORMAN: Well, because we, you know we went into Selma in 1963 and the way that it carried over into Selma was that Dr. King was asked or it was my understanding you know that that to, to, to participate to try to strengthen the '64 Civil Rights Act, but the Fifth Circuit Court of Appeals was already, had already decided as a, to hand down a lot of injunctions, you know which would strengthen the '65, '64 Civil Rights Act. And the key thing that I'm talking about is the literacy requirements. The United States Justice Department wanted a provision that would have some degree of literacy requirements, and in the Student Nonviolent Coordinating Committee we objected to that. We felt that all of these literacy requirements were unconstitutional, unnecessary and that people should just present themselves and once they present themselves, they should be able to vote. Now the conditions for that, I mean of course were certainly heightened by a result of the Selma march, but, but mind you that the differences occurred I mean like uh, the Monday before Bloody Tuesday, uh, when we met with Dr. King in Montgomery, um, and discussed the proposal of Judge Johnson that an injunction would be handed down if we called off the march. And we voted against that. We voted that the march should continue and then when we got to Selma of course, Dr. King said to the people that the march would continue. Well, I mean we, you know, even though we knew that he had agreed to this injunction, so we felt that the thing to do then was to have a meeting with him and to try to get him to be consistent, to keep the march going, I mean the march on Turnaround Tuesday, you know, and not to say to people, that, that the march wouldn't continue.

INTERVIEWER: GO BACK TO WHEN . . . SELMA WHEN YOU'RE THERE AND SCLC COMES IN AND GIVE ME IN SELMA, GENERICALLY HOW THE DIFFERENCES IN LEADERSHIP UM, UH CAUSED CONFLICT, OR, OR JUST DESCRIBE FOR ME WHAT THE DIFFERENCES IN LEADER-SHIP WERE. TRYING TO GET AT THE BEGINNING OF THE SELMA . . .

JAMES FORMAN: Well, I recall definitely a meeting with Dr. King. A lot of us had meetings, and we kept explaining to him the necessity to try to develop this indigenous leadership and we also tried to explain to him the danger, OK, the real danger in trying to project a charismatic leader as the leader of the movement because of a possible assassination. I mean that, this is still a very, that in 1965 conditions were very difficult and that the uh uh uh um people were being, still being killed. You know and if you didn't have broad based movement, the assassination of a leader could lead to a decapitation or a reduction of the movement and we didn't want that, I mean we had, you know we wanted you know a movement that would survive the loss of our lives. And then therefore then, the uh uh, the necessity to build a broad based movement, and not just a charismatic leader.

INTERVIEWER: I'M GOING TO LET YOU PICK RIGHT UP.

JAMES FORMAN: Well, in Selma, Alabama, the differences with the Southern Christian Leadership Conference did become acute. And these differences revolved around the nature of the cooperation with the federal government, um, the um, the style of leadership as well as the the the forms of protest, ok. Now, we had been trying to, excuse me, to get people throughout the South not to have a lot of confidence, you know, that the federal government was going, not that the state governments I mean were going to say to them, we, we were operating on two, two levels, I think that to try to make it clear. That inside the states uh, we felt that federal government should be utilized to break the power of the reactionary racist state governments, because people were living in a climate of fear on the, uh, on the, uh, from the state governors and sheriffs and so forth. And that we had to have some fire to break this grip of fear and this torture and terror which it was inflicted throughout the South. And we felt that the federal government was the agency by which to do that. We were fighting for a strong central federal government OK, and we were successful in that. However, we did not agree that people should collaborate and and and cooperate to the detriment of the long range interests of the people and we felt that by agreeing to injunctions, you know, on the part of the federal government or by not fighting those as it happened in in in Albany, Georgia, I mean we explained to Dr. King that, that when the, when the federal courts were handing down injunctions, that those injunctions should be fought. OK, so consequently we did not feel that that there should be any types of deals worked out with the Justice Department or so forth that you should take, find out what's the principle and fight for the principle. And so therefore then in Selma,

Alabama when he was agreeing to various things we were rejecting that but when he picked up the phone at 5 o'clock in the morning and called the United States Justice Department and said I have to go against the injunction, you know we felt that that was a tremendous victory, and that he should be supported, you know and that meant that we should participate actively in the demonstrations you know. And so on the other hand then as a result of Turnaround Tuesday you know the uh uh uh we felt that something, I mean we knew for instance, I mean we had heard all morning you know that, that well the . . . the march may be called off but so but we felt that people had to be mobilized to continue to march.

Source: James Forman, interview with Blackside, December 11, 1985, Henry Hampton Collection, Film and Media Archive, Washington University Libraries, http://digital.wustl.edu/e/eop/eopweb/for0015.0489.039jamesforman.html.

FURTHER READING

Andrews, Kenneth T. *Freedom Is a Constant Struggle: The Mississippi Civil Rights Movement and Its Legacy*. Chicago: University of Chicago Press, 2004.

Bolton, Charles C. *The Hardest Deal of All: The Battle over School Integration in Mississippi, 1870–1980*. Jackson: University Press of Mississippi, 2005.

Brooks, Maegan Parker. *Fannie Lou Hamer: America's Freedom Fighting Woman*. Lanham, MD: Rowman & Littlefield, 2020.

Crawford, Vicki. "African American Women in the Mississippi Freedom Democratic Party." In *Sisters in the Struggle: African American Women in the Civil Rights–Black Power Movement*, edited by Bettye Collier-Thomas and V. P. Franklin, 121–38. New York: New York University Press, 2001.

Crosby, Emilye. *A Little Taste of Freedom: The Black Struggle for Freedom in Claiborne County, Mississippi*. Chapel Hill: University of North Carolina Press, 2005.

Dittmer, John. *Local People: The Struggle for Civil Rights in Mississippi*. Urbana: University of Illinois Press, 1995.

Doyle, William. *An American Insurrection: The Battle of Oxford, Mississippi, 1962*. New York: Anchor Books, 2001.

Eagles, Charles W. *The Price of Defiance: James Meredith and the Integration of Ole Miss*. Chapel Hill: University of North Carolina Press, 2014.

Evers, Myrlie, and Manning Marable. *The Autobiography of Medgar Evers: A Hero's Life and Legacy Revealed through His Writings, Letters, and Speeches*. New York: Basic Civitas Books, 2005.

Evers, Myrlie, and William Peters. *For Us, the Living*. Jackson: University Press of Mississippi, 2007.

Fairclough, Adam. *To Redeem the Soul of America: The Southern Christian Leadership Conference and Martin Luther King, Jr*. Athens: University of Georgia Press, 1987.

Forner, Karlyn. *Why the Vote Wasn't Enough for Selma*. Durham, NC: Duke University Press, 2017.

Gallagher, Henry. *James Meredith and the Ole Miss Riot: A Soldier's Story*. Jackson: University Press of Mississippi, 2012.

Garrow, David. *Protests at Selma: Martin Luther King, Jr., and Voting Rights of 1965*. New Haven, CT: Yale University Press, 2009.

Hamlin, Francoise. *Crossroads at Clarkdale: The Black Freedom Struggle in the Mississippi Delta after World War II*. Chapel Hill: University of North Carolina Press, 2014.

Hogan, Wesley. *Many Minds, One Heart: SNCC's Dream for a New America*. Chapel Hill: University of North Carolina Press, 2007.

Holsaert, Faith S., et al., eds. *Hands on the Freedom Plow: Personal Accounts by Women in SNCC*. Urbana: University of Illinois Press, 2012.

LaFayette, Bernard, and Kathryn Lee Johnson. *In Peace and Freedom: My Journey in Selma*. Lexington: University Press of Kentucky, 2015.

Lee, Chana Kai. *For Freedom's Sake: The Life of Fannie Lou Hamer*. Urbana: University of Illinois Press, 2000.

Lewis, John, and Mike D'Orso. *Walking with the Wind: A Memoir of the Movement*. San Diego: Harcourt Brace, 1998.

Meredith, James, and William Doyle. *A Mission from God: A Memoir and Challenge for America*. New York: Atria Books, 2016.

Meredith, James, and Aram Goudsouzian. *Three Years in Mississippi*. Jackson: University Press of Mississippi, 2019.

Mills, Kay. *This Little Light of Mine: The Life of Fannie Lou Hamer*. Lexington: University Press of Kentucky, 2007.

Newman, Mark. *Divine Agitators: The Delta Ministry and Civil Rights in Mississippi*. Athens: University of Georgia Press, 2004.

Ownby, Ted, ed. *The Civil Rights Movement in Mississippi*. Jackson: University Press of Mississippi, 2013.

Payne, Charles. *I've Got the Light of Freedom: The Organizing Tradition and the Mississippi Freedom Struggle*. Berkeley: University of California Press, 1995.

Pratt, Robert A. *Selma's Bloody Sunday: Protest, Voting Rights, and the Struggle for Racial Equality*. Baltimore: Johns Hopkins University Press, 2017.

7

Economic Dimensions of the Civil Rights Movement

The Black freedom struggle in the 1930s focused on labor and economic issues. What was the nature of the struggle for African American labor and economic freedom after the Second World War? To what extent did the focus on economic inequality differ from the fight for desegregation and voting rights within the movement? What areas of economic inequality did civil rights activists across the country target? And how well did federal civil rights and antipoverty legislation address Black demands for jobs, fair housing, education, and welfare rights?

On August 28, 1963, Martin Luther King Jr. gave his now-iconic "I Have a Dream" speech. In it, as many celebrate, he stated: "I have a dream that one day down in Alabama . . . little black boys and black girls will be able to join hands with little white boys and white girls as sisters and brothers." But his speech did more than call for racial unity. King made radical statements (radical for the time, of course) calling for the end of economic discrimination and disenfranchisement. He spoke: "We cannot be satisfied as long as the Negro's basic mobility is from a smaller ghetto to a larger one." John Lewis also spoke at the March on Washington and made similar comments. He opened his speech, in fact, with: "We march today for jobs and freedom, but we have nothing to be proud of. For hundreds and thousands of our brothers are not here. For they are receiving starvation wages, or no wages at all."

It is clear, then, that civil rights activists understood that freedom meant more than ending discrimination in public accommodations and at the polls. It also meant economic freedom. Activists' efforts facilitated the creation and implementation of President Lyndon B. Johnson's War on Poverty, which Johnson hoped would eradicate forms of rural and urban poverty. Johnson's Equal Opportunity Act of 1964 created the Office of Economic Opportunity and established jobs training programs, community action grants, greater access to legal aid, and the Food Stamp Act.

One year after Johnson introduced his War on Poverty, in mid-1965, King joined the Chicago Freedom Movement, which demanded open housing in the city of Chicago. While the movement faced many difficulties and setbacks, it is credited for inspiring the Fair Housing Act of 1968. This act is part of the Civil Rights Act of 1968. It prohibits housing discrimination based on race, color, religion, or national origin with regards to the sale, rental, and advertising of homes.

In 1966, the Southern Christian Leadership Conference chose Chicago as the site for a new chapter of Operation Breadbasket, a civil rights organization led by ministers that came to be known as the economic arm of the SCLC. Operation Breadbasket utilized strategies from earlier phases of the Black freedom struggle by boycotting businesses that operated in Black communities but refused to hire Black workers or stock Black products. Likewise, Operation Breadbasket engaged local communities in fighting for more financial institutions and Black businesses to serve their communities.

Black women were at the helm of efforts petitioning federal and state governments for economic assistance for impoverished families. The National Welfare Rights Organization was inaugurated in 1967 and brought together the organizing efforts of Johnnie Tillmon, Beulah Sanders, and other welfare rights activists. Long excluded from federal and state assistance programs or subject to greater restrictions, Black women in the NWRO sought greater assistance from and more rights under the welfare system. The organizations used direct and legal action to advance and protect the rights of welfare recipients, the majority of whom were women and children.

The SCLC's shift in focus to economic inequality was most notable through its Poor People's Campaign in 1968. Prior to his assassination in April 1968, King and the SCLC announced plans to lead thousands of poor people to Washington, D.C., to bring national awareness and action to the vast amount of Americans who remained poor despite civil rights legislation and antipoverty programs. King hoped that the next phase of nonviolent protest would be aimed against poverty and that taking the Poor People's Campaign to the nation's capital would inspire similar protests around the country.

In early April 1968, King traveled to Memphis, Tennessee, to lend support to city sanitation workers, who were on strike for better wages, working conditions, and measures to end discrimination toward its largely African American male workforce. King and the SCLC saw the strike by Black workers in Memphis as in line with their organization's growing focus on attacking economic inequality. However, on April 4, 1968, the day after giving one of his most memorable speeches, King was assassinated while standing on the balcony of his room at the Lorraine Motel. Days of violent protests across the nation followed King's assassination. James Earl Ray, a segregationist with a long criminal history, was ultimately convicted of killing King. Despite King's death, the Poor People's Campaign continued under the leadership of Ralph Abernathy. In May 1968, more than three thousand people traveled to Washington, D.C., and established a tent community on the National Mall named "Resurrection City" where they would reside for six weeks. Along with Resurrection City, members of the Poor People's Campaign marched and held public demonstrations across Washington, D.C., and attended congressional meetings in hopes of forcing more federal action on antipoverty measures.

DOCUMENT 7.1

March on Washington Program (1963)

Twenty-two years after the planned, but not executed, 1941 March on Washington, civil rights leaders planned the 1963 March on Washington for Jobs and Freedom. The goal of the march was to pressure the federal government and the Kennedy administration to back a stronger civil rights platform that would include measures against racial segregation and for greater economic, political, and legal rights for Black Americans. A. Philip Randolph and Bayard Rustin, architects of the 1941 March on Washington Movement, played integral roles in organizing the march. The program below illustrates the breadth of organizations involved in the 1963 march, but belies the many tensions that existed around the march such as those between older and younger civil rights activists and between male and female civil rights leaders. Nevertheless, the march did apply pressure to the Kennedy administration and, along with ongoing civil rights struggles across the nation, helped push passage of federal civil rights legislation. Some two hundred thousand people attended the march.

MARCH ON WASHINGTON FOR JOBS AND FREEDOM
AUGUST 28, 1963

LINCOLN MEMORIAL PROGRAM

1.	The National Anthem	*Led by* Marian Anderson.
2.	Invocation	The Very Rev. Patrick O'Boyle, *Archbishop of Washington.*
3.	Opening Remarks	A. Philip Randolph, *Director March on Washington for Jobs and Freedom.*
4.	Remarks	Dr. Eugene Carson Blake, *Stated Clerk, United Presbyterian Church of the U.S.A.; Vice Chairman, Commission on Race Relations of the National Council of Churches of Christ in America.*
5.	Tribute to Negro Women Fighters for Freedom Daisy Bates Diane Nash Bevel Mrs. Medgar Evers Mrs. Herbert Lee Rosa Parks Gloria Richardson	Mrs. Medgar Evers
6.	Remarks	John Lewis, *National Chairman, Student Nonviolent Coordinating Committee.*
7.	Remarks	Walter Reuther, *President, United Automobile, Aerospace and Agricultural Implement Wokers of America, AFL-CIO; Chairman, Industrial Union Department, AFL-CIO.*
8.	Remarks	James Farmer, *National Director, Congress of Racial Equality.*
9.	Selection	Eva Jessye *Choir*
10.	Prayer	Rabbi Uri Miller, *President Synagogue Council of America.*
11.	Remarks	Whitney M. Young, Jr., *Executive Director, National Urban League.*
12.	Remarks	Mathew Ahmann, *Executive Director, National Catholic Conference for Interracial Justice.*
13.	Remarks	Roy Wilkins, *Executive Secretary, National Association for the Advancement of Colored People.*
14.	Selection	Miss Mahalia Jackson
15.	Remarks	Rabbi Joachim Prinz, *President American Jewish Congress.*
16.	Remarks	The Rev. Dr. Martin Luther King, Jr., *President, Southern Christian Leadership Conference.*
17.	The Pledge	A Philip Randolph
18.	Benediction	Dr. Benjamin E. Mays, *President, Morehouse College.*

"WE SHALL OVERCOME"

Source: March on Washington, August 28, 1963, program, Bayard Rustin Papers, John F. Kennedy Library, National Archives and Records Administration, https://www.archives.gov /milestone-documents/official -program-for-the-march-on -washington.

DOCUMENT 7.2

John Lewis, Speech at the March on Washington (1963)

In 1963, John Lewis was the leader of the Student Nonviolent Coordinating Committee, an organization that came to embody the perspectives of student and youth civil rights activists as well as those who favored a more grassroots, community-based form of civil rights organizing. Lewis's original speech was more militant in tone than what follows. He criticized the Kennedy administration for being too slow and too timid in supporting civil rights and argued that SNCC would take a more direct, confrontational approach to securing Black freedoms in the South. A. Philip Randolph, Martin Luther King Jr., and others persuaded Lewis to adapt his tone for the speech. What follows are the remarks Lewis gave at the march.

We march today for jobs and freedom, but we have nothing to be proud of. For hundreds and thousands of our brothers are not here. For they are receiving starvation wages, or no wages at all. While we stand here, there are sharecroppers in the Delta of Mississippi who are out in the fields working for less than three dollars a day, twelve hours a day. While we stand here there are students in jail on trumped-up charges. Our brother James Farmer, along with many others, is also in jail. We come here today with a great sense of misgiving.

It is true that we support the administration's civil rights bill. We support it with great reservations, however. Unless Title III is put in this bill, there is nothing to protect the young children and old women who must face police dogs and fire hoses in the South while they engage in peaceful demonstrations. In its present form, this bill will not protect the citizens of Danville, Virginia, who must live in constant fear of a police state. It will not protect the hundreds and thousands of people that have been arrested on trumped charges. What about the three young men, SNCC field secretaries in Americus, Georgia, who face the death penalty for engaging in peaceful protest?

As it stands now, the voting section of this bill will not help the thousands of black people who want to vote. It will not help the citizens of Mississippi, of Alabama and Georgia, who are qualified to vote, but lack a sixth-grade education. "One man, one vote" is the African cry. It is ours too. It must be ours!

We must have legislation that will protect the Mississippi sharecropper who is put off of his farm because he dares to register to vote. We need a bill that will provide for the homeless and starving people of this nation. We need a bill that will ensure the equality of a maid who earns five dollars a week in a home of a family whose total income is $100,000 a year. We must have a good FEPC [Fair Employment Practices Commission] bill.

My friends, let us not forget that we are involved in a serious social revolution. By and large, American politics is dominated by politicians who build their careers on immoral compromises and ally themselves with open forms of political, economic, and social exploitation. There are exceptions, of course. We salute those. But what political leader can stand up and say, "My party is the party of principles"? For the party of Kennedy is also the party of Eastland. The party of Javits is also the party of

Goldwater. Where is our party? Where is the political party that will make it unnecessary to march on Washington?

Where is the political party that will make it unnecessary to march in the streets of Birmingham? Where is the political party that will protect the citizens of Albany, Georgia? Do you know that in Albany, Georgia, nine of our leaders have been indicted, not by the Dixiecrats, but by the federal government for peaceful protest? But what did the federal government do when Albany's deputy sheriff beat Attorney C.B. King and left him half-dead? What did the federal government do when local police officials kicked and assaulted the pregnant wife of Slater King, and she lost her baby?

To those who have said, "Be patient and wait," we have long said that we cannot be patient. We do not want our freedom gradually, but we want to be free now! We are tired. We are tired of being beaten by policemen. We are tired of seeing our people locked up in jail over and over again. And then you holler, "Be patient." How long can we be patient? We want our freedom and we want it now. We do not want to go to jail. But we will go to jail if this is the price we must pay for love, brotherhood, and true peace.

I appeal to all of you to get into this great revolution that is sweeping this nation. Get in and stay in the streets of every city, every village and hamlet of this nation until true freedom comes, until the revolution of 1776 is complete. We must get in this revolution and complete the revolution. For in the Delta in Mississippi, in southwest Georgia, in the Black Belt of Alabama, in Harlem, in Chicago, Detroit, Philadelphia, and all over this nation, the black masses are on the march for jobs and freedom.

They're talking about slow down and stop. We will not stop. All of the forces of Eastland, Barnett, Wallace, and Thurmond will not stop this revolution. If we do not get meaningful legislation out of this Congress, the time will come when we will not confine our marching to Washington. We will march through the South; through the streets of Jackson, through the streets of Danville, through the streets of Cambridge, through the streets of Birmingham. But we will march with the spirit of love and with the spirit of dignity that we have shown here today. By the force of our demands, our determination, and our numbers, we shall splinter the segregated South into a thousand pieces and put them together in the image of God and democracy. We must say: "Wake up America! Wake up!" For we cannot stop, and we will not and cannot be patient.

Source: John Lewis, "Text of Speech to Be Delivered at Lincoln Memorial," August 28, 1963, Student Nonviolent Coordinating Committee Papers, Martin Luther King Jr. Library and Archives. Courtesy of the Estate of John Lewis.

Lyndon B. Johnson, "War on Poverty Speech" (1964)

In President Lyndon B. Johnson's first State of the Union address on January 8, 1964, he declared a "War on Poverty." His vision of a War on Poverty involved the expansion of social-welfare legislation and the creation of reform programs to assist financially struggling Americans in line with the administration's Great Society reforms. Johnson positioned poverty as a societal problem to be solved, not one produced by individual shortcomings. Black activists and civil rights leaders viewed the War on Poverty as a potential vehicle through which to address long-standing racial inequities in access to jobs, fair housing, education, health care, and other quality-of-life measures. The War on Poverty faced significant hurdles, including widespread skepticism from conservatives and the allocation of far more resources to the Vietnam War.

We are citizens of the richest and most fortunate nation in the history of the world . . . [W]e have never lost sight of our goal: an America in which every citizen shares all the opportunities of his society, in which every man has a chance to advance his welfare to the limit of his capacities. We have come a long way toward this goal. We still have a long way to go.

The distance which remains is the measure of the great unfinished work of our society. To finish that work I have called for a national war on poverty. Our objective: total victory.

There are millions of Americans—one fifth of our people—who have not shared in the abundance which has been granted to most of us, and on whom the gates of opportunity have been closed.

What does this poverty mean to those who endure it? It means a daily struggle to secure the necessities for ever a meager existence. It means that the abundance, the comforts, the opportunities they see all around them are beyond their grasp. Worst of all, it means hopelessness for the young.

The young man or woman who grows up without a decent education, in a broken home, in a hostile and squalid environment, in ill health or in the face of racial injustice—that young man or woman is often trapped in a life of poverty. He does not have the skills demanded by a complex society. He does not know how to acquire those skills. He faces a mounting sense of despair which drains initiative and ambition and energy . . .

[W]e must also strike down all the barriers which keep many from using those exits. The war on poverty is not a struggle simply to support people, to make them dependent on the generosity of others. It is a struggle to give people a chance. It is an effort to allow them to develop and use their capacities, as we have been allowed to develop and use ours, so that they can share, as others share, in the promise of this nation.

We do this, first of all, because it is right that we should . . . We do it also because helping some will increase the prosperity of all. Our fight against poverty will be an investment in the most valuable of our resources—the skills and strength of our people . . . It strikes at the causes, not just the consequences of poverty.

Source: Lyndon B. Johnson, "War on Poverty Speech," 1965, *Public Papers of the Presidents of the United States* (Washington, DC: Government Printing Office, 1966).

Demands of the Chicago Freedom Movement (1966), Taped to the Door of City Hall by Martin Luther King Jr.

In July 1965, local Chicago civil rights activists under the umbrella Coordinated Council of Community Organizations invited Dr. King to participate in a demonstration against discrimination and segregation in Chicago that permeated many areas of Black life from education and housing to jobs and health care. In 1966, the CCCO, led by Al Raby, decided to focus its efforts on housing and invited Dr. King and the SCLC to partner on a campaign, the Chicago Freedom Movement, that would openly challenge, through demonstrations and demands, widespread housing discrimination in Chicago and its suburbs. In pushing for "open housing," the Chicago Freedom Movement revealed both the virulent racism of white segregationists in the North and the difficulty of challenging the racial politics of the Richard J. Daley machine. Many, however, credit the Chicago Freedom Movement with contributing to the passage of the Fair Housing Act of 1968.

REAL ESTATE BOARDS & BROKERS
1. Public statements that all listings will be available on a nondiscriminatory basis.

BANKS & SAVINGS INSTITUTIONS
1. Public statements of a nondiscriminatory mortgage policy so that loans will be available to any qualified borrower without regard to the racial composition of the area.

THE MAYOR & CITY COUNCIL
1. Publication of headcounts of whites, Negroes and Latin Americans for all city departments and for all firms from which city purchases are made.
2. Revocation of contracts with firms that do not have a full scale fair employment practice.
3. Creation of a citizens review board for grievances against police brutality and false arrests or stops and seizures.
4. Ordinance giving ready access to the names of owners and investors for all slum properties.
5. A saturation program of increased garbage collection, street cleaning, and building inspection services in the slum properties.

POLITICAL PARTIES
1. The requirement that precinct captains be residents of their precincts.

CHICAGO HOUSING AUTHORITY & CHICAGO DWELLING ASSOCIATION
1. Program to rehabilitate present public housing including such items as locked lobbies, restrooms in recreation areas, increased police protection and child care centers on every third floor.
2. Program to increase vastly the supply of low-cost housing on a scattered basis for both low and middle income families.

BUSINESS

1. Basic headcounts, including white, Negro and Latin American, by job classification and income level, made public.
2. Racial steps to upgrade and to integrate all departments, all levels of employment.

UNIONS

1. Headcounts in unions for apprentices, journeymen and union staff and officials by job classification. A crash program to remedy any inequities discovered by the headcount.
2. Indenture of at least 400 Negro and Latin American apprentices in the craft unions.

GOVERNOR

1. Prepare legislative proposals for a $2.00 state minimum wage [equal to $14.61 in 2014] law and for credit reform, including the abolition of garnishment and wage assignment.

ILLINOIS PUBLIC AID COMMISSION & COOK COUNTY DEPARTMENT OF PUBLIC AID

1. Encouragement of grievance procedures for the welfare recipients so that recipients know that they can be members of and represented by a welfare union or a community organization.
2. Institution of a declaration of income system to replace the degrading investigation and means test for welfare eligibility.

FEDERAL GOVERNMENT

1. Executive enforcement of Title I of the 1964 Civil Rights Act regarding the complaint against the Chicago Board of Education.
2. An executive order for Federal supervision of the nondiscriminatory granting of loans by banks and savings institutions that are members of the Federal Deposit Insurance Corporation or by the Federal Deposit Insurance Corporation.
3. Passage of the 1966 Civil Rights Act without any deletions or crippling amendments.
4. Direct funding of Chicago community organizations by the Office of Economic Opportunity.

PEOPLE

1. Financial support of the Freedom Movement.
2. Selective buying campaigns against businesses that boycott the products of Negro-owned companies.
3. Participation in the Freedom Movement target campaigns for this summer, including volunteer services and membership in one of the Freedom Movement Organizations.

Source: Demands of the Chicago Freedom Movement, 1966,
Civil Rights Movement Archive, https://www.crmvet.org/docs/66chi.htm.

Operation Breadbasket Flyer (ca. late 1960s)

The SCLC launched Operation Breadbasket in Chicago in tandem with the Chicago Freedom Movement as a way to challenge racist practices in hiring, employment, and supply contracts. The SCLC chose Jesse Jackson, a young civil rights activist and aspiring minister, to lead Operation Breadbasket in 1966. Operation Breadbasket challenged prevailing practices like those of supermarket giant A&P in which companies operating in Black communities and profiting off of Black dollars failed to hire Blacks in representative numbers, sell products made by Black-owned companies, invest financially in local community institutions, or employ Black workers in the construction, renovation, and upkeep of their stores. In many ways, Operation Breadbasket harked back to the "Don't Buy" campaigns of the 1930s, often employing boycotts to pressure businesses to adopt more equitable labor and economic practices.

Source: SCLC Operation Breadbasket, "A&P Signs Pact," circa 1968, flyer, box 5, folder 2, Rev. Martin L. Deppe Papers, Special Collections, Chicago Public Library.

Dr. Martin Luther King Jr., "Statement Announcing the Poor People's Campaign" (1967)

With the announcement of the Poor People's Campaign, Dr. King and the SCLC signaled an important shift from efforts focused on desegregation and the procurement of civil and political rights to a focus on economic inequality in the United States that acutely impacted not only Blacks but Americans of many different racial and ethnic backgrounds. In the statement, King links urban rebellions to inequality between the affluent and the poor and criticizes the United States' investment in the Vietnam War and other measures that failed to address the nation's most economically marginalized groups. King speaks frequently of going to Washington, D.C., to pressure federal officials to act. He did not, however, make it to Washington, D.C., that following summer, as he was assassinated on April 4, 1968, while in Memphis, Tennessee, to support the sanitation workers' strike.

Statement by Dr. Martin Luther King Jr.
President, Southern Christian Leadership Conference
Atlanta, Georgia

December 4, 1967

Ladies and Gentlemen:

Last week the staff of the Southern Christian Leadership Conference held one of the most important meetings we have ever convened. We had intensive discussions and analyses of our work and of the challenges which confront us and our nation, and at the end we made a decision which I wish to announce today.

The Southern Christian Leadership Conference will lead waves of the nation's poor and disinherited to Washington, D. C., next spring to demand redress of their grievances by the United States government and to secure at least jobs or income for all.

We will go there, we will demand to be heard, and we will stay until America responds. If this means forcible repression of our movement, we will confront it, for we have done this before. If this means scorn or ridicule, we embrace it, for that is what America's poor now receive. If it means jail, we accept it willingly, for the millions of poor already are imprisoned by exploitation and discrimination. But we hope, with growing confidence, that our campaign in Washington will receive at first a sympathetic understanding across our nation, followed by dramatic expansion of nonviolent demonstrations in Washington and simultaneous protests elsewhere. In short, we will be petitioning our government for specific reforms, and we intend to build militant nonviolent actions until that government moves against poverty.

We have now begun preparations for the Washington campaign. Our staff soon will be taking new assignments to organize people to go to Washington from 10 key cities and 5 rural areas. This will be no mere one-day march in

Washington, but a trek to the nation's capital by suffering and outraged citizens who will go to stay until some definite and positive action is taken to provide jobs and income for the poor.

We are sending our staff into these key areas to meet with the local leadership of these areas to discuss their readiness to cooperate with us in this venture.

In the coming weeks we will disclose our detailed plans on mobilizing this massive campaign and on the specific proposals which we are formulating.

Today I would like to tell you why the Southern Christian Leadership Conference has decided to undertake this task with the advice and participation we anticipate from other organizations and thousands of individuals.

America is at a crossroads of history, and it is critically important for us, as a nation and a society, to choose a new path and move upon it with resolution and courage.

It is impossible to under-estimate the crisis we face in America. The stability of a civilization, the potential of free government, and the simple honor of men are at stake.

Those who serve in the human-rights movement, including our Southern Christian Leadership Conference, are keenly aware of the increasing bitterness and despair and frustration that threaten the worst chaos, hatred and violence any nation has ever encountered.

In a sense, we are already at war with and among ourselves. Affluent Americans are locked into suburbs of physical comfort and mental insecurity; poor Americans are locked inside ghettoes of material privation and spiritual debilitation; and all of us can almost feel the presence of a kind of social insanity which could lead to national ruin.

Consider, for example, the spectacle of cities burning while the national government speaks of repression instead of rehabilitation. Or think of children starving in Mississippi while prosperous farmers are rewarded for not producing food. Or Negro mothers leaving children in tenements to work in neighborhoods where people of color can not live. Or the awesome bombardment, already greater than the munitions we exploded in World War II, against a small Asian land, while political brokers de-escalate and very nearly disarm a timid action against poverty. Or a nation gorged on money while millions of its citizens are denied a good education, adequate health services, decent housing, meaningful employment, and even respect, and are then told to be responsible.

The true responsibility for the existence of these deplorable conditions lies ultimately with the larger society, and much of the immediate responsibility for removing the injustices can be laid directly at the door of the federal government.

This is the institution which has the power to act, the resources to tap, and the duty to respond. And yet, this very government now lacks the will to make reforms which are demanded by a rising chorus across the nation.

According to the Harris Poll, for example, a substantial majority of Americans believe that we must proceed at once to tear down and rebuild the slums, and a solid majority feel that everyone should have a job. Concerned leaders of industry, civil-rights organizations, labor unions and churches are joining in such groups as the new Urban Coalition to urge progressive economic measures at the national level. Many urban political leaders are ready to carry out enlightened programs if only the federal government will provide the needed financial support. Newsweek magazine recently devoted an entire issue to the problem of racism in America and set forth some sound proposals for dealing with this situation.

I cite these facts merely to show that a clear majority in America are asking for the very things which we will demand in Washington.

We have learned from hard and bitter experience in our movement that our government does not move to correct a problem involving race until it is confronted directly and dramatically. It required a Selma before the fundamental right to vote was written into the federal statutes. It took a Birmingham before the government moved to open doors of public accomodations [*sic*] to all human beings.

What we now need is a new kind of Selma or Birmingham to dramatize the economic plight of the Negro, and compel the government to act.

Unrest among the poor of America, and particularly among Negroes, is growing rapidly. In this age of technological wizardry and political immorality, the poor are demanding that the basic need of people be met as the first priority of our domestic programs. Poor people can not long be placated by the glamour of multi-billion-dollar exploits in space. Poor people who encounter racial discrimination every day in every aspect of their lives can not be fooled by patronizing gestures and half-way promises. Poor people who are treated with derision and abuse by an economic system soon conclude with elementary logic that they have no rational interest in killing people 12, 000 miles away in the name of defending that system.

We intend to channelize the smouldering rage and frustration of Negro people into an effective, militant and nonviolent movement of massive proportions in Washington and other areas. Similarly, we will be calling on the swelling masses of young people in this country who are disenchanted with this materialistic society, and asking them to join us in our new Washington movement. We also look for participation by representatives of the millions of non-Negro poor—Indians, Mexican-Americans, Puerto Ricans, Appalachians, and others. And we shall welcome assistance from all Americans of good will.

And so, we have decided to go to Washington and to use any means of legitimate nonviolent protest necessary to move our nation and our government on a new course of social, economic, and political reform. As I said before, the power to initiate this reform resides in Washington. The President and the Congress have a primary responsibility for low minimum wages, for a degrading system of inadequate welfare, for subsidies of the rich and unemployment and underemployment of the poor, for a war mentality, for slums and starvation, and racism. The survival of a free society depends upon the guarantee and survival of freedom and equality. This is what we seek.

In the final analysis, SCLC decided to go to Washington because, if we did not act, we would be abdicating our responsibilities as an organization committed to nonviolence and freedom. We are keeping that commitment, and we shall call on America to join us in our forthcoming Washington campaign. In this way, we can work creatively against the despair and indifference that have so often caused our nation to be immobilized during the cold winter and shaken profoundly in the hot summer.

Memphis Sanitation Workers' Demonstrations (1968)

In this photograph from the 1968 Memphis Sanitation Workers Strike, Black men raise signs with what would become an iconic slogan embodying the struggle for Black rights: "I AM A MAN." The slogan was adopted by the sanitation workers to highlight their humanity and dignity and became a symbol for men and women in the Black freedom struggle in Memphis.

Source: Richard L. Copley, *1968 Iconic Image "I AM A MAN,"* 1968. Used by permission of Richard L. Copley.

William "Bill" Lucy on the Memphis Sanitation Workers' Strike and the Assassination of Dr. Martin Luther King Jr. (2013)

In the 1950s, Bill Lucy joined the American Federation of State, County and Municipal Employees (AFSCME) and would become one of its most visible and influential Black leaders. In the following excerpt, Lucy discusses the reasons for the strike and the support given to the sanitation workers by community members, especially Black women. Lucy draws on the relationship between labor and civil rights activism and describes the support that AFSCME lent to the strike, as well as the devastating impact of Dr. King's assassination.

[**Emilye Crosby**]: How did you end up being involved in the Memphis strike?

[**William Lucy**]: Well, like a lot of people, I got caught in the wrong place at the wrong time. [Laughter] I was, as I say, doing legislation and community affairs, which is something that I was in the learning phase of. This was in 1968. I ran into the president in the hallway one day, and he says, "What are you doing for the next couple of days?" And I said, "What I've been doing for the last couple of days."

EC: [Laughs]

WL: He said, "Well, I'd like for you to go to Detroit and do some work there," and I agreed to do it. And he called me back a little while later and says, "There's something going on in Memphis. You're from Memphis. Perhaps you could go down, take a look and see what it means."

The Sanitation Department in Memphis, Tennessee, was sort of in turmoil. You had men who had worked there the better part of their adult life and still earning wages that allowed them to qualify for every poverty program that existed there. As Dr. King once said, it was really the true story of the working poor. They were caught in a political squeeze between a brand-new mayor, who had got elected in a brand-new system of government. And he won his election on probably some of the strongest racial themes that had been seen for a long time. So, he felt he owed the black community nothing and certainly in his newfound power was not going to tolerate a union, talk about safety and health and wages and those kinds of things. So, a stalemate developed between a brand-new mayor and a brand-new system of city government.

Prior to the strike starting, there had been an attempt by these workers to influence the city, and they were enjoined by the local court from that. The catalyst to this new effort was men getting killed in the back of their garbage truck by the packing mechanism that scooped up the garbage and forced it into the back of the truck. This system and the equipment had been complained about for some time, but the city—new government, new mayor, old problems—they didn't see the need to address any of those problems at this time. This sort of festered for a while, and then the catalyst, as I said, was the men being crushed in the back of the truck. The remaining workforce just said, "We've just had enough of this."

Well, the last thing you need in a city like Memphis, Tennessee, in February is a garbage strike. I mean, strikes don't come because workers are mad. Strikes come because they are frustrated and have no ability to resolve the issues that contribute to their frustration. So, they were preparing to strike or to do something. And I went from Detroit to Memphis just to get sort of a look at what was going on. And it was clear that this was a major issue that wasn't going to resolve itself in 24 hours, because the city was entrenched in its position and the workers were in theirs.

And I sort of passed this on to the president, and we thought about it for a minute. We were subsequently notified by the *Washington Post*, a fellow from the *Washington Post*. I can't recall his name now, but he was coming back, oddly enough, from a meeting in Marks, Mississippi, that Dr. King had been in as a part of his early movement towards the Poor People's Campaign. And so, they called us and said, "Looks like there's a strike in Memphis, Tennessee." We said, "What do you mean, a strike in Memphis, Tennessee?' They said, "You ought to check it out." So, we did again, and it was true. The men were in the process of refusing to go to work. And ultimately, they took that position.

And I was there to work with them, myself; a fellow by the name of Jesse Epps, out of Clarksdale, Mississippi; one other fellow by the name of Joe Paisley, out of East Tennessee, I think, Nashville. And what we tried to do was just give some direction and some support to the workers until we figured out exactly what we were up against. And the strike just got bigger and bigger. It was a classic confrontation between a city with total power and a group of workers with no power, other than a good idea.

And the strike lasted for 67 days. And clearly the story was Dr. King ultimately saw this as a great contradiction, you know, in the rich nations and certainly rich cities, yet you have people working for wages for which will not allow them to bring themselves out of poverty. I mean, if you work every day, you ought to earn a wage sufficient to allow you to raise our family and so forth.

During the course of the strike, in the early days, Roy Wilkins came down, Bayard Rustin, ultimately Dr. King. This was a very quiet strike. I mean, it was not well-known outside of the city of Memphis. And we tried to ask people to come down and take a look, identify with it, who would bring some press with them, because the southern press don't give you a whole lot of play on workers' activities. When Dr. King came, because he was traveling with the national press, people had the opportunity to see exactly what was taking place. And my hat and heart goes out to the men who participated in that, because, I mean, whatever they had, it was on the line in that struggle.

EC: How did having Dr. King come in change the dynamics of the strike and what you were trying to do or able to do?

WL: Well, we had spent a good deal of time trying to keep this as an employer and employee issue. And because we felt pretty strongly that if it became a question of a racial polarization, that there would be little sympathy for the men themselves because nobody knew anything about sanitation workers. But it was impossible to do that. I mean, all of the elements, you know, suggested that you were going to ultimately wind up there. What Dr. King did was made this analogy that here is the problem in America. You've got people who work every day that don't earn a sufficient enough wage to get themselves out of poverty. We did an analysis of all the workers in that participation and 85 to 90 percent qualified for public aid, yet they worked every day.

And, as we sort of talked to people, we really began to understand that people had no sense of the role that sanitation workers play in the social service system. I think many of them thought that they just put their garbage out and it just disappeared overnight, as opposed to somebody getting up at four o'clock in the morning and coming by, picking it up, putting it on their shoulder, taking it around front and throwing it in the truck.

. . .

EC: There was quite a bit of organizing throughout the Memphis community in relation to this strike.

WL: We had to first get people to understand what was taking place, because these men, as I said before, had never been seriously thought of. What we asked them to do, because they touched every home in the city once or twice a week, and we asked them if they would do two things if they had decided to make this confrontation. First of all, they needed to go back home and talk to their wives, because the last thing you need is home pressure if you're in the middle of a confrontation. And the second thing is to take a simple leaflet and leave it at the home of every home you touch in the course of your day's work and explain to people what it is that's taking place. So, at least they're neutral at best, and hopefully some would be supportive.

And that's what we got. We got pretty much solid support in the African American community, because these are the people who live next door. We got lukewarm support in the white community, because, bear in mind, they just had an election for a new form of government and new political leadership, and the belief was that the national union had come down to take advantage of the city of Memphis, some of this fostered by the Justice Department under the leadership of J. Edgar Hoover. But, for a union that's somewhat mature, the last thing you're going to have in the winter is a garbage strike in Memphis, Tennessee.

EC: Right.

WL: And we were able slowly but surely to attract the religious community, at least to listen to the discussion and debate. Ultimately, we wanted them to support us, too. But, I mean, it took a while, because the South, not just in the white community, but in the black community, also, was not tuned into public sector trade unionism.

EC: I know that the slogan that you see on the signs, "I am a man," and I know a historian who's written some interesting things about sort of what that means in terms of men and women, and that some people have really focused on this as something about manhood. And she says you can look at pictures and see the huge numbers of women out on the streets, protesting this, and so, she argues that it's a lot more complex than that.

WL: Oh, it is. In spite of the wages and benefits and lack of safety and all that kind of stuff, there were no tangible demands on the table that was the core of the strike. It was the lack of respect, the absence of dignity, that caused these workers to say, "We've just had enough." And it was just really so hard to define. I mean, if you talk to a reporter, and he says, "What's this about?" And you say, "Respect and dignity," and he says, "Oh, yeah, right." Well, there was just no understanding of it. And the men themselves you could listen to them talk and you could see that, for many of them, this is their first stand against a system that had virtually robbed them of any self-respect, both as workers and even in their homes, you know, children who really didn't believe they were doing anything worthwhile.

And so, James Lawson, who joined the strike in the early days, had a press conference one day, and he was defining racism. And he says that racism, in the context of what we're talking about was when a person treats a man like he's not a man. And we didn't think about that much at that point, but it became very clear that we had to have something that held this thing together. So, one of the local ministers and myself was charged with going out, figuring out something. [Laughs] So, we sat down one evening at the Peabody Hotel there in Memphis, Tennessee, and we just started sort of playing with words and what-have-you. And what came to us was the statement that James Lawson had made earlier, and we tried to put it as simple as possible. And if you've seen one of the signs, they're sort of block letters, you know, four words, and it simply said, "I am a man."

And the impact of that on the *workers*, I mean, it defined for them *all* that they were about, because these were not young workers. These were men who were middle-aged or older at that time. And I think they were replaying some of the disrespect they had heard, because, you know, in the South you could go from boy to uncle to grandpa, without ever stopping at man. And so, they were so proud that this sign defined what they saw as their struggle.

EC: And can you talk about how you can have that slogan, and my understanding is it doesn't exclude women, that they're still—that the women identify with this issue, not in the same way, but in a significant way that invites their participation?

WL: Well, I mean, if it had not been for the women, we'd still be on strike in Memphis. I mean, women—wives and neighbors—did so much to give their support to the effort. This was in no way a sort of a macho kind of thing. It was much more an emotional kind of thing and an expression of the frustrations that they had experienced over time, not being able to play the simple role that a man would play in a family setting. There was just tremendous women support, and everybody had a role to play.

EC: Can you talk more about the different kinds of contributions different people, different groups made?

WL: Well, by the time we got into about midway the strike, we had logistical needs like you wouldn't believe. We had feeding needs. We had all kinds of economic needs. The churches' role became sort of spiritual. Every day we had to have an activity that gave people a chance to vent. So, the women would cook, the women would do the office work, the women would march on the picket lines. I mean, they did everything that they needed in order to make the strike successful. And, I mean, there's a tremendous story that needs to be told about the role that women played in the Memphis sanitation strike.

EC: And what about Reverend Lawson? You mentioned him a minute ago.

WL: James Lawson was one of the unique individuals who had been a longtime aide and ally of Dr. King. Jim had studied Gandhi tactics, or studied under Gandhi, I'm not sure which one, maybe both. But was a very strong spiritual leader in the Memphis community. And he identified with the strike very early and sort of earned the reputation of becoming the most hated African American in Memphis, [laughter] which was fine with Jim.

But he brought to the strike a sort of new kind of vision, in a very both emotional and intellectual context. And he helped to mobilize other ministers to come to the aid of the strikers. The story that the black church was right there instantly is sort of, you know, literary license by whoever writes it. Because the African American church had little if any experience with unions, period, and public sector unions, probably none whatsoever. And so, people did not want to be dragged into a fight that they didn't understand.

So, it took some time for them to become very clear on what the issues were and why the issues were having such impact on these men. I mean, many people thought they would go back to work the next day. But they didn't. They chose to strike. And no union can force people to strike. Workers strike out of frustration that their problems are not being dealt with. . . .

About Memphis. Dr. King saw this, as I said, as the ultimate contradiction for people who work every day, but still cannot lift themselves out of poverty. So, he aligned the Memphis strike with the Poor People's Campaign and he was just totally committed to it. He came to Memphis twice. The first speech he gave was just, as we say, a barnburner. And his second preparation for the march—he was killed on April fourth—Dr. King gave what has now come to be known as the "Mountaintop Speech," which was one of the better bringing-together of the struggle of workers and contrasting it with the richness of the country, the freedom, the struggles, because many of these men had fought for the country in World War II. He just saw this as the great contradiction.

And the tragedy is that the powers-that-be in Memphis did not listen to what he was suggesting, because his assassination did not have to take place. And I'm not one of those who still convinced that that James Earl Ray as a lone person did this. I mean, you've got a burglar who gets from Memphis to Europe with no support. That's kind of a stretch. . . .

Source: William Lucy, oral history interview conducted by Emilye Crosby in Washington, D.C., June 25, 2013, U.S. Civil Rights History Project, American Folklife Center, Library of Congress, https://www.loc.gov/item/afc2010039_crhp0094/.

Resurrection City, Washington, D.C. (1968)

One of the most well-known demonstrations of the Poor People's Campaign was the occupation of the National Mall in Washington, D.C., known as Resurrection City. For forty-two days beginning in May 1968, a coalition of poor people from diverse racial and ethnic backgrounds built more than three thousand wooden tents and camped out on the National Mall. They organized demonstrations in the city; met with federal government officials in housing, labor, and agriculture; and served as a constant reminder of the nation's inability to adequately address economic inequality. Residents disbanded the city when demonstration permits expired in late June. Ralph Abernathy, King's successor in the SCLC, led the Poor People's Campaign.

Residents outside their shelters relax in the shadow of the Washington Monument in Resurrection City, a three-thousand-person tent city on the Washington Mall set up as part of the Poor People's Campaign protest, Washington, D.C., May 1968.

Source: Jill Freedman, untitled, May 12, 1968, photograph. Courtesy of the Jill Freedman Estate. https://abernathysclcppc.weebly.com/poor-peoples-campaign.html.

DOCUMENT 7.10

Gautreaux Decision on Public Housing Desegregation (1

In 1965, the Illinois Chapter of the American Civil Liberties Union, led by
Polikoff, filed suit against the Chicago Housing Authority for housing discr
that the CHA intentionally built and placed public housing projects in predominantly
communities to avoid placing Blacks in white communities. Black applicants to public housing
were mostly denied the ability to live in public housing projects in white communities. In the
U.S. District Court ruling below, the judges partially sided with the plaintiffs in the case, who
were African American public housing residents, and placed restrictions on the CHA, requiring the agency to construct public housing outside of predominantly minority communities,
unless they built housing both within and outside of those communities. The CHA also had
to cease building dense high-rise projects in communities and had to establish a program for
assigning new tenants on a nondiscriminatory basis, the latter of which would eventually evolve
into the Gautreaux Program.

304 F.Supp. 736

United States District Court, N.D. Illinois, Eastern Division.

Dorothy GAUTREAUX, Odell Jones, Doreatha R. Crenchaw, Eva Rodgers, James Rodgers,
Robert M. Fairfax and Jimmie Jones, Plaintiffs,

v.

The CHICAGO HOUSING AUTHORITY, a corporation, and C. E. Humphrey, Executive
Director, Defendants.

Civ. A. No. 66 C 1459. | July 1, 1969.

Negro tenants in or applicants for public housing brought suits alleging that city
housing authority and its executive director had violated their rights under Fourteenth Amendment. The District Court, Austin, J., 296 F.Supp. 907, denied defendants' motions for summary judgment, granted plaintiffs summary judgment as
to count one and denied plaintiffs' summary judgment motion on count two. In
supplemental judgment order, the District Court held that Chicago Housing
Authority would not be permitted to cause construction of public housing in part
of county, which lay within census tracts having 30% Or more nonwhite population, or within distance of one mile from outer perimeter of such tracts, unless
within three months following commencement of construction at least 75% Of
total units caused to be commenced by authority were outside of that part of
county.

Order accordingly.

Source: *Gautreaux v. Chicago Housing Authority* (U.S. District Court for the Northern District
of Illinois), Judgment Order July 1, 304 F.Supp. 736 (Ill. 1969). https://www.clearinghouse
.net/chDocs/public/PH-IL-0001–0047.pdf.

Ashmore, Susan Y. *Carry It On: The War on Poverty and the Civil Rights Movement in Alabama, 1964–1972*. Athens: University of Georgia Press, 2008.

Deppe, Martin L. *Operation Breadbasket: An Untold Story of Civil Rights in Chicago, 1966–1971*. Athens: University of Georgia Press, 2017.

Finley, Mary Lou, Bernard Lafayette Jr., and James Ralph Jr., eds. *The Chicago Freedom Movement: Martin Luther King Jr. and Civil Rights Activism in the North*. Lexington: University Press of Kentucky, 2016.

Garrow, David. *Bearing the Cross: Martin Luther King, Jr., and the Southern Christian Leadership Conference*. New York: William Morrow Paperbacks, 2004.

Green, Laurie. *Battling the Plantation Mentality: Memphis and the Black Freedom Struggle*. Chapel Hill: University of North Carolina Press, 2007.

Hinton, Elizabeth. *From the War on Poverty to the War on Crime: The Making of Mass Incarceration in America*. Cambridge, MA: Harvard University Press, 2016.

Honey, Michael. *Going Down Jericho Road: The Memphis Strike, Martin Luther King's Last Campaign*. New York: W. W. Norton, 2008.

Jones, William P. *The March on Washington: Jobs, Freedom and the Forgotten History of Civil Rights*. New York: W. W. Norton, 2014.

Laurent, Sylvie. *King and the Other America: The Poor People's Campaign and the Quest for Economic Equality*. Berkeley: University of California Press, 2019.

Lewis, John, and Michael D'Orzo. *Walking with the Wind: A Memoir of the Movement*. New York: Simon & Schuster, 2015.

Orleck, Annelise, and Lisa Gayle Hazirjian, eds. *The War on Poverty: A New Grassroots History, 1964–1980*. Athens: University of Georgia Press, 2011.

Polikoff, Alexander. *Waiting for Gautreaux: A Story of Segregation, Housing, and the Black Ghetto*. Evanston, IL: Northwestern University Press, 2006.

Quadagno, Jill. *The Color of Welfare: How Race Undermined the War on Poverty*. Oxford: Oxford University Press, 1996.

Ralph, James, Jr. *Northern Protest: Martin Luther King, Jr., Chicago and the Civil Rights Movement*. Cambridge, MA: Harvard University Press, 1993.

Rubinowitz, Leonard S. "The Chicago Freedom Movement and the Federal Fair Housing Act." In *The Chicago Freedom Movement: Martin Luther King Jr. and Civil Rights Activism in the North*, edited by Mary Lou Finley et al. Louisville: University of Kentucky Press, 2016.

Taylor, Keeanga-Yamahtta. *Race for Profit: How Banks and the Real Estate Industry Undermined Black Homeownership*. Chapel Hill: University of North Carolina Press, 2019.

Valk, Anne M. "Black Women, Motherhood, and Welfare Rights in Washington, D.C." In *Sharing the Prize: The Economics of the Civil Rights Revolution in the American South*, by Gavin Wright. Cambridge, MA: Belknap Press of Harvard University Press, 2018.

8

Black Power

What conditions/circumstances facilitated the rise of Black Power politics? How did it differ from mainstream civil rights? How did it impact African American life culturally, economically, socially, and politically? To what extent was Black Power considered a help or a hindrance to the Black freedom struggle?

In the mid-1960s, Black activists within and outside of the southern civil rights movement began to challenge the integrationist approach by calling for Black Power, a term rooted in the idea of Black nationalism. At its core, Black nationalism advocated for Black cultural, economic, and political institutions separate from white society, along with a greater cultural pride and self-sufficiency. Black nationalism was not a novel idea and had its roots in nineteenth-century Black abolitionism as well as the early-twentieth-century Garveyism movement. Black nationalism reemerged in the 1960s alongside the civil rights movement. The most prominent Black nationalist in the early 1960s was Malcolm X. Born Malcolm Little in 1925, Malcolm was exposed to the idea of Black nationalism through his parents who adhered to Garveyism. Though a gifted student, Malcolm engaged in a number of criminal acts during his early adulthood and was sentenced to ten years in prison in 1946. While in prison, Malcolm became exposed to and subsequently joined the Nation of Islam.

Following his release from prison in 1952, Malcolm X rose up the ranks of the NOI and became its most visible leader. Malcolm X called for Black nationalism, a right to self-defense, cultural pride, and Pan-Africanism. In the spring of 1964, Malcolm X broke with the NOI and formed his own organizations, including the Organization of Afro-American Unity. Though Malcolm X became less imprisoned by the racial binaries of America, he did not turn away from Black nationalism. In February 1965, less than a year after his break from the NOI, Malcolm X was assassinated by three members of the group. Though controversial to mainstream America and integrationists within the civil rights movement, Malcolm X's calls for Black nationalism inspired generations of Black Americans and provided other pathways through which they might achieve freedom, dignity, and justice.

Arguably, the Watts Riots and James Meredith's March against Fear encouraged a more militant approach to civil rights. The Watts Riots began when Marquette Frye, a young

African American motorist, and his brother were pulled over and arrested for suspicion of driving while under the influence by the California Highway Patrol on August 11, 1965. Their mother came to the scene, wanting to know what was going on and trying to free her sons from arrest. The California Highway Patrol then arrested Frye, his brother, and his mother, alleging that Frye tried to reach for an officer's weapon. Onlookers disputed this version of events, and a violent exchange ensued. Violence continued for six days and resulted in more than $200 million in damages. Retail establishments, especially those owned by middle- and upper-class whites, received most of the brunt of the riot. Churches, homes, libraries, and Black-owned stores were left relatively untouched.

The Watts Riots were the largest, costliest, and most destructive riots of the 1960s. However, they were neither the first nor the last. Riots in Rochester, Harlem, and Philadelphia occurred in 1964 following incidents of police brutality. And in the year following the Watts Riots, riots occurred in Cleveland, Omaha, and Detroit. Following the assassination of Martin Luther King in 1968, a wave of riots occurred across the country in cities such as Chicago, Detroit, Baltimore, Kansas City, Louisville, and Washington, D.C.

One year after the Watts Riots, in June 1966, James Meredith, who had integrated the University of Mississippi four years prior, decided to conduct a one-man march from Memphis, Tennessee, to Jackson, Mississippi, to promote Black voter registration. The march was called the "March against Fear." Just two days into his march, Meredith was shot by an unknown gunman. He survived but was unable to complete his mission. The Student Nonviolent Coordinating Committee, Southern Christian Leadership Conference, and Congress of Racial Equality decided to continue the march, which ultimately took three weeks to complete. During the march, protesters routinely used the slogan "Black Power." But the slogan did not gain nationwide attention until Stokely Carmichael, SNCC chairman at the time, joined the march and told marchers: "The only way we're going to stop them white men from whipping us is to take over. We've been saying 'Freedom' for six years, and we ain't got nothing. What we're going to start saying now is 'Black Power.'" On June 26, marchers finally reached Jackson and added thousands of new Black voters to the state's voting rolls. This march was the last great one of the southern civil rights movement.

In October 1966, after hearing the call for Black Power, Huey Newton and Bobby Seale, college students at Merritt College in Oakland, California, started the Black Panther Party for Self-Defense (BPP). Newton became the party's minister of defense, while Seale became its chairman. Not long thereafter, Newton and Seale recruited Eldridge Cleaver to help grow the party and become its minister of information. Chapters of the BPP quickly emerged in American cities, including Chicago, New York, Los Angeles, Seattle, and Philadelphia.

By the late 1960s, the BPP was the new image of Black protest. Many former members of SNCC joined the party in the late 1960s, including Stokely Carmichael, H. Rap Brown, and James Forman. Its philosophy and approach were grounded in Marxist ideology; it viewed the struggle of African Americans in light of U.S. imperialism and was concerned with global citizenship, called for militancy and armed self-defense, and touted that "Black is beautiful."

Black women were essential to the formation, rise, and growth of the Black Panther Party, though they often encountered sexism and misogyny. As more women such as Elaine Brown, Kathleen Neal Cleaver, and Ericka Huggins joined the party and climbed its ranks, the Black Panther Party's gender ideology transformed and created space for women to lead the party's efforts. (Brown would eventually become the party's chairperson in 1974; Newton appointed her to this position when he fled to Cuba to avoid criminal charges.) Because of Black women's influence and leadership, the party became committed to social work and community organizing. It created after-school, hot-breakfast, and literacy programs; organized free health clinics in poor Black communities; and offered tests for sickle-cell anemia (a disease that disproportionately affects African Americans).

Not everyone, however, favored Black Power politics. Martin Luther King Jr., in particular, had mixed feelings: on the one hand, he felt that there was no real definition of Black Power and that the movement would alienate white allies; on the other hand, however, King welcomed Black Power's promotion of Black political and economic power and cultural pride. Many whites—both protesters and politicians who had participated in the civil rights movement—focused primarily on the BPP's rhetoric of self-defense, which they saw as solely the promotion of violence, and felt as though they no longer had a place or purpose in the Black freedom movement.

The federal government also saw Black Power politics and the Black Panther Party specifically as a threat. J. Edgar Hoover, leader of the FBI, utilized its existing Counterintelligence Program (COINTELPRO) to investigate domestic extremist groups. The Black Panther Party was categorized as a Black extremist group and targeted. As a result, agents infiltrated the party; spread lies, rumors, and discord; and then watched the Panthers destroy themselves.

Black Power politics also emerged in artistic expression. In 1965, Amiri Baraka opened the Black Arts Repertory Theater in Harlem and sparked the Black Arts Movement (BAM). The movement embodied the cultural nationalism at the heart of Black Power. Black poets, musicians, writers, artists, and actors embraced and defined what it meant to be Black in America from both historical and contemporary standpoints. Black artists emphasized the beauty and dynamism of Black history and culture, all with the hope of activating a revolutionary and liberatory consciousness among Black Americans. The Black Arts Movement was most popular in the Northeast and Midwest and on the West Coast. Artists like Baraka, Gwendolyn Brooks, Nikki Giovanni, Gil Scott-Heron, James Baldwin, Maya Angelou, Audre Lorde, June Jordan, and many others were affiliated with the Black Arts Movement. By 1975, the movement collapsed, but many of the artists associated with it continued to produce art, music, and literature that captured Black humanity.

At the same time, the FBI's COINTELPRO, federal surveillance on civil rights activists and infiltration of the Black Panther Party, shed light on increasing attacks by local and federal law enforcement on Black activists challenging racial capitalism and white supremacy in the late 1960s and 1970s. The incarceration of Black political prisoners, however, coincided with an increase in incarceration rates for low-income Black and Brown people that mass-incarceration historian Elizabeth Hinton argues can be traced to the Johnson administration's "War on Crime." Hinton argues in *From the War on Poverty to the War on Crime*, "The expansion of the carceral state should be understood as the federal government's response to the demographic transformation of the nation at mid-century, the gains of the African American civil rights movement, and the persistent threat of urban rebellion."[1] Federal, state, and local law enforcement institutions worked together to criminalize poverty as well as the actions of Black activists who challenged systemic racism and economic inequalities.

Some of the strongest voices to emerge against the growing carceral state and criminal justice system were prisoners. On September 9, 1971, prisoners at the Attica Correctional Facility in New York staged one of the largest prison riots in American history. More than half of the prison population at Attica was Black. The prisoners took more than forty guards and civilians as hostages and produced a set of demands asking for better living conditions, greater political rights, and protections from racist prison guards. After a four-day standoff, state police eventually gained control of Attica. The uprising resulted in the deaths of forty-three people, the majority of whom were inmates. Though the state of New York agreed to some of the demands of the prisoners, the growth of the carceral state would only increase in the decades after Attica with the continuation of the War on Crime, the creation of the War on Drugs, and increased privatization of the prison industry.

NOTES

1. Elizabeth Hinton, *From the War on Poverty to the War on Crime* (Cambridge, MA: Harvard University Press, 2016), 11.

DOCUMENT 8.1

Malcolm X, "The Ballot or the Bullet" (1964)

On April 3, 1964, activist Malcolm X delivered the speech "The Ballot or the Bullet" at Cory Methodist Church in Cleveland, Ohio. In it, Malcolm X called for Black nationalism rather than maintaining faith in the American political system. Specifically, he advised African Americans to be careful and judicious when exercising their vote and cautioned the government that, should it continue to obstruct Black political enfranchisement and prevent them from securing full equality, African Americans may be forced to take up arms. The speech was given approximately one month after his break from the Nation of Islam. Ten days thereafter, Malcolm X made his pilgrimage to Mecca, where he would have a stunning change of heart regarding race relations.

> . . . At present I am the minister of the newly founded Muslim Mosque Incorporated, which has its offices in the Theresa Hotel right in the heart of Harlem, that's the black belt in New York City. And when we realize that Adam Clayton Powell, is a Christian minister, he has Abyssinian Baptist Church, but at the same time he's more famous for his political struggling. And Dr. King is a Christian minister from Atlanta Georgia, or in Atlanta Georgia, but he's become more famous for being involved in the civil rights struggle. . . . [A]ll of these are Christian ministers but they don't come to us as Christian ministers, they come to us as fighters in some other category.
>
> . . . The same as they are Christian ministers, I'm a Muslim minister. And I don't believe in fighting today on any one front, but on all fronts. In fact, I'm a Black Nationalist freedom fighter. . . .
>
> So today, though Islam is my religious philosophy, my political, economic and social philosophy is black nationalism. . . .
>
> The political philosophy of black nationalism only means that the black man

should control the politics and the politicians in his own community. The time when white people can come in our community and get us to vote for them so that they can be our political leaders and tell us what to do and what not to do is long gone. . . . By the same token, the time when that same white man, knowing that your eyes are too far open, can send another Negro in the community, and get you and me to support him, so that he can use him to lead us astray, those days are long gone too.

The political philosophy of black nationalism only means that if you and I are going to live in a black community—and that's where we're going to live, 'cause as soon as you move into one of their. . . . soon as you move out of the black community into their community, it's mixed for a period of time, but they're gone and you're right there all by yourself again.

. . .

The economic philosophy of black nationalism only means that we should own and operate and control the economy of our community. You would never have found—you can't open up a black store in a white community. White man won't even patronize you. And he's not wrong. He got sense enough to look out for himself. It's you who don't have sense enough to look out for yourself.

. . . [T]he economic philosophy of black nationalism only means that we have to become involved in a program of reeducation, to educate our people into the importance of knowing that when you spend your dollar out of the community in which you live, the community in which you spend your money becomes richer and richer, the community out of which you take your money becomes poorer and poorer. And because these Negroes, who have been misled, misguided, are breaking their necks to take their money and spend it with the Man, the Man is becoming richer and richer, and you're becoming poorer and poorer. And then what happens? The community in which you live becomes a slum. It becomes a ghetto. The conditions become rundown. And then you have the audacity to complain about poor housing in a rundown community, while you're running down yourselves when you take your dollar out.

And you and I are in a double trap because not only do we lose by taking our money someplace else and spending it, when we try and spend it in our own community we're trapped because we haven't had sense enough to set up stores and control the businesses of our community. The man who is controlling the stores in our community is a man who doesn't look like we do. He's a man who doesn't even live in the community. . . .

. . .

So our people not only have to be reeducated to the importance of supporting black business, but the black man himself has to be made aware of the importance of going into business. And once you and I go into business, we own and operate at least the businesses in our community. What we will be doing is developing a situation, wherein, we will actually be able to create employment for the people in the community. And once you can create some employment in the community where you live, it will eliminate the necessity of you and me having to act ignorantly and disgracefully, boycotting and picketing some cracker someplace else trying to beg him for a job.

Whether you are a Christian or a Muslim or a nationalist, we all have the same problem. They don't hang you because you're a Baptist; they hang you 'cause you're black. They don't attack me because I'm a Muslim. They attack me 'cause I'm black. They attacked all of us for the same reason. All of us catch hell from the same enemy. We're all in the same bag, in the same boat.

. . . The government itself has failed us. And the white liberals who have been posing as our friends have failed us. And once we see that all of these other sources to which we've turned have failed us, we stop turning to them and turn to ourselves. We need a self-help program, a do-it-yourself philosophy. . . . Black nationalism is a self-help philosophy.

What's so good about it—you can stay right in the church where you are and still take black nationalism as your philosophy. You can stay in any kind of civic organization that you belong to and still take black nationalism as your philosophy. You can be an atheist and still take black nationalism as your philosophy. This is a philosophy that eliminates the necessity for division and argument, 'cause if you're black, you should be thinking black. And if you're black and you not thinking black at this late date, well, I'm sorry for you.

. . .

When we look at other parts of this Earth upon which we live, we find that black, brown, red and yellow people in Africa and Asia are getting their independence. They're not getting it by singing, "We Shall Overcome." No, they're getting it through nationalism. It is nationalism that brought about the independence of the people in Asia. Every nation in Asia gained its independence through the philosophy of nationalism. Every nation on the African continent that has gotten its independence brought it about through the philosophy of nationalism. And it will take black nationalism to bring about the freedom of 22 million Afro-Americans, here in this country, where we have suffered colonialism for the past 400 years.

. . .

I'm one of the 22 million black victims of the Democrats. One of the 22 million black victims of the Republicans and one of the 22 million black victims of Americanism. And when I speak, I don't speak as a Democrat or a Republican, nor an American. I speak as a victim of America's so-called democracy. You and I have never seen democracy—all we've seen is hypocrisy.

. . .

You, today, are in the hands of a government of segregationists. Racists, white supremacists, who belong to the Democratic party but disguise themselves as Dixiecrats. A Dixiecrat is nothing but a Democrat. Whoever runs the Democrats is also the father of the Dixiecrats. And the father of all of them is sitting in the White House. I say, and I'll say it again, you got a president who's nothing but a southern segregationist from the state of Texas. They'll lynch in Texas as quick as they'll lynch you in Mississippi. Only in Texas they lynch you with a Texas accent, in Mississippi they lynch you with a Mississippi accent.

· · ·

Up here in the North you have the same thing. The Democratic Party don't—they don't do it that way. They got a thing they call gerrymandering. They maneuver you out of power. Even though you can vote they fix it so you're voting for nobody. They got you going and coming. In the South they're outright political wolves, in the North they're political foxes. A fox and a wolf are both canine, both belong to the dog family. . . . You going to choose a northern dog or a southern dog? Because either dog you choose, I guarantee you, you'll still be in the doghouse.

This is why I say it's the ballot or the bullet. It's liberty or it's death. It's freedom for everybody or freedom for nobody. America today finds herself in a unique situation. Historically, revolutions are bloody, oh yes they are. . . . You don't have a revolution in which you love your enemy. And you don't have a revolution in which you are begging the system of exploitation to integrate you into it. Revolutions overturn systems. Revolutions destroy systems.

· · ·

So those of us whose political and economic and social philosophy is black nationalism have become involved in the civil rights struggle. We have injected ourselves into the civil rights struggle. And we intend to expand it from the level of civil rights to the level of human rights. As long as you fight it on the level of civil rights, you're under Uncle Sam's jurisdiction. You're going to his court expecting him to correct the problem. He created the problem. He's the criminal! You don't take your case to the criminal, you take your criminal to court.

· · ·

So our next move is to take the entire civil rights struggle—problem—into the United Nations and let the world see that Uncle Sam is guilty of violating the human rights of 22 million Afro-Americans right down to the year of 1964 and still has the audacity or the nerve to stand up and represent himself as the leader of the free world? Not only is he a crook, he's a hypocrite.

· · ·

So I say in my conclusion, the only way we're going to solve it: we got to unite. We got to work together in unity and harmony. And black nationalism is the key. How we gonna overcome the tendency to be at each other's throats that always exists in our neighborhood? And the reason this tendency exists—the strategy of the white man has always been divide and conquer. He keeps us divided in order to conquer us. He tells you, I'm for separation and you for integration, and keep us fighting with each other. No, I'm not for separation and you're not for integration, what you and I are for is freedom. Only, you think that integration will get you freedom; I think that separation will get me freedom. We both got the same objective, we just got different ways of getting' at it. . . .

Source: Malcolm X, "The Ballot or the Bullet," speech, April 12, 1964, King Solomon Baptist Church, Detroit, from Malcolm X, *Malcolm X Speaks* (Atlanta: Pathfinder Press, 1989). Copyright © 1965, 1989 by Betty Shabazz and Pathfinder Press. Reprinted by permission.

National Advisory Commission on Civil Disorders Report Summary (1968)

The summary of the National Advisory Commission on Civil Disorders Report, commonly known as the Kerner Report, follows. In 1967, as the Detroit Riot raged, President Lyndon B. Johnson appointed an eleven-person commission chaired by Governor Otto Kerner. The commission was charged with investigating racial upheavals and incidents of civil disobedience that left hundreds dead, thousands injured, and thousands of buildings destroyed in the 1960s. Seven months later, on February 29, 1968, the commission released its 426-page report, which became a best-selling book. In it, the group argued that urban violence was caused by a lack of economic opportunity, failed social service programs, police brutality, racism and discrimination, and white media bias. The commission suggested that preventive measures should include the creation of new jobs and new housing, improvement and expansion of social service programs, and hiring of more diverse and sensitive police officers in urban areas. One month after its release, more than one hundred riots broke out after Dr. Martin Luther King Jr. was assassinated.

REPORT OF THE NATIONAL ADVISORY COMMISSION ON CIVIL DISORDERS
SUMMARY OF REPORT
INTRODUCTION

The summer of 1967 again brought racial disorders to American cities, and with them shock, fear and bewilderment to the nation.

The worst came during a two-week period in July, first in Newark and then in Detroit. Each set off a chain reaction in neighboring communities.

On July 28, 1967, the President of the United States established this Commission and directed us to answer three basic questions:

What happened?

Why did it happen?

What can be done to prevent it from happening again?

. . .

This is our basic conclusion: Our nation is moving toward two societies, one black, one white—separate and unequal.

Reaction to last summer's disorders has quickened the movement and deepened the division. Discrimination and segregation have long permeated much of American life; they now threaten the future of every American.

This deepening racial division is not inevitable. The movement apart can be reversed. Choice is still possible. Our principal task is to define that choice and to press for a national resolution.

To pursue our present course will involve the continuing polarization of the American community and, ultimately, the destruction of basic democratic values.

The alternative is not blind repression or capitulation to lawlessness. It is the realization of common opportunities for all within a single society.

This alternative will require a commitment to national action—compassionate, massive and sustained, backed by the resources of the most powerful and the richest nation on this earth. From every American it will require new attitudes, new understanding, and, above all, new will.

. . .

Violence and destruction must be ended—in the streets of the ghetto and in the lives of people.

Segregation and poverty have created in the racial ghetto a destructive environment totally unknown to most white Americans.

What white Americans have never fully understood but what the Negro can never forget—is that white society is deeply implicated in the ghetto. White institutions created it, white institutions maintain it, and white society condones it.

. . . It is time to adopt strategies for action that will produce quick and visible progress. It is time to make good the promises of American democracy to all citizens— urban and rural, white and black, Spanish-surname, American Indian, and every minority group.

. . .

The "typical" riot did not take place. The disorders of 1967 were unusual, irregular, complex and unpredictable social processes. Like most human events, they did not unfold in an orderly sequence. However, an analysis of our survey information leads to some conclusions about the riot process. In general:

- The civil disorders of 1967 involved Negroes acting against local symbols of white American society, authority and property in Negro neighborhoods—rather than against white persons.

. . .

- Initial damage estimates were greatly exaggerated. In Detroit, newspaper damage estimates at first ranged from $200 million to $500 million; the highest recent estimate is $45 million. In Newark, early estimates ranged from $15 to $25 million. A month later damage was estimated at $10.2 million, over 80 percent in inventory losses.

. . .

- Disorder did not erupt as a result of a single "triggering" or "precipitating" incident. Instead, it was generated out of an increasingly disturbed social atmosphere, in which typically a series of tension-heightening incidents over a period of weeks or months became linked in the minds of many in the Negro community with a reservoir of underlying grievances. . . .

- "Prior" incidents, which increased tensions and ultimately led to violence, were police actions in almost half the cases; police actions were "final" incidents before the outbreak of violence in 12 of the 24 surveyed disorders.

. . .

- The typical rioter was a teenager or young adult, a lifelong resident of the city in which he rioted, a high school dropout; he was, nevertheless, somewhat better educated than his nonrioting Negro neighbor, and was usually underemployed or employed in a menial job. He was proud of his race, extremely hostile to both whites and middle-class Negroes and, although informed about politics, highly distrustful of the political system.

. . .

• Most rioters were young Negro males. Nearly 53 percent of arrestees were between 15 and 24 years of age; nearly 81 percent between 15 and 35.

. . .

• What the rioters appeared to be seeking was fuller participation in the social order and the material benefits enjoyed by the majority of American citizens. Rather than rejecting the American system, they were anxious to obtain a place for themselves in it.

. . .

• The proportion of Negroes in local government was substantially smaller than the Negro proportion of population. Only three of the 20 cities studied had more than one Negro legislator; none had ever had a Negro mayor or city manager. In only four cities did Negroes hold other important policy-making positions or serve as heads of municipal departments.

• Although almost all cities had some sort of formal grievance mechanism for handling citizen complaints, this typically was regarded by Negroes as ineffective and was generally ignored.

. . .

The background of disorder is often as complex and difficult to analyze as the disorder itself. But we find that certain general conclusions can be drawn:

• Social and economic conditions in the riot cities constituted a clear pattern of severe disadvantage for Negroes compared with whites, whether the Negroes lived in the area where the riot took place or outside it. Negroes had completed fewer years of education and fewer had attended high school. Negroes were twice as likely to be unemployed and three times as likely to be in unskilled and service jobs. Negroes averaged 70 percent of the income earned by whites and were more than twice as likely to be living in poverty. Although housing cost Negroes relatively more, they had worse housing—three times as likely to be overcrowded and substandard. . . .

. . .

In addressing the question "Why did it happen?" we shift our focus from the local to the national scene, from the particular events of the summer of 1967 to the factors within the society at large that created a mood of violence among many urban Negroes.

These factors are complex and interacting; they vary significantly in their effect from city to city and from year to year; and the consequences of one disorder, generating new grievances and new demands, become the causes of the next. . . .

. . .

Race prejudice has shaped our history decisively; it now threatens to affect our future.

White racism is essentially responsible for the explosive mixture which has been accumulating in our cities since the end of World War II. Among the ingredients of this mixture are:

- Pervasive discrimination and segregation in employment, education and housing, which have resulted in the continuing exclusion of great numbers of Negroes from the benefits of economic progress.

- Black in-migration and white exodus, which have produced the massive and growing concentrations of impoverished Negroes in our major cities, creating a growing crisis of deteriorating facilities and services and unmet human needs.

- The black ghettos where segregation and poverty converge on the young to destroy opportunity and enforce failure. Crime, drug addiction, dependency on welfare, and bitterness and resentment against society in general and white society in particular are the result. At the same time, most whites and some Negroes outside the ghetto have prospered to a degree unparalleled in the history of civilization. Through television and other media, this affluence has been flaunted before the eyes of the Negro poor and the jobless ghetto youth.

. . .

- Frustrated hopes are the residue of the unfulfilled expectations aroused by the great judicial and legislative victories of the Civil Rights Movement. . . .

- A climate that tends toward approval and encouragement of violence as a form of protest has been created by white terrorism directed against nonviolent protest; by the open defiance of law and federal authority by state and local officials resisting deseg-regation; and by some protest groups engaging in civil disobedience who turn their backs on nonviolence, go beyond the constitutionally protected rights of petition and free assembly, and resort to violence to attempt to compel alteration of laws and poli-cies with which they disagree.

- The frustrations of powerlessness have led some Negroes to the conviction that there is no effective alternative to violence as a means of achieving redress of grievances, and of "moving the system." These frustrations are reflected in alienation and hostility toward the institutions of law and government and the white society which controls them, and in the reach toward racial consciousness and solidarity reflected in the slogan "Black Power."

- A new mood has sprung up among Negroes, particularly among the young, in which self-esteem and enhanced racial pride are replacing apathy and submission to "the system."

- The police are not merely a "spark" factor. To some Negroes police have come to sym-bolize white power, white racism and white repression. And the fact is that many police do reflect and express these white attitudes. The atmosphere of hostility and cynicism is reinforced by a widespread belief among Negroes in the existence of police brutality and in a "double standard" of justice and protection—one for Negroes and one for whites.

. . .

No American—white or black—can escape the consequences of the continuing social and economic decay of our major cities.

Only a commitment to national action on an unprecedented scale can shape a future compatible with the historic ideals of American society.

· · ·

The major goal is the creation of a true union—a single society and a single American identity. Toward that goal, we propose the following objectives for national action:

- Opening up opportunities to those who are restricted by racial segregation and discrimination, and eliminating all barriers to their choice of jobs, education and housing.

- Removing the frustration of powerlessness among the disadvantaged by providing the means for them to deal with the problems that affect their own lives and by increasing the capacity of our public and private institutions to respond to these problems.

- Increasing communication across racial lines to destroy stereotypes, to halt polarization, end distrust and hostility, and create common ground for efforts toward public order and social justice.

We propose these aims to fulfill our pledge of equality and to meet the fundamental needs of a democratic and civilized society—domestic peace and social justice. . . .

Source: Kerner Commission, *Report of the National Advisory Commission on Civil Disorders* (Washington, DC: U.S. Government Printing Office, 1968), 1–29.

DOCUMENT 8.3
Stokely Carmichael, "What We Want" (1966)

In 1966, Stokely Carmichael (later Kwame Toure) delivered the speech "What We Want" before a crowd in Greenwood, Mississippi. At the time, Carmichael was chairman of SNCC, which was still actively engaged in rights struggles in Mississippi; Lowndes County, Alabama; and across the South. Carmichael called for "Black Power" in the speech; although he was not the first to use the phrase, he popularized it.

One of the tragedies of the struggle against racism is that up to now there has been no national organization which could speak to the growing militancy of young black people in the urban ghetto. There has been only a civil rights movement, whose tone of voice was adapted to an audience of liberal whites. It served as a sort of buffer zone between them and angry young blacks. None of its so-called leaders could go into a rioting community and be listened to. In a sense, I blame ourselves—together with the mass media—for what has happened in Watts, Harlem, Chicago, Cleveland, Omaha. Each time the people in those cities saw Martin Luther King get slapped, they became angry; when they saw four little black girls bombed to death, they were angrier; and when nothing happened, they were steaming. We had nothing to offer that they could see, except to go out and be beaten again. We helped to build their frustration.

For too many years, black Americans marched and had their heads broken and got shot. They were saying to the country, "Look, you guys are supposed to be nice guys and we are only going to do what we are supposed to do—why do you beat us up, why don't you give us what we ask, why don't you straighten yourselves out?" We cannot be expected any longer to march and have our heads broken in order to say to whites: come on, you're nice guys. For you are not nice guys. We have found you out.

An organization which claims to speak for the needs of a community—as does the Student Nonviolent Coordinating Committee—must speak in the tone of that community, not as somebody else's buffer zone. This is the significance of black power as a slogan. For once, black people are going to use the words they want to use—not just the words whites want to hear. . . .

BLACK POWER can be clearly defined for those who do not attach the fears of white America to their questions about it. We should begin with the basic fact that black Americans have two problems: they are poor and they are black. All other problems arise from this two-sided reality: lack of education, the so-called apathy of black men. Any program to end racism must address itself to that double reality.

. . .

. . . [T]he concept of "black power" is not a recent or isolated phenomenon: It has grown out of the ferment of agitation and activity by different people and organizations in many black communities over the years. . . . Where Negroes lack a majority, black power means proper representation and sharing of control. It means the creation of power bases from which black people can work to change statewide or nationwide patterns of oppression through pressure from strength—instead of weakness. Politically, black power means what it has always meant to SNCC: the coming-together of black people to elect representatives and *to force those representatives to speak to their needs.* . . .

ULTIMATELY, the economic foundations of this country must be shaken if black people are to control their lives. The colonies of the United States—and this includes the black ghettoes within its borders, north and south—must be liberated. . . . For racism to die, a totally different America must be born.

This is what the white society does not wish to face; this is why that society prefers to talk about integration. But integration speaks not at all to the problem of poverty, only to the problem of blackness. Integration today means the man who "makes it," leaving his black brothers behind in the ghetto as fast as his new sports car will take him. . . .

Integration, moreover, speaks to the problem of blackness in a despicable way. As a goal, it has been based on complete acceptance of the fact that *in order to have* a decent house or education, blacks must move into a white neighborhood or send their children to a white school. This reinforces, among both black and white, the idea that "white" is automatically better and "black" is by definition inferior. This is why integration is a subterfuge for the maintenance of white supremacy. It allows the nation to focus on a handful of Southern children who get into white schools, at great price, and to ignore the 94 per cent who are left behind in unimproved all-black schools. Such situations will not change until black people have power—to control their own school boards, in this case. Then Negroes become equal in a way that means something, and integration ceases to be a one-way street. Then integration doesn't mean draining skills and energies from the ghetto into white neighborhoods. . . .

...

To most whites, black power seems to mean that the Mau Mau are coming to the suburbs at night. The Mau Mau are coming, and whites must stop them. Articles appear about plots to "get Whitey," creating an atmosphere in which "law and order must be maintained." Once again, responsibility is shifted from the oppressor to the oppressed. Other whites chide, "Don't forget—you're only 10 per cent of the population; if you get too smart, we'll wipe you out." If they are liberals, they complain, "what about me?—don't you want my help any more?" These are people supposedly concerned about black Americans, but today they think first of themselves, of their feelings of rejection. Or they admonish, "you can't get anywhere without coalitions," when there is in fact no group at present with whom to form a coalition in which blacks will not be absorbed and betrayed. Or they accuse us of "polarizing the races" by our calls for black unity, when the true responsibility for polarization lies with whites who will not accept their responsibility as the majority power for making the democratic process work.

White America will not face the problem of color, the reality of it. The well-intended say: "We're all human, everybody is really decent, we must forget color." But color cannot be "forgotten" until its weight is recognized and dealt with. White America will not acknowledge that the ways in which this country sees itself are contradicted by being black—and always have been. Whereas most of the people who settled this country came here for freedom or for economic opportunity, blacks were brought here to be slaves. When the Lowndes County Freedom Organization chose the black panther as its symbol, it was christened by the press "the Black Panther Party"—but the Alabama Democratic Party, whose symbol is a rooster, has never been called the White Cock Party. . . . The furor over that black panther reveals the problems that white America has with color and sex; the furor over "black power" reveals how deep racism runs and the great fear which is attached to it.

. . .

From birth, black people are told a set of lies about themselves. We are told that we are lazy—yet I drive through the Delta area of Mississippi and watch black people picking cotton in the hot sun for fourteen hours. We are told, "If you work hard, you'll succeed"—but if that were true, black people would own this country. We are oppressed because we are black—not because we are ignorant, not because we are lazy, not because we're stupid (and got good rhythm), but because we're black.

. . .

The need for psychological equality is the reason why SNCC today believes that blacks must organize in the black community. Only black people can convey the revolutionary idea that black people are able to do things themselves. Only they can help create in the community an aroused and continuing black consciousness that will provide the basis for political strength. In the past, white allies have furthered white supremacy without the whites involved realizing it—or wanting it, I think. Black people must do things for themselves; they must get poverty money they will control and spend themselves, they must conduct tutorial programs themselves so that black children can identify with black people. This is one reason Africa has such importance:

The reality of black men ruling their own natives gives blacks elsewhere a sense of possibility, of power, which they do not now have.

This does not mean we don't welcome help, or friends. But we want the right to decide whether anyone is, in fact, our friend. . . . We cannot have the oppressors telling the oppressed how to rid themselves of the oppressor.

. . . One of the most disturbing things about almost all white supporters of the movement has been that they are afraid to go into their own communities—which is where the racism exists—and work to get rid of it. They want to run from Berkeley to tell, us what to do in Mississippi; let them look instead at Berkeley. They admonish blacks to be nonviolent; let them preach non-violence in the white community. They come to teach me Negro history; let them go to the suburbs and open up freedom schools for whites. Let them work to stop America's racist foreign policy; let them press this government to cease supporting the economy of South Africa.

There is a vital job to be done among poor whites. We hope to see, eventually, a coalition between poor blacks and poor whites. That is the only coalition which seems acceptable to us, and we see such a coalition as the major internal instrument of change in American society. SNCC has tried several times to organize poor whites; we are trying again now, with an initial training program in Tennessee. It is purely academic today to talk about bringing poor blacks and whites together, but the job of creating a poor-white power bloc must be attempted. The main responsibility for it falls upon whites. Black and white can work together in the white community where possible; it is not possible, however, to go into a poor Southern town and talk about integration. Poor whites everywhere are becoming more hostile—not less—partly because they see the nation's attention focused on black poverty and nobody coming to them. . . .

Black people do not want to "take over" this country. They don't want to "get whitey"; they just want to get him off their backs, as the saying goes. It was for example the exploitation by Jewish landlords and merchants which first created black resentment toward Jews—not Judaism. The white man is irrelevant to blacks, except as an oppressive force. Blacks want to be in his place, yes, but not in order to terrorize and lynch and starve him. They want to be in his place because that is where a decent life can be had.

But our vision is not merely of a society in which all black men have enough to buy the good things of life. When we urge that black money go into black pockets, we mean the communal pocket. We want to see money go back into the community and used to benefit it. We want to see the cooperative concept applied in business and banking. We want to see black ghetto residents demand that an exploiting store keeper sell them, at minimal cost, a building or a shop that they will own and improve cooperatively; they can back their demand with a rent strike, or a boycott, and a community so unified behind them that no one else will move into the building or buy at the store. The society we seek to build among black people, then, is not a capitalist one. It is a society in which the spirit of community and humanistic love prevail. . . . The love we seek to encourage is within the black community, the only American community where men call each other "brother" when they meet. . . .

Source: Stokely Carmichael, "What We Want," 1966, speech, box 1, folder 5, Michael J. Miller Civil Rights Collection, University of Southern Mississippi Library.

DOCUMENT 8.4

Bobby Seale on the Formation of the Black Panther Party (1988)

In this document, Black Panther Party cofounder Bobby Seale discusses the founding and agenda of the Black Panther Party for Self-Defense. Seale and fellow Merritt College student Huey P. Newton established the party in October 1966, after learning about the Lowndes County Freedom Organization and Stokely Carmichael's call for "Black Power." The party was grounded in Marxist ideology and quickly became the new image of Black protest in the mid-twentieth century.

. . .

INTERVIEWER: Okay, how did you come up with the symbol of, the, the name Black Panther. How did you come up with the name Black Panther?

BOBBY SEALE: Actually we had written the Ten-Point Platform and Program of the organization but yet didn't have a name. A couple of days later, Huey Newton and I was trying to figure out why it was that on a Lowndes County Freedom Organization—it was Lowndes County, Mississippi, a pamphlet we had—why did they have this charging black panther as a logo? And Huey come up with some notion that if you drive a panther into a corner, if he can't go left and he can't go right, then it will tend to come out of that corner to wipe out or stop its aggressor. So I says, that's just like Black people, all the civil rights people are getting' brutalized across this country for exercising the First Amendment of the Constitution which is the law of the land, they can't go left. Other people have tried to control the police with law books and tape recorders, they've been brutalized, they can't go right. Even the young Whites who were protesting, I said, who was in support of the Black people, can't go left, can't go right. I said, we're just like the Black Panthers. And in effect Huey P. Newton and I named our organization the Black Panther Party, but at first it was the Black Panther Party for Self-Defense. Later, we dropped the self-defense aspect because we didn't want to be classified as a paramilitary organization.

. . .

INTERVIEWER: OK, I'm trying to put the Panthers in some sort of, in some sort of line with other struggles for, for, for Black freedom. Where did the, the philosophy of the Panthers come from? How were you influenced by Malcolm X, your were talking about Martin, and Elijah Muhammad?

BOBBY SEALE: Huey and I had been involved for some time, off and on, studying Black history, what have you, what Malcolm had done, where Martin Luther King had come from. I was highly influenced by Martin Luther King at first, and then later Malcolm X. Largely, the Black Panther Party come out of a lot of readings, Huey and I putting scrutiny to everything going on in the United States of America. It was like we must've subscribed to twenty-some-odd different periodicals, off-beat periodicals like *The Liberator, Freedom Ways*, what have you, even some periodicals out of Africa. But we had read and digested Frantz Fanon's *The Wretched of the Earth*. I mean, we knew Lerone Bennett's *Before the Mayflower*. I knew about the 250 slave revolts and that included Gabriel Prosser and Nat Turner and Denmark Vesey. I mean, I, Frederick Douglass, everything, the Nation of Islam, what had happened in the 1930's, what have you, and so on. And there we were with all this knowledge about our history, our struggle against racism, and when we started the Black Panther Party it was more or less based on where Malcolm was coming from, where our struggle was, an argument about the civil rights movement, not learning to own property, and then Stokely Carmichael in 1965, '66 talkin' about Black Power, and we thought we needed a functional definition of just the word "power" alone. . . .

INTERVIEWER: Did . . . Malcolm X have a particular influence on the Panthers?

. . .

BOBBY SEALE: Malcolm X had a particular influence on the Panthers in the sense that earlier he had stated that the civil rights people down South who were exercising the First Amendment of the Constitution, that's what he alluded to, are gonna be violated by racists and every Black man who has a shotgun in his home has a right to defend himself. Even the Deacons for the Defense in this context had an influence there. Even as we read the history of Robert Williams, also had an influence there. So, you see this has been rollin' since '59 in terms of how we see the history, even with respect to the slavery votes historically. So, it comes to a point that if the civil rights people who were peacefully protesting, if their rights are gonna be violated, then we're gonna have to move to a higher level, and take the position that we have a right to defend ourself based on the Constitution of the United States.

. . .

INTERVIEWER: OK. Could you talk about com-community control and how that became a policy and a program for the Panther Party, particularly, with, with the police, community control?

BOBBY SEALE: Well, community control was in a vague way from the initial point of the, that was all related to the functional definition of power. But we initiated a program where we got some research teams out of the University of California and some other places and put together a real referendum to the ballot for community control of police, really to decentralize the police and have five commissioners duly elected by the people, a form of more participatory democracy here. And we finally did get it on the ballot in the City of Berkeley, it lost by one percentage point. But that was one aspect, along with selling the Black Panther Party newspaper and dealing with a lot of other problems in the community, that was one of the key political electoral aspects in 1968 that we attempted to initiate.

. . .

INTERVIEWER: OK. When did the Panther Party begin to start moving on a, on a national front that, become a, become a national organization effectively?

BOBBY SEALE: Effectively as a national organization, the Black Panther Party began to move, well, originally, you have to understand that when I did the California, when I went to the California State Capital that caused us first to have international notoriety. But in terms of on a organizational level, the Black Panther Party really spread from, prior to the murder of Mart—the assassination of Brother Martin Luther King, we only had about 700 members in six or seven chapters and branches, largely on the West Coast. Following the assassination of Martin Luther King our organization grew from 700 to 5,000 members plus. And with the assassination of Robert Kennedy later that year the young White radicals readily coalesced with us at our direction, they couldn't direct us. They coalesced with us. So it was whoever in the power structure who murdered Martin Luther King caused a lot of people who sided with Martin Luther King to say, The heck with it, let's join the Panthers, and they in effect tagged us as the vanguard of the revolution.

. . .

INTERVIEWER: OK. Could you talk about the, the, the breakfast programs and, and the development of the survival programs? How did they, how did they begin?

BOBBY SEALE: Young man standing out in front of the Black Panther Party office that sold papers at McClymonds High School, a Black school, said something about the fact that some teachers was tryin' to get free lunches for high school students. And I said, Well, what about the little kids? They need to eat too. So, I initiated with the central committee that we wanted a free breakfast for children program. Eldridge Cleaver called it a sissy program. I says, Who's the greatest revolution in the, revolutionary in the world to you, Eldridge Cleaver? He says Mao Tse-Tung. I said, When you read the material it says, "Always serve the people." But mine and Huey's concept related to that was that the recipients of the program, in effect, become educated and understand that they have to organize in opposition to the racist power structure. But the breakfast programs initiated in Reverend Neil's church in West Oakland, California, spreaded around this country to a point where we was feeding over two hu—two, a couple hundred thousand kids free breakfast. Later, Willie Brown and some other state legislators in California moved and got a bill through, even with the override for $5 million for all the schools in the poor and wo—working class communities for free breakfast for children.

. . .

INTERVIEWER: OK. I'm gonna go to some Fred Hampton questions now. What, what are your personal recollections, what personal recollections do you have of Fred Hampton as a party leader?

BOBBY SEALE: My own personal recollections of Fred Hampton as a party leader was the time when I went to Chicago to see firsthand what brother Fred Hampton and, and, and, and Bobby Rush and organized. It blew my mind. Fred Hampton's charismatic ability to teach and rap to young brothers and sisters, have a thousand young brothers and sisters in the church all saying, Power to the people! Power to the people! Power to the people! And to even would find out that Fred Hampton had previously been in the NAACP and here was, you know, had all these breakfast programs, health clinics rolling and everything and to speak. And I remember later telling party members that, If anything ever happened to me, because I know sooner or later these racists are gonna wanna to kill me, that since Fred Hampton is deputy chairman under me with the Illinois Chapter of the Black Panther Party then he will become the chairman of our national organization. Please make sure you always consider him. And I was telling members of the central committee that. And Fred Hampton was just one of those young brothers who could articulate, bring home, capture the feeling of young people and break it down. He could break, I, I was good at breaking all this theory down so the average person'd understand it, but Fred Hampton, he was twice as good as I was.

. . .

INTERVIEWER: OK. The police and the FBI raided the Chicago Panther headquarters several times in 1969 and at one point they, like, broke in and knocked it down. Could you just tell that story about the time that they just tore the place apart and what you advised them to do and what the community did in, in response to what happened afterward?

BOBBY SEALE: In 1969, practically every branch and chapter of the Black Panther Party throughout the United States was attacked not less than once and as much as five times particularly in Chicago. . . . The Chicago Chapter of the Black Panther Party was attacked several times. And one particular time, I remember they raided the Black Panther Party office and they had a short shootout. And of course, we had a rule that we would take an arrest so somehow or another, you know, it was another [incident] so they took the arrest but what the police did is they went in like Eliot Ness with sledgehammers. I mean, our press, all of our IBM typewriters that had been donated by the White radicals, our newspapers, I mean our mimeograph papers by the caseload, and then set the whole building on fire. This is what the FBI and the Chicago Police did. Now, the idea on the part of the police was to psyche the community out. They called me up the next day, I says, Is the office open? Well, no the police boarded the place up. I said, Open it back up. You got the lease to the place. What? I says, Open it up. Take all that boarding down, paint that place. And the Black Panther Party members started working for a couple of days. The next thing you know the community started bringing wood, paint, and everything, and opened that Black Panther Party office right back up. And of course, this was an attempt to terrorize us out of existence. . . .

INTERVIEWER: How, how were your suspicions and, and fears of the FBI and other federal and local police forces changing in those years, in, in '68 and '69? How were you becoming more aware and more suspicious of them?

BOBBY SEALE: Actually, through the year '69 we had big purge in the Black Panther Party because we had grown by early '69 to seven, eight thousand Black Panth—Black people in the Black Panther Party. And we had too many provocateur agents and then too many incidents and things were happening, you know, like $42 service station robbery in the Black Panther Party newspaper truck with bold, black, one-foot letters that says "The Black Panther Black Community News Service." For forty-two bucks and I'm bringing in twenty-five thousand dollars a year to the Black Panther Party, every penny going into the treasurer of the Black Panther Party. What do we need with forty-two bucks, you see? So, this was a lot of provocateur agent activity that was going on, that in effect was an attempt on the part of the FBI to make us look bad in the eyes of not only the public but the Black community in particular. So, we were very leery and we began to kick people out. Even if people fooled around and wouldn't pass some leaflets out, kick 'em out. We got too many people in the organization, we didn't know what was happening because sometimes you would have some people passing out leaflets and then you find a stack of 'em them in a trash can somewhere. . . . We, we were too big. In fact, I think we reduced, by the end of that year, we reduced our membership by fifty percent. . . .

Source: Bobby Seale, interview with Blackside, Inc., November 4, 1988, Eyes on the Prize Interviews II, Henry Hampton Collection, Film and Media Archive, Washington University Libraries, http://digital.wustl.edu/e/eii/eiiweb/sea5427.0172.147bobbyseale.html.

DOCUMENT 8.5

Black Panther Party Ten-Point Program (1966)

The Ten-Point Program of the Black Panther Party, the Black Panther Party's governing document, is presented here. According to Bobby Seale, he and Huey P. Newton drafted the first version of the program at the North Oakland Neighborhood Service Center. "The Ten Point Platform and Program of 'What We Want, What We Believe,'" he states, "culminating with the opening paragraphs of the United States Declaration of Independence, reflected the objectives of the party."[1]

- *We Want Freedom. We Want Power To Determine The Destiny Of Our Black Community.*
  We believe that Black people will not be free until we are able to determine our destiny.

- *We Want Full Employment For Our People.*
  We believe that the federal government is responsible and obligated to give every man employment or a guaranteed income. We believe that if the White American businessmen will not give full employment, then the *means* of production should be taken from the businessmen and placed in the community so that the people of the community can organize and employ all of its people and give a high standard of living.

- *We Want An End To The Robbery By The Capitalists Of Our Black Community.*
  We believe that this racist government has robbed us, and now we are demanding the overdue debt of forty acres and two mules. Forty acres and two mules were promised 100 years ago as restitution for slave labor and mass murder of Black people. We will accept the payment in currency which will be distributed to our many communities. The Germans are now aiding the Jews in Israel for the genocide of the Jewish people. The Germans murdered six million Jews. The American racist has taken part in the slaughter of over fifty million Black people; therefore, we feel that this is a modest demand that we make.

- *We Want Decent Housing Fit For The Shelter Of Human Beings.*
  We believe that if the White Landlords will not give decent housing to our Black community, then the housing and the land should be made into cooperatives so that our community, with government aid, can build and make decent housing for its people.

- *We Want Education For Our People That Exposes The True Nature Of This Decadent American Society. We Want Education That Teaches Us Our True History And Our Role In The Present-Day Society.*
  We believe in an educational system that will give to our people a knowledge of self. If a man does not have knowledge of himself and his position in society and the world, then he has little chance to relate to anything else.

- *We Want All Black Men To Be Exempt From Military Service.*
  We believe that Black people should not be forced to fight in the military service

to defend a racist government that does not protect us. We will not fight and kill other people of color in the world who, like Black people, are being victimized by the White racist government of America. We will protect ourselves from the force and violence of the racist police and the racist military, by whatever means necessary.

- *We Want An Immediate End To Police Brutality And Murder Of Black People.*
  We believe we can end police brutality in our Black community by organizing Black self-defense groups that are dedicated to defending our Black community from racist police oppression and brutality. The Second Amendment to the Constitution of the United States gives a right to bear arms. We therefore believe that all Black people should arm themselves for self-defense.

- *We Want Freedom For All Black Men Held In Federal, State, County And City Prisons And Jails.*
  We believe that all Black people should be released from the many jails and prisons because they have not received a fair and impartial trial.

- *We Want All Black People When Brought To Trial To Be Tried In Court By A Jury Of Their Peer Group Or People From Their Black Communities, As Defined By The Constitution Of The United States.*
  We believe that the courts should follow the United States Constitution so that Black people will receive fair trials. The Fourteenth Amendment of the U.S. Constitution gives a man a right to be tried by his peer group. A peer is a person from a similar economic, social, religious, geographical, environmental, historical and racial background. To do this the court will be forced to select a jury from the Black community from which the Black defendant came. We have been, and are being, tried by all-White juries that have no understanding of the "average reasoning man" of the Black community.

- *We Want Land, Bread, Housing, Education, Clothing, Justice And Peace.*
  When, in the course of human events, it becomes necessary for one people to dissolve the political bands which have connected them with another, and to assume, among the powers of the earth, the separate and equal station to which the laws of nature and nature's God entitle them, a decent respect of the opinions of mankind requires that they should declare the causes which impel them to the separation.

  We hold these truths to be self-evident, that all men are created equal; that they are endowed by their Creator with certain inalienable rights; that among these are life, liberty, and the pursuit of happiness. That, to secure these rights, governments are instituted among men, deriving their just powers from the consent of the governed; that, whenever any form of government becomes destructive of these ends, it is the right of the people to alter or abolish it, and to institute a new government, laying its foundation on such principles, and organizing its powers in such form, as to them shall seem most likely to effect their safety and happiness. Prudence, indeed, will dictate that governments long established should not be changed for light and transient causes; and, accordingly, all experience hath shown that mankind are more disposed to suffer, while evils are sufferable, than to right themselves by abolishing the forms to which they are accustomed. But, when a long train of abuses and usurpations, pursuing invariably the same object, evinces a design to reduce them under absolute despotism, it is their right, it is their duty, to throw off such government, and to provide new guards for their future security.

Source: Huey P. Newton, "The Ten-Point Program," first printed in *The Black Panther*, May 15, 1967.

NOTES

1. Stephen Shames and Bobby Seale, *Power to the People: The World of the Black Panthers* (New York: Abrams, 2016), 23.

DOCUMENT 8.6

Roy Wilkins and Ramsey Clark, "Search and Destroy: A Report by the Commission of Inquiry into the Black Panthers and the Police" (1973)

In "Search and Destroy: A Report by the Commission of Inquiry into the Black Panthers and the Police," Roy Wilkins, the former executive director of the NAACP, and Ramsey Clark, attorney general in the President Lyndon B. Johnson administration, investigate the murders of Illinois Chapter Black Panthers Fred Hampton and Mark Clark. On December 4, 1969, two years after the Federal Bureau of Information identified Hampton as a radical threat, local and state police with cooperation from the FBI via William McNeil, an informant within the Black Panther Party, raided the Chicago branch of the Black Panther Party and murdered Hampton and Clark at around 4:45 a.m. At the time, Hampton was sleeping beside his pregnant girlfriend, Deborah Johnson (now known as Akua Njeri), when he was shot and killed; Clark was killed when he opened the door of the headquarters. Hampton and Clark were only two of many African Americans working for social change who were targeted by the FBI.

PREFACE

Those of us who want to love our country are not anxious to ask whether our police are capable of murder. So we do not ask. We do not dare concede the possibility.

But we live here, and we are aware, however dimly, that hundreds of us are killed every year by police. We assume the victims are mad killers and that the officers fired in self-defense or to save lives.

Then came Orangeburg, the Algiers Motel incident, the Kent State killings, and reasonable persons were put on notice. Official conduct bears investigation. In a free society the police must be accountable to the people. Often, instead of seeking facts, we tend, largely in ignorance, to polarize, with ardent emotional commitment to the state and order on the one side, and equally passionately, the oppressed and justice on the other.

This report pursues the truth of an episode that occurred early on December 4, 1969, at 2337 West Monroe Street in Chicago, Illinois. It was a time of darkness, cold, rage, fear, and violence. Facts are not easily found in such company.

The early dawn stillness had been broken at about 4:45 a.m. by heavy gunfire, eighty rounds or more, which lasted over a period of ten minutes. When it stopped, two young men, Fred Hampton and Mark Clark, were dead. Four other occupants of the premises, the Illinois Black Panther Party headquarters, were seriously wounded. Two police officers were injured, one by glass, the other by a bullet in the leg.

Of the total of perhaps one hundred shots fired that fatal night, probably one bullet was discharged by a Panther. It is possible that no Panther fired a shot, or that two or even three shots were fired by them. But it is highly unlikely that any Panther fired more than a single shot. The physical evidence does indicate that one shot was fired by them; and bullets fired inside a house make their mark.

Fred Hampton may or may not have been drugged or asleep throughout the episode; one can never be sure. Still, the probability is that he was unconscious at the time of his death. Nor can we be positive whether he was shot in the head by a policeman standing in full view of his prostrate body or by blind police gunfire from another room. But we must not weight the probabilities with our wishes. If Hampton never awakened, if he was murdered, it is better to know it. . . .

There is no chance that needed reforms will be made until the people have the opportunity and the will to understand the facts about official violence. Many will simply refuse to believe officials are capable of unlawful violence. Others will believe such violence and support it. But surely most Americans will not knowingly accept police lawlessness. If official violence is to be renounced, the truth must finally overcome our natural reluctance to incriminate government. It is our hope that this report will serve that end.

Of all violence, official violence is the most destructive. It not only takes life, but it does so in the name of the people and as the agent of the society. It says, therefore, this is our way, this is what we believe, we stand for nothing better. Official violence practices violence and teaches those who resist it that there is no alternative, that those who seek change must use violence. Violence, the ultimate human degradation, destroys our faith in ourselves and our purposes. When society permits its official use, we are back in the jungle.

. . . We do not value others' lives as we do our own. The Vietnamese, the black students, the convicts and their guards are expendable. Until we understand that George Jackson and Mark Clark and Fred Hampton, as well as the victims of Kent State and nameless and faceless victims of Jackson State and on all sides in the Indochina War, are human beings equal in every way to our children and ourselves, we will see no wrong in using violence to control or destroy them.

Fred Hampton and Mark Clark were valuable young men. They could have enriched our lives. If they spoke of violence, suffered it, or used it, we should not be surprised. It was not foreign to their environment, nor did their government eschew it. And talented or not, violent or nonviolent, they were human beings whose lives and legal rights must be cherished by a just society. . . .

THE PLAN FOR AND PURPOSE OF THE RAID

The federal grand jury's *Report* concluded that the raid was "ill-conceived." The Commission considers that characterization of the raid to be a vast understatement, and has found that there is probable cause to believe that the predawn raid, carried out by officers with heavy armament but without tear gas, sound equipment, or lighting equipment, involved criminal acts on the part of the planners of the raid.

The infiltrator who reportedly informed the police and/or the FBI that illegal weapons were likely to be found in the Panthers' apartment was also reported to have informed them that the apartment was likely to be unoccupied at 8 p.m. on the evening preceding the raid. If the object of the raid had been, as stated, to search the premises for illegal weapons, that purpose could best have been accomplished without violence when the apartment was empty. Assuming that the search had disclosed illegal weapons, appropriate arrests could have been made thereafter.

Alternatively, the police could have surrounded the apartment, and communicated with the residents either by telephone or loudspeaker, told them that the apartment was surrounded and ordered them to come out. The residents might have surrendered if given a chance. And the firepower available to the police department was surely more than ample to have permitted such an approach with no more danger to the police than was presented by the course of action actually followed.

Instead, however, the police chose to serve the warrant at 4:45 a.m., heavily armed and dressed in plainclothes. It is probable that the method chosen to execute the search warrant not only failed to avert violence, but instead actually maximized the likelihood of violence and clearly endangered the lives of the Panthers in the apartment. Moreover, it is probable that the purpose of the raid was to conduct a surprise attack on the Panthers, and that serving the search warrant was merely a guise. . . .

THE PATTERN OF THE SHOOTING

Approximately six shots were apparently fired as the police entered the living room through the front door—two by Sergeant Groth, three by Officer Davis, and one by Mark Clark. The FBI's ballistics analysis shows that during the remainder of the raid between seventy-seven and ninety-four shots were fired by the police—and none by the apartment's occupants. Accordingly, with the exception of one shot, the police testimony of gunfire directed at them from the occupants must be rejected.

. . .

The Commission finds that attribution of culpability in the killing of Mark Clark and the wounding of Brenda Harris may be less clearly definable in the context of the already-begun raid. Clark apparently did fire at the police—regardless of whether his shot was the initial shot. . . . The Commission is convinced, however, that both the killing of Clark and the wounding of Harris would have been avoided by proper planning, and that while no culpability is necessarily assignable to the officers who did the shooting, there is probable cause to believe that the planning of the raid was so inadequate as to constitute criminal conduct.

THE SHOOTING OF FRED HAMPTON

The death of Fred Hampton appears to the Commission to have been isolated from the killing of Mark Clark and the wounding of Brenda Harris on the one hand, and from the wounding of Ronald Satchel, Verlina Brewer, and Blair Anderson on the other. The Commission has concluded that there is probable cause to believe that Fred Hampton was murdered—that he was shot by an officer or officers who could see his prostrate body lying on the bed. Unfortunately, the inadequate investigation by the police and the other officials and their inadequate examination of the available evidence make it impossible to know which officer or officers actually fired the fatal bullets.

The Commission has been unable to determine whether the purpose, or a purpose, of the raid was specifically to kill Hampton. There is some evidence that Hampton was shot after the other occupants of the rear bedroom were removed. If that was not the sequence of events, it seems likely that he was the sole target of the police shooting from the doorway of the bedroom. Neither of those consequences, however, would establish that Hampton's death was an object of the raid.

On the other hand, the fact that Hampton appears from virtually all of the testimony never to have moved during the raid, the fact that after the police entered the apartment all the testimony placed him in bed, and the possibility that his failure to move was caused by his having been drugged are relevant to the question of the purpose of the raid.

WHETHER HAMPTON WAS DRUGGED

The Commission has been unable to determine whether Hampton was drugged at the time of his murder, but considers it more probable than not that he was. The blood tests performed in connection with the second autopsy reportedly showed that Hampton had been drugged with a massive dose of secobarbital. The blood test reportedly conducted by the Cook County coroner failed to show the presence of any barbiturate, but there is a substantial doubt whether that test was ever conducted. The federal grand jury accepted as conclusive the findings of an FBI blood analysis which did not show the presence of any drugs. But the experts consulted by the Commission unanimously expressed the opinion that the FBI test, because of the embalming procedure used on Hampton's body, the instability of secobarbital in solution, and the long time during which the blood was stored without having been frozen, should not have been accepted as conclusive. In addition, certain of the experts concluded affirmatively that the blood did show the presence of a barbiturate, and that the FBI results were not just inadequate but wrong. In short, although the Commission has concluded that it is probable that Hampton was drugged, a final resolution of the issue is beyond the Commission's competence. . . .

SUMMARY

The federal grand jury report found instances of official misfeasance, malfeasance, and nonfeasance related to investigations of the raid. It also established what the Commission deems to be a prima facie case of illegal denial of the constitutional rights of the residents of the apartment. Nonetheless, the federal grand jury and the first state grand jury failed to return any indictments against the officials, and, instead, the first state grand jury indicted the survivors. The attitude of both grand juries appears to have been that the Panthers were dangerous, and, consequently, that any excesses by the police against them could be excused. The Commission deplores that approach.

One of the primary purposes of the criminal law is deterrence. If no attempt is made to prosecute the police in instances of apparent misconduct, such as appear to be present in this case, then it seems likely that police misconduct will continue in the future. . . .

DOCUMENT 8.7

"Northwestern University Student Demands" (1968)

The Black Studies Movement at Northwestern University is the focus of this document. In late April 1968, For Members Only and Afro-American Student Union, Black student organizations at Northwestern, presented a list of demands to the university's administration. Demands included an increase in Black student enrollment and financial aid, access to campus housing and other resources, and the creation of a Black-studies program. When their demands were not met, more than one hundred Black students peacefully occupied the university's Bursar Office on May 3, 1968. The occupation lasted thirty-eight hours before a resolution was reached. The resolution provided for the development of advisory boards to oversee the admissions process, increased recruitment of Black students to the university, a review of their financial-aid packages, equitable on- and off-campus housing, and the creation of the Department of African American Studies and a Black student union, among others.

BLACK STUDENT STATEMENT AND PETITION TO NORTHWESTERN UNIVERSITY ADMINISTRATORS, RECEIVED MONDAY, APRIL 22, 1968

We, the Black students at Northwestern University have found the academic, cultural, and social conditions for us on the campus deplorably limited. In order to counteract the physical, emotional, and spiritual strains we have been subjugated to, in order to find some meaning and purpose in our being here, we demand that the following conditions be immediately met

I POLICY STATEMENT:

We demand, firstly, that a policy statement be issued from the administration deploring the viciousness of "white racism" and insuring that all conscious or unconscious racist policies, practices, and institutions existing now on campus will no longer be tolerated. This statement should make it clear that Northwestern is willing to go to any extent to enforce such a policy and also to protect the interests of the Black students on campus who have been negatively affected by such racist attitudes and practices. Furthermore, this statement should express Northwestern's readiness to exert its influences (both political and financial, in uprooting racism in the city of Evanston).

II ADMISSION:

Considering that Black people account for 12% of the total American population, we demand that Northwestern initiate a project which guarantees the gradual increase of the number of Black students to a more "realistic" figure which we shall decide. We demand also that we have some say in the development and initiation of such a project with Black students of our own choosing on the steering committee. We further demand that at least half (1/2) of each year's incoming Black students be from the inner school systems.

As for now, we demand a complete list containing the names of all Black students enrolled at Northwestern as of Fall Quarter 1967.

III SCHOLARSHIPS:

We demand that our scholarships be increased to cover what is now included in our "required jobs" and to include funds for those who want or need to attend summer school. We have found that students who work because they want to, and not because they have to, perform much better academically and with less mental tension and frustration. Furthermore, we have found it a contradiction that in view of the fact that we inadequately prepared for the type of competition we encountered here at Northwestern, we were still expected to keep up and hold down a job simultaneously. We strongly feel, as well, that those Black students who want to continue their intellectual pursuits through the summer should have the same opportunity to do so as any other Northwestern student. The University should not deny them that opportunity by requiring that they work instead, in order to substantiate their scholarships for the other three quarters.

IV HOUSING:

We demand that the University provide a living unit(s) for those Black students who want to live together. We demand that immediate action be taken to provide such a unit(s) by Fall Quarter 1968.

Inasmuch as that Black freshman women do not usually room with each other, we demand that they receive the same treatment as their white roommates. In the past, upon receiving room assignments, a white girl or her parents have been allowed to object to having a Negro for a roommate and upon either of their requests a shift in room assignments took place. We contend that if the girl or her parents wanted to be assured that she would not be roaming with a Negro, she should have stated on her housing form her preference of a Caucasian roommate to a Negro one. Black students did not even have the option to request another Black student for a roommate. We were told from the start that it was the University's intention to split us up and that we would not be allowed to room with each other.

Due to contradictory (racist) housing policies and practices, to the definite differences in social and cultural differences between us and our white roommates, and to the general tenseness of the racial situation, we demand that this Black living unit be made available to us by Fall quarter to help alleviate some of the tension of being "a Black student at a white university."

V CURRICULUM:

We demand that a Black Studies Course be added to the curriculum including studies in Black history, literature, and art in view of the fact that Black accomplishments have been underplayed and Black history misconstrued, we demand to have the ultimate decision in the choice of professors to be hired to teach these courses. There is no doubt, that since they inevitably must be "Black" professors, no one on the administration is capable of adequately judging their qualifications.

VI COUNSELLING:

We demand that a Black Counselor be provided by the University in order to help us properly cope with the psychological, mental, and academic tensions resulting from the dualism of our existence as "black college students." There is a definite need for Black students seeking to overcome the contradictions of the demands placed on us by this white community, which offers little for us to identify with, and the demands of our own people and our native communities which look to us for some kind of inspiration, guidance, and instruction in the struggle to overcome white oppression, to have someone who can relate to us and understand us out of a common experience. The "Great White Father" image the university has been projecting must be destroyed if any real communication is to develop.

VII FACILITIES:

We demand a Black Student Union, a place to be used for social and recreational activities, as well as, a place to office F.M.O. and all other Black organizations on campus. Black students have nothing at Northwestern to call our own. We need a place where we will feel free to come and to go as we please, a place which will substitute for the lack of fraternity and sorority houses and provide us with the necessary facilities to function as independently as the Student Senate office.

VIII OPEN OCCUPANCY:

We are aware that Northwestern University has taken a stand in favor of Open Occupancy. However, what good, we ask, is such a stand when Northwestern is in effect the main promoter of segregation in the City of Evanston? We demand that the University immediately cease with this hypocrisy and take the necessary steps to desegregate all of its real estate holdings. We further demand that evidence be presented to us, verifying that Northwestern is doing more than taking "a stand on Open Occupancy," and that monthly reports be turned over to the president of F.M.O. indicating N.U.'s subsequent progressive measures.

There has been too much idle talk about how to solve some of the problems facing Black students here at Northwestern. Indeed, there has been too much talk and too little action in regard to the general racial situation. We are not about to solve America's race problems, if there is in fact a solution; however, we are concerned about the problem as it affects us on campus and in the city of Evanston.

Northwestern was wrong to assume that in bringing us here, we would be able to disassociate ourselves from the injustices, sufferings, and mounting frustration of our people. Like them, we, too, are tired of being talked about and we are weary of talking to people who cannot or refuse to do anything else but talk.

It would be useless to engage in further discussion—there are some things which will never be understood, and even if they were understood, it would make little difference anyway. These are our demands of the University. We are willing to confer with the administration, but we have no intention of debating or conceding our stand. We have been to the administration before but with very little consequence. We want tangible results, not excuses or even promises. The University either responds to our demands or we have no other alternative but to respond to its lack of response. The University has until 5:00 p.m. Friday, April 26, 1968, to notify us of its decision.

CONTACT: Kathryn Ogletree (F.M.O.), James Turner (A.A.S.U.)

Source: For Members Only and the Afro-American Student Union, "Black Student Statement and Petition to Northwestern University Administrators," 1968, Records of the Bursars Takeover, Northwestern University Archives, https://www.northwestern.edu/bursars-takeover /documents/April%2022%20Demands.pdf. Courtesy of McCormick Library of Special Collections & University Archives, Northwestern University.

Margaret Burroughs, "What Shall I Tell My Children Who Are Black (Reflections of an African-American Mother)" (1963)

Margaret Burroughs's "What Shall I Tell My Children Who Are Black" (1963) is representative of the poetry from the Black Arts Movement. BAM was a movement of Black artists, writers, poets, and musicians who stressed Black beauty and pride in their work in the 1960s and 1970s. Although the movement is said to have officially started in 1965, Burroughs expressed a commitment to Black artistic expression and institution building in Chicago much earlier than the aforementioned date. Like Burroughs, BAM artists created politically engaged work that bridged the history, politics, and culture of African Americans and transformed the way that African Americans were portrayed in cultural forms. Burroughs's poem was published on the occasion of the one hundredth anniversary of the Emancipation Proclamation and tells the story of Black motherhood and child rearing—the experiences and emotions they evoke—in the 1960s.

> What shall I tell my children who are black
> Of what it means to be a captive in this dark skin
> What shall I tell my dear one, fruit of my womb,
> Of how beautiful they are when everywhere they turn
> They are faced with abhorrence of everything that is black.
> Villains are black with black hearts.
> A black cow gives no milk. A black hen lays no eggs.
> Bad news comes bordered in black, black is evil
> And evil is black and devils' food is black . . .
> What shall I tell my dear ones raised in a white world
> A place where white has been made to represent
> All that is good and pure and fine and decent.
> Where clouds are white, and dolls, and heaven
> Surely is a white, white place with angels
> Robed in white, and cotton candy and ice cream
> and milk and ruffled Sunday dresses
> And dream houses and long sleek cadillacs
> And angel's food is white . . . all, all . . . white.
> What can I say therefore, when my child
> Comes home in tears because a playmate
> Has called him black, big lipped, flatnosed
> and nappy headed? What will he think
> When I dry his tears and whisper, "Yes, that's true.
> But no less beautiful and dear."
> How shall I lift up his head, get him to square
> His shoulders, look his adversaries in the eye,
> Confident of the knowledge of his worth,
> Serene under his sable skin and proud of his own beauty?

What can I do to give him strength
That he may come through life's adversities
As a whole human being unwarped and human in a world
Of biased laws and inhuman practices, that he might
Survive. And survive he must! For who knows?
Perhaps this black child here bears the genius
To discover the cure for . . . Cancer
Or to chart the course for exploration of the universe.
So, he must survive for the good of all humanity.
He must and will survive.
I have drunk deeply of late from the foundation
Of my black culture, sat at the knee and learned
From Mother Africa, discovered the truth of my heritage,
The truth, so often obscured and omitted.
And I find I have much to say to my black children.
I will lift up their heads in proud blackness
With the story of their fathers and their fathers
Fathers. And I shall take them into a way back time
of Kings and Queens who ruled the Nile,
And measured the stars and discovered the
Laws of mathematics. Upon whose backs have been built
The wealth of continents. I will tell him
This and more. And his heritage shall be his weapon
And his armor; will make him strong enough to win
Any battle he may face. And since this story is
Often obscured, I must sacrifice to find it
For my children, even as I sacrificed to feed,
Clothe and shelter them. So this I will do for them
If I love them. None will do it for me.
I must find the truth of heritage for myself
And pass it on to them. In years to come I believe
Because I have armed them with the truth, my children
And my children's children will venerate me.
For it is the truth that will make us free!

Source: Margaret Burroughs, "What Shall I Tell My Children Who Are Black,"
poem, in *What Shall I Tell My Children Who Are Black?* (Chicago: MAAH Press, 1968).
Courtesy of the Estate of Dr. Margaret Burroughs.

Amiri Baraka, "Black People: This Is Our Destiny" (1967)

Amiri Baraka's "Black People: This Is Our Destiny" (1967) is another poem from the Black Arts Movement. Baraka (née LeRoi Jones) started the Black Arts Movement in 1965 when he founded the Black Arts Repertory Theater in Harlem, New York, as a place for Black expression. He believed that Black artists should produce art for Black people that advances the Black freedom movement.

The road run straight with no turning, the circle runs complete as it is in the storm of
peace, the all embraced embracing in the circle complete turning road straight like a
burning straight with the circle complete as in a peaceful storm, the elements, the niggers'
voices harmonized with creation on a peak in the holy black man's eyes that we rise, whose
race is only direction up, where we go to meet the realization of makers knowing
who we are and the war in our hearts but the purity of the holy world that we long for,
knowing how to live, and what life is, and who God is, and the many revolutions we must
spin through in our

Seven adventures in the endlessness of all existing feeling, all existing forms of life, the
gases, the plants, the ghost minerals the spirits the souls the light in the stillness where the
storm the glow the nothing in God is complete except there is

Nothing
to be incomplete the pulse and change of rhythm, blown flight to be anything at all . . .
vibration holy nuance beating against itself, a rhythm a playing re-understood
now by one of the 1st race . . .

DOCUMENT 8.10

Attica Prisoners' Demands (1971)

In the late 1960s and 1970s, a prisoners' rights movement began to grow, and Attica Prison was a major site of protest. In September 1971, days after a series of relatively minor conflicts occurred between prisoners and guards, a group of inmates from Cell Block D broke through a gate with a defective weld and took over one of the four prison yards, held forty guards hostage, and demanded the removal of the prison warden, amnesty for those who participated in the revolt, better conditions, adequate medical care and legal representation at parole hearings, and access to employment and labor unions, among others. To the dismay of the prisoners, the state agreed to some but not all of their demands. After five days, New York governor Nelson Rockefeller approved a military attack on the prison, whereby one thousand armed National Guardsmen, prison guards, and local police attacked unarmed prisoners. Thirty-three prisoners were killed, numerous prisoners were beaten and tortured by guards, and ten guards died by friendly fire. Other prison rebellions in the nation followed.

We, the men of Attica Prison, have been committed to the New York State Department of Corrections by the people of society for the purpose of correcting what has been deemed as social errors in behaviour. Errors which have classified us as socially unacceptable until reprogrammed with new values and more thorough understanding as to our values and responsibilities as members of the outside community. The Attica Prison program in its structure and conditions have been enslaved on the pages of this Manifesto of Demands with the blood, sweat, and tears of the inmates of this prison. . . .

MANIFESTO OF DEMANDS

1. We Demand the constitutional rights of legal representation at the time of all parole board hearings and the protection from the procedures of the parole authorities whereby they permit no procedural safeguards such as an attorney for cross-examination of witnesses, witnesses in behalf of the parolee, at parole revocation hearings.

2. We Demand a change in medical staff and medical policy and procedure. The Attica Prison hospital is totally inadequate, understaffed, and prejudiced in the treatment of inmates. There are numerous "mistakes" made many times; improper and erroneous medication is given by untrained personnel. We also demand periodical check-ups on all prisoners and sufficient licensed practitioners 24 hours a day instead of inmates' help that is used now.

3. We Demand adequate visiting conditions and facilities for the inmate and families of Attica prisoners. The visiting facilities at the prison are such as to preclude adequate visiting for inmates and their families.

4. We Demand an end to the segregation of prisoners from the mainline population because of their political beliefs. Some of the men in segregation units are confined there solely for political reasons and their segregation from other inmates is indefinite.

5. We Demand an end to the persecution and punishment of prisoners who practice the Constitutional Right of peaceful dissent. Prisoners at Attica and other

New York prisons cannot be compelled to work as these prisons were built for the purpose of housing prisoners and there is no mention as to the prisoners being required to work on prison jobs in order to remain in the mainline population and/or be considered for release. Many prisoners believe their labour power is being exploited in order for the state to increase its economic power and to continue to expand its correctional industries (which are million-dollar complexes), yet do not develop working skills acceptable for employment in the outside society, and which do not pay the prisoner more than an average of forty cents a day. Most prisoners never make more than fifty cents a day. Prisoners who refuse to work for the outrageous scale, or who strike, are punished and segregated without the access to the privileges shared by those who work; this is class legislation, class division, and creates hostilities within the prison.

6. We Demand an end to political persecution, racial persecution, and the denial of prisoner's rights to subscribe to political papers, books, or any other educational and current media chronicles that are forwarded through the U.S. Mail.

7. We Demand that industries be allowed to enter the institutions and employ inmates to work eight hours a day and fit into the category of workers for scale wages. The working conditions in prisons do not develop working incentives parallel to the many jobs in the outside society, and a paroled prisoner faces many contradictions of the job that add to his difficulty in adjusting. . . .

8. We Demand that inmates be granted the right to join or form labour unions.

9. We Demand that inmates be granted the right to support their own families; at present, thousands of welfare recipients have to divide their checks to support their imprisoned relatives, who without outside support, cannot even buy toilet articles or food. Men working on scale wages could support themselves and families while in prison.

10. We Demand that correctional officers be prosecuted as a matter of law for any act of cruel and unusual punishment where it is not a matter of life and death.

11. We Demand that all institutions using inmate labour be made to conform with the state and federal minimum wage laws.

12. We Demand an end to the escalating practice of physical brutality being perpetrated upon the inmates of New York State prisons.

13. We Demand the appointment of three lawyers from the New York State Bar Association to full-time positions for the provision of legal assistance to inmates seeking post-conviction relief, and to act as a liaison between the administration and inmates for bringing inmates' complaints to the attention of the administration.

14. We Demand the updating of industry working conditions to the standards provided for under New York State law.

15. We Demand the establishment of inmate worker's insurance plan to provide compensation for work-related accidents.

16. We Demand the establishment of unionized vocational training programs comparable to that of the Federal Prison System which provides for union instructions, union pay scales, and union membership upon completion of the vocational training course.

17. We Demand annual accounting of the inmates Recreational Fund and formulation of an inmate committee to give inmates a voice as to how such funds are used.

18. We Demand that the present Parole Board appointed by the Governor be eradicated and replaced by the parole board elected by popular vote of the people. In a world where many crimes are punished by indeterminate sentences and where authority acts within secrecy and within vast discretion and given heavy weight to accusations by prison employees against inmates, inmates feel trapped unless they are willing to abandon their desire to be independent men.

19. We Demand that the state legislature create a full-time salaried board of overseers for the State Prisons. The board would be responsible for evaluating allegations made by inmates, their families, friends and lawyers against employers charged with acting inhumanely, illegally or unreasonably. The board should include people nominated by a psychological or psychiatric association, by the State Bar Association or by the Civil Liberties Union and by groups of concerned involved laymen.

20. We Demand an immediate end to the agitation of race relations by the prison administration of this State.

21. We Demand that the Dept. of Corrections furnish all prisoners with the services of ethnic counsellors for the needed special services of the Brown and Black population of this prison.

22. We Demand an end to the discrimination in the judgment and quota of parole for Black and Brown people.

23. We Demand that all prisoners be present at the time their cells and property are being searched by the correctional officers of state prisons.

24. We Demand an end to the discrimination against prisoners when they appear before the Parole Board. Most prisoners are denied parole solely because of their prior records. Life sentences should not confine a man longer than 10 years as 7 years is the considered statute for a lifetime out of circulation, and if a man cannot be rehabilitated after a maximum of ten years of constructive programs, etc., then he belongs in a mental hygiene centre, not a prison.

25. We Demand that better food be served to the inmates. The food is a gastronomical disaster. We also demand that drinking water be put on each table and that each inmate be allowed to take as much food as he wants and as much bread as he wants, instead of the severely limited portions and limited (4) slices of bread. Inmates wishing a pork-free diet should have one, since 85% of our diet is pork meat or pork-saturated food.

26. We Demand an end to the unsanitary conditions that exist in the mess hall: i.e., dirty trays, dirty utensils, stained drinking cups and an end to the practice of putting food on the table's hours before eating time without any protective covering over it.

27. We Demand that there be one set of rules governing all prisons in this state instead of the present system where each warden makes rules for his institution as he sees fit.

IN CONCLUSION

We are firm in our resolve and we demand, as human beings, the dignity and justice that is due to us by our right of birth. We do not know how the present system of brutality and dehumanization and injustice has been allowed to be perpetrated in this day of enlightenment, but we are the living proof of its existence and we cannot allow it to continue.

The taxpayers who just happen to be our mothers, fathers, sisters, brothers, daughters and sons should be made aware of how their tax dollars are being spent to deny their sons, brothers, fathers and uncles of justice, equality and dignity.

Source: "The Attica Liberation Faction Manifesto of Demands and Anti-depression Platform,"
September 9, 1971, written by the imprisoned and read by L. D. Barkley,
https://freedomarchives.org/Documents/Finder/DOC510_scans/Attica/510.Prisons
.AtticaManifesto.pdf.

DOCUMENT 8.11

Angela Davis, "Political Prisoners, Prisons, and Black Liberation" (1971)

Revolutionary Angela Davis takes a historical look at the relationship between Black political repression and incarceration. Davis wrote this piece while incarcerated at the Women's Detention Center in Marin County for being involved in seventeen-year-old Jonathan Jackson's kidnapping of superior court judge Harold Haley from the Marin County Civic Center. Jackson sought to use the kidnapping as a tool for negotiating the release of the Soledad Brothers (George Jackson, Fleeta Drumgo, and John Clutchette, who were charged with the murder of a prison guard at the Soledad Prison in California). The weapons Jonathan used were said to be Angela Davis's. Davis has continued to be an outspoken voice in the prison abolition movement.

... [T]he history of the United States has been marred from its inception by an enormous quantity of unjust laws, far too many expressly bolstering the oppression of Black people. Particularized reflections of existing social inequities, these laws have repeatedly borne witness to the exploitative and racist core of the society itself. For Blacks, Chicanos, for all nationally oppressed people, the problem of opposing unjust laws and the social conditions which nourish their growth, has always had immediate practical implications. Our very survival has frequently been a direct function of our skill in forging effective channels of resistance. In resisting, we have sometimes been compelled to openly violate those laws which directly or indirectly buttress our oppression. But even when containing our resistance within the orbit of legality, we have been labeled criminals and have been methodically persecuted by a racist apparatus.

... There is a distinct and qualitative difference between one breaking a law for one's own individual self-interest and violating it in the interests of a class or a people whose oppression is expressed either directly or indirectly through that particular law. The former might be called a criminal (though in many instances he is a victim), but the latter, as a reformist or revolutionary, is interested in universal social change. Captured, he or she is a political prisoner.

. . .

A deep-seated ambivalence has always characterized the official response to the political prisoner. Charged and tried for a criminal act, his guilt is always political in nature. . . .

Even in all of Martin Luther King's numerous arrests, he was not so much charged with the nominal crimes of trespassing, disturbance of the peace, etc., but rather with being an enemy of Southern society, an inveterate foe of racism. When Robert Williams was accused of a kidnapping, this charge never managed to conceal his real offense—the advocacy of Black people's incontestable right to bear arms in their own defense.

The offense of the political prisoner is his political boldness, his persistent challenging—legally or extra-legally—of fundamental social wrongs fostered and reinforced by the state. He has opposed unjust laws and exploitative, racist social conditions in general, with the ultimate aim of transforming these laws and this society into an order harmonious with the material and spiritual needs and interests of the vast majority of its members.

. . . In the Spring of 1970, Los Angeles Panthers took up arms to defend themselves from an assault initiated by the local police force on their office and on their persons. They were charged with criminal assault. If one believed the official propaganda, they were bandits and rogues who pathologically found pleasure in attacking policemen. It was not mentioned that their community activities—educational work, services such as free breakfast and free medical programs—which had legitimized them in the Black community, were the immediate reason for which the wrath of the police had fallen upon them. In defending themselves from the attack waged by some 600 policemen (there were only 11 Panthers in the office) they were defending not only their lives, but even more important their accomplishments in the Black community surrounding them, and in the boarded thrust for Black liberation. Whenever Blacks in struggle have recourse to self-defense, particular armed self-defense, it is twisted and distorted on official levels and ultimately rendered synonymous with criminal aggression. On the other hand, when policemen are clearly indulging in acts of criminal aggression, officially they are defending themselves through "justifiable assault" or "justifiable homicide."

. . .

As the Black Liberation Movement and other progressive struggles increase in magnitude and intensity, the judicial system and its extension, the penal system, consequently become key weapons in the state's fight to preserve the existing conditions of class domination, therefore racism, poverty and war.

. . .

The prison is a key component of the state's coercive apparatus, the overriding function of which is to ensure social control. . . . The penitentiary was projected as the locale for doing penitence for an offense against society, the physical and spiritual purging of proclivities to challenge rules and regulations which command total obedience. While cloaking itself with the bourgeois aura of universality—imprisonment was supposed to cut across all class lines, as crimes were to be defined by the act, not the perpetrator—the prison has actually operated as an instrument of class domination, a means of prohibiting the have-nots from encroaching upon the haves.

The occurrence of crime is inevitable in a society in which wealth is unequally distributed, as one of the constant reminders that society's productive forces are being channeled in the wrong direction. The majority of criminal offenses bear a direct relationship to property. Contained in the very concept of property, crimes are profound but suppressed social needs which express themselves in anti-social modes of action....

. . .

Racist oppression invades the lives of Black people on an infinite variety of levels. Blacks are imprisoned in a world where our labor and toil hardly allow us to eke out a decent existence, if we are able to find jobs at all. When the economy begins to falter, we are forever the first victims, always the most deeply wounded. When the economy is on its feet, we continue to live in a depressed state. Unemployment is generally twice as high in the ghettos as it is in the country as a whole and even higher among Black women and youth. The unemployment rate among Black youth has presently skyrocketed to 30 percent. If one-third of America's white youths were without a means of livelihood, we would either be in the thick of revolution or else under the iron rule of fascism....

. . .

The announced function of the police, "to protect and serve the people," becomes the grotesque caricature of protecting and preserving the interests of our oppressors and serving us nothing but injustice. They are there to intimidate Blacks, to persuade us with their violence that we are powerless to alter the conditions of our lives. Arrests are frequently based on whims. Bullets from their guns murder human beings with little or no pretext, aside from the universal intimidation they are charged with carrying out.... They encircle the community with a shield of violence, too often forcing the natural aggression of the Black community inwards. Fanon's analysis of the role of colonial police is an appropriate description of the function of the police in America's ghettos.

It goes without saying that the police would be unable to set into motion their racist machinery were they not sanctioned and supported by the judicial system. The courts not only consistently abstain from prosecuting criminal behavior on the part of the police, but they convict, on the basis of biased police testimony, countless Black men and women. Court-appointed attorneys, acting in the twisted interests of overcrowded courts, convince 85 percent of the defendants to plead guilty. Even the manifestly innocent are advised to cop a plea so that the lengthy and expensive process of jury trials is avoided. This is the structure of the apparatus which summarily railroads Black people into jails and prisons....

... The only effective guarantee against the victory of fascism is an indivisible mass movement which refuses to conduct business as usual as long as repression rages on. It is only natural that Blacks and other Third World peoples must lead this movement, for we are the first and most deeply injured victims of fascism. But it must embrace all potential victims and most important, all working-class people, for the key to the triumph of fascism is its ideological victory over the entire working class. . . .

. . . No potential victim of the fascist terror should be without the knowledge that the greatest menace to racism and fascism is unity!

MARIN COUNTY JAIL

May, 1971

Source: Angela Y. Davis, "Political Prisoners, Prisons, and Black Liberation," in *If They Come in the Morning: Voices of Resistance*, edited by Angela Davis (New York: Verso, 1971), 27–43. Copyright © National United Committee to Free Angela Davis, 1971, 2016. Reproduced with permission of Verso Books through PLSclear.

FURTHER READING

Biondi, Martha. *The Black Revolution on Campus*. Berkeley: University of California Press, 2012.

Bloom, Joshua, and Waldo E. Martin. *Black against Empire: The History and Politics of the Black Panther Party*. Berkeley: University of California Press, 2013.

Brown, Elaine. *A Taste of Power: A Black Woman's Story*. New York: Pantheon Books, 1992.

Brown, Scot. *Fighting for US: Maulana Karenga, the US Organization, and Black Cultural Nationalism*. New York: New York University Press, 2003.

Carmichael, Stokely, and Charles Hamilton. *Black Power: The Politics of Liberation in America* New York: Vintage Books, 1967.

Carson, Clayborne. *SNCC and the Black Awakening of the 1960s*. Cambridge, MA: Harvard University Press, 1981.

Churchill, Ward. *To Disrupt, Discredit and Destroy: The FBI's Secret War against the Black Panther Party*. New York: Routledge, 2009.

Churchill, Ward, and Jim Vander Wall. *Agents of Repression: The FBI's Secret Wars against the Black Panther Party and the American Indian Movement*. Boston: South End Press, 2002.

———. *The COINTELPRO Papers: Documents from the FBI's Secrets Wars against Dissent in the United States*. Boston: South End Press, 1990.

Cleaver, Eldridge. *Soul on Ice*. Menlo Park, CA: Ramparts, 1968.

———. *Target Zero: A Life in Writing*. Edited by Kathleen Cleaver. London: St. Martin's Press, 2006.

Collier-Thomas, Bettye, and V. P. Franklin. *Sisters in the Struggle: African American Women in the Civil Rights–Black Power Movement*. New York: New York University Press, 2001.

Davis, Angela. *Angela Davis: An Autobiography*. New York: Random House, 1974.

Douglas, Emory, Bobby Seale, and Kathleen Cleaver. *Black Panther: The Revolutionary Art of Emory Douglas*. Edited by Sam Durant. New York: Rizzoli, 2007.

Foner, Philip S., ed. *The Black Panthers Speak: The Manifesto of the Party; The First Complete Documentary Record of the Panthers' Program*. Boston: Da Capo Press, 1995.

Haas, Jeffrey. *The Assassination of Fred Hampton: How the FBI and the Chicago Police Murdered a Black Panther*. Chicago: Lawrence Hill Books, Chicago Review Press, 2010.

Horne, Gerald. *The Fire This Time: The Watts Uprising and the 1960s*. Charlottesville: University Press of Virginia, 1995.

Jefferies, Hasan Kwame. *Bloody Lowndes: Civil Rights and Black Power in Alabama Black Belt*. New York: New York University Press, 2009.

Jones, Charles E., ed., *The Black Panther Party (Reconsidered)*. Baltimore: Black Classic Press, 1998.

Joseph, Peniel E. *The Black Power Movement: Rethinking the Civil Rights–Black Power Era*. New York: Routledge, 2006.

———. *Dark Days, Bright Nights: From Black Power to Barack Obama*. New York: Basic Books, 2010.

———. *Sword and the Shield: The Revolutionary Lives of Malcolm X and Martin Luther King, Jr*. New York: Basic Books, 2020.

———. *Waiting 'til the Midnight Hour: A Narrative History of Black Power in America*. New York: Henry Holt, 2006.

Kelley, Robin D. G. *Freedom Dreams: The Black Radical Imagination*. Boston: Beacon Press, 2002.

Murch, Donna Jean. *Living for the City: Migration, Education, and the Rise of the Black Panther Party in Oakland, California*. Chapel Hill: University of North Carolina Press, 2010.

Neal, Larry. "The Black Arts Movement." *Drama Review* 12 (Summer 1968): 29–39.

Newton, Frederika S., and David Hilliard, eds. *To Die for the People: The Writings of Huey P. Newton*. New York: Random House, 1972.

Newton, Frederika S., Donald Weise, and David Hilliard, eds. *The Huey P. Newton Reader*. New York: Seven Stories Press, 2003.

Newton, Huey P. *Revolutionary Suicide*. Somerset, MA: Writers and Readers, 1973.

Newton, Michael. *Bitter Grain: Huey Newton and the Black Panther Party*. New York: Holloway House, 1980.

Ogbar, Jeffrey O. G. *Black Power: Radical Politics and African American Identity*. Baltimore: Johns Hopkins University Press, 2004.

Pearson, Hugh. *The Shadow of the Panther: Huey Newton and the Price of Black Power in America*. Boston: Addison-Wesley, 1994.

Phillips, Mary. "The Feminist Leadership of Ericka Huggins in the Black Panther Party." *Black Diaspora Review* 4, no. 1 (2014): 187–218.

Seale, Bobby. *Seize the Time: The Story of the Black Panther Party and Huey Newton*. Baltimore: Black Classic Press, 1991.

Self, Robert O. *American Babylon: Race and the Struggle for Postwar Oakland*. Princeton, NJ: Princeton University Press, 2003.

Shakur, Assata. *Assata: An Autobiography*. Chicago: Lawrence Hill Books, Chicago Review Press, 1987.

Smethurst, James. *The Black Arts Movement: Literary Nationalism in the 1960s and 1970s*. Chapel Hill: University of North Carolina Press, 2005.

———. *Brick City Vanguard: Amiri Baraka, Black Music, Black Modernity*. Amherst: University of Massachusetts Press, 2020.

Spencer, Robyn C. "Engendering the Black Freedom Struggle: Revolutionary Black
      Womanhood and the Black Panther Party in the Bay Area, California." *Journal
      of Women's History* 20, no. 1 (2008): 90–113. https://muse.jhu.edu/article
      /233236.
———. *The Revolution Has Come: Black Power, Gender, and the Black Party in Oakland.*
      Durham, NC: Duke University Press, 2016.
Street, Joe. *The Culture War in the Civil Right Movement.* Gainesville: University Press of
      Florida, 2007.
Williams, Jakobi. *From the Bullet to the Ballot: The Illinois Chapter of the Black Panther
      Party and Racial Coalition Politics in Chicago.* Chapel Hill: University of North
      Carolina Press, 2013.
Williams, Rhonda. *Concrete Demands: The Search for Black Power in the 20th Century.*
      New York: Routledge, 2015.
X, Malcolm, and Alex Haley. *The Autobiography of Malcolm X: As Told to Alex Haley.*
      New York: Random House, 1964.

9

Gender and Sexuality

What was the role of gender and sexuality in the civil rights and Black Power movements? How were gender and sexuality conceptualized by activists and their opponents? In what ways was Black liberation gendered? How did patriarchy, masculinity, respectability politics, and women's liberation inform the Black freedom movement? How were gender and sexuality battlegrounds in the Black freedom movement? Moreover, to what extent was the Black freedom movement both a predecessor and an ally for the gay liberation movement that emerged in the 1970s? How did Black men and women reconcile their various or intersectional identities while remaining committed to the Black freedom struggle?

Gender, sex, and Jim Crow were intricately intertwined in deeply pathological ways. As discussed in the third chapter, African American men were often falsely accused of sexually assaulting white women and were lynched as a result. African American women, however, were often the true victims of sexual assault at the hands of white men. Stories of sexual violence abound in the historical record. For example, in 1944, twenty-four-year-old Recy Taylor from Abbeville, Alabama, was walking back from church on a September evening accompanied by a couple of friends and their son. A group of white men stopped them, abducted Ms. Taylor, and the six of them gang-raped her. Rosa Parks, who then worked as secretary of the Montgomery NAACP, was dispatched to cover the story and denounce the impunity with which white men assaulted Black women. The Committee for Equal Justice for Mrs. Recy Taylor garnered national attention and was coined the "strongest campaign for equal justice to be seen in a decade" by the *Chicago Defender*. The violence Ms. Taylor endured was part of the white supremacist apparatus that operated on various levels and whose effect on Black women has long been understated in scholarship on the violence of Jim Crow.

The intense reality of everyday physical, emotional, psychological, and sexual violence pushed many women, including Fannie Lou Hamer and Ella Baker, to reject the gradualist approach embraced by advocates of "waiting." Black women spoke out publicly about being raped and waged radical claims for first-class citizenship, protection, and respect. African American community members often rallied to their defense. Too often, however, Black women's dignity and access to justice were not upheld by courts of law.

Gender informed the nature and organization of civil rights activism in other ways, however. Going as far back as the abolition movement and well into the mid-twentieth-century Black freedom movement, African American women obeyed the tenets of respectability to challenge racial discrimination and segregation. Respectability entailed certain representations of gender norms, middle-class appearance, and heterosexuality. For example, during the sit-in movement, civil rights demonstrators embraced "respectability politics," dressing in their "Sunday best" to convince white Americans that African Americans were deserving of equal rights and protections.

Gender and sexuality also impacted the organization and leadership of civil rights organizations. This often meant that African American women were not the face of the organization but relegated to the ranks of organizers and supporters even when their ideas, thoughts, and strategies were indicative of leadership. For example, while A. Philip Randolph, Martin Luther King Jr., and other male leaders were front and center at the March on Washington in 1963, Anna Arnold Hedgeman did much of the planning, organization, and recruitment for the march. In fact, Randolph and other male leaders refused to include women on an equal basis or even fully acknowledge women's contributions to the movement. Hedgeman, Dorothy Height (head of the National Council of Negro Women [(NCNW]), and other women leaders considered the march too important of an event not to push for at least one woman speaker and found it "unnerving to be given the argument that women were members of the National Urban League and all of the other organizations, and so, they were represented." In spite of lively debates behind the scenes, women remained absent from the list of speakers, with the exception of Daisy Bates, who delivered a tribute to the women segment. Most women leaders were seated on the platform, visually representing the "backbone" of the movement.

Civil rights organizer Ella Baker's involvement in the NAACP, Southern Christian Leadership Conference, and other national organizations further illustrates some of the movement's gender dynamics. In both the NAACP and the SCLC, Baker encountered male-centered, top-down leadership, which she opposed. As a result, in 1960, she helped organize the Student Nonviolent Coordinating Committee, which was organized around the goal of a participatory democracy (group-centered leadership). Despite this laudable goal, by 1964, women within SNCC often found themselves, as one observer noted, "in the same position as that token Negro hired in a corporation."

Black women also faced challenges in the women's movement of the 1960s and 1970s. Many second-wave feminist groups failed to adequately speak to the interlocking oppressions faced by women who were not middle class and white. Thus, African Americans founded or led groups like the National Welfare Rights Organization, Combahee River Collective, National Black Women's Organization, National Black Feminist Organization, and Black Women Organized for Political Action, among others. Black feminists urged that any movement seeking to improve the lives of Black women had to consider the intersectional oppression of race, gender, class, and sexuality.

Gay and lesbian African American activists understood the danger of belonging to other oppressed communities while fighting for civil rights, yet still called attention to the plight of gays and lesbians as oppressed peoples. For example, in 1957, Lorraine Hansberry supported the publication of the *Ladder*, the first national lesbian newspaper, and understood the necessity of addressing the concerns of lesbian women in particular. Also, during the 1960s, despite being the "brains" of several campaigns, Bayard Rustin, an openly gay civil rights activist, found that his involvement made many Black men in the movement, including Martin Luther King Jr., uneasy. He was often a victim of homophobia and relegated to the shadows of the movement, like African American women. Toward the end of the movement and thereafter, Rustin grew more vocal about gay rights and became an influential leader in the gay liberation movement.

The movement's reluctance to address gender and sexuality politics receded slowly. For example, in 1974, Huey Newton, cofounder of the Black Panther Party, appointed Elaine Brown as the organization's first chairwoman. The appointment of a woman was fitting given his advocacy for coalition building with the women's liberation and gay liberation movement and the labor of African American women in the party. Similar to many of the civil rights national organizations, the BPP also held a majority female membership. Women in the BPP did much of the work in running party initiatives, like the free-breakfast programs and community clinics, as well as advocating for Black self-defense and community empowerment. Brown remained chairwoman for three years, during which the party's leadership became less male centered. On the issues of race and sexuality, James Baldwin, who published the seminal *Giovanni's Room* in 1956, declared: "The sexual question and the racial question have always been entwined, you know. If Americans can mature on the level of racism, they have to mature on the level of sexuality."

DOCUMENT 9.1

Lorraine Hansberry, Selections of Anonymous Letters to the *Ladder* (1957)

In 1959, playwright and writer Lorraine Hansberry became the first African American woman to produce a play on Broadway when *A Raisin in the Sun* debuted. Written in 1957, the play was inspired by the Hansberry family's real-life experience with racially restrictive covenants and housing discrimination in Chicago. Though married for several years to songwriter and producer Robert Nemiroff, Hansberry struggled with her sexuality and openly embraced lesbianism near the end of her life. After Hansberry's death in 1965 at the age of thirty-four due to pancreatic cancer, Nemiroff donated her papers to the New York Public Library and restricted access to materials discussing Hansberry's sexuality for fifty years. In 2013, the materials became accessible, revealing Hansberry's lesbianism as well as her support for and engagement with gay and lesbian publications like the *Ladder*.

L.H.N., LETTER TO THE EDITOR, *THE LADDER*, MAY 1957, PP. 26–28.

Please find enclosed a money order for $2.00. I should like to receive as many of your back issues as that amount will cover. In the event $2.00 is in excess of the cost of six issues—well, fine. Those few cents may stand as a mere downpayment toward sizeable (for me, that is) donations I know already that I shall be sending to you.

I hope you are somewhat interested in off-the-top-of-the-head reactions from across the country because I would like to offer a few by way of the following:

(1) I'm glad as heck that you exist. You are obviously serious people and I feel that

women, without wishing to foster any strict *separatist* notions, homo or hetero, indeed have a need for their own publications and organizations. Our problems, our experiences as women are profoundly unique as compared to the other half of the human race. Women, like other oppressed groups of one kind of another, have particularly had to pay a price for the intellectual impoverishment that the second class status imposed on us for centuries created and sustained. Thus, I feel that THE LADDER is a fine, elementary step in a rewarding direction.

(2) Rightly or wrongly (in view of some of the thought provoking discussions I have seen elsewhere in a homosexual publication) I could not help but be encouraged and relieved by one of the almost subsidiary points under Point I of your declaration of purpose, "(to advocate) a mode of behaviour and dress acceptable to society." As one raised in a cultural experience (I am a Negro) where those within were and are forever lecturing to their fellows about how to appear acceptable to the dominant social group, I know something about the shallowness of such a view as an end in itself.

The most splendid argument is simple and to the point, Ralph Bunche, with all his clean fingernails, degrees, and, of course, undeniable service to the human race, could still be insulted, denied a hotel room or meal in many parts of our country. (Not to mention the possibility of being lynched on a lonely Georgia road for perhaps having demanded a glass of water in the wrong place.)

What ought to be clear is that one is oppressed or discriminated against because one is different, not "wrong" or "bad" somehow. This is perhaps the bitterest of the entire pill. HOWEVER, as a matter of facility, of expediency, one has to take a critical view of revolutionary attitudes which in spite of the BASIC truth I have mentioned above, may tend to aggravate the problems of a group.

I have long since passed that period when I felt personal discomfort at the sight of an ill-dressed or illiterate Negro. Social awareness has taught me where to lay the blame. Someday, I expect, the "discreet" Lesbian will not turn her head on the streets at the sight of the "butch" strolling hand in hand with her friend in their trousers and definitive haircuts. But for the moment, it still disturbs. It creates an impossible area for discussion with one's most enlightened (to use a hopeful term) heterosexual friends. Thus, I agree with the inclusion of that point in your declaration to the degree of wanting to comment on it.

(3) I am impressed by the general tone of your articles. The most serious fault being at this juncture that there simply is too little.

(4) Would it be presumptuous or far-fetched to suggest that you try for some overseas communications? One hears so much of publications and organizations devoted to homosexuality and homosexuals in Europe; but as far as I can gather these seem to lean heavily toward male questions and interests.

Just a little afterthought: considering Mattachine; Bilitis, ONE; all seem to be cropping up on the West Coast rather than here where a vigorous and active gay set almost bump one another off the streets—what is it in the air out there? Pioneers still? Or a tougher circumstance which inspires battle? Would like to hear speculation, lighthearted or otherwise.

L.H.N., New York, N.Y.

"I want to thank you for giving the Denver chapter's newsletter a write-up in THE LADDER. We are going to give DOB a write-up, too, very soon . . .

"We don't know any women here. If any of your group have contacts in the Denver area they would like to refer to us, or have us contact them, we would appreciate it. I always exhibit THE LADDER at our meetings. We will seek to place it in the hands of interested women when we have contact with them."

CARL B. HARDING, SECRETARY
Mattachine Society
P.O. Box 7035
Capitol Hill Station,
Denver 6, Colorado

Regarding that manuscript on Lesbian marriage we never got around to writing for the Mattachine Review, please be advised that if it ever comes into being it will be run in THE LADDER. After all, . . .-ED.

* * * * *

"Enclosed you will find a money order for five dollars which is to help make good a so far neglected earlier promise of financial support. . . .

"With the last two copies of the publication I am more convinced than ever of the depth and sincerity and—dignity—you people are determined to pursue your work with. I cannot tell you how encouraging it is. From where you are getting the energy and courage is something of a mystery to me, but please know it begins to inspire similar qualities in those who read THE LADDER.

"In the issue before the last I was particularly struck with and interested in the article by Osbourne and Stephens. I remarked at some length in my first (rather talky, I'm afraid) letter on my views on transvestism. I am now pleased to see that there are those who have given and are giving attention to the question in a most serious way. Good. I feel I am learning how to think all over again.

"Most of all I wanted to leap into the questions raised in Nancy Osbourne's so very important bit on heterosexually married lesbians. (I am one of those, incidentally, who is going to stick to lower-case, until somebody convinces me that what the homosexual wants and needs is not autonomy from the human race—but utter integration into it. I feel, however, that I could be wrong about it.) I was equally interested in Marion Bradley's contributions on the theme in the current issue, though frankly I understood what she was saying far less. I felt the piece was of serious and intelligent intentions but made some rather precarious suggestions. Speaking personally as well as abstractly here, may I ask when did the problem of saying to oneself, or to one's husband, or anyone else that finds "other women interesting" get to be any kind of a problem at all? With the very best circumspect motivations I am sure, it does seem to me that Miss Bradley misstates the problem of the homosexual woman (married or otherwise) so crucially as to almost approach the comical. I mean really, unless I am afflicted with the worst kind of misunderstanding, the homosexual impulse does transcend 'interest' in other women. Isn't the problem of the married lesbian woman that of an individual who finds that, despite her conscious will ofttimes, she is inclined to have her most intense emotional and physical reactions directed toward other women, quite beyond any comparative thing she might have ever felt for her husband—whatever her sincere affection for him? And isn't that the problem? How one quite admits that to oneself—and to one's husband? And isn't it necessary to state it so before we can pretend to discuss it?

"Further, to assert that such women ought to be able to 'put genuine truth in her statement that her interest in other women will affect her marriage no more than the heterosexual woman's interest in other men is making an equation of two decidedly different social circumstances that simply have no equality in life. A woman of strength and honesty may, if she chooses, sever her marriage and marry a new male mate and society will be upset that the divorce rate is rising so—but there are few places in the United States, in any event, where she will be anything remotely akin to an 'outcast'. Obviously this is not true for a woman who would end her marriage to take up life with another woman.

"I very loudly agree, on the other hand, with the writer's view that women who violate their marriages freely because the violations involve women rather than men deserve the condemnation of both society and lesbian opinion. Not so much because of any sacredness of our dubious social morality, but rather because it involves the deception of another human being—and that, as always, is intolerable. Also I think it is very nice if somehow lesbian women in general might lend themselves amiably to showing that all relationships between women need not be those of 'cats' tearing at one another—but in this particular discussion it seems rather beside the point.

"I suspect that the problem of the married woman who would prefer emotional-physical relationships with other women is proportionally much higher than a similar statistic for men. (A statistic surely no one will ever really have.) This because the estate of woman being what it is, how could we ever begin to guess the numbers of women who are not prepared to risk a life alien to what they have been taught all their lives to believe was their 'natural' destiny—AND—their only expectation for ECONOMIC security. It seems to me that this is why the question has an immensity that it does not have for male homosexuals. We must, as noted above, take a dim view of anyone who treats a married partner without respect; but at the same time I should imagine that we would have a particularly sensitive and sympathetic awareness of the nature of the 'social trap' (I cannot think of a better set of words at the moment) which the fundamental position of women as a sex is likely to force many women into—homosexual or heterosexual.

"I am suggesting here that perhaps it is pat and even unfair to suggest that all that remains for the married lesbian, already nursing her frustrations and confusions, is somehow to get rid of her 'self-pity' and self-excuses' and make a 'happy marriage without in anyway denying her nature'. I am afraid that homosexuality, whatever its origins, is far more real than that, far more profound in the demands it makes; otherwise it could hardly deserve to be called a problem at all. I don't think people start out in this world to be 'bad'—they start out to be happy. Frankly, I haven't the least idea in the world what a 'solution' to the question might be at this particular moment in history. And I guess in the face of that kind of an admission it seems a little presumptious [sic] to have charged into Miss Bradley's really quite worthwhile efforts. But maybe that is what I was trying to say—let us not get lost in answers which cannot possibly exist at the moment; but rather, exhaust ourselves in the dissection of previous views. For instance, the whole realm of morality and ethics is something that has escaped the attention of women by and large. And, it needs the attention of intellectual women most desperately. I think it is about time that equipped women began to take on some of the ethical questions which a male dominated culture has produced and dissect and analyze them quite to pieces in a serious fashion. It is time that 'half the human race' had something to say about the nature of its existence. Otherwise—without revised basic thinking—the woman intellectual is likely to find herself trying to draw conclusions—moral conclusions—based on acceptance of a social moral superstructure which has never admitted to the equality of women and is therefore immoral itself. As per marriage, as per sexual practices, as per the rearing of children, etc. In this kind of work there may be women to emerge who will be able to formulate a new and possible concept that homosexual persecution and condemnation has at its roots not only social ignorance, but a philosophically active anti-feminist dogma. But that is but a kernel of a speculative embryonic idea improperly introduced here."

L.N., New York, N.Y.

DOCUMENT 9.2

Dorothy Height, "We Wanted the Voice of a Woman to Be Heard" (2001)

For forty years, Dorothy Height served as the president of the National Council of Negro Women, an organization founded in 1935 by Mary McLeod Bethune to increase the quality of life for Black women, their families, and their communities. Despite serving as advocates for civil rights and women's rights and as leaders in national and local civil rights organizations, Height and other women were overlooked and denied the opportunity to speak at the 1963 March on Washington, even as they recruited thousands of marchers. In the following excerpt, Height details the conflict between male and female leaders leading up to and during the march.

... [W]hen the 1963 March on Washington was being planned, people quite naturally asked me, "What's going to happen?" Many prominent women were concerned about the visible participation and representation of women leaders in the program. Most of these women thought that the CUCRL was organizing the March and making decisions about the platform. When the question was raised, we were always referred to Bayard Rustin, the Executive Director of the March, appointed by A. Philip Randolph, who first issued the call.

I went along with Anna Arnold Hedgeman, a woman with a long history of working for freedom and equality, to meet with Bayard Rustin. We discussed the women's participation in the March. We were amazed to hear the response, "Women are included." Rustin asserted that, "Every group has women in it, labor, church," and so on. When we asked Rustin who was doing the planning, he referred to the heads of the National Council of Churches, NAACP, National Urban League, several Jewish groups, and other organizations. When the question was raised in the CUCRL meetings, it was always referred back to Bayard Rustin. There was an all-consuming focus on race. We women were expected to put all our energies into it. Clearly, there was a low tolerance level for anyone raising the questions about the women's participation, per se.

The men seemed to feel that women were digressing and pulling the discussion off the main track. But it wasn't just a male attitude. There were black women who felt that we needed to stick with the "real" issue of race. It was thought that we were making a lot of fuss about an insignificant issue, that we did not recognize that the March was about racism, not sexism. We knew all that. But, we made it clear that we wanted to hear at least one woman in the March dealing with jobs and freedom. We knew, first-hand, that most of the Civil Rights Movement audiences were largely comprised of women, children, and youth.

Prior to the 1963 March on Washington, whenever there was a civil rights rally, the platform was filled predominantly by males. When we said that we wanted the voice of a woman to be heard, and gave the names of women to be considered, such as Deborah Partridge Wolfe, and Anna Arnold Hedgeman, and mentioned that there were a number of possibilities, Rustin and others would say that they did not know who to choose. The women were quick to say that they were ready to make a selection or nomination, but we could never get to that point. We knew that other groups had not had the question raised on who they would choose. But it came up around the concerns of women.

It was unnerving to be given the argument that women were members of the National Urban League and all of the other organizations, and so, they were represented. As the time approached, there was no agreement on having the students speak either. SNCC was carrying on direct action protest activities. Roy Wilkins said that at times the SNCC students were upsetting all the good work that the NAACP had done. He emphasized that the NAACP worked through the courts. There was real tension in the meetings of the Council of Civil Rights Leadership at the beginning of the discussions about the March. But, as a woman, I just kept saying that I did not see how we could leave our young people out. We needed them around the table. Unlike the women, SNCC more aggressively pursued the issue of having a student speaker at the March. When John Lewis demanded to speak, the students were prepared to demonstrate. The organizers of the March held out, right up to the end. The students made threats. Their prepared remarks were questioned. . . .

Nothing that women said or did broke the impasse blocking their participation. I've never seen a more immovable force. We could not get women's participation taken seriously. The March organizers proffered many excuses. They said, "We have too many speakers as it is. The program is too long. You are already represented."

They said, "We have Mahalia Jackson." Oh yes, we said, "But she is not speaking. She's not speaking on behalf of women, or on behalf of civil rights. She's singing."

To address the issue, the organizers gave a number of us prominent seats on the platform. We were seated. In all the March on Washington pictures, we're right there on the platform. There were several women who just refused to do anything. Some were so angry that they didn't really want to take part. The women represented a cross section of organizations, including labor, religion, and social welfare groups. What actually happened was so disappointing, because actually women were an active part of the whole effort. Indeed, women were the backbone of the movement. A look at the pictures gives the impression that we were intimately involved.

Within the CUCRL, I think that Whitney Young, Martin Luther King, Jr., and James Farmer showed the greatest concern. But even they did not take an active stand. They passed the question on. They said, "We'll check with Mr. Randolph, and check with Bayard." . . .

Our white sisters find it hard to understand the positions we often take. It is characteristic of black women to put the race issue ahead of everything else, so that when we confront sexism, we are not an angry caucus. We fully supported the 1963 March on Washington because we felt it would strike a major blow against racism. However, it did not go down easily that the young people were only reluctantly admitted. I think the women began to say that "this March has to speak up for jobs and freedom," ironic as that may seem.

. . .

Despite the fact that the March organizers and many of the male leaders asked groups not to call any meetings, and not to organize gatherings with the people who came to Washington, NCNW had set up a meeting called "After the March, What?" This proved especially important because women were able, once again, to get some perspective. Over and above the planned agenda, women talked freely of their concern about women's participation. We could hardly believe that after all we were doing in the Civil Rights Movement, the men leaders could conclude, "You have a place in all of the participating national organizations, so you are represented." Those who supported the demand for direct representation showed no sensitivity to the need to move on the issue. What was most discouraging was that there was no sign of remorse among the male leadership, no feeling that there was any injustice. They believed that this was the right thing to do. After all, there were speakers from a diversity of national bodies, Protestants, Catholics, Jews, the NAACP, the Urban League, Labor, and the Southern Christian Leadership Conference. The organizers had stressed that in all of these organizations, women carried vital roles. As we worked through the meeting, again and again, the point was made that women were fully supportive of the March. Once we saw we were not going to prevail, we did so with our eyes open, and the experience itself helped open our eyes.

It did not go unnoticed that some of the male leaders wanted to act as though Bayard Rustin had made a unilateral decision. There was no easy way to find out who made the decision. It simply had been decided. That was one thing, but it also put us on guard that if we didn't speak up, nobody would. And we began to realize that if we did not address issues such as this, if we did not demand our rights, we were not going to get them. The women became much more aware and much more aggressive in facing up to sexism in our dealings with the male leadership in the movement.

Following this meeting to assess the status of the movement, and to chart the next steps, the NCNW held a Leadership Conference on November 14, 1963. One invited speaker was Pauli Murray, a noted legal scholar, educator, and well-known activist in a number of civil rights groups. . . . The NCNW invited Murray to speak about black women's struggle for equality.

In her speech, "The Negro Woman in the Quest for Equality," Pauli Murray captured the feeling of black women about their exclusion from direct participation in the March on Washington, as well as their feelings about their treatment in the overall movement. Her speech was well received, and elicited a great deal of discussion. Murray traced the history of black women and their struggle for equality from slavery to freedom, noting the similarities and differences in their status from that of white women, race being the main distinction. She noted that in their quest for equality, black women had been willing to overlook gender discrimination in order to gain racial equality. . . . Looking back on the March on Washington, most people remember Dr. King's great "I Have a Dream" speech. However, for many black women who were actively involved in the Civil Rights Movement, especially those in leadership positions, the blatantly insensitive treatment of black women leaders was a new awakening. We began to reflect upon the importance of black women in our community. They are the backbone of the churches. The evidence of their work can be seen everywhere. It made some of us sit up and think in new and different ways. We were forced to recognize that, traditionally, black women, through their unstinting support of race movements and their willingness to play frequently unquestioned subordinate roles, and to put the men out front, made it seem that this was acceptable. Little or no thought had been given to ourselves as women.

. . . [T]he March on Washington experience, as proud as everybody was of Mahalia Jackson, brought into bold relief the different perspectives of men and women on the whole issue of gender. Though every statistic showed us that a number of our families were headed by women, we were still dominated by the view that if men were given enough, the women would be better off. There was not that sense of equal partnership. For many of us, the March opened that sense of equal partnership. For many of us, the March opened up the dialogue. It made it necessary. We had to talk about it.

Source: Dorothy Height, "We Wanted the Voice of a Woman to Be Heard,"
in *Sisters in the Struggle: African American Women in the Civil Rights–Black Power Movement*, edited by Bettye Collier-Thomas and V. P. Franklin (New York: New York University Press, 2001), 83–92.
Copyright © 2001 by Bettye Collier-Thomas and V. P. Franklin. Used by permission.

DOCUMENT 9.3

SNCC Position on Women in the Movement (1964)

Within the student- and youth-centered SNCC, similar questions about restrictions on women and sexism within civil rights organizations came to the fore. In the spring of 1964, Black and white women staged a protest in the SNCC Atlanta office, challenging the fact that women were always selected to take the meeting minutes and act as secretaries. When SNCC chairman James Forman tasked group members with submitting position papers for discussions at a retreat in the fall of 1964, four white women—Elaine DeLott, Casey Hayden, Mary King, and Emmie Schrader—authored the following paper that discusses evidence of sexism within the organization and compares the damaging impact of race and sex discrimination. Other SNCC women, including Judy Richardson and Ruby Doris Smith-Robinson, felt that the organization was deeply shaped by women like Ella Baker and gave space to young Black women to lead and organize, even if they did not occupy the leadership ranks of SNCC.

1. Staff was involved in Crucial constitutional revisions at the Atlanta staff meeting in October. A large committee was appointed to present revisions to the staff. The committee was all men.

2. Two organizers were working together to form a farmers league. Without asking any questions, the male organizer immediately assigned the clerical work to the female organizer although both had equal experience in organizing campaigns.

3. Although there are women in Mississippi project who have been working as long as some of the men, the leadership group in COFO is all men.

4. A woman in a field office wondered why she was held responsible for day to day decisions, only to find out later that she had been appointed project director but not told.

5. A fall 1964 personnel and resources report on Mississippi projects lists the number of people in each project. The section on Laurel however, lists not the number of persons, but "three girls."

6. One of SNCC's main administrative officers apologizes for appointment of a woman as interim project director in a key Mississippi project area.

7. A veteran of two years work for SNCC in two states spends her day typing and doing clerical work for other people in her project.

8. Any woman in SNCC, no matter what her position or experience, has been asked to take minutes in a meeting when she and other women are outnumbered by men.

9. The names of several new attorneys entering a state project this past summer were posted in a central movement office. The first initial and last name of each lawyer was listed. Next to one name was written: (girl).

10. Capable, responsible and experienced women who are in leadership positions can expect to have to defer to a man on their project for final decision making.

11. A session at the recent October staff meeting in Atlanta was the first large meeting in the past couple of years where a woman was asked to chair.

Undoubtedly this list will seem strange to some, petty to others, laughable to most. The list could continue as far as there are women in the movement. Except that most women don't talk about these kinds of incidents, because the whole subject is discussable—strange to some, petty to others, laughable to most.

The average white person finds it difficult to understand why the Negro resents being called "boy", or being thought of as "musical" and "athletic," because the average white person doesn't realize that he assumes he is superior. And naturally he doesn't understand the problem of paternalism. So too the average SNCC worker finds it difficult to discuss the woman problem because of the assumption of male superiority. Assumptions of male superiority are as widespread and deep rooted and every much as crippling to the woman as the assumptions of white supremacy are to the Negro. Consider why it is in SNCC that women who are competent, qualified and experienced, are automatically assigned to the "female" kinds of jobs such as: typing, desk work, telephone work, filing, library work, cooking and the assistant kind of administrative work but rarely the "executive" kind.

The woman in SNCC is often in the same position as that token Negro hired in a corporation. The management thinks that it has done its bit. Yet, every day the Negro bears an atmosphere, attitudes and actions which are tinged with condescension and paternalism, the most telling of which are when he is not promoted as the equally or less skilled whites are.

This paper is anonymous. Think about the kinds of things the author, if made known, would have to suffer because of rasing [sic] this kind of discussion. Nothing so final as being fired or outright exclusion, but the kinds of things which are killing to the insides—insinuations, ridicule, overexaggerated compensations.

This paper is presented anyway because it needs to be made know [sic] that many women in the movement are not "happy and contented" with their status. It needs to be made known that much talent and experience are being wasted by this movement when women are not given jobs commensurate with their abilities. It needs to be known that just as Negroes were the crucial factor in the ecnomy [sic] of the cotton South, so too in SNCC, women are the crucial factor that keeps the movement running on a day to day basis. Yet they are not given equal say-so when it comes to day to day decision making. What can be done? Probably nothing right away. Most men in this movement are probably too threatened by the possibility of serious discussion on this subject. Perhaps this is because they have recently broken away from a matriarchal framework under which they may have grown up. Then too, many women are as unaware and insensitive to this subject as men, just as there are many Negroes who don't understand they are not free or who want to be part of white America. They don't understand that they have to give up their souls and stay in their place to be accepted. So too, many women, in order to be accepted by men, or men's terms, give themselves up to that caricature of what a woman is—unthinking, pliable, an ornament to please the man.

Maybe the only thing that can come out of this paper is discussion—amidst the laughter—but still discussion. (Those who laugh the hardest are often those who need the crutch of male supremacy the most.) And maybe some women will begin to recognize tday [sic] to day discriminations. And maybe sometime in the future the whole of the women in this movement will become so alert as to force the rest of the movement to stop the discrimination and start the slow process of changing values and ideas so that all of us gradually come to understand that this is no more a man's world than it is a white world.

Source: "Student Nonviolent Coordinating Committee Position Paper: Women in the Movement," November 1964, 1964 Organizing & Political Materials Collection, Freedom Movement Organizing & Political Materials, Civil Rights Movement Archive, http://www.crmvet.org /docs/6411w_us_women.pdf.

DOCUMENT 9.4

Interview with Elaine Brown on Women in the Black Panther Party (1988)

Elaine Brown discusses women in the Black Panther Party. Born in Philadelphia in 1943, Brown initially aspired to be a songwriter and moved to Los Angeles to pursue her dream. But Brown became radicalized through personal and professional relationships and attended her first Black Panther Party meeting in 1968. Brown helped set up some of the party's signature programs (including the free-breakfast and legal-aid programs), edited party publications, wrote and recorded songs for the party, and ran unsuccessfully for a local city council position in Oakland. When BPP chairman Huey Newton ran into legal troubles in 1974, he fled the country and appointed Brown to lead the BPP, the only woman ever to do so. As chairwoman, Brown led the party to deepen its institutional roots by founding the Panthers' Liberation School and supported Lionel Wilson's successful bid to become Oakland's first Black mayor. In 1977, Newton returned from exile, and Brown stepped down shortly thereafter when Newton failed to condemn men in the party who viciously attacked a female administrator at the Panthers' Liberation School for reprimanding a male colleague.

. . .

LOUIS MASSIAH: How did you see the Panther party transform—you were talking about guys in the Slausons in L.A., and also folks in Oakland, around the country. How did you see it transforming young Black men and women?

ELAINE BROWN: Well, you know, the Panther party first of all was dominated by men. So it, it, no point in talking too much about the women, because there weren't a lot of women in the party, the party. There were a lot of women, but there weren't a lot of women. I mean, we were, the party was dominated by men. And it was a male-dominated organization in terms of attitude and everything, and the paramilitary, ah, you know, atmosphere and so forth. But I think that, the simple fact is the Black Panther gave all those gang people, the Slausons in L.A., the Peace Stone Nation in, in um, in Chicago, it focused their attention away from what they were doing, and onto this more serious issue. In other words, the reason gangs form is not just so that people can have camaraderie, as many sociologists would like to suggest. You know, there's this sort of, everybody's happy just being a part of something. Well we could be part of something other than a street gang, and go around robbing and maiming and mugging people and stuff and so forth. But there was that sense, and I know from Philadelphia, from, from the Avenue Gang and Norris Street, and all the gangs in my neighborhood, that it was, it wasn't just a matter of belonging, it was standing for something, it was having territory, it was having a sense of your own dignity in a, in a world that denied your existence. What the Black Panther party said is you can do the same thing—

. . .

LOUIS MASSIAH: And you as a woman, what was particular, what brought women into the party?

ELAINE BROWN: Well, for me, it was the idea that Black men were actually deciding that they wanted to be men as I, as I put it, in the sense of, um, I was denounced as a matter of fact by some of the women's groups because, um, you know, the question of feminism seemed to not allow for this element, this return to the, the return to the community of the Black male. And I had grown up in a neighborhood where there were two fathers that I could name off the top of my head, that we knew of, that were still in the home and married or whatever. The rest of, most people I knew, and most people in most Black, many Black communities had divorced parents long before these statistics were popular. Or fathers who, the image that we had at least was the father wasn't there. Or the father didn't do this, or there was the, the Black male who was the weak figure and so forth. Here were men who were saying, "Listen, we are willing to take charge of our lives. We are willing to stand up, we are willing"—I mean, there was the appeal that Malcolm had in many ways, and it was the appeal that other people have had, but, but for me, the Black Panthers were the, the ultimate. And so it was the men that I saw and the sense of being part of them and being ha—so happy to see that they cared about me, and I as a child who had no father at home, that had a certain subjective appeal to my psyche and to my emotional need, to say yes, there were men in this world who, who cared, ah, Black men, who, ah, who cared about the community and wanted to, to do something and were willing to, to take it to the, to, to the last, ah, degree.

. . .

LOUIS MASSIAH: What were the expectations of women in the party, and was it any different from the expectations of men?

ELAINE BROWN: No. Um, I don't think we saw ourselves differently in the beginning at least. We thought that we were revolutionaries, um, and we thought that we would, ah, we would, ah, participate in the same level as men. The one thing we did know is that we weren't really, there was really no difference in the beginning at least. At least we thought of ourselves as, as, as the same as the men in terms of our commitment, and in terms of what we had to do. So our expectations were that we really thought, of course, as, as did the men, that, um, that we would introduce, ah, revolution into the United States. . . .

Source: Elaine Brown, interview with Louis Massiah, October 14, 1988, Henry Hampton Collection, Eyes on the Prize II Interviews, Film and Media Archive, Washington University Libraries.

Pauli Murray, "The Negro Woman in the Quest for Equality" (1964)

On November 14, 1963, civil rights and women's rights activist Pauli Murray delivered the speech "The Negro Woman in the Quest for Equality" to the National Council of Negro Women in Washington, D.C. Murray, who was also a lawyer, addressed the lack of Black women speakers at the recently held March on Washington, as well as the significant hurdles Black women faced in employment and marriage. Given their plight, Murray implored Black women to fight for civil rights and women's rights.

THE DILEMMA

Recent disquieting events have made imperative an assessment of the role of the Negro woman in the quest for equality. The civil rights revolt, like many social upheavals, has released powerful pent-up emotions, cross currents, rivalries and hostilities. . . . There is much jockeying for position as ambitious men push and elbow that way to leadership roles. . . .

What emerges most clearly from events of the past several months is the tendency to assign women to a secondary, ornamental or "honoree" role instead of the partnership role in the civil rights movement which they have earned by their courage, intelligence, and dedication. It was bitterly humiliating for Negro women on August 28 to see themselves accorded little more than token recognition in the historic March on Washington. Not a single woman was invited to make one of the major speeches or to be part of the delegation of leaders who went to the White House. This omission was deliberate. Representations for recognition of women were made to the policy-making body sufficiently in advance of the August 28 arrangements to have permitted the necessary adjustments of the program. What the Negro women leaders were told is revealing: that no representation was given to them because they would not be able to agree on a delegate. How familiar was this excuse! It is a typical response from an entrenched power group.

Significantly, two days before the March, A. Philip Randolph, leader of the March, accepted an invitation to be guest speaker at a luncheon given by the National Press Club in Washington in the face of strong protest by organized newspaper women that the National Press Club excludes qualified newspaper women from membership and sends women reporters who cover its luncheons to the balcony. Mr. Randolph apparently saw no relationship between being sent to the balcony and being sent to the back of the bus. Perhaps if he had been able to understand what an affront it is to one's personal dignity to be sent to the balcony at a meeting concerned primarily with the issue of human dignity, he would set as a condition for his appearance a non-segregated gathering. He failed to see that he was supporting the violation of the very principle for which he was fighting: that human rights are indivisible.

. . . [T]he great mass of magazine and newsprint expended upon the civil rights crisis, national editors have selected Negro men almost exclusively to articulate the aspirations of the Negro community. There has been little or no public discussion of the problems, aspirations and role of Negro women. Moreover, the undertone of news stories of recent efforts to create career opportunities for Negroes in government and industry seems to be that what is being talked about is jobs for Negro men only. The fact that Negro women might be available and, as we shall see, are qualified and in need of employment, is ignored. While this is in keeping with the general tenor of a male-dominated society, it has grave consequences for Negro women.

At the very moment in history when there is an international movement to raise the status of women and a recognition that women generally are underemployed, are Negro women to be passed over in the social arrangements which are to create new job opportunities for Negroes? Moreover, when American women are seeking partnership in our society, are Negro women to take a backward step and sacrifice their equalitarian tradition? Negro women have tremendous power. How shall they use their power? How can they help Negro men and themselves to achieve mature relationship in the wider community without impairing this tradition? Or is it inherent in the struggle that Negro men can achieve maturity only at the price of destroying in Negro women the very characteristics which are stressed as part of American tradition and which have been indispensable to the Negro's steep climb out of slavery? And if these qualities are suppressed in the women, what will be the effect upon the personalities of future generations of Negro children? What are the alternatives to matriarchal dominance on the one hand and male supremacy on the other hand?

MATRIARCHAL OR MATELESS?

. . . The statistical profile of a Negro woman which emerges from the latest census reports is that she has a harder time finding a mate, remains single more often, bears more children, is in the labor market longer, has less education, earns less, is widowed earlier and carries a heavier economic burden as a family head than her white sister.

The explosive social implications of an excess of more than half a million Negro girls and women over 14 years of age are obvious in a society in which mass media intensify notions of glamour and expectations of romantic love and marriage, while at the same barriers are erected against interracial marriages. The problem of an excess female population is a familiar one in European countries which have experienced heavy male casualties during wars, but an excess female ethnic minority as an enclave within a larger population raises important social issues. What is there in the American environment which is hostile to both the birth and survival of Negro males? How much of the tensions and conflicts traditionally associated with the matriarchal frame-work of Negro society are in reality due to this imbalance and the pressures it generates? Does this excess explain the active competition between Negro professional men and women seeking employment in markets which have limited or excluded Negroes? And does this competition intensify the stereotype of the matriarchal society and female dominance?

We have seen from Dr. Noble's study that the higher educational rank and earning power than that of their husbands has created feelings of guilt in some Negro women and that some even failed to go on to higher degrees in order to preserve the marital relationship from the destructive effects of envy and jealousy on the part of their husbands. It is nothing less than tragic that a ceiling should be set upon education for

Negro women at a time when more education for all is being stressed in the wider society.

Equality for the Negro woman must mean equal opportunity to compete for jobs and to find a mate in the total society. For as long as she is confined to an area in which she must compete fiercely for a mate, she will remain the object of sexual exploitation and the victim of all of the social evils which such exploitation involves.

In short, many of the 645,000 excess Negro women will never marry at all unless they marry outside of the Negro community. And many others will marry men whose educational and cultural standards may not be the same as their own. Add to the large reservoir of unmarried nonwhite women (22.3%), a higher proportion of widowed, separated and divorced nonwhite women than of white women, and you have factors which have combined to make the Negro woman the responsible family head in more than one fifth of all nonwhite families.

The point I am trying to make here is that the Negro woman cannot assume with any degree of confidence that she will be able to look to marriage for either economic or emotional support. She must prepare to be self-supporting and to support others, perhaps, for a considerable period or for life. In these circumstances, while efforts to raise educational and employment levels for Negro men will certainly ease some of the economic and social burdens now carried by many Negro women today, these burdens will not be eased for a large and growing minority. These burdens will continue and may even be aggravated if there continues to be a large numerical imbalance between the sexes. Bearing in mind that everything possible must be done to encourage Negro males to develop their highest educational potential and to accept their family responsibilities and feel secure in their marital relationships, Negro women have no alternative but to insist upon equal opportunities without regard to sex in training, education and employment at every level. This may be a matter of sheer survival. And these special needs must be articulated by the civil rights movement so that they are not overlooked.

EDUCATION AND EMPLOYMENT

The Negro woman worker is triply handicapped. She is largely concentrated in non-union employment and thus has few of the benefits to be derived from labor organization or social legislation. She is handicapped because of her race and sex. On the whole she is further handicapped because of inadequate education and training. Thus, in 1960 a little over half of all nonwhite women had completed eight grades of elementary school (56.7%) as compared to more than four out of five white women (82.1%). More significantly, less than a fourth of nonwhite women had completed high school (23.2%) as compared to nearly half of all white women (44.7%). Twice as many white women, proportionally, have completed college (6%) as nonwhite women (3.6%). When we consider that presently the bulk of Negro women are non-skilled or semi-skilled, that there is a steady pool of 4.6 million unemployed in the United States, and that automation continues to eliminate jobs in the semiskilled categories, the present outlook for the Negro woman is dark indeed unless she is encouraged to increase her educational level and to develop wider skills.

... The Negro woman can no longer postpone or subordinate the fight against discrimination because of sex to the civil rights struggle but must carry on both fights simultaneously. She must insist upon a partnership role in the integration movement. ... [T]he full participation and leadership of Negro women is necessary to the success of the civil rights revolution.

Moreover, Negro women should seek to communicate and cooperate with white women wherever possible. Their common problems and interests as women provide a bridge to span initial self-consciousness. Many white women today are earnestly seeking to make common cause with Negro women and are holding out their hands. All too often they find themselves rebuffed. Integration, however, is a two-way effort and Negro women must be courageous enough to grasp the hand whenever it is held out.

The path ahead will not be easy; the challenges to meet new standards of achievement in the search for equality will be many and bewildering. For a time, even, the casualties of integration may be great. But as Negro women in the United States enter their second century of emancipation from chattel slavery, let them be proud of their heritage and resolute in their determination to pass the best of it along to their children. As Lorraine Hansberry, the gifted playwright, has said, "For above all, in behalf of an ailing world which sorely needs our defiance, may we, as Negroes or women, never accept the notion of—'our place.'"

DOCUMENT 9.6

Loving v. Virginia Decision (1967)

Laws banning interracial marriage in Virginia dated back to the colonial era before the United States was even a nation. In June 1958, Richard Loving, a white man, and Mildred Jeter, an African American and Native American woman, married in Washington, D.C., but decided to reside in their home state of Virginia. Shortly after returning to the state, the two were arrested for violating Virginia's antimiscegenation laws that prohibited interracial marriage and sentenced to prison for one year. The case worked its way to the Supreme Court, which ruled unanimously that Virginia's state laws violated the Fourteenth Amendment and the freedom of individuals to marry. In addition to striking down similar laws in other states, the Supreme Court's ruling in the case set a precedent for same-sex marriage cases nearly fifty years later.

Mr. Chief Justice WARREN delivered the opinion of the Court.

1

This case presents a constitutional question never addressed by this Court: whether a statutory scheme adopted by the State of Virginia to prevent marriages between persons solely on the basis of racial classifications violates the Equal Protection and Due Process Clauses of the Fourteenth Amendment. For reasons which seem to us to reflect the central meaning of those constitutional commands, we conclude that these statutes cannot stand consistently with the Fourteenth Amendment.

2

In June 1958, two residents of Virginia, Mildred Jeter, a Negro woman, and Richard Loving, a white man, were married in the District of Columbia pursuant to its laws. Shortly after their marriage, the Lovings returned to Virginia and established their marital abode in Caroline County. At the October Term, 1958, of the Circuit Court of Caroline County, a grand jury issued an indictment charging the Lovings with violating Virginia's ban on interracial marriages. On January 6, 1959, the Lovings pleaded guilty to the charge and were sentenced to one year in jail; however, the trial judge suspended the sentence for a period of 25 years on the condition that the Lovings leave the State and not return to Virginia together for 25 years. . . .

4

After their convictions, the Lovings took up residence in the District of Columbia. On November 6, 1963, they filed a motion in the state trial court to vacate the judgment and set aside the sentence on the ground that the statutes which they had violated were repugnant to the Fourteenth Amendment. The motion not having been decided by October 28, 1964, the Lovings instituted a class action in the United States District Court for the Eastern District of Virginia requesting that a three-judge court be convened to declare the Virginia antimiscegenation statutes unconstitutional and to enjoin state officials from enforcing their convictions. On January 22, 1965, the state trial judge denied the motion to vacate the sentences, and the Lovings perfected an appeal to the Supreme Court of Appeals of Virginia. On February 11, 1965, the three-judge District Court continued the case to allow the Lovings to present their constitutional claims to the highest state court.

5

The Supreme Court of Appeals upheld the constitutionality of the antimiscegenation statutes and, after modifying the sentence, affirmed the convictions. The Lovings appealed this decision. . . .

6

The Lovings were convicted of violating § 20–58 of the Virginia Code:

7

'Leaving State to evade law.—If any white person and colored person shall go out of this State, for the purpose of being married, and with the intention of returning, and be married out of it, and afterwards return to and reside in it, cohabiting as man and wife, they shall be punished as provided in § 20–59, and the marriage shall be governed by the same law as if it had been solemnized in this State. The fact of their cohabitation here as man and wife shall be evidence of their marriage.'

8

Section 20–59, which defines the penalty for miscegenation, provides:

9

'Punishment for marriage.—If any white person intermarry with a colored person, or any colored person intermarry with a white person, he shall be guilty of a felony and shall be punished by confinement in the penitentiary for not less than one nor more than five years.'

10

Other central provisions in the Virginia statutory scheme are § 20–57, which automatically voids all marriages between 'a white person and a colored person' without any judicial proceeding, and §§ 20–54 and 1–14 which, respectively, define 'white persons' and 'colored persons and Indians' for purposes of the statutory prohibitions....

11

Virginia is now one of 16 States which prohibit and punish marriages on the basis of racial classifications. Penalties for miscegenation arose as an incident to slavery and have been common in Virginia since the colonial period. The present statutory scheme dates from the adoption of the Racial Integrity Act of 1924, passed during the period of extreme nativism which followed the end of the First World War.

I

13

... [T]he State contends that, because its miscegenation statutes punish equally both the white and the Negro participants in an interracial marriage, these statutes, despite their reliance on racial classifications do not constitute an invidious discrimination based upon race. The second argument advanced by the State assumes the validity of its equal application theory. The argument is that, if the Equal Protection Clause does not outlaw miscegenation statutes because of their reliance on racial classifications, the question of constitutionality would thus become whether there was any rational basis for a State to treat interracial marriages differently from other marriages....

14

Because we reject the notion that the mere 'equal application' of a statute containing racial classifications is enough to remove the classifications from the Fourteenth Amendment's proscription of all invidious racial discriminations, we do not accept the State's contention that these statutes should be upheld if there is any possible basis for concluding that they serve a rational purpose....

17

There can be no question but that Virginia's miscegenation statutes rest solely upon distinctions drawn according to race. The statutes proscribe generally accepted conduct if engaged in by members of different races. Over the years, this Court has consistently repudiated '(d)]istinctions between citizens solely because of their ancestry' as being 'odious to a free people whose institutions are founded upon the doctrine of equality.' . . . At the very least, the Equal Protection Clause demands that racial classifications, especially suspect in criminal statutes, be subjected to the 'most rigid scrutiny' . . . and, if they are ever to be upheld, they must be shown to be necessary to the accomplishment of some permissible state objective, independent of the racial discrimination which it was the object of the Fourteenth Amendment to eliminate. . . .

18

There is patently no legitimate overriding purpose independent of invidious racial discrimination which justifies this classification. The fact that Virginia prohibits only interracial marriages involving white persons demonstrates that the racial classifications must stand on their own justification, as measures designed to maintain White Supremacy. We have consistently denied the constitutionality of measures which restrict the rights of citizens on account of race. There can be no doubt that restricting the freedom to marry solely because of racial classifications violates the central meaning of the Equal Protection Clause.

II

19

These statutes also deprive the Lovings of liberty without due process of law in violation of the Due Process Clause of the Fourteenth Amendment. The freedom to marry has long been recognized as one of the vital personal rights essential to the orderly pursuit of happiness by free men.

20

Marriage is one of the 'basic civil rights of man,' fundamental to our very existence and survival. . . . To deny this fundamental freedom on so unsupportable a basis as the racial classifications embodied in these statutes, classifications so directly subversive of the principle of equality at the heart of the Fourteenth Amendment, is surely to deprive all the State's citizens of liberty without due process of law. The Fourteenth Amendment requires that the freedom of choice to marry not be restricted by invidious racial discriminations. Under our Constitution, the freedom to marry or not marry, a person of another race resides with the individual and cannot be infringed by the State.

21

These convictions must be reversed. It is so ordered.

Source: Judge Earl Warren and the Supreme Court of the United States, *U.S. Reports: Loving v. Virginia,* 388 U.S. 1 (1967), periodical, https://www.loc.gov/item/usrep388001/.

Frances Beal, "Double Jeopardy: To Be Black and Female" (1970)

The idea that Black women and women of color experienced a double bind or dual oppression on account of their race and sex dates back to the nineteenth century with the testimonies of antislavery activists like Maria Stewart, Sojourner Truth, and Harriet Tubman and the efforts of Black suffragists to gain voting rights. Beal, who was only thirty years old when she authored "Double Jeopardy," drew on her activism in civil rights, peace, and leftist organizations as well as her experience as a Black feminist involved in Black women's liberation organizations to give voice to the multiple oppressions women of color faced, which included race, sex, and class, to say the least. In the excerpt below, Beal discusses the many ways in which Black women are oppressed and the costs of their exploitation.

. . . Unfortunately, there seems to be some confusion in the Movement today as to who has been oppressing whom. Since the advent of Black Power, the black male has exerted a more prominent leadership role in our struggle for justice in this country. He sees the System for what it really is for the most part, but where he rejects its values and mores on many issues, when it comes to women, he seems to take his guidelines from the pages of *Ladies' Home Journal*. Certain black men are maintaining that they have been castrated by society but that black women somehow escaped this persecution and even contributed to this emasculation. Let me state here and now that the black woman in America can justly be described as a "slave of a slave." By reducing the black man in America to such abject oppression, the black woman had no protector and was used, and is still being used in some cases, as the scapegoat for the evils that this horrendous system has perpetrated on black men. Her physical image has been maliciously maligned; she has been sexually molested and abused by the white colonizer; she has suffered the worse kind of economic exploitation, having been forced to serve as the white woman's maid and wet-nurse for white offspring while her own children were more often than not starving and neglected. It is the depth of degradation to be socially manipulated, physically raped, used to undermine your own household, and to be powerless to reverse this syndrome.

It is true that our husbands, fathers, brothers, and sons have been emasculated, lynched, and brutalized. They have suffered from the cruelest assault on mankind that the world has ever known. However, it is a gross distortion of fact to state that black women have oppressed black men. The capitalist system found it expedient to enslave and oppress them and proceeded to do so without consultation or the signing of any agreements with black women.

It must also be pointed out at this time that black women are not resentful of the rise to power of black men. We welcome it. We see in it the eventual liberation of all black people from this corrupt system of capitalism. Nevertheless, this does not mean that you have to negate one for the other. This kind of thinking is a product of miseducation; that it's either X or it's Y. It is fallacious reasoning that in order for the black man to be strong, the black woman has to be weak.

Those who are exerting their "manhood" by telling black women to step back into a domestic, submissive role are assuming a counterrevolutionary position. Black women likewise have been abused by the system, and we must begin talking about the elimination of all kinds of oppression. If we are talking about building a strong nation, capable of throwing off the yoke of capitalist oppression, then we are talking about the total involvement of every man, woman, and child, each with a highly developed political consciousness. We need our whole army out there dealing with the enemy and not half an army.

There are also some black women who feel that there is no more productive role in life than having and raising children. This attitude often reflects the conditioning of the society in which we live and is adopted from a bourgeois white model. Some young sisters who have never had to maintain a household and accept the confining role which this entails tend to romanticize (along with the help of a few brothers) this role of housewife and mother. Black women who have had to endure this kind of function are less apt to have these utopian visions.

Those who project in an intellectual manner how great and rewarding this role will be and who feel that the most important thing that they can contribute to the black nation is children are doing themselves a great injustice. This line of reasoning completely negates the contributions that black women have historically made to our struggle for liberation.

We live in a highly industrialized society, and every member of the black nation must be as academically and technologically developed as possible. To wage a revolution, we need competent teachers, doctors, nurses, electronics experts, chemists, biologists, physicists, political scientists, and so on and so forth. Black women sitting at home reading bedtime stories to their children are just not going to make it.

ECONOMIC EXPLOITATION OF BLACK WOMEN

Those industries which employ mainly black women are the most exploitive in the country. Domestic and hospital workers are good examples of this oppression; the garment workers in New York City provide us with another view of this economic slavery. The International Ladies Garment Workers Union (ILGWU), whose overwhelming membership consists of Black and Puerto Rican women, has a leadership that is nearly all lily-white and male. This leadership has been working in collusion with the ruling class and has completely sold its soul to the corporate structure.

To add insult to injury, the ILGWU has invested heavily in business enterprises in racist, apartheid South Africa—with union funds. Not only does this bought-off leadership contribute to our continued exploitation in this country by not truly representing the best interests of its membership, but it audaciously uses funds that black and Puerto Rican women have provided to support the economy of a vicious government that is engaged in the economic rape and murder of our black brothers and sisters in our Motherland, Africa.

The entire labor movement in the United States has suffered as a result of the superexploitation of black workers and women. The unions have historically been racist and chauvinistic. They have upheld racism in this country and have failed to fight the white skin privileges of white workers. They have failed to fight or even make an issue against the inequities in the hiring and pay of women workers. There has been virtually no struggle against either the racism of the white worker or the economic exploitation of the working woman, two factors that have consistently impeded the advancement of the real struggle against the ruling class.

BEDROOM POLITICS

I have briefly discussed the economic and psychological manipulation of black women, but perhaps the most outlandish act of oppression in modern times is the current campaign to promote sterilization of nonwhite women in an attempt to maintain the population and power imbalance between the white haves and the nonwhite have-nots.

These tactics are but another example of the many devious schemes that the ruling-class elite attempt to perpetrate on the black population in order to keep itself in control. It has recently come to our attention that a massive campaign for so-called birth control is presently being promoted not only in the underdeveloped nonwhite areas of the world, but also in black communities here in the United States. However, what the authorities in charge of these programs refer to as "birth control" is in fact nothing but a method of outright surgical genocide.

The United States has been sponsoring sterilization clinics in nonwhite countries, especially in India, where already some three million young men and boys in and around New Delhi have been sterilized in makeshift operating rooms set up by the American Peace Corps workers. Under these circumstances, it is understandable why certain countries view the Peace Corps not as a benevolent project, not as evidence of America's concern for underdeveloped areas, but rather as a threat to their very existence. This program could more aptly be named the Death Corps.

Vasectomy, which is performed on males and takes only six or seven minutes, is a relatively simple operation. The sterilization of a woman, on the other hand, is admittedly major surgery. This operation (salpingectomy)* must be performed in a hospital under general anesthesia. This method of "birth control" is a common procedure in Puerto Rico. Puerto Rico has long been used by the colonist exploiter, the United States, as a huge experimental laboratory for medical research before allowing certain practices to be imported and used here. When the birth control pill was first being perfected, it was tried out on Puerto Rican women and selected black women (poor), using them as human guinea pigs, to evaluate its effect and its efficiency.

These sterilization clinics are cropping up around the country in the black and Puerto Rican communities. These so-called maternity clinics specifically outfitted to purge black women or men of their reproductive possibilities are appearing more and more in hospitals and clinics across the country.

Threatened with the cut-off of relief funds, some black welfare women have been forced to accept this sterilization procedure in exchange for a continuation of welfare benefits. Black women are often afraid to permit any kind of necessary surgery because they know from bitter experience that they are more likely than not to come out of the hospital without their insides.

These outrageous Nazi-like procedures on the part of medical researchers are but another manifestation of the totally amoral and dehumanizing brutality that the capitalist system perpetrates on black women. The sterilization experiments carried on in concentration camps some twenty-five years ago have been denounced the world over, but no one seems to get upset by the repetition of these same racist tactics today in the United States of America—land of the free and home of the brave. This campaign is as nefarious a program as Germany's gas chambers, and, in a long-term sense, as effective and with the same objective.

The rigid laws concerning abortions in this country are another vicious means of subjugation and, indirectly, of outright murder. Rich white women somehow manage to obtain these operations with little or no difficulty. It is the poor black and Puerto Rican woman who is at the mercy of the local butcher. Statistics show us that the non-white death rate at the hands of the unqualified abortionist is substantially higher than for white women. Nearly half of the childbearing deaths in New York City are attributed to abortion alone, and out of these, seventy-nine percent are among nonwhites and Puerto Rican women.

We are not saying that black women should not practice birth control. *Black women have the right and the responsibility to determine when it is in the interest of the struggle to have children or not to have them, and this right must not be relinquished to anyone.* It is also her right and responsibility to determine when it is in her own best interests to have children, how many she will have, and how far apart.

The lack of the availability of safe birth control methods, the forced sterilization practices, and the inability to obtain legal abortions are all symptoms of a decadent society that jeopardizes the health of black women (and thereby the entire black race) in its attempts to control the very life processes of human beings. This is a symptom of a society that believes it has the right to bring political factors into the privacy of the bed-chamber. The elimination of these horrendous conditions will free black women for full participation in the revolution, and, thereafter in the building of the new society.

Source: Frances Beal, "Double Jeopardy," in *Words of Fire: An Anthology of African American Feminist Thought,* edited by Beverly Guy-Sheftall (New York: New Press, 1995), 146–55. Courtesy of Frances Beal.

DOCUMENT 9.8

Johnnie Tillmon, "Welfare Is a Women's Issue" (1972)

The concerns of poor women, especially those who needed government assistance and relied on welfare, began to permeate both the civil rights and the women's rights movements in the 1960s. When Johnnie Tillmon, a divorced single mother who could no longer work due to illness, applied for and began receiving welfare, she gained firsthand insight into the many restrictions placed on women on welfare and the ways in which they were often derided by the welfare system and wider society. Black women, in particular, had historically had a difficult relationship with this system—more often than not being excluded from receiving welfare benefits. Tillmon subsequently founded Aid to Needy Children (ANC) Mothers Anonymous in 1963 as an organization to advocate for women on welfare and their children. In 1972, she wrote a powerful essay on poverty as a feminist issue for *Ms. Magazine.* That same year, she succeeded George Wiley as executive director of the National Welfare Rights Organization and led the organization until its dissolution in 1975. The NWRO used direct and legal action to advance and protect the rights of welfare recipients, the majority of whom were women and children.

I'm a woman. I'm a black woman. I'm a poor woman. I'm a fat woman. I'm a middle-aged woman. And I'm on welfare.

In this country, if you're any one of those things—poor, black, fat, female, middle-aged, on welfare—you count less as a human being. If you're all those things, you don't count at all. Except as a statistic.

I am a statistic.

I am 45 years old. I have raised six children.

I grew up in Arkansas, and I worked there for fifteen years in a laundry, making about $20 or $30 a week, picking cotton on the side for carfare. I moved to California in 1959 and worked in a laundry there for nearly four years. In 1963 I got too sick to work anymore. Friends helped me to go on welfare.

They didn't call it welfare. They called it A.F.D.C.—Aid to Families with Dependent Children. Each month I got $363 for my kids and me. I pay $128 a month rent; $30 for utilities, which include gas, electricity, and water; $120 for food and nonedible household essentials; $50 for school lunches for the three children in junior and senior high school who are not eligible for reduced-cost meal programs.

There are millions of statistics like me. Some on welfare. Some not. And some, really poor, who don't even know they're entitled to welfare. Not all of them are black. Not at all. In fact, the majority—about two-thirds—of all the poor families in the country are white.

Welfare's like a traffic accident. It can happen to anybody, but especially it happens to women.

And that is why welfare is a women's issue. For a lot of middle-class women in this country, Women's Liberation is a matter of concern. For women on welfare it's a matter of survival.

Forty-four percent of all poor families are headed by women. That's bad enough. But the *families* on A.F.D.C. aren't really families. Because 99 percent of them are headed by women. That means there is no man around. In half the states there really can't be men around because A.F.D.C. says if there is an "able-bodied" man around, then you can't be on welfare. If the kids are going to eat, and the man can't get a job, then he's got to go. So his kids can eat.

The truth is that A.F.D.C. is like a supersexist marriage. You trade in a man for *the* man. But you can't divorce him if he treats you bad. He can divorce you, of course, cut you off anytime he wants. But in that case, *he* keeps the kids, not you.

The man runs everything. In ordinary marriage, sex is supposed to be for your husband. On A.F.D.C., you're not supposed to have any sex at all. You give up control of your own body. It's a condition of aid. You may even have to agree to get your tubes tied so you can never have more children just to avoid being off welfare.

The man, the welfare system, controls your money. He tells you what to buy, what not to buy, where to buy it, and how much things cost. If things—rent, for instance—really cost more than he says they do, it's just too bad for you.

There are other welfare programs, other kinds of people on welfare—the blind, the disabled, the aged. (Many of them are women too, especially the aged.) Those others make up just over a third of all the welfare caseloads. We A.F.D.C. are two-thirds.

But when the politicians talk about the "welfare cancer eating at our vitals," they're not talking about the aged, blind, and disabled. Nobody minds them. They're the "deserving poor." Politicians are talking about A.F.D.C. Politicians are talking about us—the women who head up 99 percent of the A.F.D.C. families—and our kids. We're the "cancer," the "undeserving poor." Mothers and children.

In this country we believe in something called the "work ethic." That means that your work is what gives you human worth. But the work ethic itself is a double standard. It applies to men and to women on welfare. It doesn't apply to all women. If you're a society lady from Scarsdale and you spend all your time sitting on your prosperity paring your nails, well, that's okay.

The truth is a job doesn't necessarily mean an adequate income. A woman with three kids—not twelve kids, mind you, just three kids—that woman earning the full federal minimum wage of $2.00 an hour, is still stuck in poverty. She is below the Government's own official poverty line. There are some ten million jobs that now pay less than the minimum wage, and if you're a woman, you've got the best chance of getting one.

The President keeps repeating the "dignity of work" idea. What dignity? Wages are the measure of dignity that society puts on a job. Wages and nothing else. There is no dignity in starvation. Nobody denies, least of all poor women, that there is dignity and satisfaction in being able to support your kids through honest labor.

We wish we could do it.

The problem is that our country's economic policies deny the dignity and satisfaction of self-sufficiency to millions of people—the millions who suffer everyday [sic] in underpaid dirty jobs and still don't have enough to survive.

People still believe that old lie that A.F.D.C. mothers keep on having kids just to get a bigger welfare check. On the average, another baby means another $35 a month—barely enough for food and clothing. Having babies for profit is a lie that only men could make up, and only men could believe. Men, who never have to bear the babies or have to raise them and maybe send them to war.

There are a lot of other lies that male society tells about welfare mothers; that A.F.D.C. mothers are immoral, that A.F.D.C. mothers are lazy, misuse their welfare checks, spend it all on booze and are stupid and incompetent.

If people are willing to believe these lies, it's partly because they're just special versions of the lies that society tells about all women. . . .

On TV, a woman learns that human worth means beauty and that beauty means being thin, white, young and rich.

She learns that her body is really disgusting the way it is, and that she needs all kinds of expensive cosmetics to cover it up.

She learns that a "real woman" spends her time worrying about how her bathroom bowl smells; that being important means being middle class, having two cars, a house in the suburbs, and a minidress under your maxicoat. In other words, an A.F.D.C. mother learns that being a "real woman" means being all the things she isn't and having all the things she can't have.

Either it breaks you, and you start hating yourself, or you break it.

There's one good thing about welfare. It kills your illusions about yourself, and about where this society is really at. It's laid out for you straight. You have to learn to fight, to be aggressive, or you just don't make it. If you can survive being on welfare, you can survive anything. It gives you a kind of freedom, a sense of your own power and togetherness with other women.

Maybe it is we poor welfare women who will really liberate women in this country. We've already started on our welfare plan.

Along with other welfare recipients, we have organized together so we can have some voice. Our group is called the National Welfare Rights Organization (N.W.R.O.). We put together our own welfare plan, called Guaranteed Adequate Income (G.A.I.), which would eliminate sexism from welfare.

There would be no "categories"—men, women, children, single, married, kids, no kids—just poor people who need aid. You'd get paid according to need and family size only—$6,500 for a family of four (which is the Department of Labor's estimate of what's adequate), and that would be upped as the cost of living goes up.

If I were president, I would solve this so-called welfare crisis in a minute and go a long way toward liberating every woman. I'd just issue a proclamation that "women's" work is *real* work.

In other words, I'd start paying women a living wage for doing the work we are already doing—child-raising and house-keeping. And the welfare crisis would be over, just like that. Housewives would be getting wages, too—a legally determined percentage of their husband's salary—instead of having to ask for and account for money they've already earned.

For me, Women's Liberation is simple. No woman in this country can feel dignified, no woman can be liberated, until all women get off their knees. That's what N.W.R.O. is all about—women standing together, on their feet.

Source: Johnnie Tillmon, "Welfare Is a Women's Issue," *Ms. Magazine*, Spring 1972, https://www .bitchmedia.org/sites/default/files/documents/tillmon_welfare.pdf. Reprinted by permission of *Ms. Magazine*, copyright © 1972.

DOCUMENT 9.9

The Combahee River Collective, a Black Feminist Statement (1977)

In 1973, a group of Black lesbian feminists, including Barbara Smith and Demita Frazier, met at regional meeting in Boston of the National Black Feminist Organization and decided to author a statement that reflected their more radical politics and centered their struggles against oppression on the basis of their race, class, sex, and sexuality. In the next year, the women continued to meet and adopted their name from the Combahee River Raid led by Harriet Tubman during the Civil War in which hundreds of enslaved peoples were freed. The Combahee River Collective statement became one of the defining declarations of Black feminism and intersectionality. The collective operated from 1974 to 1980.

THE COMBAHEE RIVER COLLECTIVE STATEMENT

Combahee River Collective

We are a collective of Black feminists who have been meeting together since 1974. During that time we have been involved in the process of defining and clarifying our politics, while at the same time doing political work within our own group and in coalition with other progressive organizations and movements. The most general statement of our politics at the present time would be that we are actively committed to struggling against racial, sexual, heterosexual, and class oppression, and see as our particular task the development of integrated analysis and practice based upon the fact that the major systems of oppression are interlocking.... As Black women we see Black feminism as the logical political movement to combat the manifold and simultaneous oppressions that all women of color face....

1. THE GENESIS OF CONTEMPORARY BLACK FEMINISM

Before looking at the recent development of Black feminism we would like to affirm that we find our origins in the historical reality of Afro-American women's continuous life-and-death struggle for survival and liberation. Black women's extremely negative relationship to the American political system (a system of white male rule) has always been determined by our membership in two oppressed racial and sexual castes.... There have always been Black women activists—some known, like Sojourner Truth, Harriet Tubman, Frances E. W. Harper, Ida B. Wells Barnett, and Mary Church Terrell, and thousands upon thousands unknown—who have had a shared awareness of how their sexual identity combined with their racial identity to make their whole life situation and the focus of their political struggles unique. Contemporary Black feminism is the outgrowth of countless generations of personal sacrifice, militancy, and work by our mothers and sisters.

A Black feminist presence has evolved most obviously in connection with the second wave of the American women's movement beginning in the late 1960s. Black, other Third World, and working women have been involved in the feminist movement from its start, but both outside reactionary forces and racism and elitism within the movement itself have served to obscure our participation. In 1973, Black feminists, primarily located in New York, felt the necessity of forming a separate Black feminist group. This became the National Black Feminist Organization (NBFO).

Black feminist politics also have an obvious connection to movements for Black liberation, particularly those of the 1960s and 1970s. Many of us were active in those movements (Civil Rights, Black nationalism, the Black Panthers), and all of our lives Were greatly affected and changed by their ideologies, their goals, and the tactics used to achieve their goals. It was our experience and disillusionment within these liberation movements, as well as experience on the periphery of the white male left, that led to the need to develop a politics that was anti-racist, unlike those of white women, and anti-sexist, unlike those of Black and white men.

... Black feminists and many more Black women who do not define themselves as feminists have all experienced sexual oppression as a constant factor in our day-to-day existence. As children we realized that we were different from boys and that we were treated differently. For example, we were told in the same breath to be quiet both for the sake of being "ladylike" and to make us less objectionable in the eyes of white people. As we grew older we became aware of the threat of physical and sexual abuse by men....

Black feminists often talk about their feelings of craziness before becoming conscious of the concepts of sexual politics, patriarchal rule, and most importantly, feminism, the political analysis and practice that we women use to struggle against our oppression. The fact that racial politics and indeed racism are pervasive factors in our lives did not allow us, and still does not allow most Black women, to look more deeply into our own experiences and, from that sharing and growing consciousness, to build a politics that will change our lives and inevitably end our oppression. Our development must also be tied to the contemporary economic and political position of Black people. The post World War II generation of Black youth was the first to be able to minimally partake of certain educational and employment options, previously closed completely to Black people. Although our economic position is still at the very bottom of the American capitalistic economy, a handful of us have been able to gain certain tools as a result of tokenism in education and employment which potentially enable us to more effectively fight our oppression.

A combined anti-racist and anti-sexist position drew us together initially, and as we developed politically we addressed ourselves to heterosexism and economic oppression under capItalism [*sic*].

2. WHAT WE BELIEVE

Above all else, Our politics initially sprang from the shared belief that Black women are inherently valuable, that our liberation is a necessity not as an adjunct to somebody else's. . . . This may seem so obvious as to sound simplistic, but it is apparent that no other ostensibly progressive movement has ever consIdered [*sic*] our specific oppression as a priority or worked seriously for the ending of that oppression. Merely naming the pejorative stereotypes attributed to Black women (e.g. mammy, matriarch, Sapphire, whore, bulldagger), let alone cataloguing the cruel, often murderous, treatment we receive, Indicates how little value has been placed upon our lives during four centuries of bondage in the Western hemisphere. We realize that the only people who care enough about us to work consistently for our liberation are us. Our politics evolve from a healthy love for ourselves, our sisters and our community which allows us to continue our struggle and work.

This focusing upon our own oppression is embodied in the concept of identity politics. We believe that the most profound and potentially most radical politics come directly out of our own identity, as opposed to working to end somebody else's oppression. In the case of Black women this is a particularly repugnant, dangerous, threatening, and therefore revolutionary concept because it is obvious from looking at all the political movements that have preceded us that anyone is more worthy of liberation than ourselves. We reject pedestals, queenhood, and walking ten paces behind. To be recognized as human, levelly human, is enough.

We believe that sexual politics under patriarchy is as pervasive in Black women's lives as are the politics of class and race. We also often find it difficult to separate race from class from sex oppression because in our lives they are most often experienced simultaneously. We know that there is such a thing as racial-sexual oppression which is neither solely racial nor solely sexual, e.g., the history of rape of Black women by white men as a weapon of political repression.

Although we are feminists and Lesbians, we feel solidarity with progressive Black men and do not advocate the fractionalization that white women who are separatists demand. Our situation as Black people necessitates that we have solidarity around the fact of race, which white women of course do not need to have with white men, unless it is their negative solidarity as racial oppressors. We struggle together with Black men against racism, while we also struggle with Black men about sexism.

We realize that the liberation of all oppressed peoples necessitates the destruction of the political-economic systems of capitalism and imperialism as well as patriarchy. We are socialists because we believe that work must be organized for the collective benefit of those who do the work and create the products, and not for the profit of the bosses. Material resources must be equally distributed among those who create these resources. We are not convinced, however, that a socialist revolution that is not also a feminist and anti-racist revolution will guarantee our liberation. We have arrived at the necessity for developing an understanding of class relationships that takes into account the specific class position of Black women who are generally marginal in the labor force, while at this particular time some of us are temporarily viewed as doubly desirable tokens at white-collar and professional levels. We need to articulate the real class situation of persons who are not merely raceless, sexless workers, but for whom racial and sexual oppression are significant determinants in their working/economic lives. Although we are in essential agreement with Marx's theory as it applied to the very specific economic relationships he analyzed, we know that his analysis must be extended further in order for us to understand our specific economic situation as Black women.

A political contribution which we feel we have already made is the expansion of the feminist principle that the personal is political. In our consciousness-raising sessions, for example, we have in many ways gone beyond white women's revelations because we are dealing with the implications of race and class as well as sex. Even our Black women's style of talking/testifying in Black language about what we have experienced has a resonance that is both cultural and political. We have spent a great deal of energy delving into the cultural and experiential nature of our oppression out of necessity because none of these matters has ever been looked at before. No one before has ever examined the multilayered texture of Black women's lives. An example of this kind of revelation/conceptualization occurred at a meeting as we discussed the ways in which our early intellectual interests had been attacked by our peers, particularly Black males. We discovered that all of us, because we were "smart" had also been considered "ugly," i.e., "smart-ugly." "Smart-ugly" crystallized the way in which most of us had been forced to develop our intellects at great cost to our "social" lives. The sanctions In the Black and white communities against Black women thinkers is comparatively much higher than for white women, particularly ones from the educated middle and upper classes.

As we have already stated, we reject the stance of Lesbian separatism because it is not a viable political analysis or strategy for us. It leaves out far too much and far too many people, particularly Black men, women, and children. We have a great deal of criticism and loathing for what men have been socialized to be in this society: what they support, how they act, and how they oppress. But we do not have the misguided notion that it is their maleness, per se—i.e., their biological maleness—that makes them what they are. As Black [sic] women we find any type of biological determinism a particularly dangerous and reactionary basis upon which to build a politic. . . .

3. PROBLEMS IN ORGANIZING BLACK FEMINISTS

During our years together as a Black feminist collective we have experienced success and defeat, joy and pain, victory and failure. We have found that it is very difficult to organize around Black feminist issues, difficult even to announce in certain contexts that we are Black feminists. We have tried to think about the reasons for our difficulties, particularly since the white women's movement continues to be strong and to grow in many directions. In this section we will discuss some of the general reasons for the organizing problems we face and also talk specifically about the stages in organizing our own collective.

The major source of difficulty in our political work is that we are not just trying to fight oppression on one front or even two, but instead to address a whole range of oppressions. We do not have racial, sexual, heterosexual, or class privilege to rely upon, nor do we have even the minimal access to resources and power that groups who possess anyone [*sic*] of these types of privilege have. . . .

Feminism is, nevertheless, very threatening to the majority of Black people because it calls into question some of the most basic assumptions about our existence, i.e., that sex should be a determinant of power relationships. Here is the way male and female roles were defined in a Black nationalist pamphlet from the early 1970s:

> We understand that it is and has been traditional that the man is the head of the house. He is the leader of the house/nation because his knowledge of the world is broader, his awareness is greater, his understanding is fuller and his application of this information is wiser . . . After all, it is only reasonable that the man be the head of the house because he is able to defend and protect the development of his home . . . Women cannot do the same things as men— they are made by nature to function differently. Equality of men and women is something that cannot happen even in the abstract world. Men are not equal to other men, i.e. ability, experience or even understanding. The value of men and women can be seen as in the value of gold and silver—they are not equal but both have great value. We must realize that men and women are a complement to each other because there is no house/family without a man and his wife. Both are essential to the development of any life.

The material conditions of most Black women would hardly lead them to upset both economic and sexual arrangements that seem to represent some stability in their lives. Many Black women have a good understanding of both sexism and racism, but because of the everyday constrictions of their lives, cannot risk struggling against them both.

The reaction of Black men to feminism has been notoriously negative. They are, of course, even more threatened than Black women by the possibility that Black feminists might organize around our own needs. They realize that they might not only lose valuable and hardworking allies in their struggles but that they might also be forced to change their habitually sexist ways of interacting with and oppressing Black women. Accusations that Black feminism divides the Black struggle are powerful deterrents to the growth of an autonomous Black women's movement. . . .

4. BLACK FEMINIST ISSUES AND PROJECTS

During our time together we have identified and worked on many issues of particular relevance to Black women. The inclusiveness of our politics makes us concerned with any situation that impinges upon the lives of women, Third World and working people. We are of course particularly committed to working on those struggles in which race, sex, and class are simultaneous factors in oppression. We might, for example, become involved in workplace organizing at a factory that employs Third World women or picket a hospital that is cutting back on already inadequate heath care to a Third World community, or set up a rape crisis center in a Black neighborhood. Organizing around welfare and daycare concerns might also be a focus. The work to be done and the countless issues that this work represents merely reflect the pervasiveness of our oppression.

Issues and projects that collective members have actually worked on are sterilization abuse, abortion rights, battered women, rape and health care. We have also done many workshops and educationals on Black feminism on college campuses, at women's conferences, and most recently for high school women.

One issue that is of major concern to us and that we have begun to publicly address is racism in the white women's movement. As Black feminists we are made constantly and painfully aware of how little effort white women have made to understand and combat their racism, which requires among other things that they have a more than superficial comprehension of race, color, and Black history and culture. Eliminating racism in the white women's movement is by definition work for white women to do, but we will continue to speak to and demand accountability on this issue.

In the practice of our politics we do not believe that the end always justifies the means. Many reactionary and destructive acts have been done in the name of achieving "correct" political goals. As feminists we do not want to mess over people in the name of politics. We believe in collective process and a nonhierarchical distribution of power within our own group and in our vision of a revolutionary society. We are committed to a continual examination of our politics as they develop through criticism and self-criticism as an essential aspect of our practice. . . .

Source: The Combahee River Collective, "The Combahee River Collective Statement," April 1977, Women's and Gender Studies Web Archive, Library of Congress. https://www.loc.gov/item/lcwaN0028151/.

DOCUMENT 9.10

Huey P. Newton, Speech on Women's and Gay Liberation Movement (1970)

Huey Newton, cofounder of the Black Panther Party, delivered the following speech in New York City in which he called for unity among Black, women's, and gay liberation groups as all three were oppressed peoples. Newton argued that revolutionary thought and action within the women's liberation and gay liberation movements could lead to potential alliances. His remarks departed from widespread assumptions that the Panthers and other Black liberation groups were both homophobic and sexist. Contradictory gender politics on the part of Newton and other male party members did exist, as women in the Black Panther Party did experience varying levels of sexism and violence.

During the past few years strong movements have developed among women and among homosexuals seeking their liberation. There has been some uncertainty about how to relate to these movements.

Whatever your personal opinions and your insecurities about homosexuality and the various liberation movements among homosexuals and women (and I speak of the homosexuals and women as oppressed groups), we should try to unite with them in a revolutionary fashion.

I say "whatever your insecurities are" because as we very well know, sometimes our first instinct is to want to hit a homosexual in the mouth, and want a woman to be quiet. We want to hit a homosexual in the mouth because we are afraid that we might be homosexual; and we want to hit the women or shut her up because we are afraid that she might castrate us, or take the nuts that we might not have to start with.

We must gain security in ourselves and therefore have respect and feelings for all oppressed people. We must not use the racist attitude that the white racists use against our people because they are Black and poor. Many times the poorest white person is the most racist because he is afraid that he might lose something, or discover something that he does not have. So you're some kind of a threat to him. This kind of psychology is in operation when we view oppressed people and we are angry with them because of their particular kind of behavior, or their particular kind of deviation from the established norm.

Remember, we have not established a revolutionary value system; we are only in the process of establishing it. I do not remember our ever constituting any value that said that a revolutionary must say offensive things towards homosexuals, or that a revolutionary should make sure that women do not speak out about their own particular kind of oppression. As a matter of fact, it is just the opposite: we say that we recognize the women's right to be free. We have not said much about the homosexual at all, but we must relate to the homosexual movement because it is a real thing. And I know through reading, and through my life experience and observations that homosexuals are not given freedom and liberty by anyone in the society. They might be the most oppressed people in the society.

And what made them homosexual? Perhaps it's a phenomenon that I don't understand entirely. Some people say that it is the decadence of capitalism. I don't know if that is the case; I rather doubt it. But whatever the case is, we know that homosexuality is a fact that exists, and we must understand it in its purest form: that is, a person should have the freedom to use his body in whatever way he wants.

That is not endorsing things in homosexuality that we wouldn't view as revolutionary. But there is nothing to say that a homosexual cannot also be a revolutionary. And maybe I'm now injecting some of my prejudice by saying that "even a homosexual can be a revolutionary." Quite the contrary, maybe a homosexual could be the most revolutionary.

When we have revolutionary conferences, rallies, and demonstrations, there should be full participation of the gay liberation movement and the women's liberation movement. Some groups might be more revolutionary than others. We should not use the actions of a few to say that they are all reactionary or counter-revolutionary, because they are not.

We should deal with the factions just as we deal with any other group or party that claims to be revolutionary. We should try to judge, somehow, whether they are operating in a sincere revolutionary fashion and from a really oppressed situation. (And we will grant that if they are women they are probably oppressed.) If they do things that are unrevolutionary or counter-revolutionary, then criticize that action.

If we feel that the group in spirit means to be revolutionary in practice, but they make mistakes in interpretation of the revolutionary philosophy, or they do not understand the dialectics of the social forces in operation, we should criticize that and not criticize them because they are women trying to be free. And the same is true for homosexuals. We should never say a whole movement is dishonest when in fact they are trying to be honest. They are just making honest mistakes. Friends are allowed to make mistakes. The enemy is not allowed to make mistakes because his whole existence is a mistake, and we suffer from it. But the women's liberation front and gay liberation front are our friends, they are our potential allies, and we need as many allies as possible.

We should be willing to discuss the insecurities that many people have about homosexuality. When I say "insecurities," I mean the fear that they are some kind of threat to our manhood. I can understand this fear. Because of the long conditioning process which builds insecurity in the American male, homosexuality might produce certain hang-ups in us. I have hang-ups myself about male homosexuality. But on the other hand, I have no hang-up about female homosexuality. And that is a phenomenon in itself. I think it is probably because male homosexuality is a threat to me and female homosexuality is not.

We should be careful about using those terms that might turn our friends off. The terms "faggot" and "punk" should be deleted from our vocabulary, and especially we should not attach names normally designed for homosexuals to men who are enemies of the people, such as [Richard] Nixon or [John] Mitchell. Homosexuals are not enemies of the people.

We should try to form a working coalition with the gay liberation and women's liberation groups. We must always handle social forces in the most appropriate manner. And this is really a significant part of the population, both women, and the growing number of homosexuals that we have to deal with.

ALL POWER TO THE PEOPLE!

Source: Huey P. Newton, "A Letter from Huey to the Revolutionary Brothers and Sisters about the Women's Liberation and Gay Liberation Movements," in pamphlet, *Gay Flames*, 7 (1970). Open JSTOR Collection, CC BY-NC 4.0 (https://creativecommons.org/licenses/by-nc/4.0/).

James Baldwin Discusses Homosexuality, Homophobia, and Racism (1984)

Born in Harlem in 1924, James Baldwin became a preeminent writer and playwright whose works like *Go Tell It on the Mountain* and *If Beale Street Could Talk* explored Black life in America and the pervasiveness of racism. Yet unlike many of his other writings, Baldwin's second novel, *Giovanni's Room*, explored love through a white male homosexual couple. Baldwin, who was gay and a prominent civil rights activist, could not find an American publisher who would back the novel due to its content, so it was published in 1956 by a publisher in England. Though Baldwin would continue to write about and speak out on racism in America, he eventually relocated to Paris; he died in France in 1987. In the following interview with Richard Goldstein, Baldwin discusses his thoughts on homosexuality, homophobia, and racism in America.

GOLDSTEIN: When I consider what a risk it must have been to write about homosexuality when you did . . .

BALDWIN: You're talking about *Giovanni's Room*. Yeah, that was rough. But I had to do it to clarify something for myself.

GOLDSTEIN: What was that?

BALDWIN: Where I was in the world. I mean, what I'm made of. Anyways, *Giovanni's Room* is not really about homosexuality. It's the vehicle through which the book moves. *Go Tell It on the Mountain*, for example, is not about a church, and *Giovanni* is not really about homosexuality. It's about what happens to you if you're afraid to love anybody. Which is much more interesting than the question of homosexuality.

. . .

GOLDSTEIN:: Did people advise you not to write the book so candidly?

BALDWIN: I didn't ask anybody. When I turned the book in, I was told I shouldn't have written it. I was told to bear in mind that I was a young Negro writer with a certain audience, and I wasn't supposed to alienate that audience. And if I published the book, it would wreck my career. They wouldn't publish the book, they said, as a favor to me. So I took the book to England and I sold it there before I sold it here.

. . .

GOLDSTEIN: I don't think straight people realize how frightening it is to finally admit to yourself that this is going to be you forever.

BALDWIN: It's very frightening. But the so-called straight person is no safer than I am really. Loving anybody and being loved by anybody is a tremendous danger, a tremendous responsibility. Loving of children, raising of children. The terrors homosexuals go through in this society would not be so great if the society itself did not go through so many terrors which it doesn't want to admit. The discovery of one's sexual preference doesn't have to be a trauma. It's a trauma because it's such a traumatized society.

. . .

GOLDSTEIN: Is there a particularly American component of homophobia?

BALDWIN: I think Americans are terrified of feeling anything. And homophobia is simply an extreme example of the American terror that's concerned with growing up. I never met a people more infantile in my life.

. . .

GOLDSTEIN: Are you as apocalyptic about the prospects for sexual reconciliation as you are about racial reconciliation?

BALDWIN: Well, they join. The sexual question and the racial question have always been entwined, you know. If Americans can mature on the level of racism, then they have to mature on the level of sexuality.

GOLDSTEIN: I think we would agree there's a retrenchment going on in race relations. Do you sense that happening also in sex relations?

BALDWIN: Yeah. There's what we would have to call a backlash which, I'm afraid, is just beginning.

GOLDSTEIN: I suspect most gay people have fantasies about genocide.

BALDWIN: Well, it's not a fantasy exactly since the society makes its will toward you very, very clear. Especially the police, for example, or truck drivers. I know from my own experience that the macho men—truck drivers, cops, football players—these people are far more complex than they want to realize. That's why I call them infantile. They have needs which, for them, are literally inexpressible. They don't dare look into the mirror. And that is why they need faggots. They've created faggots in order to act out a sexual fantasy on the body of another man and not take any responsibility for it. Do you see what I mean? I think it's very important for the male homosexual to recognize that he is a sexual target for other men, and that is why he is despised, and why he is called a faggot. He is called a faggot because other males need him.

GOLDSTEIN: Why do you think homophobia falls so often on the right of the political spectrum?

BALDWIN: It's a way of controlling people. Nobody really cares who goes to bed with whom, finally. I mean, the State doesn't really care, the Church doesn't really care. They care that you should be frightened of what you do. As long as you feel guilty about it, the State can rule you. It's a way of exerting control over the universe, by terrifying people.

GOLDSTEIN: Why don't black ministers need to share in this rhetoric?

BALDWIN: Perhaps because they're more grown-up than most white ministers.

GOLDSTEIN: Did you never hear antigay rhetoric in church?

BALDWIN: Not in the church I grew up in. I'm sure that's still true. Everyone is a child of God, according to us.

GOLDSTEIN: Didn't people ever call you "faggot" uptown?

BALDWIN: Of course. But there's a difference in the way it's used. It's got less venom, at least in my experience. I don't know of anyone who has ever denied his brother or his sister because they were gay. No doubt it happens. It must happen. But in the generality, a black person has got quite a lot to get through the day without getting entangled in all the American fantasies.

GOLDSTEIN: Do black gay people have the same sense of being separate as white gay people do? I mean, I feel distinct from other white people.

BALDWIN: Well, that I think is because you are penalized, as it were, unjustly; you're placed outside a certain safety to which you think you were born. A black gay person who is a sexual conundrum to society is already, long before the question of sexuality comes into it, menaced and marked because he's black or she's black. The sexual question comes after the question of color; it's simply one more aspect of the danger in which all black people live. I think white gay people feel cheated because they were born, in principle, into a society in which they were supposed to be safe. The anomaly of their sexuality puts them in danger, unexpectedly. Their reaction seems to me in direct proportion to the sense of feeling cheated of the advantages which accrue to white people in a white society. There's an element, it has always seemed to me, of bewilderment and complaint. Now that may sound very harsh, but the gay world as such is no more prepared to accept black people than anywhere else in society. It's a very hermetically sealed world with very unattractive features, including racism.

· · ·

GOLDSTEIN: Do you think black people have heightened capacity for tolerance, even acceptance, in its truest sense?

BALDWIN: Well, there is a capacity in black people for experience, simply. And that capacity makes other things possible. It dictates the depth of one's acceptance of other people. The capacity for experience is what burns out fear. Because the homophobia we're talking about really is a kind of fear. It's a terror of flesh. It's really a terror of being able to be touched.

· · ·

GOLDSTEIN: Do you think of the gay world as being a false refuge?

BALDWIN: I think perhaps it imposes a limitation which is unnecessary. It seems to me simply a man is a man, a woman is a woman, and who they go to bed with is nobody's business but theirs. I suppose what I am really saying is that one's sexual preference is a private matter. I resent the interference of the State, or the Church, or any institution in my only journey to whatever it is we are journeying toward. But it has been made a public question by the institutions of this country. I can see how the gay world comes about in response to that. And to contradict myself, I suppose, or more precisely, I hope that it is easier for the transgressor to become reconciled with himself or herself than it was for many people in my generation—and it was difficult for me. It is difficult to be despised, in short. And if the so-called gay movement can cause men and women, boys and girls, to come to some kind of terms with themselves more speedily and with less pain, then that's a very great advance. I'm not sure it can be done on that level. My own point of view, speaking out of black America, when I had to try to answer that stigma, that species of social curse, it seemed a great mistake to answer in the language of the oppressor. As long as I react as a "nigger," as long as I protest my case on evidence or assumptions held by others, I'm simply reinforcing those assumptions. As long as I complain about being oppressed, the oppressor is in consolation of knowing that I know my place, so to speak.

Source: James Baldwin, interview with Richard Goldstein, June 26, 1984, in James Baldwin, *James Baldwin: The Last Interview and Other Conversations*, with contributions by Quincy Troupe et al. (Brooklyn: Melville House, 2014), 57–74. http://www.richardgoldsteinonline.com/uploads/2/5/3/2/25321994/richardgoldstein -jamesbaldwininterview.pdf. Courtesy of Richard Goldstein.

Bayard Rustin, "From Montgomery to Stonewall" (1986)

Bayard Rustin was a skilled civil rights strategist whose efforts contributed to the 1941 March on Washington Movement, the 1947 Journey of Reconciliation, and the 1963 March on Washington. He was also involved in the labor movement and at various points in his life was a member of the Quakers and communist organizations. In 1953, Rustin was arrested and served time in jail for engaging in sexual activity with a man in a parked car in California. Martin Luther King and members of the SCLC valued his contributions to the movement, but remained uncomfortable with his sexuality. As an openly gay man, Rustin often worked behind the scenes in the civil rights movement, fearing that his sexuality would be used against the movement and the initiatives he was involved in. In the 1980s, Rustin became more outspoken about the struggles of gay men and women and argued that their struggles, similar to the struggle of Blacks, was a struggle for human rights. He writes about this in his 1986 essay, "From Montgomery to Stonewall."

In 1955 when Rosa Parks sat down and began the Montgomery Bus Protest, if anyone had said that it would be the beginning of a most extraordinary revolution, most people, including myself, would have doubted it.

But revolutionary beginnings are often unpredictable. Consider, for example, Russia. In 1917 Lenin was in Switzerland writing a book indicating that the Russian Revolution could not possibly begin before 1925. Then, a most unusual thing happened. Some women in a factory were cold, and to warm themselves they decided to go out into the street and parade around the plaza. Some Russian soldiers, upon seeing these women, assumed that they were making a protest and joined them. Thus the Russian Revolution began!

Consider now gay rights. In 1969, in New York of all places, in Greenwich Village, a group of gay people were in a bar. Recall that the 1960s was a period of extreme militancy—there were antiwar demonstrations, civil rights demonstrations, and women's rights demonstrations. The patrons of the bar added gay rights demonstration to the list. The events began when several cops moved into the bar to close it down, a very common practice in that period, forcing many gay bars to go underground. The cops were rough and violent, and, for the first time in the history of the United States, gays, as a collective group, fought back—and not just that night but the following night, and the next, and the night after that.

That was the beginning of an extraordinary revolution, similar to the Montgomery Bus Boycott in that it was not expected that anything extraordinary would occur. As in the case of the women who left the Russian factory, and as in the case of Rosa Parks who sat down in the white part of the bus, something began to happen. People began to protest. They began to fight for the right to live in dignity, the right to resist arbitrary behavior on the part of authorities, the right essentially to be one's self in every respect, and the right to be protected under law. In other words, people began to fight for their human rights.

Gay people must continue this protest. This will not be easy, in part because homosexuality remains an identity that is subject to a "we/they" distinction. People who would not say, "I am like this, but black people are like that," or "we are like this, but women are like that," or "we are like this, but Jews are like that," find it extremely simple to say, "homosexuals are like that, but we are like this." That's what makes our struggle the central struggle of our time, the central struggle for democracy and the central struggle for human rights. If gay people do not understand that, they do not understand the opportunity before them, nor do they understand the terrifying burdens they carry on their shoulders.

There are four burdens, which gays, along with every other despised group, whether it is blacks following slavery and reconstruction, or Jews fearful of Germany, must address. The first is to recognize that one must overcome fear. The second is overcoming self-hate. The third is overcoming self-denial. The fourth burden is more political. It is to recognize that the job of the gay community is not to deal with extremists who would castrate us or put us on an island and drop an H-bomb on us. The fact of the matter is that there is a small percentage of people in America who understand the true nature of the homosexual community. There is another small percentage who will never understand us. Our job is not to get those people who dislike us to love us. Nor was our aim in the civil rights movement to get prejudiced white people to love us. Our aim was to try to create the kind of America, legislatively, morally, and psychologically, such that even though some whites continued to hate us, they could not openly manifest that hate. That's our job today: to control the extent to which people can publicly manifest antigay sentiment.

Well, what do we have to do that is concrete? We have to fight for legislation wherever we are, to state our case clearly, as blacks had to do in the South when it was profoundly uncomfortable. Some people say to me, "Well, Mr. Rustin, how long is it going to take?" Let me point out to you that it doesn't take a law to get rid of a practice. The NAACP worked for sixty years to get an antilynch law in this country. We never got an antilynch law, and now we don't need one. It was the propaganda for the law we never got that liberated us.

Source: Bayard Rustin, "From Montgomery to Stonewall," adapted from a 1986 speech at the University of Pennsylvania, in *Time on Two Crosses: The Collected Writings of Bayard Rustin*, edited by Devon W. Carbado and Donald Weise (San Francisco: Cleis Press, 2003), 271–72. Courtesy of the Estate of Bayard Rustin.

FURTHER READING

Brown, Elaine. *A Taste of Power: A Black Women's Story*. New York: Anchor Books, 1992.

Carbado, Devon, and Donald Weise, eds. *Time on Two Crosses: The Collected Writings of Bayard Rustin*. Jersey City, NJ: Cleis Press, 2015.

Cashin, Sheryll. *Loving: Interracial Intimacy in America and the Threat to White Supremacy*. Boston: Beacon Press, 2018.

Collier-Thomas, Bettye, and V. P. Franklin. *Sisters in the Struggle: African American Women in the Civil Rights–Black Power Movement*. New York: New York University Press, 2001.

Crawford, Vicki L., et al. *Women in the Civil Rights Movement: Trailblazers and Torch-bearers, 1941–1965.* Bloomington: Indiana University Press, 1993.

Gore, Dayo, Jeanne Theoharis, and Komozi Woodard, eds. *Want to Start a Revolution? Radical Women in the Black Freedom Struggle.* New York: New York University Press, 2009.

Hansberry, Lorraine. *To Be Young, Gifted and Black.* Edited by Robert Nemiroff. New York: Vintage Books, 1995.

Height, Dorothy. *Open Wide the Gates of Freedom: A Memoir.* New York: PublicAffairs, 2005.

Hill Collins, Patricia. *Black Feminist Thought: Knowledge, Consciousness and the Politics of Empowerment.* New York: Routledge, 2008.

Holsaert, Faith S., et al. *Hands on the Freedom Plow: Personal Accounts by Women in SNCC.* Urbana: University of Illinois Press, 2012.

Houck, Davis W., and David E. Dizon, eds. *Women and the Civil Rights Movement, 1954–1965.* Jackson: University Press of Mississippi, 2009.

Leeming, David. *James Baldwin: A Biography.* New York: Arcade, 2015.

Ling, Peter, and Sharon Monteith, eds. *Gender and the Civil Rights Movement.* New Brunswick, NJ: Rutgers University Press, 2004.

McGuire, Danielle. *At the Dark End of the Street: Black Women, Rape, and Resistance—a New History of the Civil Rights Movement from Rosa Parks to the Rise of Black Power.* New York: Vintage Books, 2011.

Mumford, Kevin. *Not Straight, Not White: Black Gay Men from the March on Washington to the AIDS Crisis.* Chapel Hill: University of North Carolina Press, 2016.

Murray, Pauli. *Song in a Weary Throat: Memoir of an American Pilgrimage.* New York: Liveright, 2018.

Perry, Imani. *Looking for Lorraine Hansberry: The Radiant and Radical Life of Lorraine Hansberry.* Boston: Beacon Press, 2018.

Phelps, Christopher. "The Sexuality of Malcolm X." *Journal of American Studies* 51, no. 3 (2017): 659–90.

Ransby, Barbara. *Ella Baker and the Black Freedom Movement.* Chapel Hill: University of North Carolina Press, 2005.

Robnett, Belinda. *How Long? How Long? African American Women in the Struggle for Civil Rights.* Oxford: Oxford University Press, 2000.

Rosenberg, Rosalind. *Jane Crow: The Life of Pauli Murray.* Oxford: Oxford University Press, 2020.

Spencer, Robyn C. *The Revolution Has Come: Black Power, Gender and the Black Panther Party in Oakland.* Durham, NC: Duke University Press, 2016.

Taylor, Keeanga-Yamahtta. *How We Get Free: Black Feminism and the Combahee River Collective.* Chicago: Haymarket Books, 2017.

Tuuri, Rebecca. *Strategic Sisterhood: The National Council of Negro Women in the Black Freedom Struggle.* Chapel Hill: University of North Carolina Press, 2018.

Wallenstein, Peter. *Race, Sex and the Freedom to Marry: "Loving v. Virginia."* Lawrence: University Press of Kansas, 2014.

10

Culture and the Movement

What was the role of culture in the civil rights movement? How did African Americans use cultural art forms like music and theater to project their struggles for freedom to the nation and the larger world? How did Blacks and whites employ culture in their efforts to improve the Black condition in the twentieth century? In what ways did culture reflect the nation's race problem? And to what extent did mainstream media engage civil rights struggles and efforts to integrate sites of cultural production?

Since slavery, African Americans have used song, dance, the press, and other cultural forms of expression to protest the violence of being Black in the United States. During the civil rights movement, activists and leaders understood that culture could unite and galvanize support, foster racial solidarity, offer relief from the labors of protest, be used to reject centuries-old racial stereotypes, and showcase African American artistic talents.

Culture was also used to depict a modern Black life and encourage interracialism. For example, *Ebony*, first published in late fall of 1945 by John H. Johnson, aimed "to mirror the deeds of black men, to help blend America's black and whites into interracial understanding through mutual admiration of all that is good in both." He stressed that "*Ebony* is a magazine of, by, and for Negroes who are proud of their color. Therefore, the name—*Ebony*." More than this, however, *Ebony* offered African Americans opportunities to reflect on racial politics and receive counsel on issues such as economic instability and housing discrimination. It promoted Black celebrity—a "dream world of successes, romances, and life routines of recognizable Black personalities," like Lena Horne—in an effort to project a different vision of Black life. This vision celebrated the Black community's triumphs, not its dysfunctions, and inspired African Americans to imagine and work toward a better existence not only for themselves but also for their community and the nation.

Like *Ebony*, Motown Records, was hugely successful. Both became lucrative businesses patronized by Blacks and whites throughout the country and the world. Detroit native and songwriter Berry Gordy founded Motown in 1959. He established his company to challenge the exploitation of Black musical artists, many of whom had their music covered by white singers but never received their deserved recognition or royalties. Top artists and acts on the Motown label included Smokey Robinson, the Supremes, the Temptations, and Marvin Gaye. During the company's first decade, Motown artists personified Black respectability politics and were in many ways unpolitical, meaning they were not consciousness raising. This approach made African Americans artists on the Motown label not only digestible to white listeners but also extremely popular among Blacks and whites.

As Motown gained prominence, so too did other forms of African American musical expression. Within the civil rights movement, freedom songs emerged as a way to begin mass meetings and demonstrations, as well as a way to help carry activists through imprisonment and tense moments. Freedom songs often originated from Negro spirituals dating back to the nineteenth century, and words and phrases were altered to reflect the mid-twentieth-century Black freedom struggle. For example, "Ain't Gonna Let Nobody Turn Me 'Round" was a freedom song based off of the Negro spiritual "Don't Let Nobody Turn Me Round." In the spiritual, the goal is to stay on the straight and narrow path toward salvation by avoiding obstacles, whereas the freedom song positions jail and segregationist police and politicians as the obstacles one must overcome to achieve freedom and equality. Freedom songs gained even greater notoriety with the founding of the Freedom Singers in 1962 in Albany, Georgia. According to scholar Joe Street, freedom songs "linked the present struggle with previous struggles for freedom, reaffirming the value of cultural forms to sustaining a political and social movement. Audiences were encouraged to understand the political and cultural roots of the southern movement, including its relationship with black Christianity; to empathize with those singing the songs (both in the hall and in the jails); and to come to terms with the political significance of the movement."[1]

Freedom songs, however, were not the only form of musical expression directly addressing the civil rights struggle. Protest music also emerged in the 1960s as a form of popular music that called attention to racial discrimination. Black and white musicians composed and performed music addressing the murders of Emmett Till and Medgar Evers, the violence of segregation, and the need for Black Americans to embrace racial pride. In 1964, jazz and blues musician Nina Simone wrote "Mississippi Goddam"—a political anthem and a scathing critique of southern racism and racial violence, respectability politics, and the gradualist approach to civil rights. The song, historian Ruth Feldstein writes, "also challenged principles strongly associated with liberal civil rights activism: religion as a source of solace and protest for African Americans, and the viability of a beloved community of whites and blacks."[2] By the late 1960s, even Motown loosened its ties toward producing "crossover music" and gave its artists greater leeway to produce protest music on issues ranging from civil rights to antiwar to environmentalism.

In addition to print media and music, African American culture was expressed and celebrated through community-based theater. In 1963, students at Tougaloo College in Mississippi formed the Free Southern Theater (FST). Students at Tougaloo, a private historically Black college, were highly active in the struggle for civil rights and staged sit-ins at local restaurants and engaged in high-profile marches and public demonstrations against segregation. The Free Southern Theater was founded by John O'Neal, Doris Derby, and Gilbert Moses as a way to bring theater to southerners who had no access to it or similar forms of cultural expression. Plays produced by the Free Southern Theater promoted Black culture and social protest. The Free Southern Theater later became affiliated with the Black Arts Movement before dissolving in the late 1970s.

African Americans also recognized that certain sites of cultural production, like television and film, also carried power and could sway public opinion on integration. With the increasing availability and affordability of television, more Americans owned televisions in the 1960s than in the 1950s. Even as some local television outlets in the South refused to or shied away from covering civil rights demonstrations, many national media outlets did cover the explosive scenes in Birmingham in early 1963 and the March on Washington later that same year. Television had the capability of bringing the civil rights movement into American homes. Likewise, the increasing presence of Black actors as feature and nonstereotypical characters in prime-time television shows such as *I Spy*, *Julia*, an *Star Trek* or as musicians performing on white mainstays like *The Ed Sullivan Show* challenged, albeit sometimes minimally, the marginalization of Black culture on the big and small screens. In 1968, new ground was broken when *Star Trek,* a science fiction television show, featured an interracial kiss between costars Nichelle Nichols and William Shatner (who played Uhura and Captain Kirk, respectively).

At the movie theater, African Americans proved that their loves and lives, including the harsh realities of race relations, could be popular and profitable. Message films like *The Defiant Ones* (1958) and *Guess Who's Coming to Dinner* (1967) told groundbreaking stories of interracial friendships and romances, while *A Raisin in the Sun* (1961), *Nothing but a Man* (1964), and *In the Heat of the Night* (1967) depicted the racial and economic struggles of being Black in America. By the end of the 1960s and early 1970s, Hollywood films like *Sweet Sweetback's Baadasssss* (1971) and *Shaft* (1971), both of which are considered blaxploitation films, incorporated Black Power ideology and became box-office hits.

NOTES

1. Joe Street, *The Culture War in the Civil Rights Movement* (Gainesville: University Press of Florida, 2007), 49.
2. Ruth Feldstein, *How It Feels to Be Free: Black Women Entertainers and the Civil Rights Movement* (Oxford: Oxford University Press, 2013), 84.

Lena Horne on the Cover of *Ebony* Magazine (1956)

African American actress and civil rights activist Lena Horne graced the cover of *Ebony* magazine in February 1956. She was a frequent and favorite cover girl of the publication. *Ebony* was founded and run by African Americans inspired by *Life* magazine, the nation's leading photo-editorial magazine, and was launched in November 1945 to be the Black *Life*. In its first issue, editors stated: "As you can gather, we're rather jolly folks, we *Ebony* editors. We like to look at the zesty side of life. Sure, you can get all hot and bothered about the race question (and don't think we don't) but not enough is said about all the swell things we Negroes can do and will accomplish. Ebony will try to mirror the happier side of Negro life—the positive, everyday achievements from Harlem to Hollywood. But when we talk race as the No. 1 problem of America, we'll talk turkey."

In the 1940s, Horne appeared in several films including *Stormy Weather* (1943), *Cabin in the Sky* (1943), and *Ziegfeld Follies* (1945). In the 1950s, as she became disenchanted with Hollywood and more involved in the civil rights movement, Horne was targeted by Senator Joseph McCarthy, and her name was eventually placed on the Red Channels blacklist of performers suspected of aiding communism. *Ebony* magazine continued to feature Horne, however, because she was a glamorous "working mother" and outspoken proponent of Black civil rights.

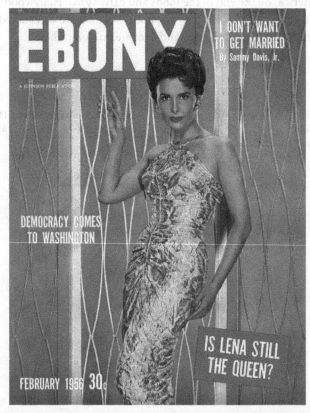

Source: Cover of *Ebony*, February 1956. Special thanks to Ebony Media Group, LLC. All Rights Reserved.

Cover of *Ebony* Magazine Featuring the March on Montgomery (1965)

For a better part of its early years, *Ebony* magazine focused on African American celebrity and sports. As the civil rights movement gained momentum, however, the publications not only featured major moments in the struggle including the March on Montgomery (Alabama) in 1965 as portrayed here, but also became more vocal and arguably radical on the issue of race and racism.

Source: Cover of *Ebony*, May 1965. Special thanks to Ebony Media Group, LLC. All Rights Reserved.

DOCUMENT 10.3

The Freedom Singers (1963)

Emerging out of the Albany Movement, the Freedom Singers were founded as a student quartet at Albany College in 1962. Original group members consisted of Cordell and Bernice Reagon, Rutha Mae Harris, and Charles Neblett; they were occasionally joined by Bertha Gober. The Freedom Singers toured the country and sang traditional freedom songs, including "We Shall Overcome," "We Shall Not Be Moved," and "Ain't Gonna Let Nobody Turn Me 'Round," as well as original songs written by Student Nonviolent Coordinating Committee members. Notable appearances include a SNCC fund-raiser with gospel artists Mahalia Jackson in June 1963, Newport Folk Festival with Bob Dylan in July 1963, and the March on Washington for Jobs and Freedom in August 1963. The money they made was used to fund the civil rights movement. In October 1963 they recorded a studio album after having signed to Mercury Records.

Source: Joe Alper, *Freedom Singers*, 1963, photograph. Courtesy of Joe Alper Photo Collection LLC.

Flyer for the "Pre-march Freedom Rally" for the Meredith Marchers (1966)

Singers, actresses, and other entertainers often lent their voices and support to the civil rights movement. In 1966, James Meredith, who integrated the University of Mississippi in 1962, began a one-man "March against Fear" from Memphis, Tennessee, to Jackson, Mississippi. On the second day of the march, Meredith was shot and wounded by Aubrey James Norvell. Civil rights organizations immediately rallied in support and vowed to complete the march on Meredith's behalf. Before the second march began, a premarch freedom rally for Meredith Marchers was held on Tougaloo's campus on Saturday, June 25, 1966. At the rally, singers Sammy Davis, James Brown, Nina Simone, and Eartha Kitt, as well as actors Marlon Brando and Burt Lancaster, performed.

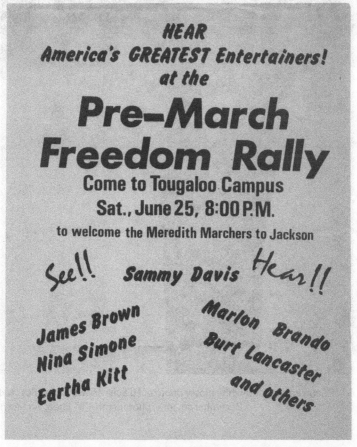

Source: Flyer for a premarch Freedom Rally for the Meredith Marchers, 1966, ink on paper, Gift from the Trumpauer-Mulholland Collection, Smithsonian National Museum of African American History and Culture, https://nmaahc.si.edu/object/nmaahc_2011.109.5?destination=/explore /collection/search%3Fedan_q%3Dnina%2520simone%26page%3D1.

The Supremes with Television Host Ed Sullivan (1969)

Below is a photograph of Diane Ross & the Supremes (Cindy Birdsong and Mary Wilson), a Motown Records musical act with hits such as "Come See about Me" and "You Can't Hurry Love," and Ed Sullivan, television personality. This image was likely captured either onstage or backstage during one of the group's appearances on *The Ed Sullivan Show* in New York City.

Source: Black-and-white glossy photo of Ed Sullivan with Diana Ross & the Supremes, December 20, 1969, photograph, CBS Photo Archive/Getty Images.

Denise Nicholas, "A Grand Romantic Notion" (2010)

Denise Nicholas, a college student from Michigan and at the time the wife of Gilbert Moses (one of the four founders of the Freedom Southern Theater), recalls her involvement in the FST in Jackson, Mississippi. While participating in FST, Nicholas "went from being an idealistic integrationist actress 'molded' by her husband to being a pragmatic advocate of black consciousness who planned and implemented community programs."[1] She was part of the FST from 1964 to 1967. After she left, Nicholas starred in films and television shows, including *It Takes a Thief* in 1968, *Love, American Style* in 1972, *Rhoda* in 1975, and *In the Heat of the Night* from 1989 to 1995.

MISSISSIPPI SPIRIT

The Free Southern Theater (FST) was in the beginning stages when I arrived in Jackson. We were operating out of Tougaloo College and the Council of Federated Organizations (COFO) office in Jackson. SNCC folk had mixed feelings about a theater. Some people felt the theater and the arts, basically, were frivolous in the face of what needed to be done in terms of voter registration. They couldn't see how it would help or how it could be anything but a nuisance to have us running around all over the place with our sets, props, and costumes. It was an interesting challenge even from the inside. Gil and John O'Neal (co-founder of the FST) and Doris Derby had put out the word that they were looking for people among the summer volunteers who were theater majors or who had an interest in the theater. That's how we got the first group. I wasn't there as an actress; I was reading scripts and writing critiques. After much heated provocation from actress-activist Madeleine Sherwood, John and Gil decided to do Martin Duberman's play *In White America* that summer. They needed a black actress. They asked me to read for it. I read, though I didn't know what I was doing. They said, "Well, that's good enough." What a start!

By the time I arrived in Jackson, James Chaney, Andy Goodman, and Mickey Schwerner were missing. We were afraid, but I think because everybody believed very much in what we were doing, we tightened up and we just kept going. We went all over Mississippi that first summer, performing in seventeen cities. They found those boys on August 4. I remember, from pictures or television, seeing these white sheriffs with body bags, like Vietnam body bags, bringing in the remains. I have that in my head, right with the Emmett Till photo. Those visuals never, ever go away. There were other unforgettable moments when Rita Schwerner, Mickey Schwerner's wife, who was also working in Mississippi that summer, came to a number of our performances and spoke at the churches where we were. Her fragile appearance contrasted with her strength as she stood there assuring us that she would not leave Mississippi that summer, but would stay and do the work we all had come to do.

That first summer there was violence everywhere. We could feel it in the air all the time. Even when we were dancing and letting off steam in some Dew Drop Inn with a jukebox that was leaning over three feet to the side, danger was always part of the equation. It was always there. In McComb, someone threw a bomb at the stage. In another location—Holmes County, I think—men with shotguns sat on the porch all night guarding us while we slept.

Once we performed in a half-finished community center building. Some young builders from California had come out to reconstruct it after the original one had been bombed. When we performed, half the roof was there, the posts were there, but the walls were not up yet. It was incredible and beautiful. We did *In White America* in that space, and local people guarded us while we performed. Our performances were held in the early evening. We had to follow all the regulations and rules coming out of Jackson, just as the COFO and SNCC workers did, as far as being on the road—for example, making sure the cars were serviced, because you didn't want to have a breakdown on the road in a rural area; driving a little bit under the speed limit, and being very polite with people all the time. We walked around with our necks so stiff from tension. We were having this extraordinary experience, but, at the same time, we were always riding on top of terror, constantly trying to leap up on top of our own fear and do the things were there to do.

The Free Southern Theater toured towns where there was a COFO project, places like Canton, Greenville, Meridian, and Hattiesburg. People on our staff worked with the COFO people in the towns we went to. Our housing, how things would be set up, what church we would perform in, publicity, all of these kinds of necessities were worked out between our staff, the local people, and the COFO volunteers in that particular town. COFO workers and local people helped us with advertising by handing out flyers. Young people from the town helped us unload the equipment, do the setup, then helped us take it down and load it onto the truck. Older people in these communities housed and fed us; they really took care of us.

In most of the communities we toured to, the local people had no conception of the conventions of the theater. Often people spoke to us from the audience during performances. During one tour we were doing a one-act that Gil Moses had written, and in that play my character, Dottie, is onstage trying to open a jar but can't get it open. The husband character takes it, but he can open it either and gives it back to her. Dottie tries again. At that point, an older, slightly built man came right up on the stage from the audience and said, "I'll help you," took the jar, and opened it. It was so sweet and kind. Things like that happened all the time.

People reacted with joy to our performances. They were happy to have us there and said so. I think it was all a part of the world opening to them, letting them know that we cared enough to come see about them. It was beautiful. It was beautiful to be in the place, to be there. We had discussions after all the performances, so people had an opportunity to voice what they got from the experience of the play and how it and we connected to their lives and how we connected to the political changes that were going on in the South. The theater, like literature, can be a tool of community, of illumination of the human condition.

There was so much energy that first summer in Mississippi; even backwater, teenyweeny little places picked up the zeal of what was going on in the whole state. In a sense it was like the entire state was in performance. It was uplifting, very uplifting. That whole summer was an incredible moment. We went to places like Mound Bayou, an all-black town with no paved streets. As a young woman from Detroit and Ann Arbor, I saw how poor, rural, and forgotten some places were, but at the same time I saw how wonderful these people and these places were. The spirit was so strong. It was us picking up their spirit and giving back what we had. It was an exchange, a pure exchange.

I was always very shy. It is hard to believe now, because theater made me into a talker. Theater is a group experience, which gave me courage and helped me to develop a personality. I don't think I projected a whole lot; I wasn't pushed through to myself until I'd worked for a while in the theater. I've heard other actors say this also, that the theater experience, the act of doing it, this group experience, developed them as personalities.

NEW ORLEANS

Gil Moses and John O'Neal decided that Mississippi was so hard, so harsh and unrelenting that we would probably do better basing the theater in New Orleans and touring into Mississippi. However, the worst incident I experienced personally took place in New Orleans. We had two apartments in a building on Burgundy Street (Bur-GUN-dy, as black people say). SNCC people would come in and use the apartments for rest and relaxation days. On this weekend, there were a bunch of SNCC folk in town, and two SNCC photographers went across the street to a little store to get cigarettes. There was a shoeshine stand directly opposite that the police used. Watching from one of the apartment balconies overlooking the street, I saw the two photographers go over to the corner store and come back out, but they never came up the stairs to the apartment. I thought, "Oh, God, something has happened!" So I walked downstairs. As I walked out the door, a cop pulled his gun out and put it to my head, saying, "If you take one more step, I will blow your effing brains out." You pay attention to something like that.

I thought, "Oh God, this is it." I could see the photographers in the back of the police car that was pulled up on the curb under the balcony. I just stood there. I couldn't move. I've never been so frightened in my life. I remember thinking I hope I don't pee on myself out here. I prayed. I hope I don't die right here on this street. After a few terrifying minutes, other people from the Free Southern Theater came downstairs and the cop let me go.

. . . When the black power movement took hold in the late sixties, we went through an extraordinary, raging change. The Free Southern Theater had always been a mixed group, and there were a couple of white people who had been integral to making this project happen. People you'd come to know and love were suddenly being excluded. It was very, very difficult time. The Movement was changing, and we had to change with it. It wasn't long after that, September 1966, that I moved to New York.

Source: Denise Nicholas, "A Grand Romantic Notion," in *Hands on the Freedom Plow: Personal Accounts by Women in SNCC*, edited by Faith Holsaert et al. (Urbana: University of Illinois Press, 2010), 259–62. Copyright © 2010 by Denise Nicholas. Used with permission of the University of Illinois Press.

NOTES

1. Clarissa Myrick-Harris, "Behind the Scenes: Doris Derby, Denise Nicholas, and the Free Southern Theater," in *Women in the Civil Rights Movement: Trailblazers and Torchbearers, 1941–1965*, ed. Vicki Crawford, Jacqueline Rouse, and Barbara Woods (Bloomington: Indiana University Press, 1993), 225.

Free Southern Theater Program Cover (ca. late 1960s)

Playbill for the Free Southern Theater's production of *In White America*, *The Rifles of Senora Carrar*, and *The Shadow of a Gunman*.

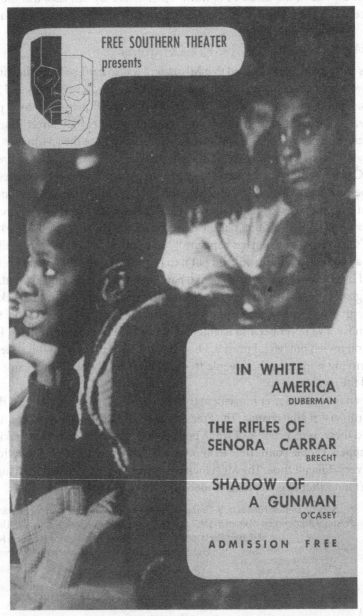

Source: *Free Southern Theater Presents*, Free Southern Theater, ca. late 1960s, program, Judy Richardson Papers, SNCC and Civil Rights Movement Series, Duke University. https://repository.duke.edu/dc/richardsonjudy/jrpst002032. Courtesy of Judy Richardson and Denise Nicholas.

NBC Crew Televises the March on Washington (1963)

WNBQ/NBC's television crew (channel 5) filmed the March on Washington in Washington, D.C., on August 28, 1963. This photograph depicts the role of the press in the civil rights movement.

Source: Rowland Scherman, *Civil Rights March on Washington, D.C.—WNBQ/National Broadcasting Company Television Crew (Channel 5)*, August 8, 1963, photograph, Miscellaneous Subjects Series, Staff and Stringer Photographs, compiled 1961–74, Record Group 306: Records of the U.S. Information Agency, 1900–2003, National Archives at College Park, catalog.archives.gov/id/542008.

Clifford Mason, "Why Does White America Love Sidney Poitier So?" (1967)

In "Why does White America Love Sidney Poitier So?," published in the *New York Times* on September 10, 1967, Clifford Mason considers the popularity of Bahamian actor Sidney Poitier who starred in the era's most notable message films, including *The Defiant Ones* (1958), *A Raisin in the Sun* (1961), *Guess Who's Coming to Dinner* (1967), and *In the Heat of the Night* (1967). Poitier became the first Black actor to win an Academy Award for Best Actor and the Golden Globe Award for Best Actor for his role in *Lilies of the Field* (1963). He was the second Black actor to ever win an Academy Award; Hattie McDaniel won the first in 1940 for her supporting-actress role in *Gone with the Wind* (1939).

There are two Sidney Poitiers. One is the man dedicated to the improvement of the Negro image in general and to rectifying the wrongs perpetrated against black women in particular. The other is the Negro movie star that all white America loves. And why do they love him so? Because he's a good actor? Partly. Because he's worked hard to get where he is? Maybe. Because he stands for a proud, black image, something all of us who are non-white have needed in this country for a long, long time? Noooooo.

But then the question of what makes for a proud image and what makes for a demeaning one is itself open to all sorts of argument. It seems this is the year for clichés in theatrical thought. According to a recent interview, Mr. Poitier had trouble with his conscience or self-respect or whatever in making both "Porgy and Bess" and "The Long Ships." And yet there is no record of his feeling similar misgivings in doing things like "Lilies of the Field," "A Patch of Blue," "The Bedford Incident," "Duel at Diablo," or "To Sir, With Love."

I submit that the Negro (or black, if you will) image was subverted by his roles in these films much more so than it was in the two films he seems worried about. Honesty is still the most important ingredient in art. The black writer Loften Mitchell has said that Arthur Miller's "Death of a Salesman" would have been an even greater play had Miller in fact used his Jewishness as forthrightly as O'Neill used his Irishness in "Long Day's Journey Into Night." And it is a schizophrenic flight from identity and historical fact that makes anybody imagine, even for a moment, that the Negro is best served by being a black version of the man in the gray flannel suit, taking on white problems and a white man's sense of what's wrong with the world.

I, too, am tired of "Porgy and Bess." But at least it doesn't try to fool us. Even though its Negroes are frankly stereotypes, at least we have a man, a real man, fighting for his woman and willing to follow her into the great unknown, the big city, poor boy from Catfish Row that he is. What did we have in "The Bedford Incident," by comparison? Poitier as a black correspondent who went around calling everyone sir. Did anyone ever see Gary Cooper or Greg Peck call anyone sir when *they* played foreign correspondents? And after Richard Widmark (who starred with Poitier in the film) barks at him and pushes him around all over the submarine for almost two hours, the only thing he gets to do at the end is shout at bad Dicky Widmark. And why do they allow him to shout at Widmark? Because Widmark has just gotten the whole ship stuck in the path of an onrushing torpedo that blows them all to heaven the next instant! For that kind of mistake, Poitier should at least have been allowed to bust him one in the jaw.

And yet, listening to the things Poitier says, one wonders if he would have thought it appropriate. In "Duel at Diablo" he did little more than hold James Garner's hat, and this after he had won the Academy Award. What white romantic actor would take a part like that? He gets to kill a few Indians, but Garner gets the girl and does all the real fighting. Poitier was simply dressed up in a fancy suit, with a cigar stuck in his mouth and a new felt hat on his head.

"To Sir, With Love" had the all-time Hollywood reversal act. Instead of putting a love interest into a story that had none, they took it out. But "A Patch of Blue" was probably the most ridiculous film Poitier ever made. He's a newspaper reporter who befriends a blind white girl from the slums, a girl whom he doesn't even make love to. He gets her away from her whoring mother and sends her off to a home for the blind, and the little symbolism at the end with the music box makes it clear that they'll never see each other again. And why does he go to the park day after day and sit with her and string her beads and buy her lunch? Because he's running his private branch of the ASPCA, the Black Society for the Prevention of Cruelty to Blind White Girls, the BSPCBWG?

All this Mr. Poitier endures, and more, without a murmur of protest. Now there are those who will say there's nothing else he can do. *They* won't let him make anything else. I used to console myself with the fact that that was probably true. And it may very well be true. But truer than that is the fact that he thinks these films have really been helping to change the stereotypes that black actors are subjected to. In essence, they are merely contrivances, completely lacking in any real artistic merit. In all of these films he has been a showcase nigger, who is given a clean suit and a complete purity of motivation so that, like a mistreated puppy, he has all the sympathy on his side and all those mean whites are just so many Simon Legrees.

Gradualism may have some value in politics. But in art it just represents a stale, hackneyed period, to be forgotten as soon as we can get on to the real work at hand. And artistic NAACPism is all that this whole period of Sidney Poitier moviemaking stands for. At least the villain he played in "The Long Ships" was a fighter—on his own mission, in his own world. And even though there was the nonsense about a vow that kept him from making love to Rossana Schiaffino, her attempt to warn him of danger and his death at Richard Widmark's hands were handled with great care for the importance of his role. He was not killed as a mean, despicable villain, but rather as a noble enemy. Even more important, he was nobody's eunuch or black mammy busting his gut for white folks as if their problems were all that's important in the world. And so the stern "I hated it" that he uttered in a recent interview to tell how he felt about doing "The Long Ships" shows the confusion in his mind as to what constitutes dignity for Negroes in films.

The rabid rumor—indeed, it's an incontestable fact by now—that Poitier actually kisses the white girl *and* marries her in his next opus, "Guess Who's Coming to Dinner," should presumably refute all of my arguments up to this point. But what should seem obvious is that the prime concern is not with the manipulation of black and white bodies before the camera. So close today and closer tomorrow. They can give him the girl, all the girls, and have him kill ten rednecks and still make a bad picture. And that is the essence of the argument. Until the concern of movies is for the dignity, the manhood, the thinking of the Negro in *his* world, with its historical past, its turbulent present and its hopeful future, there can be no true portrait of the Negro and no true art. Whites may or may not play a part in this world; the crucial need however is for a break with the concept that the world is only white, and that the Negro exists only in the white man's view of him.

Now Poitier may very well say that he is sacrificing his career so that eventually all God's chillun will be able to do what white folks have been doing for years. That would be a cute point, and I'd like to think it *was* true. But until the day of complete honesty comes, white critics will gladly drag out a double standard and applaud every "advance" in movies like "Lilies of the Field" as so much American-style, democratic goodwill. Which is what the road to hell is paved with.

Finally—and this brings us completely up to date as far as Negroes in films are concerned, because Poitier is really all we have, there being room for only one of us at a time—there is "In the Heat of the Night." Even though the acting, his and Rod Steiger's particularly, is excellent, we have the same old Sidney Poitier syndrome: a good guy in a totally white world, with no wife, no sweetheart, no woman to love or kiss, helping the white man solve the white man's problem. True, the nature of his purpose is an improvement over what it was in "Lilies of the Field": there is some racial justification for his working to solve the murder in "In the Heat of the Night." The white victim was a Northerner who had planned to employ Negroes as well as whites in a factory in Mississippi. And this time out, Poitier actually gets to slap a white Southern aristocrat. Of course, he only does it after the aristocrat slaps *him*.

But he remains unreal, as he has for nearly two decades, playing essentially the same role, the antiseptic, one-dimensional hero. If he keeps it up, he'll soon be able to give Sean Connery lessons in how to do the same role year after year after year. I can just see the two of them now: Connery, toothless and doddering, but still killing Asians, Turks and some white Communists, while 50 girls try to get his courage up. And Poitier, finally going to flesh, but still pure, still nonplussed by white arrogance and wanting only to be left alone but, because of his innate goodness, finally making that fateful decision to solve the problem for "them," good nigger that he is.

Source: Clifford Mason, "Why Does White America Love Sidney Poitier So?," *New York Times*, September 10, 1967. https://archive.nytimes.com/www.nytimes.com/packages/html/movies/bestpictures/heat-ar.html?scp=8&sq=Fact&st=cse#:~:text=There%20are%20two%20Sidney%20Poitiers,that%20all%20white%20America%20loves. Courtesy of Clifford Mason.

Julia **Publicity Photo (ca. 1968)**

A promotional photograph for *Julia*, a television series that starred African American actress and singer Diahann Carroll in the title role, follows. (It is believed that the photo is from the show's first-season Christmas episode, "I'm Dreaming of a Black Christmas.") *Julia* premiered September 1968 and ended its run in 1971. Carroll played a mother, widow, and professional nurse, living with her son in the suburbs—making *Julia* the first sitcom to portray an African American in a nonstereotypical role (such as a maid, prostitute, or slave). For this reason, many viewers and critics celebrated *Julia* as a revolutionary sitcom; others, however, criticized the show for not engaging the politics of the civil rights movement on a deeper level. (Three years prior to *Julia*'s premiere, *I Spy* was the first television drama to feature a Black actor in the lead role. *I Spy*, an international secret-agent show, starred African American actor and comedian Bill Cosby and white actor Robert Culp. *I Spy* ran on NBC from 1965 to 1968.)

Source: Diahann Carroll and Marc Copage from an episode of *Julia*, ca. 1968, photograph, NBC Television, Wisconsin Center for Film and Theater Research, University of Wisconsin–Madison and Wisconsin Historical Society.

Harriet Glickman Writes Charles Schulz (1968)

On April 15, 1968, Harriet Glickman wrote to Charles Schulz, the creator of the *Peanuts* comic strip, imploring him to add an African American character. Franklin Armstrong, the first African American character in *Peanuts*, made his debut on July 31, 1968. In this comic strip, Franklin returns a beach ball to Charlie Brown and helps him build a sandcastle. The addition of Franklin garnered criticism from white southerners, in particular, but it was also celebrated by African Americans and their white allies.

Mrs. Harriet Glickman   4933 Wortser Ave. Sherman Oaks, Calif/ 91403

Mr. Charles Schulz
United Features Syndicate
220 E. 42nd St.
New York, N.Y. 10017

April 15,1968

Dear Mr. Schulz,

Since the death of Martin Luther King, I've been asking myself
what I can do to help change those conditions in our society
which led to the assassination and which contribute to the
vast sea of misunderstanding, fear, hate and violence.

As a suburban housewife; the mother of three children and a
deeply concerned and active citizen, I am well aware of the
very long and tortuous road ahead. I believe that it will
be another generation before the kind of open friendship,
trust and mobility will be an accepted part of our lives.

In thinking over the areas of the mass media which are of
tremendous importance in shaping the unconscious attitudes of
our kids, I felt that something could be done through our
comic strips and even in that violent jungle of horrors known
as Children's Television.

You need no reassurances from me that Peanuts is one of the
most adored, well-read and quoted parts of our literate society.
In our family, teen-age Kathy has posters and sweat shirts...
pencil holders and autograph books. Paul, who's ten and
our Charlie Brown Little Leaguer....has memorized every
paper back book...has stationery, calendars, wall hangings
and a Snoopy pillow. Three and a half year old Simon has
his own Snoopy which lives, loves, eats, paints, digs, bathes
and sleeps with him. My husband and I keep pertinent Peanuts
cartoons on desks and bulletin boards as guards against pomposity.
You see...we are a totally Peanuts-oriented family.

It occurred to me today that the introduction of Negro children
into the group of Schulz characters could happen with a minimum
of impact. The gentleness of the kids,..even Lucy, is a perfect
setting. The baseball games, kite-flying...yes, even the
Psychiatric Service cum Lemonade Stand would accommodate the
the idea smoothly.

Sitting alone in California suburbia makes it all seem so easy
and logical. I'm sure one doesn't make radical changes in so
important an institution without a lot of shock waves from
syndicates, clients, etc. You have, however, a stature and
reputation which can withstand a great deal.

Lastly; should you consider this suggestion, I hope that the
result will be more than one black child....Let them be as
adorable as the others...but please...allow them a Lucy!

Sincerely,

Source: Harriet Glickman to Charles Schulz, April 15, 1968, Peanuts Worldwide LLC/Harriet Glickman Collection, Courtesy of the Charles M. Schulz Museum and Research Center, Santa Rosa, California.

FURTHER READING

Bodroghkozy, Aniko. *Equal Time: Television and the Civil Rights Movement*. Urbana: University of Illinois Press, 2012.

Bracey, John, Jr., Sonia Sanchez, and James Smethurst. *SOS—Calling All Black People: A Black Arts Movement Reader*. Amherst: University of Massachusetts Press, 2014.

Classen, Steven D. *Watching Jim Crow: The Struggles over Mississippi TV, 1955–1969*. Durham, NC: Duke University Press, 2004.

Crawford, Vicki, Jacqueline Anne Rouse, and Barbara Woods, eds. *Women in the Civil Rights Movement: Trailblazers & Torchbearers, 1941–1965*. Bloomington: Indiana University Press, 1993.

Cripps, Thomas. *Making Movies Black: The Hollywood Message Movie from World War II to the Civil Rights Era*. Oxford: Oxford University Press, 1993.

Davis, Angela. *Blues Legacies and Black Feminism: Gertrude "Ma" Rainey, Bessie Smith, and Billie Holiday*. New York: Vintage Books, 1999.

Donovan, Robert J., and Ray Scherer. *Unsilent Revolution: Television News and American Public Life, 1948–1991*. Cambridge: Cambridge University Press, 1992.

Eyerman, Ron, and Andrew Jamison. *Music and Social Movements: Mobilizing Traditions in the Twentieth Century*. Cambridge: Cambridge University Press, 1998.

Feldstein, Ruth. *How It Feels to Be Free: Black Women Entertainers and the Civil Rights Movement*. Oxford: Oxford University Press, 2013.

Graham, Allison. *Framing the South: Hollywood, Television, and Race during the Civil Rights Struggle*. Baltimore: Johns Hopkins University Press, 2003.

Green, Adam. *Selling the Race: Culture, Community, and Black Chicago, 1940–1955*. Chicago: University of Chicago Press, 2009.

Green, Laurie. *Battling the Plantation Mentality: Memphis and the Black Freedom Struggle*. Chapel Hill: University of North Carolina Press, 2009.

Kurlansky, Mark. *Ready for a Brand New Beat: How "Dancing in the Street" Became the Anthem for a Changing America*. New York: Penguin, 2014.

Rabaka, Reiland. *Civil Rights Music: The Soundtracks of the Civil Rights Movement*. Lanham, MD: Lexington Books, 2016.

Reed, Thomas Vernon. *The Art of Protest: Culture and Activism from the Civil Rights Movement to the Streets of Seattle*. Minneapolis: University of Minnesota, 2005.

Scott, Ellen C. *Cinema Civil Rights: Regulation, Repression, and Race in the Classical Hollywood Era*. New Brunswick, NJ: Rutgers University Press, 2015.

Smith, Suzanne E. *Dancing in the Street: Motown and the Cultural Politics of Detroit*. Cambridge, MA: Harvard University Press, 2009.

Street, Joe. *The Culture War in the Civil Right Movement*. Gainesville: University Press of Florida, 2007.

Torres, Sasha. *Black, White, and in Color: Television and Black Civil Rights*. Princeton, NJ: Princeton University Press, 2003.

Ward, Brian. *Just My Soul Responding: Rhythm and Blues, Black Consciousness and Race Relations*. Berkeley: University of California Press, 1998.

West, E. James. *"Ebony" Magazine and Lerone Bennett Jr.: Popular Black History in Postwar America*. Urbana: University of Illinois Press, 2020.

Williams, Megan E. *"The "Crisis" Cover Girl: Lena Horne, the NAACP, and Representations of American Femininity, 1941–1945." American Periodicals* 16, no. 2 (2006): 200–218.

11

Black Power Politics and Reform in the 1970s and 1980s

How did the civil rights and Black Power movements shape the Black political landscape in the 1970s and 1980s? What strategies, reforms, or policies did Black activists push for in order to secure first-class citizenship? In what ways were their efforts challenged? How were the successes of the Black freedom movement undermined in the 1970s and 1980s?

In the decades following the passage of the Civil Rights Act of 1964 and the Voting Rights Act of 1965, more and more African Americans were elected to public office, facilitating the growth of Black political power in the late twentieth century. According to the historian Adam Fairclough, "Black voters were becoming increasingly important in local, state, and congressional elections. By 1969, the Voting Rights Act had added 900,000 black voters in the covered states; by 1976, black voter registration in the South stood at 63 percent—only five percentage points below the white level. Congress renewed the Voting Rights Act in 1970 and again in 1975." Too, "The Supreme Court . . . greatly widened the scope of the Voting Rights Act, barring racial discrimination in electoral arrangements, as well as the discrimination that hampered or prevented blacks from registering and voting."[1]

The 1960s, 1970s, and 1980s saw the election of many Black firsts. In 1964, George D. Carroll became the first African American mayor of a U.S. city, governing over Richmond, California. Three years later, in 1967, Carl Stokes was elected mayor of Cleveland, Ohio; Richard G. Hatcher was elected mayor of Gary, Indiana; and Shirley Chisholm was elected to the U.S. House of Representative for the state of New York. Chisholm would later run for the Democratic Party presidential bid in 1972, making her the first woman of any race to run as a presidential candidate from a major political party. That same year, the First National Black Political Convention was held in Gary, and Barbara Jordan became the first southern woman elected to the House of Representatives. In 1983, Harold Washington was elected the first African American mayor of Chicago. One year later, Jesse Jackson became the first African American man to seek the Democratic nomination for president. And in 1989,

L. Douglas Wilder was elected governor of Virginia, becoming the first Black governor in any state since Reconstruction. Efforts to grow Black political power through electoral politics revealed the difficulties that many Black political "firsts" in this era faced. Black elected leaders in cities inherited urban centers challenged by deindustrialization, struggling infrastructures, and entrenched city machine politics that relied on Black voters but failed to produce equitable resources for Black communities. Still, Black voters and others who supported Black political candidates championed these victories as steps in the right direction toward a more representative and equitable democracy.

As Black political power grew, so did efforts to dismantle gains made by the civil rights and Black Power movements—most notably, those made in education and employment. Despite the *Brown v. Board of Education* decision, the problem of segregated schools persisted. In the late 1960s and early 1970s, civil rights organizations pushed to finally end the problem by busing students across district lines. In Ocean Hill–Brownsville in 1968, the local school was predominantly African American as a result of New York City's failure to racially integrate its public schools. African American parents decided that, if not integrated, they should have full control over the school—meaning the teachers and the curriculum should be Black—and initiated a one-day boycott. White teachers and administrators took exception to their call and boycotted with the support of the United Federation of Teachers. Scholars have marked the Ocean Hill–Brownsville conflict as "the end of the school integration movement."[2]

Boston was the site of another vicious confrontation over school busing. In this New England city, the all-white Boston School Committee controlled the local schools. And under its governance, Black schools received less funding than their white counterparts; they were housed in derelict buildings, seriously overcrowded, and deficient in supplies and equipment. In the late 1960s and early 1970s, frustrated Black students organized demonstrations and strikes, demanding the recruitment of Black teachers and guidance counselors, the commission of an independent study on racial patterns in the city's schools, an end to the harassment of Black students, and amnesty to all striking students. Their demands were ignored. Eventually, a group of Black parents and children, with the assistance of the NAACP, filed a class-action lawsuit—*Morgan v. Hennigan*—against the Boston School Committee in federal court, alleging racial segregation in Boston public schools.

On June 21, 1974, U.S. district judge W. Arthur Garrity Jr. ruled in favor of the Black parents and children. He found the "School Committee had engaged in deliberate segregation," and thus it was guilty of violating the Equal Protection Clause of the Fourteenth Amendment. Garrity also ruled that, to achieve racial balance, students (numbering in the several thousands) should be bused between the mostly white South Boston, Hyde Park, and Dorchester and the mostly Black Roxbury and "the feeder system, which fed black students into high school in ninth grade and white students in tenth grade, to be eliminated," beginning the following September.[3]

White segregationists in Boston (of both the middle and working classes) fiercely opposed the ruling. White parents refused to let their children attend school, they organized boycotts and demonstrations, and they verbally and physically harassed prosegregation Black and white Bostonians. Their actions continued through the beginning of the school year. In fact, the start of the school year marked some of the "most angry and violent demonstrations against desegregation in the nation's history. Buses were stoned, children attacked, and mobs of whites demonstrated their opposition across the city." White students, however, were not welcomed the same way when they came to Black schools.[4]

Despite the court's decision, the Boston School Committee dug in its heels, and the federal government was forced to assume control over the city's school system. Many whites removed their children from the public school system, as a result. Nevertheless, some degree of integration was achieved, and finally in 1977 a Black candidate—John O'Bryant—won a seat on the committee.

The problem of school segregation was also ongoing in colleges and universities. As a result, the University of California–Davis School of Medicine set up such an affirmative action program, whereby up to sixteen seats out of a hundred in the first-year class were reserved for minority students. In 1974, however, its program was challenged when Allan Bakke, a white engineer, was rejected from this and other medical schools and filed suit. Bakke claimed that the school's affirmative action program discriminated against him. In 1978, with the case having reached the highest court in the land, the Supreme Court agreed and overturned the special minority admissions program at Davis.

Affirmative action programs were also challenged (less successfully) in workplaces, most notably in *Kaiser Aluminum & Chemical Corporation and United Steelworkers of America, AFL-CIO v. Brian F. Weber* (1979). In *Weber*, Brian F. Weber, a white man, challenged Kaiser Aluminum and Chemical Corporation's affirmative action policy that admitted whites and Blacks into its training program on a one-to-one basis, alleging that this policy violated Title VII of the 1964 Civil Rights Act and thus discriminated against him. The Court ruled that this program was lawful, "though it ruled narrowly, finding that Title VII's ban on discrimination 'does not condemn all private, voluntary, race-conscious affirmative action plans.'"[5]

NOTES

1. Adam Fairclough, *Better Day Coming: Blacks and Equality, 1890–2000* (New York: Penguin, 2001), 324, 325.
2. Marilyn Berube and Michael Gittell, *Confrontation at Ocean Hill–Brownsville: The New York School Strikes of 1968* (New York: Frederick A. Praeger, 1969), 13.
3. Jeanne Theoharris, "'I'd Rather Go to School in the South': How Boston's School Desegregation Complicates .the Civil Rights Paradigm," in *Freedom North: Black Freedom Struggles Outside the South, 1940–1980*, edited by Jeanne Theoharris and Komozi Woodard (New York: Palgrave Macmillan, 2003), 137.
4. Theoharris, "'I'd Rather Go to School in the South,'" 140.
5. Nancy MacLean, *Freedom Is Not Enough: The Opening of the American Workplace* (Cambridge, MA: Harvard University Press, 2008), 252.

DOCUMENT 11.1

The Gary Declaration (1972)

In March 1972—an election year—approximately ten thousand Black activists, organizers, and politicians representing differing political philosophies convened in Gary, Indiana, at the National Black Political Convention. The city had recently elected its first African American mayor, Richard Gordon Hatcher, in 1968. The convention was held with the hopes of determining a Black political strategy that would increase Black political representation and create concrete policies to address discrimination in employment, education, housing, health care, criminal justice, and other areas negatively impacting the quality of life for Black people. The following declaration, which advocated for independent Black politics as opposed to allegiance to the American two-party political system, came out of the convention.

THE BLACK AGENDA
The Gary Declaration: Black Politics at the Crossroads

INTRODUCTION

The Black Agenda is addressed primarily to Black people in America. It rises naturally out of the bloody decades and centuries of our people's struggle on these shores. It flows from the most recent surgings of our own cultural and political consciousness. It is our attempt to define some of the essential changes which must take place in this land as we and our children move to self-determination and true independence.

The Black Agenda assumes that no truly basic change for our benefit takes place in Black or white America unless we Black people organize to initiate that change. It assumes that we must have some essential agreement on overall goals, even though we may differ on many specific strategies.

Therefore, this is an initial statement of goals and directions for our own generation, some first definitions of crucial issues around which Black people must organize and move in 1972 and beyond. Anyone who claims to be serious about the survival and liberation of Black people must be serious about the implementation of the Black Agenda. . . .

BOTH PARTIES HAVE BETRAYED US

Here at Gary, let us never forget that while the times and the names and the parties have continually changed, one truth has faced us insistently, never changing: Both parties have betrayed us whenever their interests conflicted with ours (which was most of the time), and whenever our forces were unorganized and dependent, quiescent and compliant. Nor should this be surprising, for by now we must know that the American political system, like all other white institutions in America, was designed to operate for the benefit of the white race: It was never meant to do anything else.

That is the truth that we must face at Gary. If white "liberalism" could have solved our problems, then Lincoln and Roosevelt and Kennedy would have done so. But they did not solve ours nor the rest of the nation's. If America's problems could have been solved by forceful, politically skilled and aggressive individuals, then Lyndon Johnson would have retained the presidency. If the true "American Way" of unbridled monopoly capitalism, combined with a ruthless military imperialism could do it, then Nixon would not be running around the world, or making speeches comparing his nation's decadence to that of Greece and Rome.

If we have never faced it before, let us face it at Gary. The profound crisis of Black people and the disaster of America are not simply caused by men nor will they be solved by men alone. These crises are the crises of basically flawed economics and politics, and or cultural degradation. None of the Democratic candidates and none of the Republican candidates—regardless of their vague promises to us or to their white constituencies—can solve our problems or the problems of this country without radically changing the systems by which it operates.

THE POLITICS OF SOCIAL TRANSFORMATION

So we come to Gary confronted with a choice. But it is not the old convention question of which candidate shall we support, the pointless question of who is to preside over a decaying and unsalvageable system. No, if we come to Gary out of the realities of the Black communities of this land, then the only real choice for us is whether or not we will live by the truth we know, whether we will move to organize independently, move to struggle for fundamental transformation, for the creation of new directions, towards a concern for the life and the meaning of Man. Social transformation or social destruction, those are our only real choices.

If we have come to Gary on behalf of our people in America, in the rest of this hemisphere, and in the Homeland—if we have come for our own best ambitions—then a new Black Politics must come to birth. If we are serious, the Black Politics of Gary must accept major responsibility for creating both the atmosphere and the program for fundamental, far-ranging change in America. Such responsibility is ours because it is our people who are most deeply hurt and ravaged by the present systems of society....

WE ARE THE VANGUARD

The challenge is thrown to us here in Gary. It is the challenge to consolidate and organize our own Black role as the vanguard in the struggle for a new society. To accept that challenge is to move independent Black politics. There can be no equivocation on that issue. History leaves us no other choice. White politics has not and cannot bring the changes we need.

We come to Gary and are faced with a challenge. The challenge is to transform ourselves from favor-seeking vassals and loud-talking, "militant" pawns, and to take up the role that the organized masses of our people have attempted to play ever since we came to these shores. That of harbingers of true justice and humanity, leaders in the struggle for liberation.

A major part of the challenge we must accept is that of redefining the functions and operations of all levels of American government, for the existing governing structures—from Washington to the smallest county—are obsolescent. That is part of the reason why nothing works and why corruption rages throughout public life. For white politics seeks not to serve but to dominate and manipulate.

We will have joined the true movement of history if at Gary we grasp the opportunity to press Man forward as the first consideration of politics. Here at Gary we are faithful to the best hopes of our fathers and our people if we move for nothing less than a politics which places community before individualism, love before sexual exploitation, a living environment before profits, peace before war, justice before unjust "order", and morality before expediency.

This is the society we need, but we delude ourselves here at Gary if we think that change can be achieved without organizing the power, the determined national Black power, which is necessary to insist upon such change, to create such change, to seize change.

TOWARDS A BLACK AGENDA

So when we turn to a Black Agenda for the seventies, we move in the truth of history, in the reality of the moment. We move recognizing that no one else is going to represent our interests but ourselves. The society we seek cannot come unless Black people organize to advance its coming. We lift up a Black Agenda recognizing that white America moves towards the abyss created by its own racist arrogance, misplaced priorities, rampant materialism, and ethical bankruptcy. Therefore, we are certain that the Agenda we now press for in Gary is not only for the future of Black humanity, but is probably the only way the rest of America can save itself from the harvest of its criminal past.

So, Brothers and Sisters of our developing Black nation, we now stand at Gary as people whose time has come. From every corner of Black America, from all liberation movements of the Third World, from the graves of our fathers and the coming world of our children, we are faced with a challenge and a call:

Though the moment is perilous we must not despair. We must seize the time, for the time is ours.

We begin here and now in Gary. We begin with an independent Black political movement, an independent Black Political Agenda, and independent Black spirit. Nothing less will do. We must build for our people. We must build for our world. We stand on the edge of history. We cannot turn back.

Source: "Gary Declaration: Black Politics at the Crossroads," First National Black Political Convention, March 11, 1972, Gary, Indiana, https://www.blackpast.org /african-american-history/gary-declaration-national-black-political-convention-1972/.

DOCUMENT 11.2

Shirley Chisholm, "Equal Rights for Women (1969)

Shirley Chisholm was elected to the U.S. Congress in 1968 as a representative of New York and would serve in that capacity until 1983. As the first Black woman in Congress, Chisholm frequently discussed the impact of sex discrimination on her life and the lives of women across America. One notable example of this occurred on May 21, 1969, when she delivered the following congressional speech on the necessity of the Equal Rights Amendment. This proposed constitutional amendment sought to eradicate gender discrimination. In 1972, Chisholm became the first African American to run for U.S. president from a major party and the first woman to run for president as a Democrat. Chisholm's historic candidacy garnered support from the women's movement and a broad array of progressive Democrats. However, Chisholm's candidacy suffered from a lack of funding, a lack of support from mainstream and Black Democratic leadership, as well as male chauvinism.

Mr. Speaker, when a young woman graduates from college and starts looking for a job, she is likely to have a frustrating and even demeaning experience ahead of her. If she walks into an office for an interview, the first question she will be asked is, "Do you type?"

There is a calculated system of prejudice that lies unspoken behind that question. Why is it acceptable for women to be secretaries, librarians, and teachers, but totally unacceptable for them to be managers, administrators, doctors, lawyers, and Members of Congress.

The unspoken assumption is that women are different. They do not have executive ability orderly minds, stability, leadership skills, and they are too emotional.

It has been observed before, that society for a long time, discriminated against another minority, the blacks, on the same basis—that they were different and inferior. The happy little homemaker and the contented "old darkey" on the plantation were both produced by prejudice.

As a black person, I am no stranger to race prejudice. But the truth is that in the political world I have been far oftener discriminated against because I am a woman than because I am black.

Prejudice against blacks is becoming unacceptable although it will take years to eliminate it. But it is doomed because, slowly, white America is beginning to admit that it exists. Prejudice against women is still acceptable. There is very little understanding yet of the immorality involved in double pay scales and the classification of most of the better jobs as "for men only."

More than half of the population of the United States is female. But women occupy only 2 percent of the managerial positions. They have not even reached the level of tokenism yet. No women sit on the AFL-CIO council or Supreme Court. There have been only two women who have held Cabinet rank, and at present there are none. Only two women now hold ambassadorial rank in the diplomatic corps. In Congress, we are down to one Senator and 10 Representatives.

Considering that there are about 3 1/2 million more women in the United States than men, this situation is outrageous.

It is true that part of the problem has been that women have not been aggressive in demanding their rights. This was also true of the black population for many years. They submitted to oppression and even cooperated with it. Women have done the same thing. But now there is an awareness of this situation particularly among the younger segment of the population.

As in the field of equal rights for blacks, Spanish-Americans, the Indians, and other groups, laws will not change such deep-seated problems overnight. But they can be used to provide protection for those who are most abused, and to begin the process of evolutionary change by compelling the insensitive majority to reexamine it's [sic] unconscious attitudes.

It is for this reason that I wish to introduce today a proposal that has been before every Congress for the last 40 years and that sooner or later must become part of the basic law of the land—the equal rights amendment.

Let me note and try to refute two of the commonest arguments that are offered against this amendment. One is that women are already protected under the law and do not need legislation. Existing laws are not adequate to secure equal rights for women. Sufficient proof of this is the concentration of women in lower paying, menial, unrewarding jobs and their incredible scarcity in the upper level jobs. If women are already equal, why is it such an event whenever one happens to be elected to Congress?

It is obvious that discrimination exists. Women do not have the opportunities that men do. And women that do not conform to the system, who try to break with the accepted patterns, are stigmatized as "odd" and "unfeminine." The fact is that a woman who aspires to be chairman of the board, or a Member of the House, does so for exactly the same reasons as any man. Basically, these are that she thinks she can do the job and she wants to try.

A second argument often heard against the equal rights amendment is that is would eliminate legislation that many States and the Federal Government have enacted giving special protection to women and that it would throw the marriage and divorce laws into chaos.

As for the marriage laws, they are due for a sweeping reform, and an excellent beginning would be to wipe the existing ones off the books. Regarding special protection for working women, I cannot understand why it should be needed. Women need no protection that men do not need. What we need are laws to protect working people, to guarantee them fair pay, safe working conditions, protection against sickness and layoffs, and provision for dignified, comfortable retirement. Men and women need these things equally. That one sex needs protection more than the other is a male supremacist myth as ridiculous and unworthy of respect as the white supremacist myths that society is trying to cure itself of at this time.

Source: Shirley Chisholm, "Equal Rights for Women," May 21, 1969, speech,
U.S. House of Representatives, Washington, D.C.

DOCUMENT 11.3

Harold Washington, Inaugural Address (1983)

Often heralded as "the people's mayor," Harold Washington was a native Chicagoan, born and raised in Bronzeville, a cultural center of Chicago's Black South Side. After serving in World War II, Washington attended Roosevelt University as an undergraduate and later earned his law degree from Northwestern University's School of Law in 1952. Washington went on to work in local city politics under the tutelage of Ralph Metcalfe Sr. and with other Black Democratic politicians. From there, he campaigned and was elected to the Illinois House of Representatives where he served from 1965 to 1976, the Illinois Senate from 1977 to 1980, and the U.S. House of Representatives from 1981 to 1983. Washington's mayoral campaign and subsequent administrations exposed the bitter racism of the city's machine politics as well as the promise of multiracial liberal coalitions and reform politics. Washington died suddenly of a heart attack in 1987, just months after his reelection as mayor. What follows is Washington's inaugural address dated April 29, 1983.

This is a very serious vow that I've just taken before God and man, to do everything in my power to protect this City and every person who lives in it. I do not take this duty lightly. I was up late last night thinking about this moment. It went through my head hundreds and hundreds of times, and words that I was reading put me in a reflective and a somber, somber mood.

On my right hand last night was a bible, which is a very good book for a new Mayor to pay attention to. And, in front of me was a report of the City's finances which my transition team had prepared, and it did not contain very good news. To my left there was no book because the one I wanted the most does not exist. It's the one I wish had been written by my tribesman, Jean Pointe Baptiste DuSable, who settled Chicago over 200 years ago.

And, as I reflected last night for a brief period of time, I wish he had written a book about how to be a Mayor of a vast city like ours, a repository of wisdom that had been handed down from Mayor to Mayor for all these years.

Because, after reading the report about the actual state of the City's finances, I wanted some good solid, sound advice.

Then I realized that to solve the problems facing us, it will have to be decided between you and me, because every Mayor begins anew, and there is no blueprint for the future course that these cities, these municipalities must follow.

So I made a list of some of the things you told me during the election campaign, and I found out that you had given me the best and most solid advice.

The first thing you told me is to do no harm. You told me that the guiding principle of government is to do the greatest good. Your instructions which I heard from neighborhood after neighborhood, said to be patient and be fair, be candid and, in short, to continue to tell the truth.

And so, without malice, even remotely connected with my statement, but impelled by a sense of necessity so that I can continue my reputation for truth and live up to your mandate which requested the truth, I must tell you what we have inherited. I must tell you about the City's finances. As I said before, I have no good news. The immediate fiscal problem facing Chicago is both enormous and complicated.

- Our school system is not 100 million dollars short next year as we believed during the mayoral campaign. We now find that the income may be $200 million less than the expenditures of that vast bureaucracy.

- My transition team advises me that the city government is also in far worse financial condition than we thought. The City's general fund has a potential shortfall this year of as much as $150 million.

- To further complicate the matter, in the waning days of the outgoing administration, hundreds of new city jobs were passed out and hundreds of other jobs reassigned. . . .

- The City's transportation system faces a $200 million deficit and no internal solution harbors on the horizon.

All during the campaign I knew that the City had financial problems and I talked about them repeatedly, incessantly. A majority of the voters believed me and embarked on what can only be described as a great movement and revitalization labeled reform.

My election was the result of the greatest grass roots effort in the history of the City of Chicago. It may have been equaled somewhere in this country, I know not where.

My election was made possible by thousands and thousands of people who demanded that the burdens of mismanagement, unfairness and inequity be lifted so that the City could be saved.

One of the ideas that held us all together said that neighborhood involvement has to take the place of the ancient, decrepit and creaking machine. City government for once in our lifetime must be made equitable and fair. The people of Chicago have asked for more responsibility and more representation at every city level.

It's a good thing that your philosophy prevailed, because otherwise I'm not sure that the City could solve the financial crisis at hand.

Reluctantly, I must tell you that because of circumstances thrust upon us, each and everyone of us, we must immediately cut back on how much money the City can spend.

Monday, I will issue an order to freeze all City hiring and raises, in order to reduce the City expenses by millions of dollars. We will have no choice but to release several hundred new City employees who were added because of political considerations. . . .

Beginning Monday, executive salaries will be cut. Some members of my cabinet will be required to take salaries considerably less than their counterparts are now making. Holdover chiefs will be ordered to take salary cuts as well.

Unnecessary City programs are going to have to be ended, and the fat removed from all departments until there are sinew and bone left.

So that there's no confusion, these cuts will begin in the mayor's office.

But these measures are not enough to make up the enormous deficits we have inherited. Like other cities across the state, we simply cannot provide adequate public service without additional sources of revenue. During the election, I said that there was no alternative to a higher state income tax.

Chicago is not an island unto itself and other municipalities in this state suffer just as direly as we do. And municipal and state officials have joined us in this fight for more tax support. We must have new sources of income and I've joined the governor of this great state in his quest for those additional sources of income. . . .

But when it finally comes down to basic issues, I'm only going to be successful if your are involved. The neighborhoods and the people who reside in them are going to have to play an active, creative role in this administration. I am asking you now to join that team.

In the late hours last night, while contemplating the enormity of the challenge we face together, I remembered the great words of President John Fitzgerald Kennedy at his inaugural address in 1961.

"Ask not for what your country can do for you" he said. "Ask what you can do for your country."

In that same spirit, today I am asking all of you—particularly you who have taken the oath with me today—to respond to a great challenge: help me institute reforms and bring about the revival and renewal of this great City while there is still time.

Business as usual will not be accepted by the people of this City. Business as usual will not be accepted by any part of this City. Business as usual will not be accepted by this chief executive of this great City. . . .

The real challenge is in the neighborhoods, as I've said for the past several months. I'm asking the people in the neighborhoods, all of the neighborhoods, to take a direct role in the planning, development and City housekeeping so that our City becomes a finer place in which to live.

I'm calling for more leadership and more personal involvement in what goes on. We know the strength of the grassroots leadership because our election was based on it. We want this powerful infra-structure to grow because the success of tomorrow's City depends upon it, and the world and country look for an example as to how we can find the way out.

Information must flow freely from the administration to the people and back again. The City's books will be open to the public because we don't have a chance to institute fiscal reform unless we all know the hard facts. I believe in the process of collective bargaining when all the numbers are on the table and the City and its unions sit down and hammer out an agreement together. The only contracts in life are those that work and work because they are essentially fair.

Having said all this, I want you to know that the situation is serious but not desperate. I am optimistic about our future. I'm optimistic not just because I have a positive view of life, and I do, but because there is so much about this City that promises achievement.

We are a multi-ethnic, multi-racial, multi-language City and that is not a source to negate but really a source of pride, because it adds stability and strength to a metropolitan city as large as ours.

Our minorities are ambitious, and that is a sign of a prosperous city on the move. Racial fears and divisiveness have hurt us in the past. But I believe that this is a situation that will and must be overcome. . . .

I'm going to set a personal example for what we all have to do by working harder and longer than you've ever seen a mayor work before.

Most of our problems can be solved. Some of them will take brains, some of them will take patience, and all of them will have to be wrested with like an alligator in the swamp.

But there is a fine new spirit that seems to be taking root. I call it the spirit of renewal. It's like the spring coming here after a long winter. This renewal. It refreshes us and gives us new faith that we can go on.

Last night I saw the dark problems and today I see the bright promise of where we stand. Chicago has all the resources necessary for prosperity. We are at the crossroads of America—a vital transportation, economic, and business center. We are the heartland.

We have a clear vision of what our people can become, and that vision goes beyond mere economic wealth, although that is a part of our hopes and expectations.

In our ethnic and racial diversity, we are all brothers and sisters in a quest for greatness. Our creativity and energy are unequaled by any city anywhere in the world. We will not rest until the renewal of our City is done. . . .

I hope someday to be remembered by history as the Mayor who cared about people and who was, above all, fair. A Mayor who helped, who really helped, heal our wounds and stood the watch while the City and its people answered the greatest challenge in more than a century. Who saw that City renewed.

My good friends and neighbors, the oath of office that I have taken today before

God binds us all together. I cannot be successful without you. But with you, we can not fail. . . .

Thank you.

Source: Harold Washington, Inaugural Address, 1983, speech, in *Journal of the Proceedings*, Chicago City Council, April 29, 1983, 7–11, https://www.chipublib.org/mayor-harold-washington-inaugural-address-1983/.

DOCUMENT 11.4

Jesse Jackson, Speech on the Presidential Campaign Trail (1988)

In 1984, civil rights activist and minister Jesse Jackson became the second African American to run for U.S. president from a major party. At the time of his first presidential run, Jackson was the head of Rainbow/PUSH, a social justice organization based in Chicago, and known for his civil rights activism nationally and abroad. He placed third in the Democratic primary in 1984 with about 3.3 million votes, despite some controversy surrounding his campaign. Four years later in 1988, Jackson experienced even more success with nearly seven million votes. But he placed second in the Democratic primary to Massachusetts senator Michael Dukakis. What follows is one of Jackson's more noted campaign speeches in which he calls for Americans to "keep hope alive."

REVEREND JACKSON: Thank you. Thank you. Thank you.

. . . We meet tonight at the crossroads, a point of decision. Shall we expand, be inclusive, find unity and power; or suffer division and impotence?

We've come to Atlanta, the cradle of the old South, the crucible of the new South. Tonight, there is a sense of celebration, because we are moved, fundamentally moved from racial battlegrounds by law, to economic common ground. Tomorrow we'll challenge to move to higher ground.

Common ground. Think of Jerusalem, the intersection where many trails met. A small village that became the birthplace for three great religions—Judaism, Christianity, and Islam. Why was this village so blessed? Because it provided a crossroads where different people met, different cultures, different civilizations could meet and find common ground. When people come together, flowers always flourish—the air is rich with the aroma of a new spring. . . .

The only time that we win is when we come together. In 1960, John Kennedy, the late John Kennedy, beat Richard Nixon by only 112,000 votes—less than one vote per precinct. He won by the margin of our hope. He brought us together. He reached out. He had the courage to defy his advisors and inquire about Dr. King's jailing in Albany, Georgia. We won by the margin of our hope, inspired by courageous leadership. In 1964, Lyndon Johnson brought both wings together—the thesis, the antithesis, and the creative synthesis—and together we won. In 1976, Jimmy Carter unified us again, and we won. When do we not come together, we never win. In 1968, the division and despair in July led to our defeat in November. In 1980, rancor in the spring and the summer led to Reagan in the fall. When we divide, we cannot win. We must find common ground as the basis for survival and development and change and growth....

The good of our Nation is at stake. It's commitment to working men and women, to the poor and the vulnerable, to the many in the world.

With so many guided missiles, and so much misguided leadership, the stakes are exceedingly high. Our choice? Full participation in a democratic government, or more abandonment and neglect. And so this night, we choose not a false sense of independence, not our capacity to survive and endure. Tonight we choose interdependency, and our capacity to act and unite for the greater good.

Common good is finding commitment to new priorities to expansion and inclusion. A commitment to expanded participation in the Democratic Party at every level. A commitment to a shared national campaign strategy and involvement at every level....

We find common ground at the plant gate that closes on workers without notice. We find common ground at the farm auction, where a good farmer loses his or her land to bad loans or diminishing markets. Common ground at the school yard where teachers cannot get adequate pay, and students cannot get a scholarship, and can't make a loan. Common ground at the hospital admitting room, where somebody tonight is dying because they cannot afford to go upstairs to a bed that's empty waiting for someone with insurance to get sick. We are a better nation than that. We must do better.

Common ground. What is leadership if not present help in a time of crisis? And so I met you at the point of challenge. In Jay, Maine, where paper workers were striking for fair wages; in Greenville, Iowa, where family farmers struggle for a fair price; in Cleveland, Ohio, where working women seek comparable worth; in McFarland, California, where the children of Hispanic farm workers may be dying from poisoned land, dying in clusters with cancer; in an AIDS hospice in Houston, Texas, where the sick support one another, too often rejected by their own parents and friends.

Common ground. America is not a blanket woven from one thread, one color, one cloth. When I was a child growing up in Greenville, South Carolina and grandmama could not afford a blanket, she didn't complain and we did not freeze. Instead she took pieces of old cloth—patches, wool, silk, gabardine, crockersack—only patches, barely good enough to wipe off your shoes with. But they didn't stay that way very long. With sturdy hands and a strong cord, she sewed them together into a quilt, a thing of beauty and power and culture. Now, Democrats, we must build such a quilt.

Farmers, you seek fair prices and you are right—but you cannot stand alone. Your patch is not big enough.

Workers, you fight for fair wages, you are right—but your patch [of] labor is not big enough.

Women, you seek comparable worth and pay equity, you are right—but your patch is not big enough.

Women, mothers, who seek Head Start, and day care and prenatal care on the front side of life, relevant jail care and welfare on the back side of life—you are right—but your patch is not big enough.

Students, you seek scholarships, you are right—but your patch is not big enough.

Blacks and Hispanics, when we fight for civil rights, we are right—but our patch is not big enough.

Gays and lesbians, when you fight against discrimination and a cure for AIDS, you are right—but your patch is not big enough.

Conservatives and progressives, when you fight for what you believe, right wing, left wing, hawk, dove, you are right from your point of view, but your point of view is not enough. . . .

We believe in a government that's a tool of our democracy in service to the public, not an instrument of the aristocracy in search of private wealth. We believe in government with the consent of the governed, "of, for and by the people." . . .

Reaganomics: Based on the belief that the rich had too much money [*sic*]—too little money and the poor had too much. That's classic Reaganomics. They believe that the poor had too much money and the rich had too little money so they engaged in reverse Robin Hood—took from the poor, gave to the rich, paid for by the middle class. . . .

How do I document that case? Seven years later, the richest 1 percent of our society pays 20 percent less in taxes. The poorest 10 percent pay 20 percent more: Reaganomics.

Reagan gave the rich and the powerful a multibillion-dollar party. Now the party is over. He expects the people to pay for the damage. I take this principal position, convention, let us not raise taxes on the poor and the middle-class, but those who had the party, the rich and the powerful must pay for the party.

I just want to take common sense to high places. We're spending one hundred and fifty billion dollars a year defending Europe and Japan 43 years after the war is over. We have more troops in Europe tonight than we had seven years ago. Yet the threat of war is ever more remote.

Germany and Japan are now creditor nations; that means they've got a surplus. We are a debtor nation. It means we are in debt. Let them share more of the burden of their own defense. Use some of that money to build decent housing. Use some of that money to educate our children. Use some of that money for long-term health care. Use some of that money to wipe out these slums and put America back to work!

I just want to take common sense to high places. If we can bail out Europe and Japan; if we can bail out Continental Bank and Chrysler—and Mr. Iaccoca, makes $8,000 an hour, we can bail out the family farmer.

Most poor people are not lazy. They are not black. They are not brown. They are mostly White and female and young. But whether White, Black or Brown, a hungry baby's belly turned inside out is the same color—color it pain, color it hurt, color it agony.

Most poor people are not on welfare. Some of them are illiterate and can't read the want-ad sections. And when they can, they can't find a job that matches the address. They work hard everyday.

I know. I live amongst them . . . They catch the early bus. They work every day. They raise other people's children. They work everyday . . .

No job is beneath them, and yet when they get sick they cannot lie in the bed they made up every day. America, that is not right. We are a better Nation than that! . . .

We need a real war on drugs. You can't "just say no." It's deeper than that . . .

We are spending $150 billion on drugs a year. We've gone from ignoring it to focusing on the children. Children cannot buy $150 billion worth of drugs a year; a few high-profile athletes—athletes are not laundering $150 billion a year—bankers are . . .

You cannot fight a war on drugs unless until you're going to challenge the bankers and the gun sellers and those who grow them. Don't just focus on the children, let's stop drugs at the level of supply and demand. We must end the scourge on the American Culture! . . .

This generation must offer leadership to the real world. We're losing ground in Latin America, Middle East, South Africa because we're not focusing on the real world. That's the real world. We must use basic principles, support international law. We stand the most to gain from it. Support human rights; we believe in that. Support self-determination, we're built on that. Support economic development, you know it's right. Be consistent and gain our moral authority in the world. I challenge you tonight, my friends, let's be bigger and better as a Nation and as a Party! . . .

We have basic challenges—freedom in South Africa. We have already agreed as Democrats to declare South Africa to be a terrorist state. But don't just stop there. Get South Africa out of Angola; free Namibia; support the front line states. We must have a new humane human rights consistent policy in Africa. . . .

And then for our children. Young America, hold your head high now. We can win . . .

You must never stop dreaming. Face reality, yes, but don't stop with the way things are. Dream of things as they ought to be. Face pain, but love, hope, faith and dreams will help you rise above the pain. Use hope and imagination as weapons of survival and progress, but you keep on dreaming, young America . . .

Keep hope alive. Keep hope alive! Keep hope alive! On tomorrow night and beyond, keep hope alive!

Source: Jesse Jackson, "1988 Democratic National Convention Address," July 19, 1988, speech, Omni Coliseum, Atlanta, reprinted from Jesse L. Jackson, *Keeping Hope Alive: Sermons and Speeches of Rev. Jesse L. Jackson, Sr.* (Maryknoll, NY: Orbis Books, 2020). Copyright © 2020 by Jesse L. Jackson and Grace Ji-Sun Kim. Used with permission.

Ocean Hill–Brownsville Flyer on School Control (1968)

In the late 1960s, with integration efforts at a standstill in the years following the *Brown* decision and influenced by the Black Power Movement, Black and Puerto Rican communities in the Ocean Hill–Brownsville neighborhoods of Brooklyn, New York, sought to gain community control of their public schools through decentralization efforts. As stated in the flyer below, they demanded the hiring of more Black teachers and administrators, an expansion of the Black and ethnic studies curriculum, and equitable funding for the schools in their communities. They eventually gained control and dismissed the district's teachers, who were mostly white and Jewish, which pitted them against the United Federation of Teachers union and city administrators and resulted in the New York City teachers strike of 1968. Ultimately, however, the state took back Ocean Hill–Brownsville and reinstated the dismissed teachers, and racial tensions persisted.

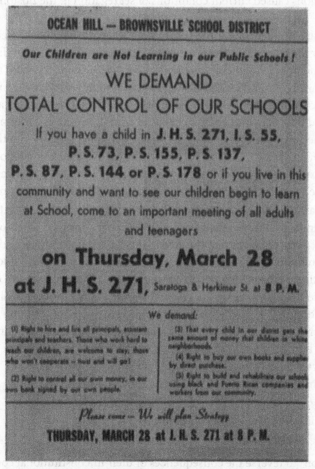

Source: Pro-community-control flyer circulated by Ocean Hill–
Brownsville governing board, March 1968, ink on paper, United
Federation of Teachers, Photograph Collection,
Robert F. Wagner Labor Archives, New York University.

Tallulah Morgan et al. v. James W. Hennigan et al. Decision (1974)

Despite the *Brown v. Board of Education* decision that ruled segregation in public schools as unconstitutional, many public school systems across the United States remained segregated twenty years later. In 1972, the Boston chapter of the NAACP filed suit on behalf of Tallulah Morgan, a parent, and several others who charged that the Boston School Committee, led by James Hennigan, intentionally maintained racially segregated schools through feeder patterns and failed to provide equitable resources to predominantly Black schools. In 1974, the U.S. District Court of Massachusetts ruled in favor of Morgan and the other plaintiffs and mandated the desegregation of Boston's public schools. An excerpt from the court's ruling follows.

... [T]he court concludes that the defendants took many actions in their official capacities with the purpose and intent to segregate the Boston public schools and that such actions caused current conditions of segregation in the Boston public schools. ...

On the issue whether substantial portions of the system have been intentionally segregated by the defendants, the court concludes that they have. Plaintiffs have proved that the defendants intentionally segregated schools at all levels ...; built new schools for a decade with sizes and locations designed to promote segregation; maintained patterns of overcrowding and underutilization which promoted segregation at 26 schools; and expanded the capacity of approximately 40 schools by means of portables and additions when students could have been assigned to other schools with the effect of reducing racial imbalance. ... Similarly every segregative transfer under open enrollment or an exception to the controlled transfer policy, whether by a white or black student, increased segregation in the sending school as well as in the receiving school. ...

Indeed plaintiffs' evidence showed, independently of reciprocal effects, that some of defendants' practices had a segregative impact on entire levels of the school system. The court concludes that the defendants have knowingly carried out a systematic program of segregation affecting all of the city's students, teachers and school facilities and have intentionally brought about and maintained a dual school system. Therefore the entire school system of Boston is unconstitutionally segregated. Accordingly, the court will contemporaneously with this opinion file a partial judgment permanently enjoining the city defendants from discriminating upon the basis of race in the operation of the Boston public schools and ordering that they begin forthwith the formulation and implementation of plans to secure for the plaintiffs their constitutional rights.

REMEDIAL GUIDELINES

It is time to turn to the future. Henceforth the defendants are under an "affirmative obligation" to reverse the consequences of their unconstitutional conduct. The defendants must eliminate all vestiges of the dual system "root and branch." ...

In order to assist the defendants in carrying out their obligations, the court will outline several remedial principles which the Supreme Court has declared to be constitutionally applicable. First, the obligation of the defendants is to proceed now to secure the rights of the plaintiffs. . . .

Second, the primary responsibility for desegregation lies with the school committee. If, in fulfilling this responsibility, policy preferences hinder or obstruct the conversion to a unitary school system, they "must give way [since they would] hinder vindication of federal constitutional guarantees." This means that a preference not to bus, or for neighborhood schools, or any other policy preference, can be validly maintained only if it will not interfere with the defendants' constitutional duty to desegregate. Also "these constitutional principles cannot be allowed to yield simply because of disagreement with them." No amount of public or parental opposition will excuse avoidance by school officials of constitutionally imposed obligations.

Third, "school authorities are 'clearly charged with the affirmative duty to take whatever steps might be necessary.'" This means that busing, the pairing of schools, redistricting with both contiguous and non-contiguous boundary lines, involuntary student and faculty assignments, and all other means, some of which may be distasteful to both school officials and teachers and parents, must be evaluated; and, if necessary to achieve a unitary school system, they must be implemented. The Supreme Court has recognized that "the remedy for such segregation may be administratively awkward, inconvenient, and even bizarre in some situations and may impose burdens on some; but all awkwardness and inconvenience cannot be avoided . . . when remedial adjustments are being made to eliminate the dual school systems." The Supreme Court has also indicated that the non-use of a more effective plan may indicate a "lack of good faith" on the part of the defendants, and any such preference places a heavy burden of justification upon them. . . .

Fourth, the Supreme Court has said, "Awareness of the racial composition of the whole school system is likely to be a useful starting point in shaping a remedy to correct past constitutional violations." In Boston the public school population is approximately two-thirds white and one-third black; ideally every school in the system would have the same racial proportions, although as a practical matter there is no prospect of achieving this 2:1 ratio in every school. The Court has also pointed out that with desegregation plans which leave any schools all or predominantly one race, white or black, the defendants must carry the burden that such treatment is genuinely nondiscriminatory. . . .

Fifth, such time as the court allows for formulation and implementation of plans to desegregate Boston's schools will not be granted at the cost of continuing the denial of the plaintiffs' rights under the Constitution. For this reason the time allowed for compliance must be only that reasonably necessary to design and evaluate plans to be presented to the court and thereafter only the time reasonably necessary, administratively, to implement the plan which is ultimately approved by the court. The Supreme Court has decreed that "the burden rests upon the defendants to establish that such time is necessary in the public interest and is consistent with good faith compliance at the earliest practicable date."

. . . The state court plan is scheduled to take effect on the opening day of school in September 1974. Our understanding is that this plan will reduce the number of majority black schools from 68 to 44 and the number of black children attending imbalanced schools from approximately 30,000 to approximately 10,000. The state plan relies on two of the traditional methods, redistricting and busing. The plan also removes one of Boston's structural obstacles to integration by converting the entire system, except for McKay junior high in East Boston, to the middle school design, i.e., all students entering the sixth grade will be in a middle school and all students entering the ninth grade will be in a high school except at McKay. Under the state board plan, Boston's high schools, except for the three examination schools, are given districts for the first time, thus eliminating many discriminatory feeder patterns. Finally, busing will be used to reduce segregation; state officials predict that approximately 6,000 students will be bused for this reason, but city officials estimate that the number will be closer to 20,000. . . .

Source: *Tallulah Morgan et al. v. James W. Hennigan et al.*, 379 F. Supp. 410 (1974); 1974 U.S. Dist. LEXIS 7973, 56–58., http://www.umass.edu/legal/Hilbink/lpsc/379_f_supp_410.pdf.

Antibusing Rally in Thomas Park, Boston (1975)

The *Morgan v. Hennigan* case resulted in a mandate to desegregate Boston's public schools through busing that involved the transfer of students from predominantly Black neighborhoods to schools in white neighborhoods and vice versa. Busing sparked immediate backlash from whites in Boston and the surrounding areas, much like their southern counterparts in the wake of the *Brown* decision. White men, women, and children engaged in public demonstrations, some of which turned violent, in order to defend their "rights" to segregated schools.

Antibusing rally at Thomas Park, South Boston, 1975.

Source: Spencer Grant, antibusing rally at Thomas Park, South Boston, 1975, photograph, Spencer Grant Collection, Boston Public Library, Digital Commonwealth, https://www.digitalcommonwealth.org/search/commonwealth:qb98mr68r. Courtesy of Spencer Grant.

Regents of the University of California v. Allan Bakke **Decision (1978)**

In the *Bakke* decision, the Supreme Court upheld affirmative action policies that considered race as one of several factors in higher-education admission policies but declared racial quotas unconstitutional. The case revolved around an admissions program at the Medical School of the University of California at Davis that was intended to increase the number of accepted minority students. A white applicant, Allan Bakke, filed suit against the university after failing to be admitted to the program on multiple occasions, despite having higher test scores and grades than minority candidates who were accepted under the university's special admissions plan. The *Bakke* case set a precedent for numerous affirmative action cases in education and employment.

OPINION

POWELL, J., Judgment of the Court

This case presents a challenge to the special admissions program of the petitioner, the Medical School of the University of California at Davis, which is designed to assure the admission of a specified number of students from certain minority groups. The Superior Court of California sustained respondent's challenge, holding that petitioner's program violated the California Constitution, Title VI of the Civil Rights Act of 1964, and the Equal Protection Clause of the Fourteenth Amendment. The court enjoined petitioner from considering respondent's race or the race of any other applicant in making admissions decisions. It refused, however, to order respondent's admission to the Medical School, holding that he had not carried his burden of proving that he would have been admitted but for the constitutional and statutory violations. The Supreme Court of California affirmed those portions of the trial court's judgment declaring the special admissions program unlawful and enjoining petitioner from considering the race of any applicant. It modified that portion of the judgment denying respondent's requested injunction and directed the trial court to order his admission.

For the reasons stated in the following opinion, I believe that so much of the judgment of the California court as holds petitioner's special admissions program unlawful and directs that respondent be admitted to the Medical School must be affirmed. . . .

I also conclude for the reasons stated in the following opinion that the portion of the court's judgment enjoining petitioner from according any consideration to race in its admissions process must be reversed. . . .

Affirmed in part and reversed in part.

. . .

. . . The guarantees of the Fourteenth Amendment extend to all persons. Its language is explicit: "No State shall . . . deny to any person within its jurisdiction the equal protection of the laws." It is settled beyond question that the "rights created by the first section of the Fourteenth Amendment are, by its terms, guaranteed to the individual. The rights established are personal rights. The guarantee of equal protection cannot mean one thing when applied to one individual and something else when applied to a person of another color. If both are not accorded the same protection, then it is not equal.

. . . We have held that, in "order to justify the use of a suspect classification, a State must show that its purpose or interest is both constitutionally permissible and substantial, and that its use of the classification is 'necessary . . . to the accomplishment' of its purpose or the safeguarding of its interest." The special admissions program purports to serve the purposes of: (i) "reducing the historic deficit of traditionally disfavored minorities in medical schools and in the medical profession"; (ii) countering the effects of societal discrimination; (iii) increasing the number of physicians who will practice in communities currently underserved; and (iv) obtaining the educational benefits that flow from an ethnically diverse student body. It is necessary to decide which, if any, of these purposes is substantial enough to support the use of a suspect classification. . . .

The State certainly has a legitimate and substantial interest in ameliorating, or eliminating where feasible, the disabling effects of identified discrimination. The line of school desegregation cases, commencing with *Brown*, attests to the importance of this state goal and the commitment of the judiciary to affirm all lawful means toward its attainment. In the school cases, the States were required by court order to redress the wrongs worked by specific instances of racial discrimination. That goal was far more focused than the remedying of the effects of "societal discrimination," an amorphous concept of injury that may be ageless in its reach into the past.

We have never approved a classification that aids persons perceived as members of relatively victimized groups at the expense of other innocent individuals in the absence of judicial, legislative, or administrative findings of constitutional or statutory violations. After such findings have been made, the governmental interest in preferring members of the injured groups at the expense of others is substantial, since the legal rights of the victims must be vindicated. In such a case, the extent of the injury and the consequent remedy will have been judicially, legislatively, or administratively defined. Also, the remedial action usually remains subject to continuing oversight to assure that it will work the least harm possible to other innocent persons competing for the benefit. Without such findings of constitutional or statutory violations, it cannot be said that the government has any greater interest in helping one individual than in refraining from harming another. Thus, the government has no compelling justification for inflicting such harm.

. . .

Hence, the purpose of helping certain groups whom the faculty of the Davis Medical School perceived as victims of "societal discrimination" does not justify a classification that imposes disadvantages upon persons like respondent, who bear no responsibility for whatever harm the beneficiaries of the special admissions program are thought to have suffered. To hold otherwise would be to convert a remedy heretofore reserved for violations of legal rights into a privilege that all institutions throughout the Nation could grant at their pleasure to whatever groups are perceived as victims of societal discrimination. . . .

Petitioner identifies, as another purpose of its program, improving the delivery of health care services to communities currently underserved. It may be assumed that in some situations a State's interest in facilitating the health care of its citizens is sufficiently compelling to support the use of a suspect classification. But there is virtually no evidence in the record indicating that petitioner's special admissions program is either needed or geared to promote that goal. The court below addressed this failure of proof:

"The University concedes it cannot assure that minority doctors who entered under the program, all of whom expressed an 'interest' in practicing in a disadvantaged community, will actually do so. It may be correct to assume that some of them will carry out this intention, and that it is more likely they will practice in minority communities than the average white doctor. Nevertheless, there are more precise and reliable ways to identify applicants who are genuinely interested in the medical problems of minorities than by race. An applicant of whatever race who has demonstrated his concern for disadvantaged minorities in the past and who declares that practice in such a community is his primary professional goal would be more likely to contribute to alleviation of the medical shortage than one who is chosen entirely on the basis of race and disadvantage. In short, there is no empirical data to demonstrate that any one race is more selflessly socially oriented or by contrast that another is more selfishly acquisitive."

. . .

The fourth goal asserted by petitioner is the attainment of a diverse student body. This clearly is a constitutionally permissible goal for an institution of higher education. Academic freedom, though not a specifically enumerated constitutional right, long has been viewed as a special concern of the First Amendment. The freedom of a university to make its own judgments as to education includes the selection of its student body. . . .

Physicians serve a heterogeneous population. An otherwise qualified medical student with a particular background—whether it be ethnic, geographic, culturally advantaged or disadvantaged—may bring to a professional school of medicine experiences, outlooks, and ideas that enrich the training of its student body and better equip its graduates to render with understanding their vital service to humanity.

Ethnic diversity, however, is only one element in a range of factors a university properly may consider in attaining the goal of a heterogeneous student body. Although a university must have wide discretion in making the sensitive judgments as to who should be admitted, constitutional limitations protecting individual rights may not be disregarded. Respondent urges—and the courts below have held—that petitioner's dual admissions program is a racial classification that impermissibly infringes his rights under the Fourteenth Amendment. As the interest of diversity is compelling in the context of a university's admissions program, the question remains whether the program's racial classification is necessary to promote this interest.

. . .

It may be assumed that the reservation of a specified number of seats in each class for individuals from the preferred ethnic groups would contribute to the attainment of considerable ethnic diversity in the student body. But petitioner's argument that this is the only effective means of serving the interest of diversity is seriously flawed. In a most fundamental sense the argument misconceives the nature of the state interest that would justify consideration of race or ethnic background. It is not an interest in simple ethnic diversity, in which a specified percentage of the student body is in effect guaranteed to be members of selected ethnic groups, with the remaining percentage an undifferentiated aggregation of students. The diversity that furthers a compelling state interest encompasses a far broader array of qualifications and characteristics of which racial or ethnic origin is but a single though important element. Petitioner's special admissions program, focused *solely* on ethnic diversity, would hinder rather than further attainment of genuine diversity . . .

The experience of other university admissions programs, which take race into account in achieving the educational diversity valued by the First Amendment, demonstrates that the assignment of a fixed number of places to a minority group is not a necessary means toward that end . . .

Race or ethnic background may be deemed a "plus" in a particular applicant's file, yet it does not insulate the individual from comparison with all other candidates for the available seats. The file of a particular black applicant may be examined for his potential contribution to diversity without the factor of race being decisive when compared, for example, with that of an applicant identified as an Italian-American if the latter is thought to exhibit qualities more likely to promote beneficial educational pluralism. Such qualities could include exceptional personal talents, unique work or service experience, leadership potential, maturity, demonstrated compassion, a history of overcoming disadvantage, ability to communicate with the poor, or other qualifications deemed important. In short, an admissions program operated in this way is flexible enough to consider all pertinent elements of diversity in light of the particular qualifications of each applicant, and to place them on the same footing for consideration, although not necessarily according them the same weight. Indeed, the weight attributed to a particular quality may vary from year to year depending upon the "mix" both of the student body and the applicants for the incoming class.

This kind of program treats each applicant as an individual in the admissions process. The applicant who loses out on the last available seat to another candidate receiving a "plus" on the basis of ethnic background will not have been foreclosed from all consideration for that seat simply because he was not the right color or had the wrong surname. It would mean only that his combined qualifications, which may have included similar nonobjective factors, did not outweigh those of the other applicant. His qualifications would have been weighed fairly and competitively, and he would have no basis to complain of unequal treatment under the Fourteenth Amendment . . .

In summary, it is evident that the Davis special admissions program involves the use of an explicit racial classification never before countenanced by this Court. It tells applicants who are not Negro, Asian, or Chicano that they are totally excluded from a specific percentage of the seats in an entering class. No matter how strong their qualifications, quantitative and extracurricular, including their own potential for contribution to educational diversity, they are never afforded the chance to compete with applicants from the preferred groups for the special admissions seats. At the same time, the preferred applicants have the opportunity to compete for every seat in the class.

The fatal flaw in petitioner's preferential program is its disregard of individual rights as guaranteed by the Fourteenth Amendment. Such rights are not absolute. But when a State's distribution of benefits or imposition of burdens hinges on ancestry or the color of a person's skin, that individual is entitled to a demonstration that the challenged classification is necessary to promote a substantial state interest. Petitioner has failed to carry this burden. For this reason, that portion of the California court's judgment holding petitioner's special admissions program invalid under the Fourteenth Amendment must be affirmed . . .

With respect to respondent's entitlement to an injunction directing his admission to the Medical School, petitioner has conceded that it could not carry its burden of proving that, but for the existence of its unlawful special admissions program, respondent still would not have been admitted. Hence, respondent is entitled to the injunction, and that portion of the judgment must be affirmed.

Source: *U.S. Reports: University of California Regents v. Bakke,* 438 U.S. 265 (1978), 269–320.
https://tile.loc.gov/storage-services/service/ll/usrep/usrep438/usrep438265/usrep438265.pdf.

DOCUMENT 11.9

United Steelworkers of America, AFL-CIO-CLC v. Brian Weber Decision (1979)

For years, Kaiser Aluminum discriminated against Black workers and failed to offer pathways for their training and promotion. In 1974, the company entered into a labor agreement with the United Steelworkers of America union that included a training program to counteract past discrimination and provide pathways to skilled work and promotions. Spots in the program were based on seniority, but half of all spots were allotted for Black employees. Brian F. Weber, a white Kaiser employee, brought a discrimination suit against the union when he was passed up for a spot despite having more seniority than a number of Black candidates. In a 5–2 ruling in its first affirmative action employment case, the Supreme Court decided that the training program was a private, voluntary agreement that did not preclude all whites and thus not a violation of the 1964 Civil Rights Act. Furthermore, the program was intended to right past wrongs. Justice William J. Brennan authored the majority opinion. In a dissenting opinion, Justice William Rehnquist argued that the affirmative action program and quotas violated the 1964 Civil Rights Act.

OPINION

BRENNAN, J., Opinion of the Court

MR. JUSTICE BRENNAN delivered the opinion of the Court.

Challenged here is the legality of an affirmative action plan collectively bargained by an employer and a union that: reserves for black employees 50% of the openings in an in-plant craft training program until the percentage of black craft-workers in the plant is commensurate with the percentage of blacks in the local labor force.

The question for decision is whether Congress, in Title VII of the Civil Rights Act of 1964, as amended, left employers and unions in the private sector free to take such race-conscious steps to eliminate manifest racial imbalances in traditionally segregated job categories. We hold that Title VII does not prohibit such race-conscious affirmative action plans . . .

In 1974, petitioner United Steelworkers of America (USWA) and petitioner Kaiser Aluminum & Chemical Corp. entered into a master collective bargaining agreement covering terms and conditions of employment at 15 Kaiser plants. The agreement contained, inter alia, an affirmative action plan designed to eliminate conspicuous racial imbalances in Kaiser's then almost exclusively white craft workforces. Black craft hiring goals were set for each Kaiser plant equal to the percentage of blacks in the respective local labor forces. To enable plants to meet these goals, on-the-job training programs were established to teach unskilled production workers—black and white—the skills necessary to become craft workers. The plan reserved for black employees 50% of the openings in these newly created in-plant training programs.

   This case arose from the operation of the plan at Kaiser's plant in Gramercy, La. Until 1974, Kaiser hired as craft workers for that plant only persons who had had prior craft experience. Because blacks had long been excluded from craft unions few were able to present such credentials. As a consequence, prior to 1974, only 1.83% (5 out of 273) of the skilled craft workers at the Gramercy plant were black, even though the workforce in the Gramercy area was approximately 39% black.

   Pursuant to the national agreement, Kaiser altered its craft hiring practice in the Gramercy plant. Rather than hiring already trained outsiders, Kaiser established a training program to train its production workers to fill craft openings. Selection of craft trainees was made on the basis of seniority, with the proviso that at least 50% of the new trainees were to be black until the percentage of black skilled craft workers in the Gramercy plant approximated the percentage of blacks in the local labor force.

   During 1974, the first year of the operation of the Kaiser-USWA affirmative action plan, 13 craft trainees were selected from Gramercy's production workforce. Of these, seven were black and six white. The most senior black selected into the program had less seniority than several white production workers whose bids for admission were rejected. Thereafter, one of those white production workers, respondent Brian Weber (hereafter respondent), instituted this class action in the United States District Court for the Eastern District of Louisiana.

   The complaint alleged that the filling of craft trainee positions at the Gramercy plant pursuant to the affirmative action program had resulted in junior black employees' receiving training in preference to senior white employees, thus discriminating against respondent and other similarly situated white employees in violation of Title VII. The District Court held that the plan violated Title VII, entered a judgment in favor of the plaintiff class, and granted a permanent injunction prohibiting Kaiser and the USWA "from denying plaintiffs, Brian F. Weber and all other members of the class, access to on-the-job training programs on the basis of race." A divided panel of the Court of Appeals for the Fifth Circuit affirmed, holding that all employment preferences based upon race, including those preferences incidental to bona fide affirmative action plans, violated Title VII's prohibition against racial discrimination in employment. We granted certiorari. We reverse.

We emphasize at the outset the narrowness of our inquiry. Since the Kaiser-USWA plan does not involve state action, this case does not present an alleged violation of the Equal Protection Clause of the Fourteenth Amendment. Further, since the Kaiser-USWA plan was adopted voluntarily, we are not concerned with what Title VII requires or with what a court might order to remedy a past proved violation of the Act. The only question before us is the narrow statutory issue of whether Title VII forbids private employers and unions from voluntarily agreeing upon bona fide affirmative action plans that accord racial preferences in the manner and for the purpose provided in the Kaiser-USWA plan . . .

Respondent argues that Congress intended in §§ 703(a) and (d) of Title VII to prohibit all race-conscious affirmative action plans. Respondent's argument rests upon a literal interpretation of the Act. Those sections make it unlawful to "discriminate . . . because of . . . race" in hiring and in the selection of apprentices for training programs . . .

Respondent's argument is not without force. But it overlooks the significance of the fact that the Kaiser-USWA plan is an affirmative action plan voluntarily adopted by private parties to eliminate traditional patterns of racial segregation . . . The prohibition against racial discrimination in §§ 703(a) and (d) of Title VII must therefore be read against the background of the legislative history of Title VII and the historical context from which the Act arose . . .

Congress' primary concern in enacting the prohibition against racial discrimination in Title VII of the Civil Rights Act of 1964 was with "the plight of the Negro in our economy." Before 1964, blacks were largely relegated to "unskilled and semi-skilled jobs." Because of automation, the number of such jobs was rapidly decreasing . . .

Congress feared that the goals of the Civil Rights Act—the integration of blacks into the mainstream of American society—could not be achieved unless this trend were reversed. And Congress recognized that that would not be possible unless blacks were able to secure jobs "which have a future" . . .

Given this legislative history, we cannot agree with respondent that Congress intended to prohibit the private sector from taking effective steps to accomplish the goal that Congress designed Title VII to achieve. The very statutory words intended as a spur or catalyst to cause "employers and unions to self-examine and to self-evaluate their employment practices and to endeavor to eliminate, so far as possible, the last vestiges of an unfortunate and ignominious page in this country's history," cannot be interpreted as an absolute prohibition against all private, voluntary, race-conscious affirmative action efforts to hasten the elimination of such vestiges . . .

Opponents of Title VII raised two related arguments against the bill. First, they argued that the Act would be interpreted to require employers with racially imbalanced workforces to grant preferential treatment to racial minorities in order to integrate. Second, they argued that employers with racially imbalanced workforces would grant preferential treatment to racial minorities, even if not required to do so by the Act. Had Congress meant to prohibit all race-conscious affirmative action, as respondent urges, it easily could have answered both objections by providing that Title VII would not require or permit racially preferential integration efforts. But Congress did not choose such a course . . . The natural inference is that Congress chose not to forbid all voluntary race-conscious affirmative action.

The reasons for this choice are evident from the legislative record. Title VII could not have been enacted into law without substantial support from legislators in both Houses who traditionally resisted federal regulation of private business . . . Clearly, a prohibition against all voluntary, race-conscious, affirmative action efforts would disserve these ends. Such a prohibition would augment the powers of the Federal Government and diminish traditional management prerogatives, while at the same time impeding attainment of the ultimate statutory goals . . .

We therefore hold that Title VII's prohibition in §§ 703(a) and (d) against racial discrimination does not condemn all private, voluntary, race-conscious affirmative action plans.

We need not today define in detail the line of demarcation between permissible and impermissible affirmative action plans. It suffices to hold that the challenged Kaiser-USWA affirmative action plan falls on the permissible side of the line. The purposes of the plan mirror those of the statute. Both were designed to break down old patterns of racial segregation and hierarchy. Both were structured to "open employment opportunities for Negroes in occupations which have been tradition- ally closed to them."

At the same time, the plan does not unnecessarily trammel the interests of the white employees. The plan does not require the discharge of white workers and their replacement with new black hirees. Nor does the plan create an absolute bar to the advancement of white employees; half of those trained in the program will be white. Moreover, the plan is a temporary measure; it is not intended to maintain racial balance, but simply to eliminate a manifest racial imbalance. Preferential selection of craft trainees at the Gramercy plant will end as soon as the percentage of black skilled craft workers in the Gramercy plant approximates the percentage of blacks in the local labor force.

We conclude, therefore, that the adoption of the Kaiser-USWA plan for the Gramercy plant falls within the area of discretion left by Title VII to the private sector voluntarily to adopt affirmative action plans designed to eliminate conspic- uous racial imbalance in traditionally segregated job categories. Accordingly, the judgment of the Court of Appeals for the Fifth Circuit is Reversed.

Source: *U.S. Reports: Steelworkers v. Weber*, 443 U.S. 193 (1979), https://www.loc.gov/item /usrep443193/.

Maynard Jackson Discusses Affirmative Action Policies in Atlanta (1988)

In 1973, Maynard Jackson was elected the first Black mayor of Atlanta and the first Black mayor of a major city in the South, at the age of thirty-five. Jackson's maternal grandfather, John Wesley Dobbs, was a civil rights and voting rights activist in Atlanta in the 1930s and 1940s and an influential member of Atlanta's Black community. Jackson followed in his grandfather's footsteps as mayor of Atlanta and sought to dismantle long-standing discrimination against Blacks. Jackson enacted affirmative action policies that saw the share of city contracts given to Black companies increase from less than 1 percent to nearly 40 percent within five years. In the following interview excerpt, Jackson describes his administration's affirmative action policies during the construction of Atlanta's new airport and opposition toward those policies.

QUESTION 6

JACKIE SHEARER: Okey doke, so let's go into this notion of your being a transition mayor.

MAYNARD JACKSON: Well, um, the obvious, of course, was 50-50 I was the first Black mayor of Atlanta. . . . When I became mayor, zero-point-five percent of all the contracts in the city of Atlanta went to Afro-Americans, in a city which at that time was, and today is about 70 percent Black. Um, there were no women department heads. Ah, this was not only a question of race, it was a question also of sexual discrimination and, you know, all the typical -isms, if there's one, normally there is a whole bunch of them, and um, they were all there. Ah, we had to change dramatically how the appointments to jobs went, ah, normal hiring practices in city government went, the, ah, contracting process, not to reduce the quality by the way, ever. We never ever, ever set up a lower standard. And those who say, "Well, affirmative action means you've got to lower the standard", that's a real insult, in my opinion, to African-Americans and other minority Americans. We never did it, didn't have to do it. We built the Atlanta Airport, biggest terminal building complex in the world, ahead of schedule, and within budget, and simultaneously rewrote the books on affirmative action. Atlanta Airport alone accounted for 89 percent of all the affirmative action in America, in all of America's airports. And the FAA told us that. We didn't know it. So you don't have to sacrifice, and we didn't. So our transition, therefore, was not just a question of race and sex and equal opportunity for women and equal opportunity for minorities, it was also a question of proving the point that we could manage well, and we did. We put new management systems in top to bottom, ah, that we could, ah, have equal rights and equal opportunity and not sacrifice quality. That we could begin to live up to our advance billing as a city, more than we did. I'm proud of Atlanta. And I'm proud of the fact that we are, I think the best in the nation among the major cities in race relations. But, the time had come for us to begin to put our money and our jobs where our mouths were. . . .

QUESTION 7

JACKIE SHEARER: So let me begin by asking you, um, to tell me about, um, ah, some specific reactions to your executive order on affirmative action.

MAYNARD JACKSON: I don't think you have enough film to go into that. Well, the, ah, ah, the reaction was immediate. It was not all White. It was Black and White. The surprise for me was, ah, the number of, ah, Black friends, well-meaning, who were frightened by the aggressiveness of this program. And who cautioned me to slow down. Ah, that they were concerned there might be a reaction against the Black community. Well, um, our, our studies indicated to us there was, the Black community was in a position that, um, for the majority of Black people, things could not get any worse. In some ways, things were excellent, and in other ways were very good or getting better, different categories, but, and better than almost any other city in the country, I keep saying that, because it was true. Atlanta was clearly head and shoulders above the rest of the na—ah, above the rest of the nation. But, not as good as we could be, and not as good as we had to be. Um, um, I had people that say, when I talked about affirmative action, and they were contracting with the city, professional firms or whatever, maybe a law firm, ah, maybe a major corporation, um, I've got a whole file of reactions. You know, one of which was, well, Maynard, ah, This was a, a major, ah, manager of a major White-run corporation, who got very upset with me about the policy on affirmative action. And um, said that "I don't see this to be necessary, we're going to do what's right, you know, you can trust us and so forth." And I said, "I have every confidence, but ah, you know, I want to trust you, but I also want you to sign on the dotted line." Ah, said, "Well, look, I'm just not to going out and hire the first Negro I see." I said, "I think that's a pretty sound personnel policy." I said, "I wouldn't either." And I said, "We're not talking about that. We're talking about a policy. An affirmative action plan." And I said, "I want to work with you." You know, "Well, I can't get it done in a month." I said, "I've never given you a timetable." "Well who do you want us to hire?" I said, "You know my policy, I never, ever recommend the person." And my reason for that is because I never wanted them to be able to say, "Well, Maynard's doing this to kind of get his buddies and his cronies into a job." So I would never recommend anybody for a particular position. But when the first of the downtown banks responded to our initiatives after a while, and, ah, came in and said, "We want to, we want to adopt an affirmative action plan, and we've spotted somebody in the bank we want to promote. It's going to take us about four or five months." I said, "That's fine, I've never said, how long you have to do it. All I want is your word." They kept their word. This was the First Georgia Bank. . . .

Source: Maynard Jackson (first Black mayor of Atlanta), interview with Jackie Shearer, October 24, 1988, Eyes on the Prize II Interviews, Henry Hammond Collection, Film and Media Archive, Washington University Libraries, http://digital.wustl.edu/e/eii/eiiweb/jac5427.0710.075maynardjackson.html.

FURTHER READING

Ball, Howard. The "Bakke" Case: Race, Education and Affirmative Action. Lawrence: University Press of Kansas, 2000.

Baugh, Joyce A. The Detroit School Busing Case: "Milliken v. Bradley" and the Controversy over Desegregation. Lawrence: University Press of Kansas, 2011.

Biles, Roger. Mayor Harold Washington: Champion of Race and Reform in Chicago. Urbana: University of Illinois Press, 2018.

Brazile, Donna, Yolanda Caraway, Leah Daughtry, Mignon Moore, and Veronica Chambers. *For Colored Girls Who Have Considered Politics*. New York: St. Vincent Press, 2018.

Chisholm, Shirley. *The Good Fight*. New York: HarperCollins, 1973.

———. *Unbought and Unbossed*. Boston: Houghton Mifflin Harcourt, 1970.

Colburn, David, and Jeffrey Adler, eds. *African American Mayors: Race, Politics and the American City*. Urbana: University of Illinois Press, 2005.

Delmont, Matthew F. *Why Busing Failed: Race, Media, and the National Resistance to School Desegregation*. Berkeley: University of California Press, 2016.

Formisano, Ronald. *Boston against Busing: Race, Class, and Ethnicity in the 1960s and 1970s*. Chapel Hill: University of North Carolina Press, 2004.

Frady, Marshall. *Jesse: The Life and Pilgrimage of Jesse Jackson*. New York: Random House, 1996.

Goldberg, David, and Trevor Griffey, eds. *Black Power at Work: Community Control, Affirmative Action, and the Construction Industry*. Ithaca, NY: ILR Press, 2010.

Guild, Joshua. "To Make Someday Come: Shirley Chisholm's Radical Politics of Possibility." In *Want to Start a Revolution*, edited by Jeanne Theoharis, Komozi Woodard, and Dayo Gore, 248–70. New York: New York University Press, 2009.

Hornsby, Alton, Jr. *Black Power in Dixie: A Political History of African Americans in Atlanta*. Gainesville: University Press of Florida, 2009.

Isaacs, Charles. *Inside Ocean Hill–Brownsville: A Teacher's Education, 1968–69*. Albany, NY: Excelsior Editions, 2014.

Podair, Jerald. *The Strike That Changed New York: Blacks, Whites, and the Ocean Hill–Brownsville Crisis*. New Haven, CT: Yale University Press, 2004.

Rivlin, Gary. *Fire on the Prairie: Harold Washington, Chicago Politics, and the Roots of the Obama Presidency*. Philadelphia: Temple University Press, 2012.

Sugrue, Thomas. "Affirmative Action from Below: Civil Rights, the Building Trades, and the Politics of Radical Equality in the Urban North, 1945–1969." *Journal of American History* (June 2004): 145–73.

Theoharris, Jeanne. "'I'd Rather Go to School in the South': How Boston's School Desegregation Complicates the Civil Rights Paradigm." In *Freedom North: Black Freedom Struggles Outside the South, 1940–1980*, edited by Jeanne Theoharis and Komozi Woodard, 125–51. New York: Palgrave Macmillan, 2003.

Todd-Breland, Elizabeth. *A Political Education: Black Politics and Education Reform in Chicago since the 1960s*. Chapel Hill: University of North Carolina Press, 2018.

Travis, Dempsey. *Harold, the People's Mayor: The Biography of Harold Washington*. Berkeley, CA: Agate Bolden, 2017.

Urofsky, Melvin. *The Affirmative Action Puzzle: A Living History from Reconstruction to Today*. New York: Pantheon Books, 2020.

Walker-McWilliams, Marcia. "Harold Washington: The People's Mayor." In *Reverend Addie Wyatt: Faith and the Fight for Labor, Gender and Racial Equality*. Urbana: University of Illinois Press, 2016.

12

The Reach of the Civil Rights Movement

How did African American civil rights activists utilize international events to shed light on the domestic Black freedom struggle? To what extent did the movement and Black freedom struggles influence other social justice movements in the United States?

The revolutionary winds of the 1960s spread across race, gender, class, age, political allegiances, and national borders. From Pan-Africanism to the antiwar movement to the women's rights movement and Chicano movement, the influences on and influence of the civil rights movement were many. At the core of these movements in the American context is a commitment to fight against discrimination and demand that the United States live up to the tenets of democracy. The 1960s and 1970s also saw renewed and novel forms of activism among American Indians, Asian Americans, gays and lesbians, advocates of disability rights, and other movements that sought to expand access to human rights and freedoms.

African Americans have always situated themselves within the African diaspora, at times in its center and at other times on its periphery. Black American activists including Paul Robeson, Josephine Baker, and W. E. B. Du Bois all spent significant periods of time outside of the United States in Europe and in Africa, in search of intellectual, artistic, political, and economic spaces free of the racial discrimination they faced in America. Similarly, activists and artists including Martin Luther King Jr., Malcolm X, and Maya Angelou journeyed to Ghana and other newly decolonized African nations in the late 1950s and early 1960s. In 1964, young delegates from the Student Nonviolent Coordinating Committee toured Africa and gained a newfound sense of connections between the Black freedom movement in America and liberation movements in Africa.

Decolonization movements in Africa and Asia began en masse after World War II, seizing upon the language of democracy and freedom over fascism and severely weakened European nations to fight for their own independence. Ghana became the first West African nation colonized by the British to secure independence in 1957. Ghana's first president,

Kwame Nkrumah, had spent several years in the United States attending college and graduate school in Pennsylvania, where he built strategic alliances among African expats and young Black American college activists. Nkrumah believed that Pan-Africanism would be the key to obtaining and maintaining independence for African nations. In these newly decolonized nations, Black Americans drew parallels between African struggles against racial, economic, and cultural oppression and the ongoing Black freedom struggle against oppression in the United States.

For the United States, newly independent nations in Africa and in Asia broadened the playing field of the Cold War. While the federal government took steps to improve the nation's image, hoping to promote democracy as a favorable alternative to communism and socialism, rising coverage of the civil rights movement and rampant racism imperiled that mission. The "blot" of American racism became worldwide news, when white Americans violently resisted peaceful civil rights protests and when it directly affected visiting African and Caribbean foreign diplomats (who to the white American gaze appeared to be African American).

The pinnacle of U.S. combat in the Cold War was its involvement in the Vietnam War from 1955 to 1975. Once the extent of U.S. involvement in the war became common knowledge in the early 1960s, African American civil rights activists protested the war for several reasons. First, the war took extensive economic resources away from antipoverty programs at the heart of local organizing campaigns. Second, the political dimensions of war threatened to overshadow the fight for civil rights legislation. Finally, large numbers of Black and Brown young men, as Martin Luther King noted, "had been crippled by our society and sending them eight thousand miles away to guarantee liberties in Southeast Asia which they had not found in southwest Georgia and East Harlem."[1]

Just as the civil rights movement in the 1960s was driven in large part by student activism, students across the nation represented a strong force in their calls for a democratic society focusing on American interventionism abroad as well as a plethora of issues within American society, including the pervasiveness of racism and white supremacy. Leftist student activists tended to support the civil rights movement, especially youth-based organizations like SNCC and their grassroots initiatives.

The Chicano movement employed many of the same nonviolent direct-action tactics of the civil rights movement such as boycotts and marches. The movement gained traction and momentum when Cesar Chavez and Dolores Huerta of the National Farm Workers Association assumed leadership of the 1965 grape strike and boycott, which ended successfully in 1970. Chavez, in particular, was inspired by Martin Luther King Jr. He once told an audience: "We advocate militant nonviolence as our means of achieving justice for our people, but we are not blind to the feelings of frustration, impatience and anger which seethe inside every farm worker."[2] Students also became a central force in the Chicano movement, which started out focusing on land rights and employment conditions and later branched into education reform and student activism, predominantly on the West Coast.

The struggles of indigenous peoples in the United States also gained greater prominence in the 1960s and 1970s, though the struggle for Native American civil rights and an end to poverty, police brutality, and colonial policies on and off reservations had a much longer history. Founded in 1968, the American Indian Movement employed both nonviolent and violent means in pursuit of greater autonomy and sustainability for Native communities. In the late 1960s and early 1970s, AIM took part in the occupation of Alcatraz penitentiary; held protests in Washington, D.C., against broken treaties with the federal government; battled with police and prosecutors to achieve justice for slain Native Americans; and led the controversial 1973 Wounded Knee standoff on the Pine Ridge Reservation in South Dakota. Asian Americans, despite being stereotyped as the "model minority," similarly contended with racism, segregation, and police brutality and staged marches, protests, and other demonstrations against injustice in the 1960s, 1970s, and 1980s.

The 1960s also witnessed the emergence of second-wave feminism. In 1966, Pauli Murray, Betty Friedan, Shirley Chisholm, Muriel Fox, and another forty-five women and men founded the National Organization for Women (NOW). The organization fashioned itself as the NAACP for women and focused many of its early initiatives aimed to dismantle sex discrimination in the workplace. NOW, in fact, was organized in part to force the newly formed Equal Employment Opportunities Commission to enforce the sex amendment of Title VII of the 1964 Civil Rights Act. It would later devote its energies to the Equal Rights Amendment, an amendment that would acknowledge equality under the law, regardless of sex. The ERA faced fierce opposition from conservative forces and the campaign to ratify the amendment as part of the U.S. Constitution continues.

The gay liberation movement also matured in the mid- to late twentieth century. The Stonewall riots are often credited for igniting this movement; the movement's origins arguably date nearly two decades prior with the founding of the Mattachine Society in 1950. The Stonewall riots, however, marked something new. They marked the start of a radical resistance movement that aimed to force America to reckon with the LGBTQIA community like never before. The riots started in Greenwich Village in New York City, after the police once again raided the Stonewall Inn, a gay club, in the early morning of June 28, 1969. Violent demonstrations by the city's gay community followed for the next several days. Like the aforementioned revolutionary movements, the gay liberation effort drew on the lessons of the civil rights movement. More than this, it also benefited from the activism of Bayard Rustin, James Baldwin, Audre Lorde, and other key civil rights activists who identified as members of the LGBTQIA community. As with the women's movement, however, this movement often failed to address race and the specific concerns of queer people of color and others who stood at the margins within these movements.

NOTES

1. Martin Luther King Jr., "Beyond Vietnam: A Time to Break the Silence," speech, Riverside Church, New York, April 4, 1967, American Rhetoric, https://www.americanrhetoric.com/speeches/mlkatimetobreaksilence.htm.
2. Cesar Chavez, "He Showed Us the Way," *Maryknoll Magazine*, April 1978, https://ufw.org/he-showed-us-the-way-by-cesar-chavez-april-1978-maryknoll-magazine/.

DOCUMENT 12.1

"Memorandum on Racial Discrimination in the U.S. and in Support of the Negro Struggle Presented by the African Nationalist Offices" (1963)

The following document illustrates how African nationalists viewed the plight of Black Americans. The events of the civil rights movement and violence shown toward Black Americans were exported internationally through news media and through channels of communication between Black American activists, expatriates, and their comrades in the diaspora. Embroiled in their own struggles against European imperialism and colonization, African nationalists expressed solidarity with and outrage on behalf of Black Americans.

MEMORANDUM ON RACIAL DISCRIMINATION IN THE U.S. AND IN SUPPORT OF THE NEGRO STRUGGLE PRESENTED BY THE AFRICAN NATIONALIST OFFICES IN CAIRO TO THE U.S. AMBASSADOR IN CAIRO.

Your Excellency,

The Representative Offices of the African Liberation movements based in Cairo view with great concern the plight of the Negro people in the United States of America. The regretable and shameful behaviour of the white Americans against the Negro people in the U.S., fills us with anger. The United States local authorities have been launching ruthless campaigns of suppression against defenceless [sic] Negroes. The beastly conduct of Governor Faubus and the intimidations against Negroes in Little Rock and Birmingham, Alabama, are fresh in our minds. So is the struggle of George Meredith to enroll at Mississippi University and continue his studies there. So is the brutal murder of Medgar Evers and John Saunders. These are only one or two incidents that get publicised and known throughout the world, but we know of greater atrocities and barbarities inflicted on the Negro people by white secret societies, like the Ku Klux Klan. These beastly acts against the Negroes are being done every day that passes in the United States, but the outside world remains ignorant of the facts. We African people shall not forget, nor shall we forgive, these atrocities against a people whose only sin is being black, and demanding equality and the enjoyment of elementary human rights.

The efforts of the United States Government to intervene on behalf of the Negroes are commendable for what they are worth, but shall not dupe us into believing that the Kennedy Administration, is sympathetic towards the cause of the Negro people. Indeed what is happening in the United States is as a result of a decadent system upheld by President Kennedy himself and his ruling clique.

Never before has the struggle of the Negroe people in the U.S. against injustices, discrimination and for full equality reached its present heights, and never before, have the Negroe people organised a mass demonstration such as to-day's March on Washington of 250,000 Negroes and other progressive white citizens, whose demand is re-cognition as equal citizens in the United States of America.

These poor victims of discriminatory laws of American states, these poor victims of day to day tortures in the hands of individuals or organised societies, these poor victims of day to day lynchings by the self-professed civilising race, have no intention of hurting anybody, but only want to have restored to them the rights to life, liberty and the pursuit of happiness guaranteed for all peoples of the United States irrespective of their colour in the United States Constitution.

For generations, the Governments of the United States have been fooling the world into believing that everything was going on well in the country, they have shouted at the top of their voices about freedom and democracy, but these have only been on paper and never practiced.

Article XIX of the United States constitution reads as follows:

> "The right of citizens of the United States to vote shall not be denied or abridged by the United States or by any state on account of race colour or previous condition of servitude."

Despite these provisions of the constitution, less than 15 percent of voting age negroes are registered in Texas, Mississippi, and South Carolina, to mention only a few.

We the people of Africa are marching today together with our brethren in the United States. We support them whole-heartedly in all the measures they take in resisting this barbarism which has come to the surface once again. We staunchly and strongly support their struggle against racial discrimination and for equality and all elementary human rights . We assure them that the African people and all democratic mankind are behind them in their struggle and shall not leave them alone.

We strongly condemn the Kennedy Administration for its pretensions at helping the Negro people, and we also vehemently condemn U.S. local authorities for their ruthless suppression of defenceless [sic] Negroes. We call upon the United States Government to act quickly to:

(a) Recognise the negroes as equal citizens of the United States and accord them all their democratic rights.

(b) re-investigate all the lynching cases and other cases of brutalities and bring the culprits to justice.

(c) exercise with greater firmness its constitutional right of intervening to put matters right in any state where the constitution is being deliberately flouted, and all humanity wronged.

Long live the struggle of the Negro people for freedom and equality.

We are,

Your Excellency,

1. African National Congress (South Africa) ············
2. Basutoland Congress Party (Basutoland)

3. UDENAMO (Mozambique)
4. South West Africa Peoples Organisation (S.W. Africa)
5. South West Africa National Union (S.W. Africa)
6. Pan Africanist Congress (South Africa)
7. Swaziland Progressive Party (Swaziland)
8. Zanzibar Nationalist Party/Zanzibar & Pemba Peoples Party (Zanzibar)
9. United National Independence Party (Northern Rhodesia)
10. Zimbabwe African Peoples Union (Southern Rhodesia)
11. Kenya African National Union (Kenya).

Source: African Nationalist & Anti-Colonial Organizations, "Memorandum on Racial Discrimination in the U.S. and in Support of the Negro Struggle Presented by the African Nationalist Offices in Cairo to the U.S. Ambassador in Cairo," ca. 1963, Civil Rights Movement Archive, http://www.crmvet.org/docs/63_african_statement.pdf.

DOCUMENT 12.2

Malcolm X, Speech at the Organization of African Unity (1964)

Following his break from the Nation of Islam, Malcolm X took a hajj, or pilgrimage, to Mecca in the spring of 1964. He also toured West Africa and gained greater insight into the Organization of African Unity and Pan-Africanism. One of the outcomes of his trip was the formation of the Organization of Afro-American Unity, modeled off of the OAU. The Organization of Afro-American Unity sought to advocate for Black human rights in the United States and across the world. In the speech, Malcolm X calls on the leaders of newly independent African nations to see the struggles of Black Americans as their struggles and to support bringing greater attention of civil rights abuses in America to the United Nations.

The Organization of Afro-American Unity has sent me to attend this historic African Summit Conference as an observer to represent the interests of 22 million African-Americans whose human rights are being violated daily by the racism of American imperialists.

The Organization of Afro-American Unity has been formed by a cross section of America's African-American community, and is patterned after the letter and spirit of the Organization of African Unity.

Just as the Organization of African Unity has called upon all African leaders to submerge their differences and unite on common objectives for the common good of all Africans, in America the Organization of Afro-American Unity has called upon Afro-American leaders to submerge their differences and find areas of agreement wherein we can work in unity for the good of the entire 22 million African Americans.

Since the 22 million of us were originally Africans, who are now in America, not by choice but only by a cruel accident in our history, we strongly believe that African problems are our problems and our problems are African problems.

We also believe that as heads of the independent African states you are the shepherds of all African peoples everywhere, whether they are still at home here on the mother continent or have been scattered abroad.

Some African leaders at this conference have implied that they have enough problems here on the mother continent without adding the Afro-American problem.

With all due respect to your esteemed positions, I must remind all of you that the Good Shepherd will leave ninety-nine sheep who are safe at home to go to the aid of the one who is lost and has fallen into the clutches of the imperialist wolf.

We in America are your long-lost brothers and sisters, and I am here only to remind you that our problems are your problems. As the African-Americans "awaken" today, we find ourselves in a strange land that has rejected us, and, like the prodigal son, we are turning to our elder brothers for help. We pray our pleas will not fall upon deaf ears.

We were taken forcibly in chains from this mother continent and have now spent over three hundred years in America, suffering the most inhuman forms of physical and psychological tortures imaginable.

During the past ten years the entire world has witnessed our men, women, and children being attacked and bitten by vicious police dogs, brutally beaten by police clubs, and washed down the sewers by high-pressure water hoses that would rip the clothes from our bodies and the flesh from our limbs.

And all of these inhuman atrocities have been inflicted upon us by the American governmental authorities, the police themselves, for no reason other than that we seek the recognition and respect granted other human beings in America.

The American Government is either unable or unwilling to protect the lives and property of your 22 million African-American brothers and sisters. We stand defenseless, at the mercy of American racists who murder us at will for no reason other than we are black and of African descent.

Last week an unarmed African-American educator was murdered in cold blood in Georgia; a few days before that three civil rights workers disappeared completely, perhaps murdered also, only because they were teaching our people in Mississippi how to vote and how to secure their political rights.

Our problems are your problems. We have lived for over three hundred years in that American den of racist wolves in constant fear of losing life and limb. Recently, three students from Kenya were mistaken for American Negroes and were brutally beaten by the New York police. Shortly after that two diplomats from Uganda were also beaten by the New York City police, who mistook them for American Negroes.

If Africans are brutally beaten while only visiting in America, imagine the physical and psychological suffering received by your brothers and sisters who have lived there for over three hundred years.

Our problem is your problem. No matter how much independence Africans get here on the mother continent, unless you wear your national dress at all time when you visit America, you may be mistaken for one of us and suffer the same psychological and physical mutilation that is an everyday occurrence in our lives.

Your problems will never be fully solved until and unless ours are solved. You will never be fully respected until and unless we are also respected. You will never be recognized as free human beings until and unless we are also recognized and treated as human beings.

Our problem is your problem. It is not a Negro problem, nor an American problem. This is a world problem, a problem for humanity. It is not a problem of civil rights, it is a problem of human rights.

We pray that our African brothers have not freed themselves of European colonialism only to be overcome and held in check now by American dollarism. Don't let American racism be "legalized" by American dollarism.

America is worse than South Africa, because not only is America racist, but she is also deceitful and hypocritical. South Africa preaches segregation and practices segregation. She, at least, practices what she preaches. America preaches integration and practices segregation. She preaches one thing while deceitfully practicing another.

South Africa is like a vicious wolf, openly hostile toward black humanity. But America is cunning like a fox, friendly and smiling, but even more vicious and deadly than the wolf.

The wolf and the fox are both enemies of humanity, both are canine, both humiliate and mutilate their victims. Both have the same objectives, but differ only in methods.

If South Africa is guilty of violating the human rights of Africans here on the mother continent, then America is guilty of worse violations of the 22 million Africans on the American continent. And if South African racism is not a domestic issue, then American racism also is not a domestic issue.

We beseech independent African states to help us bring our problem before the United Nations, on the grounds that the United States Government is morally incapable of protecting the lives and the property of 22 million African-Americans. And on the grounds that our deteriorating plight is definitely becoming a threat to world peace.

Out of frustration and hopelessness our young people have reached the point of no return. We no longer endorse patience and turning the other cheek. We assert the right of self-defense by whatever means necessary, and reserve the right of maximum retaliation against our racist oppressors, no matter what the odds against us are.

We are well aware that our future efforts to defend ourselves by retaliating- by meeting violence with violence, eye for eye and tooth for tooth-could create the type of racial conflict in America that could easily escalate into a violent, worldwide, bloody race war.

In the interests of world peace and security, we beseech the heads of the independent African states to recommend an immediate investigation into our problem by the United Nations Commission on Human Rights.

One last word, my beloved brothers at this African Summit: "No one knows the master better than his servant." We have been servants in America for over three hundred years. We have a thorough inside knowledge of this man who calls himself "Uncle Sam." Therefore, you must heed our warning. Don't escape from European colonialism only to become even more enslaved by deceitful, "friendly" American dollarism.

May Allah's blessings of good health and wisdom be upon you all.

Source: Malcolm X, "Appeal to African Heads of State" (July 17, 1964), from Malcolm X, *Malcolm X Speaks* (Atlanta: Pathfinder Press, 1989), 72–77. Copyright © 1965, 1989 by Betty Shabazz and Pathfinder Press. Reprinted by permission.

DOCUMENT 12.3

John Lewis, "SNCC Africa Trip Report" (1964)

In the fall of 1964, eleven SNCC activists—John Lewis, Jim Forman, Fannie Lou Hamer, Prathia Hall, Bob Moses, Dona Richards Moses, Julian Bond, Donald Harris, Bill Hansen, Matthew Jones, and Ruby Doris Smith-Robinson—toured newly independent West African nations. The trip, supported financially by actor and activist Harry Belafonte, was intended to help SNCC activists think about the next steps for the organization following Freedom Summer and the Mississippi Freedom Democratic Party's challenge to the American political system. One outcome of the trip was SNCC's decision to establish an African Bureau or secretariat to increase and formalize SNCC's connections to Africa. An excerpt from the trip report follows.

GHANA

On October 7th, we arrived in Accra from Liberia. We were met at the airport by relatives (Don's), Gus Kwabi and family. He was our main contact (and an excellent one) because he's a business man (Chief Accountant, Mobile Oil, Ltd.), studied in the States, and know many people in the government as well as the government influences.

First contact came with Dr. Robert E. Lee, an expatriot [*sic*] Afro-American dentist and a member of the newly-formed Afro-American Information Bureau . . . He is a militant, intellectual and activist. Through him we met Shirley Graham—Mrs. W.E.B. DuBois. For some three hours we discussed the possibilities of a strong link between the Rights Movement in the States and a direct contact with the African countries. Because of the high number of expatriot Afro-Americans in Ghana (just below 500) the country was perhaps the best informed on the continent. The purpose of the AIB was to keep the Ghana people informed about what was going on in the States and TO MAKE SURE THAT THE INFORMATION HIT THE PRESS. Mrs. DuBois is head of Ghana TV which is to begin in Jan. or Feb. 1965. She said that the AIB was also created to insure that the good situation which now exists continues and improves with time. She indicated that she would help in all and every way that she could.

Soon after we met Les Lacy an Afro-American who is studying and doing research at Legon, Ghana University. Like many of the members of AIB is a veteran with regards to demonstrations at the US Embassy. He personally spent a great deal of time with us while we were in Accra and did much to see that we got to meet people that would be most helpful to us. He, with a friend, took us on a tour of the University—a fantastic place!!!!

We had a chance to see some of the new suburbs outside of Accra—McCarthy Hill . . . seven miles outside of Accra overlooking all of the capital city (170,000 pop.) as well as the sea. Also went to Tema, the newly-built harbor 18 miles outside of Accra. A terrific new, clean, modern community full of schools, garden-type apartments, office buildings, palm trees, and happy black faces. One of the following days went to Akosombo—sight of the Volta River Dam . . . a huge complex that promises to be the most important power source in West Africa. . . .

Much of our time in Accra we spent at the African Affairs Bureau and the Pan Africanist Congress. Here at the offices of these militants . . . and nationalists . . . exiles from still dependent countries and South Africa built, began, sustained and continued revolutions against colonial, imperial and racist powers. Each time we appeared at these offices we were received warmly and enthusiastically and rarely could escape within two hours of our arrival. . . .

Finally, the day before we were to leave Accra, Julian Mayfield returned from Cairo and the Non-Allied Nations conference and we had an opportunity to meet with him at Preston King's house.

Mayfield is a writer, journalist, Afro-American expatriot who holds a great deal of respect in the government and has personal as well as business relationships with many of the people in Flagstaff House. He is also the spearhead of the AIB, if not the titled head.

We spoke with him for about two hours—was very much impressed with our reasons—the purpose of the trip. Suggested that this kind of thing should have been done long ago and saw that the AIB could work closely together. He so much as said that if the information was gotten to him he could assure that it would get into the press and on the radio. . . .

There were two factors that we had to deal with while in Ghana. The first was the fact that the Non-Allied Nations conference was taking place in Cairo at the time drawing most of the important government, party, journalist, and exiled freedom fighters away to Egypt. Even so, those that were left in Accra were wholly receptive and helpful to us and as soon as people arrived back in Ghana to put us in touch with them. In this regard, it seems we were exceptionally lucky and fortunate. The second thing we had to cope with—was that Malcolm X had just left Ghana some few days before we arrived and had made fantastic impressions. Because of this, very often peoples' first attitude or impression of us was one of skepticism and distrust. Among the first days we were in Accra someone said, "Look, you guys might be really doing something—I don't know, but if you are to the right of Malcolm, you might as well start packing right now 'cause no one'll listen to you." Among the first questions we were continually asked was, "What's your organization's relationship with Malcolm's?" We ultimately found that this situation was not peculiar to Ghana; the pattern repeated itself in every country. After a day of this we found that we must, immediately on meeting people, state our own position in regards to where we stood on certain issues—Cuba, Vietnam, the Congo, Red China and the U.N., and what SNCC's role, guidelines, and involvement in the Rights Struggle was. Malcolm's impact on Africa was just fantastic. In every country he was known and served as the main criteria for categorizing other Afro-Americans and their political views. . . .

KENYA

. . . The first person we saw on arrival at our hotel was Malcolm X, who had just come in from Tanzania with Kenyatta. This was a chance meeting, but in many ways a very important meeting.

We spent the rest of the day and evening as well as a good part of the following day talking with Malcolm about the nature of each of our trips. At that point [he] had been to eleven countries, talked with eleven heads of state and had addressed the parliaments in the majority of these countries. Although he was very tired he planned to visit five more countries. He felt that the presence of SNCC in Africa was very important and that this was significant and crucial aspect of the "human rights struggle" that the American civil rights groups had too long neglected. He pointed out (and our experience bears him correct) that the African leaders and people are strongly behind the Freedom Movement in this country; that they are willing to do all they can to support, encourage and sustain the Movement, but they will not tolerate factionalism or support particular groups or organizations within the Movement as a whole. It was with this in mind that he formed his Organization of Afro-American Unity.

Discussion also centered around Malcolm's proposed plan to bring the case of the Afro-American before the General Assembly of the United Nations and hold the United States in violation of the Human Rights Charter. The question was at that time (and ultimately was evident) that support from the civil rights [voices] in this country was not forthcoming and the American black community was too plinted to attempt such a move without looking like [complete] asses and embarrassing [our] most valuable allies. We departed with Malcolm giving us some contacts and the hope that there would be greater communication between the OAU (the U.S. version) and SNCC.

PROPOSALS:

1. That SNCC establish an international wing—specifically, an African Bureau of Secretariat. . . .
2. That the function of the African Bureau or Secretariat be to maintain and increase SNCC's contacts with Africa specifically, but also with any other countries or groups of people in other countries who can be helpful to us and the cause. . . .
3. That the African Bureau or Secretariat should be closely tied to or linked with the present communications department of SNCC. . . .
4. That at least two people be assigned to work full-time with the African Bureau or Secretariat and that one of these two persons be available to travel between Atlanta, Washington, and New York. . . .

Submitted Monday—December 14, 1964

BY: JOHN LEWIS, CHAIRMAN
DONALD HARRIS

Source: John Lewis and Donald Harris, 1964, "SNCC Africa Trip Report," Student Nonviolent Coordinating Committee, Civil Rights Movement Archive, http://www.crmvet.org/docs/64_sncc_africa_trip.pdf.

Coretta Scott King, "10 Commandments on Vietnam" (1968)

Though she spoke out against the Vietnam War several times in the 1960s, the following speech by Coretta Scott King in opposition to the war was delivered just weeks after her husband's assassination in Memphis, Tennessee. Her speech reveals some of the connections between the antiwar movement and the civil rights movement as her own values as a civil rights activist. Coretta Scott King concluded the speech by acknowledging and explicitly calling upon the power of women to help heal American society.

My dear friends of peace and freedom:

I come to New York today with a strong feeling that my dearly beloved husband, who was snatched suddenly from our midst slightly more than three weeks ago now, would have wanted me to be present today.

Though my heart is heavy with grief from having suffered an irreparable personal loss, my faith in the redemptive will of God is stronger today than ever before.

As many of you probably know my husband had accepted an invitation to speak to you today and had he been here, I am sure he would have lifted your hearts and spirits to new levels of understanding in his customary fashion.

I would like to share with you some notes taken from my husband's pockets upon his death. He carried these scraps of paper upon which he scribbled notes for his many speeches.

Among these notes was one set which he never delivered. Perhaps they were his early thoughts for the message he was to give to you today. I am sure he would have developed and delivered them in his usual eloquent and inspired fashion. I simply read them to you as he recorded them. And I quote, "Ten Commandments on Vietnam";

1. Thou shalt not believe in a military victory.
2. Thou shall not believe in a political victory.
3. Thou shall not believe that they, the Vietnamese love us.
4. Thou shall not believe that the Saigon government has the support of the people.
5. Thou shall not believe that the majority of the South Vietnamese look upon the Vietcong as terrorists.
6. Thou shalt not believe the figures of killed enemies or killed Americans.
7. Thou shall not believe that the generals know best.
8. Thou shalt not believe that the enemy's victory means communism.
9. Thou shall not believe that the world supports the United States.
10. Thou shall not kill.

These are Martin Luther King's ten commandments on Vietnam.

You who have worked with and loved my husband so much, you who have kept alive the burning issue of war in the American conscience, you who will not be deluded by talk of peace, but who press on in the knowledge that the work of peacemaking must continue until the last gun is silent.

I come to you in my grief only because you keep alive the work and dreams for which my husband gave his life. My husband arrived somewhere to his strength and inspiration from the love of all people who shared his dream, that I too now come hoping you might strengthen me for the lonely road ahead.

It was on April 4th, 1967 that my husband gave his major address against the war in Vietnam. On April 4th, 1968 he was assassinated. I remember how he agonized over the grave misunderstanding which took place as a result of his position on the Vietnam war.

His motives were questioned. His credentials were challenged and his loyalty to this nation maligned. Now, one year later we see almost unbelievable results coming from all of our united efforts.

Had we then suggested the possibility of two peace candidates as front-runners for the presidency of the United States, our sanity certainly would have been questioned. Yet I need not trace for you how many of our hopes have been realized in these 12 short months. Never in the history of this nation have the people been so forceful in reversing the policy of our government in regard to war. We are indeed on the threshold of a new day for the peacemakers.

But just as conscientious action has reversed the tide of public opinion and government policy, we must now turn our attention and the sole force of the movement of people of good will to the problems of the poor here at home.

My husband always saw the problem of racism and poverty here at home and militarism abroad as two sides of the same coin. In fact, it is even very clear that our policy at home is to try to solve social problems through military means just as we have done abroad.

The interrelatedness of domestic and foreign affairs is no longer questioned. The bombs we drop on the people of Vietnam continue to explode at home with all of their devastating potential. And so I would invite you to join us in Washington in our effort to enable the poor people of this nation to enjoy a fair share of America's blessing.

There is no reason why a nation as rich as ours should be blighted by poverty, disease, and illiteracy. It is plain that we don't care about our poor people except to exploit them as cheap labor and victimize them through excessive rents and consumer prices.

Our Congress passes laws which subsidize corporation farms, oil companies, airlines, and houses for suburbia. But when they turn their attention to the poor, they suddenly become concerned about balancing the budget and cut back on the funds for Head Start, Medicare, and mental health appropriations.

The most tragic of these cuts is the welfare section to the Social Security amendment, which freezes federal funds for millions of needy children, who are desperately poor but who do not receive public assistance. It forces mothers to leave their children and accept work or training, leaving their children to grow up in the streets as tomorrow's social problems. This law must be repealed, and I encourage you to join welfare mothers on May 12th, Mother's Day and call upon Congress to establish a guaranteed annual income, instead of these racist and archaic measures, these measures which dehumanize God's children and create more social problems than they solve.

We will be marching toward Washington soon. On Thursday, May 2nd we will return to Memphis to begin where my husband was slain and kick off his Poor People's campaign.

We will be marching toward Washington to demand that America share its abundant life with all its citizens. We should arrive in Washington by May 17th. I invite you to support the purposes of this march and to join us in Washington on May 30th for the Memorial Day weekend.

I would now like to address myself to the women. The woman power of this nation can be the power which makes us whole and heals the rotten community, now so shattered by war and poverty and racism. I have great faith in the power of women who will dedicate themselves whole-heartedly to the task of remaking our society. . . .

With this determination, with this faith, we will be able to create new homes, new communities, new cities, a new nation. Yea, a new world, which we desperately need!

Source: Coretta Scott King, "10 Commandments on Vietnam," April 27, 1968, Central Park, New York, https://www.americanrhetoric.com/speeches/corettascottkingvietnam commandments.htm. Reprinted by arrangement with The Heirs to the Estate of Martin Luther King Jr., c/o Writers House as agent for the proprietor New York, NY. Copyright © 1968 by Coretta Scott King. Renewed © 1996 by Coretta Scott King.

DOCUMENT 12.5

Cesar Chavez on Dr. Martin Luther King Jr. (1978)

The efforts of Black civil rights activists and the movement as a whole inspired the movements of other communities of color. Cesar Chavez rose to prominence as a labor leader and community organizer in California fighting for the rights of Latino farmworkers and fueling an economic arm of the Chicano movement. In the piece that follows, Chavez discusses the influence that Martin Luther King Jr. and nonviolent direct action had on the Chicano movement.

In honoring Martin Luther King, Jr.'s memory we also acknowledge non-violence as a truly powerful weapon to achieve equality and liberation, in fact, the only weapon that Christians who struggle for social change can claim as their own.

Dr. King's entire life was an example of power that nonviolence brings to bear in the real world. It is an example that inspired much of the philosophy and strategy of the farm workers' movement. This observance of Dr. King's death gives us the best possible opportunity to recall the principles with which our struggle has grown and matured.

Our conviction is that human life is a very special possession given by God to man and that no one has the right to take it for any reason or for any cause, however just it may be.

We are also convinced that nonviolence is more powerful than violence. Nonviolence supports you if you have a just and moral cause. Nonviolence provides the opportunity to stay on the offensive, and that is of crucial importance to win any contest.

If we resort to violence then one of two things will happen: either the violence will be escalated and there will be many injuries and perhaps deaths on both sides, or there will be total demoralization of the workers.

Nonviolence has exactly the opposite effect. If, for every violent act committed against us, we respond with nonviolence, we attract people's support. We can gather the support of millions who have a conscience and would rather see a nonviolent resolution to problems. We are convinced that when people are faced with a direct appeal from the poor struggling nonviolently against great odds, they will react positively. The American people and people everywhere still yearn for justice. It is to that yearning that we appeal.

But if we are committed to nonviolence only as a strategy or tactic, then if it fails our only alternative is to turn to violence. So we must balance the strategy with a clear understanding of what we are doing. However important the struggle is and however much misery, poverty and exploitation exist, we know that it cannot be more important than one human life. We work on the theory that men and women who are truly concerned about people are nonviolent by nature. These people become violent when the deep concern they have for people is frustrated and when they are faced with seemingly insurmountable odds.

We advocate militant nonviolence as our means of achieving justice for our people, but we are not blind to the feelings of frustration, impatience and anger which seethe inside every farm worker. The burdens of generations of poverty and powerlessness lie heavy in the fields of America. If we fail, there are those who will see violence as the shortcut to change.

It is precisely to overcome these frustrations that we have involved masses of people in their own struggle throughout the movement. Freedom is best experienced through participation and self-determination, and free men and women instinctively prefer democratic change to any other means.

Thus, demonstrations and marches, strikes and boycotts are not only weapons against the growers, but our way of avoiding the senseless violence that brings no honor to any class or community. The boycott, as Gandhi taught, is the most nearly perfect instrument of nonviolent change, allowing masses of people to participate actively in a cause.

When victory comes through violence, it is a victory with strings attached. If we beat the growers at the expense of violence, victory would come at the expense of injury and perhaps death. Such a thing would have a tremendous impact on us. We would lose regard for human beings. Then the struggle would become a mechanical thing. When you lose your sense of life and justice, you lose your strength.

The greater the oppression, the more leverage nonviolence holds. Violence does not work in the long run and if it is temporarily successful, it replaces one violent form of power with another just as violent. People suffer from violence.

Examine history. Who gets killed in the case of violent revolution? The poor, the workers. The people of the land are the ones who give their bodies and don't really gain that much for it. We believe it is too big a price to pay for not getting anything. Those who espouse violence exploit people. To call men to arms with many promises, to ask them to give up their lives for a cause and then not produce for them afterwards, is the most vicious type of oppression.

We know that most likely we are not going to do anything else the rest of our lives except build our union. For us there is nowhere else to go. Although we would like to see victory come soon, we are willing to wait. In this sense, time is our ally. We learned many years ago that the rich may have money, but the poor have time.

It has been our experience that few men or women ever have the opportunity to know the true satisfaction that comes with giving one's life totally in the nonviolent struggle for justice. Martin Luther King, Jr., was one of these unique servants and from him we learned many of the lessons that have guided us. For these lessons and for his sacrifice for the poor and oppressed, Dr. King's memory will be cherished in the hearts of the farm workers forever.

Source: Cesar Chavez, "He Showed Us the Way," *Maryknoll* magazine, April 1978, https://ufw.org/he-showed-us-the-way-by-cesar-chavez-april-1978-maryknoll-magazine/. Reprinted from *Maryknoll* magazine, Maryknollmagazine.org.

National Council of Students for a Democratic Society, "Resolution on SNCC" (1966)

Following SNCC's shift to Black power and greater Black control of the organization's direction and operations, the group faced widespread criticism. However, the Students for a Democratic Society (SDS) came to the group's defense and argued that because Blacks acutely felt the sting of white supremacy and racism in America, they had every right to lead and organize in ways that could support great Black empowerment, even if those ways came at the expense of white liberals.

RESOLUTION ON SNCC

Passed by National Council of Students for a Democratic Society, June 18, 1966.

SDS has long maintained fraternal relations with the Student Nonviolent Coordinating Committee. Now that SNCC is under fire from a variety of liberal organizations and publications we feel a special urgency to restate our support. Let it be clear that we are not merely supporting SNCC's right to its views, we are welcoming and supporting the thrust of SNCC's program, and expect to continue our joint work.

SNCC has emphasized "black power." This is not a magic charm or a promised land; it is a strategy for social change and a mode of organization. Both the strategy and the mode become clear if the United States is understood as an essentially racist culture. Yet at the same time Negroes have been an exploited caste, they have been taught to seek their salvation in integration—that is, in an accommodation to the dominant social values, under white leadership.

We know that not all SNCC's critics resemble George Wallace; that is precisely why we try to lay bare the liberal assumptions that lead to attacks on SNCC. We are struck with the fact that among the critics are liberals vociferous in their praise of an America in which minorities organize themselves and preserve their cultural integrity. They are now denouncing SNCC's "black consciousness" as "racism in reverse." We doubt these critics would find themselves so upset if SNCC sought to accept the major premises of American life; it is precisely because SNCC is revolutionary—because it is trying to bring about a fundamental rearrangement of power in America—that they shrink in horror.

Racism and economic exploitation confront Negroes as a group, together. So, of course, Negroes, especially in the Southern black belt and the Northern ghettoes, must act as a group in order to challenge their condition. This is not "racism in reverse" any more than American revolutionists were "colonialists in reverse." It is a recognition of the fact of common identity and the beginnings of a strategy for change. We must not simply tolerate this "black consciousness," we should encourage it.

Measured integration is very literally irrelevant, since integration assumes the integrity of the dominant (white) culture. "Black consciousness," on the other hand, understands very deeply the exploitativeness of that culture and seeks to make a beginning in reconstructing it. We agree, then, with SNCC in asking why Negroes cannot seek to live and rebuild where they wish, in their own schools, with their own economic base, without being dismissed as "racist."

Some liberal and radical critics argue that SNCC's strategy will be frustrated by the sheer fact that Negroes are a minority, even in large portions of the Deep South. To this we say that the responsibility for that frustration would lie with those whites who fail to build white movements that can at some point ally with the black movement for common goals. Whites in the civil rights movement have almost always been auxiliaries, and at the present stage they could easily frustrate the Negro movement unless they recognize the right and the need for black radicals to organize independent bases of power in Negro communities. Power means the ability to act autonomously; it is a truism that the power of black communities is limited to the extent it depends directly on white help. (This is not the only factor to be considered when the white radical thinks about organizing Negroes, but we cannot dispute its importance.)

SDS seeks to call white critics to their true tasks, not to impugn their motives. If we really want to help we will be organizing primarily among the powerless, the disenfranchised, the dependent whites—poor, working class, and middle class—toward their power in communities, unions, and professions, so that they may move toward authentic alliance with the organizations of black power. There can be no true coalition for radical change unless there exist people in many spheres, wherever they are, committed to and organized for the reconstruction of American life.

Finally, SNCC has been criticized for having a position on the Vietnam war, in the first place; and second, for having the position it does, one of deep and wholehearted opposition. But we applaud SNCC for recognizing that the enemies of deepseated social change at home are the enemies of revolution abroad, and for acting to forge alliances with the oppressed in the Third World. We are saddened to see presumed internationalists attacking SNCC for articulating its solidarity with their brothers—whether in Guatemala or South Africa or Vietnam—and we intend to work closely with them in making international contacts: without sectarianism, but also without illusions as to the real position of America in the world, or for its own poor and powerless.

Source: National Council of Students for a Democratic Society, "Resolution on SNCC," June 18, 1966, Online Archive of California, http://content.cdlib.org/view?docId=kt9s20078c&brand=calisphere&doc.view=entire_text.

DOCUMENT 12.7

National Organization for Women Statement of Purpose (1966)

The NOW statement of purpose was adopted at the organization's first national conference in Washington, D.C., on October 29, 1966. The statement of purpose articulates that the women's group aims "to bring women into full participation in the mainstream of American society now, exercising all the privileges and responsibilities thereof in truly equal partnership with men." The statement details the organization's major beliefs and interest in remaining politically independent.

We, men and women who hereby constitute ourselves as the National Organization for Women, believe that the time has come for a new movement toward true equality for all women in America, and toward a fully equal partnership of the sexes, as part of the world-wide revolution of human rights now taking place within and beyond our national borders.

The purpose of NOW is to take action to bring women into full participation in the mainstream of American society now, exercising all the privileges and responsibilities thereof in truly equal partnership with men. . . .

NOW is dedicated to the proposition that women, first and foremost, are human beings, who, like all other people in our society, must have the chance to develop their fullest human potential. We believe that women can achieve such equality only by accepting to the full the challenges and responsibilities they share with all other people in our society, as part of the decision-making mainstream of American political, economic and social life.

We organize to initiate or support action, nationally, or in any part of this nation, by individuals or organizations, to break through the silken curtain of prejudice and discrimination against women in government, industry, the professions, the churches, the political parties, the judiciary, the labor unions, in education, science, medicine, law, religion and every other field of importance in American society.

Enormous changes taking place in our society make it both possible and urgently necessary to advance the unfinished revolution of women toward true equality, now. With a life span lengthened to nearly 75 years it is no longer either necessary or possible for women to devote the greater part of their lives to child- rearing; yet childbearing and rearing which continues to be a most important part of most women's lives—still is used to justify barring women from equal professional and economic participation and advance.

Today's technology has reduced most of the productive chores which women once performed in the home and in mass-production industries based upon routine unskilled labor. This same technology has virtually eliminated the quality of muscular strength as a criterion for filling most jobs, while intensifying American industry's need for creative intelligence. In view of this new industrial revolution created by automation in the mid-twentieth century, women can and must participate in old and new fields of society in full equality—or become permanent outsiders.

Despite all the talk about the status of American women in recent years, the actual position of women in the United States has declined, and is declining, to an alarming degree throughout the 1950's and 60's. Although 46.4% of all American women between the ages of 18 and 65 now work outside the home, the overwhelming majority—75%—are in routine clerical, sales, or factory jobs, or they are household workers, cleaning women, hospital attendants. About two-thirds of Negro women workers are in the lowest paid service occupations. Working women are becoming increasingly—not less—concentrated on the bottom of the job ladder. As a consequence full-time women workers today earn on the average only 60% of what men earn, and that wage gap has been increasing over the past twenty-five years in every major industry group. In 1964, of all women with a yearly income, 89% earned under $5,000 a year; half of all full-time year round women workers earned less than $3,690; only 1.4% of full-time year round women workers had an annual income of $10,000 or more.

Further, with higher education increasingly essential in today's society, too few women are entering and finishing college or going on to graduate or professional school. Today, women earn only one in three of the B.A.'s and M.A.'s granted, and one in ten of the Ph.D.'s.

In all the professions considered of importance to society, and in the executive ranks of industry and government, women are losing ground. Where they are present it is only a token handful. Women comprise less than 1% of federal judges; less than 4% of all lawyers; 7% of doctors. Yet women represent 51% of the U.S. population. And, increasingly, men are replacing women in the top positions in secondary and elementary schools, in social work, and in libraries—once thought to be women's fields.

. . . Discrimination in employment on the basis of sex is now prohibited by federal law, in Title VII of the Civil Rights Act of 1964. But although nearly one-third of the cases brought before the Equal Employment Opportunity Commission during the first year dealt with sex discrimination and the proportion is increasing dramatically, the Commission has not made clear its intention to enforce the law with the same seriousness on behalf of women as of other victims of discrimination. Many of these cases were Negro women, who are the victims of double discrimination of race and sex. Until now, too few women's organizations and official spokesmen have been willing to speak out against these dangers facing women. Too many women have been restrained by the fear of being called ʼfeminist." There is no civil rights movement to speak for women, as there has been for Negroes and other victims of discrimination. The National Organization for Women must therefore begin to speak.

WE BELIEVE that the power of American law, and the protection guaranteed by the U.S. Constitution to the civil rights of all individuals, must be effectively applied and enforced to isolate and remove patterns of sex discrimination, to ensure equality of opportunity in employment and education, and equality of civil and political rights and responsibilities on behalf of women, as well as for Negroes and other deprived groups.

We realize that women's problems are linked to many broader questions of social justice; their solution will require concerted action by many groups. Therefore, convinced that human rights for all are indivisible, we expect to give active support to the common cause of equal rights for all those who suffer discrimination and deprivation, and we call upon other organizations committed to such goals to support our efforts toward equality for women.

. . .

WE BELIEVE that this nation has a capacity at least as great as other nations, to innovate new social institutions which will enable women to enjoy the true equality of opportunity and responsibility in society, without conflict with their responsibilities as mothers and homemakers. In such innovations, America does not lead the Western world, but lags by decades behind many European countries. We do not accept the traditional assumption that a woman has to choose between marriage and motherhood, on the one hand, and serious participation in industry or the professions on the other. We question the present expectation that all normal women will retire from job or profession for 10 or 15 years, to devote their full time to raising children, only to reenter the job market at a relatively minor level. This, in itself, is a deterrent to the aspirations of women, to their acceptance into management or professional training courses, and to the very possibility of equality of opportunity or real choice, for all but a few women. Above all, we reject the assumption that these problems are the unique responsibility of each individual woman, rather than a basic social dilemma which society must solve. True equality of opportunity and freedom of choice for women requires such practical, and possible innovations as a nationwide network of child-care centers, which will make it unnecessary for women to retire completely from society until their children are grown, and national programs to provide retraining for women who have chosen to care for their children full-time.

WE BELIEVE that it is as essential for every girl to be educated to her full potential of human ability as it is for every boy—with the knowledge that such education is the key to effective participation in today's economy and that, for a girl as for a boy, education can only be serious where there is expectation that it will be used in society. We believe that American educators are capable of devising means of imparting such expectations to girl students. Moreover, we consider the decline in the proportion of women receiving higher and professional education to be evidence of discrimination. This discrimination may take the form of quotas against the admission of women to colleges, and professional schools; lack of encouragement by parents, counselors and educators; denial of loans or fellowships; or the traditional or arbitrary procedures in graduate and professional training geared in terms of men, which inadvertently discriminate against women. . . .

WE REJECT the current assumptions that a man must carry the sole burden of supporting himself, his wife, and family, and that a woman is automatically entitled to lifelong support by a man upon her marriage, or that marriage, home and family are primarily woman's world and responsibility—hers, to dominate—his to support. We believe that a true partnership between the sexes demands a different concept of marriage, an equitable sharing of the responsibilities of home and children and of the economic burdens of their support. We believe that proper recognition should be given to the economic and social value of homemaking and child-care. To these ends, we will seek to open a reexamination of laws and mores governing marriage and divorce, for we believe that the current state of 'half-equity" between the sexes discriminates against both men and women, and is the cause of much unnecessary hostility between the sexes.

WE BELIEVE that women must now exercise their political rights and responsibilities as American citizens. They must refuse to be segregated on the basis of sex into separate-and-not-equal ladies' auxiliaries in the political parties, and they must demand representation according to their numbers in the regularly constituted party committees—at local, state, and national levels—and in the informal power structure, participating fully in the selection of candidates and political decision-making, and running for office themselves.

IN THE INTERESTS OF THE HUMAN DIGNITY OF WOMEN, we will protest, and endeavor to change, the false image of women now prevalent in the mass media, and in the texts, ceremonies, laws, and practices of our major social institutions. Such images perpetuate contempt for women by society and by women for themselves. We are similarly opposed to all policies and practices—in church, state, college, factory, or office—which, in the guise of protectiveness, not only deny opportunities but also foster in women self-denigration, dependence, and evasion of responsibility, undermine their confidence in their own abilities and foster contempt for women.

NOW WILL HOLD ITSELF INDEPENDENT OF ANY POLITICAL PARTY in order to mobilize the political power of all women and men intent on our goals. We will strive to ensure that no party, candidate, president, senator, governor, congressman, or any public official who betrays or ignores the principle of full equality between the sexes is elected or appointed to office. If it is necessary to mobilize the votes of men and women who believe in our cause, in order to win for women the final right to be fully free and equal human beings, we so commit ourselves.

WE BELIEVE THAT women will do most to create a new image of women by acting now, and by speaking out in behalf of their own equality, freedom, and human dignity—not in pleas for special privilege, nor in enmity toward men, who are also victims of the current, half-equality between the sexes—but in an active, self-respecting partnership with men. By so doing, women will develop confidence in their own ability to determine actively, in partnership with men, the conditions of their life, their choices, their future and their society.

Source: Betty Friedan, "The National Organization for Women's 1966 Statement of Purpose," 1966, National Organization for Women, first published in *It Changed My Life: Writing on the Women's Movement* (New York: Random House, 1976), 109–15.

Stonewall Activists Marsha P. Johnson and Sylvia Rivera (1973)

Marsha P. Johnson (*left*) and Sylvia Rivera (*right*) were gay rights activists involved in the 1969 Stonewall riots who eventually founded the organization Street Transvestite Action Revolutions. In the photograph, they are seen marching at the Christopher Street Gay Liberation Parade in New York City in 1973. Often ostracized from other social movements due to their identity and sexuality, LGBTQ activists established a number of organizations over the course of the 1960s and 1970s that fought for various social, civil, legal, and economic rights.

Source: Leonard Fink, *Sylvia Rivera (holding the banner) and Marsha P. Johnson (with color) of the Street Transvestite Action Revolutionaries (S.T.A.R.) at the Christopher Street Liberation Parade,* June 24, 1973, photograph, New York, Leonard Fink Photographs, box 3, folder 24, The LGBT Community Center National History Archive.

"The Process of Coming Back into the World": An American Indian Movement (A.I.M.) Activist Advocates Cultural and Political Unification (1974)

The struggle for American Indian rights to land, life, and culture have been inextricably tied to settler colonialism and efforts to erase the Native origins of the United States. In 1968, a new generation of American Indian activists formed the American Indian Movement to resist police brutality and address widespread poverty on reservations and in American Indian communities. In the following piece, AIM activist Jimmie Durham advocates for greater unity among American Indians to ward off white progressives' efforts to undermine the movement and its objectives.

AMERICAN INDIAN CULTURE: TRADITIONALISM AND SPIRITUALISM IN A REVOLUTIONARY STRUGGLE
Culture as a Way to Know the World . . .

. . . *Our societies, our culture, defines us, in large part, and our way of experiencing the world is through our culture.* Politics, economics, science and technology, language, etc., are all cultural phenomena, and finally, of course, political phenomena. Many progressive people in this country, both whites and blacks, are not critically conscious of that process, and are a part of that mass society in one degree or another.

So, when white people look critically at the Indian Movement (as they should), it should be with a critical consciousness that they are looking through their own culture, which is a particularly alienating one and therefore difficult to see through.

. . . Racism is used so effectively and insidiously as a tool of oppression that some people think that it is some absolute of human nature, or at least some absolute of white human nature. Most white progressives will freely admit that they carry some racist attitudes (whereas most Indians, also infected with racism, will not), but will not take the trouble to commit themselves to identifying and eliminating those attitudes, partly because that can be done only by the kind of praxis that U.S. culture makes so difficult. Those attitudes are especially obnoxious and destructive in white people who have the aggressiveness or self-confidence to be in leadership positions of one form or another.

Racism often takes the subtle forms of assuming Indian people to be just like white people, or *totally* different from white people, or other unspoken generalities, which further blind the people to the realities of Indian culture. It is also the primary cause of the most hateful piece of miscommunication now going on between Indians and white progressives: "political missionary-ism". Particularly, by young white Marxists who have never been in real situations of struggle in a working-class movement, who in fact have seldom worked with anyone except fellow-students, and who come to us as though we were ignorant "lumpen proletariat" in need of being "taught", not only Marxism, but the realities of our own struggle.

. . .

The second block is the colonial tool that I call "romanticism." The U.S. has used romanticism more effectively to keep Indians oppressed than it has ever been used on any other people. The basis of that romanticism is of course the concept of the "Noble Savage," but the refinements over the years have worked their way into how every non-Indian thinks about us, and how we think about ourselves. In the U.S. there is a special vocabulary of English *deliberately* developed to maintain oppression of Indians. This vocabulary has connotations of "primitiveness," backwardness, savagery, etc., and affects the ways every Indian and non-Indian in the U.S. thinks about Indians, whether or not people are conscious of them. This vocabulary has become so ingrained that the use of just one of the words conjures up the thought of Indians, and we have come to assume that these are "Indian" words, or at least direct translations from an Indian language into English.

Who decided that the word "chief," which has the connotation of meaning the head of a land or tribe, is the correct translation of the concept of the Creek Indian word "Enhomvta"? Did white people decide that was the correct word by studying the Creek political system? No. They decided because they wanted to show the Creek nation as a "primitive" body of people and "chief" carried this connotation. At first, colonists called Indian leaders "kings," as in the example of King Phillip of the Wampanoag "tribe."

Compare the two following sentences describing the same event and the reasons for a colonial vocabulary may be clearer:

1. Today Archbishop Tatanka Iotanka, Minister of Interior Affairs of the present government of the nation of Lakota and the most respected religious leader of the Lakota people, was assassinated by paid agents of the United States government.
2. Today Chief Sitting Bull, a medicine man of the Sioux Indian tribe, was killed by another Indian.

Of course, I am not suggesting that the word "archbishop" would describe Sitting Bull's position correctly or adequately, but I am saying that it describes the Lakota concept for his position just as well as the English phrase "medicine man" in the English of non-Indian people.

The romantic colonial vocabulary serves to dehumanize us, and make our affairs and political systems seem not quite as serious or advanced as those of other people. The English vocabulary used to describe us is designed to prove that we are inferior. . . .

As we in our struggle break out of isolation, we also break that language barrier, usually before the non-Indians know what has happened. Today we have learned what "tribes" really means so we refuse that definition. Non-Indians, including progressive whites, still use it. Tomorrow we will no longer speak of "full-bloods"; whites may still use that racist terminology. Those who are truly committed to liberation, however, will use the advantage of their outside position to begin an understanding of what we mean by certain words and phrases, such as "traditional," and so work in solidarity with us in the process of coming back into the world. Those whose unconscious racism makes them decide that our specialized language makes us simple-minded or romantic, or Noble Primitives will continue to enhance their own self-image by "helping" us stupid Indians.

It is not an easy situation, nor is it completely one-sided. To add to the confusion there are many young Indians today who have been brought up in cities, sometimes in white foster homes, who have been denied their own culture and the education of their people. Romantic white society gives them their concepts of what "Indianness" is. Because these young people are so alienated, they are in many ways more oppressed than the rest of us, and so their zeal and desperation makes them our "revolutionary vanguard" in many ways. They are the people most articulate and willing to talk to non-Indians. . . .

Because they are often in leadership positions and because what they say about our culture and politics fits the romantic stereotype, non-Indians sometimes take everything they say whole-cloth, and then either write off Indians as mystics or embrace Indians as fellow-mystics according to where they, the non-Indians, are politically. . . .

The Founding Fathers of the United States equated capitalism with civilization. They had to, given their mentality; to them civilization meant *their* society, which was a capitalist society. Therefore, from the earliest times the wars against Indians were not only to take over land but also to squash the threatening example of Indian communism. Jefferson was not the only man of his time to advocate imposing a capitalist and possessive society on Indians as a way to civilize them. The "bad example" was a real threat; the reason the Eastern Indian nations from Florida to New York State and from the Atlantic to Ohio and Louisiana are today so racially mixed is because indentured servants, landless poor whites and escaped black slaves chose our societies over the white societies that oppressed them. . . .

So we have always defined our struggle not only as a struggle for land but also as a struggle to retain our cultural values. Those values are "communistic" values. Our societies were and are "communistic" societies. The U.S. government has always understood that very well. It has not branded us all these years as communists because we tried to form labor unions or because we hung out with the IWW or the Communist Party but because the U.S. government correctly identified our political system. It did not make that a public issue because that would have been dangerous, and because it has been far more efficient to say that we are savages and primitives.

Marx used our societies as examples of what he meant by communism on two different occasions in his writings. He said that we are "Primitive Communists." The word "primitive" means "first," but people who have skimmed through Marx often decide, because of the *connotations* of the word "primitive" which come from political manipulation, that Marx meant that we were backward or "childlike" communists. Marx *was*, nonetheless, very Eurocentric, and he assumed that European history was the main body of humanity's history.

We do not need Marx's words to teach us how to live our lives in our own society. We do not need to go through an industrial revolution so that we can come out as communists on the other side.

We do need Marxism-Leninism as a method and system for knowing the human world as it is today and for knowing how most effectively to fight our oppressor. We do need to join forces with world Marxism-Leninism, because that is the liberation movement for the world. But we will not come into that world community as a "primitive" younger brother.

Our struggle has always been not only to maintain our own lands and culture, but to fight the political system of capitalism itself. That is evident in all the speeches and addresses given by our leaders throughout U.S./Indian history. The struggle to maintain culture is in itself a revolutionary struggle. It is a dynamic and positive struggle, not a passive holding action. We speak of our traditions, and because the romanticism of non-Indians always speaks of us in the past tense (What did the Cherokees eat?, instead of What do the Cherokees eat?), it is assumed that we are speaking of *things* that we used to do, such as "roaming the Plains" or making arrowheads. The traditions that we mean are not the exterior manifestations that are easily identified as "Indian," not the "artifacts" and objects of our culture, but what we call our "vision"—the value system that makes our culture. In short, we mean our political system (but remember we have been taught a special vocabulary), not our well-made arrowheads. . . .

Taking new ideas that are useful is a *very* Cherokee activity. It is a very Lakota activity, or Mohawk activity. We took glass beads, horses, wool blankets, wheat flour for fry-bread, etc., very early, and immediately made them identifiably "Indian" things. We are able to do that because of our cultural integrity and because our societies are dynamic and able to take in new ideas. . . .

Another of our valued traditions is to take weapons from the enemy. Thus, in the 1920's some "benign" branch of the B.I.A. decided that if properly controlled it would be a good thing if Indians sitting on barren reservations in Oklahoma were appeased and distracted by letting them hold a dance or two in the summer months. They reasoned that this would also give white people a chance to see "real Indians" doing "real Indian stuff." The B.I.A. decided that it would be easier and less dangerous if these affairs were inter-tribal. In those days the different Indian nations which had been forced into Oklahoma did not have much contact with each other, and were relative strangers to each other. Therefore the B.I.A. decided that small groups from each tribe would find it harder to communicate or plan an "uprising" than one nation of people, or two neighboring nations. The B.I.A. named these events "pow wows," after the word "P'houwah" which means "elder" or "medicine man" (the white trappers a century earlier made the mistaken translation).

To be able to sing together and dance together the Indians invented new dances and songs that did not require words in any one national language. The A.I.M. "song" is a pow wow song, but it should not be thought of as a contrivance because of that. It is a very real, valid and heartening cultural experience for us. The words are the "chant" part—the chorus—common to most Indian singing.

We were not degraded and made to feel like tourist attractions by these pow wows. We used them to create unity among us. We used the English our oppressor taught us as the most available common language. In that language we exchanged information and ideas. Now the pow wows are "our thing." We hold them all over the country all summer long, and Indians from Maine meet with Indians from New Mexico to hear a political speech from an Indian from South Dakota. This century, pow wows have been our main tool towards forming ourselves into one confederation of people and reorganizing our struggle. What was meant to alienate us we used, in our *traditional* way, to strengthen our will.

. . . Colonization and our struggle for liberation accelerated a process of unification and clarification that had already begun (witness the Iroquois Confederacy and its vision). That political process of welding together, and refining and improving a unified concept of society on the Earth, is a cultural process. It is a process that is going on right now.

But it is a process, of course, that is going on internally and is seldom seen or understood from the outside. Because it is a process in a struggle for liberation, inside the most oppressive colonization the world has ever seen, it is not a smooth, clear road towards an ideal. Remember that oppression is more than skin deep; it is not exterior to a person's inner life. It gives us confusion, self-loathing, and a natural urge to escape, which in some people takes the form of a "mental" escape—into mysticism, alcoholism, suicide, reactionism. It does that to each of us to some degree at some time or another. . . .

It is a universal truth that human beings do not exist outside of their culture, their society. A biologically human animal is not fully human without, for example, language which is a cultural/political phenomenon. To speak of an alienated society is to speak of people robbed of their culture, *always* so that some political system can exploit them. That is what makes culture so important to liberation. . . .

Progressive non-Indians in the United States cannot be either teachers or spectators in that process, but must stand with us in true solidarity, which means a commitment to clarity, Marxist criticism and analysis of actual situations. We are, by every criterion, colonized *nations of people*, whose culture is not Western. Blacks, Mexicans, Chicanos, and whites all have more in common with each other than any have with us.

Our culture and our political systems have many faults, and *had* many faults in precolonial times. We have never claimed to be perfect or to have the "secret of life". We *demand*, though, an end to romanticism, paternalism, and racism. We must include in that a demand for an end to liberalism directed against us. We demand to be taken seriously as the people we are, by the world and especially by other peoples on this continent. *We* must demand criticism of ourselves. . . .

Source: Jimmie Durham, "American Indian Culture: Traditionalism and Spiritualism in a Revolutionary Struggle," in *A Certain Lack of Coherence: Writings on Art and Cultural Politics*, edited by Jean Fisher (London: Kala Press [now Third Text], 1993), www.thirdtext.org.

DOCUMENT 12.10

Amy Uyematsu, "The Emergence of Yellow Power" (1969)

Asian Americans activists were also influenced by Black freedom struggles. In "The Emergence of Yellow Power," poet Amy Uyematsu calls on Asian Americans to embrace their identity in ways similar to how Black Power advocates called for embracing Blackness rather than attempt to assimilate or adopt white American identity and practices.

PART 1: MISTAKEN IDENTITY

. . . Within the last two years, the "yellow power" movement has developed as a direct outgrowth of the "black power" movement. The "black power" movement caused many Asian Americans to question themselves. "Yellow power" is just now at the stage of "an articulated mood rather than a program—disillusionment and alienation from white America and independence, race pride, and self-respect." Yellow consciousness is the immediate goal of concerned Asian Americans.

In the process of Americanization, Asians have tried to transform themselves into white men—both mentally and physically. Mentally, they have adjusted to the white man's culture by giving up their own languages, customs, histories, and cultural values. They have adopted the "American way of life" only to discover that this is not enough.

Next, they have rejected their physical heritages, resulting in extreme self-hatred. Yellow people share with blacks the desire to look white. Just as blacks wish to be light-complected with thin lips and unkinky hair, "yellows" want to be tall with long legs and large eyes. The self-hatred is also evident in the yellow male's obsession with obtainable white women, and in the yellow female's attempt to gain male approval by aping white beauty standards. Yellow females have their own "conking" techniques— they use "peroxide, foam rubber, and scotch tape to give them light hair, large breasts, and double-lidded eyes."

The "Black is Beautiful" cry among black Americans has instilled a new awareness in Asian Americans to be proud of their physical and cultural heritages. Yellow power advocates self-acceptance as the first step toward straightening personalities of Asian Americans.

Since the yellow power movement is thus far made up of students and young adults, it is working for Asian-American ethnic studies centers on college campuses such as Cal and UCLA. The re-establishment of ethnic identity through education is being pursued in classes like UCLA's "Orientals in America." As one student in the course relates:

> I want to take this course for a 20-20 realization, and not a passive glance in the ill-reflecting mirror; the image I see is WASP, but the yellow skin is not lily white . . . I want to find out what my voluntarily or subconsciously suppressed Oriental self is like; also what the thousands of other (suppressed?) Oriental selves are like in a much larger mind and body—America . . . I want to establish my ethnic identity not merely for the sake of such roots, but for the inherent value that such a background merits.

The problem of self-identity in Asian Americans also requires the removal of stereotypes. The yellow people in America seem to be silent citizens. They are stereotyped as being passive, accommodating, and unemotional. Unfortunately, this description is fairly accurate, for Asian Americans have accepted these stereotypes and are becoming true to them.

The "silent" Asian Americans have rationalized their behavior in terms of cultural values which they have maintained from the old country. For example, the Japanese use the term "enryo" to denote hesitation in action of expression. A young Buddhist minister, Reverend Mas Kodani of the Los Angeles Senshin Buddhist Temple, has illustrated the difference between Japanese "enryo" and Japanese-American "enryo": in Japan, if a teacher or lecturer asks, "Are there any questions?" several members of the class or audience respond; but in the United States, the same question is followed by a deathly silence. . . .

Today the Asian Americans are still scared. Their passive behavior serves to keep national attention on the black people. By being as inconspicuous as possible, they keep pressure off of themselves at the expense of the blacks. Asian Americans have formed an uneasy alliance with white Americans to keep the blacks down. They close their eyes to the latent white racism toward them which has never changed.

Frightened "yellows" allow the white public to use the "silent Oriental" stereotype against the black protest. The presence of twenty million blacks in America poses an actual physical threat to the white system. Fearful whites tell militant blacks that the acceptable criterion for behavior is exemplified in the quiet, passive Asian American.

The yellow power movement envisages a new role for Asian Americans:

> It is a rejection of the passive Oriental stereotype and symbolizes the birth
> of a new Asian—one who will recognize and deal with injustices. The shout
> of Yellow Power, symbolic of our new direction, is reverberating in the quiet
> corridors of the Asian community.

As expressed in the black power writings, yellow power also says that "When we begin to define our own image, the stereotypes—that is, lies—that our oppressor has developed will begin in the white community and end there."

Another obstacle to the creation of yellow consciousness is the well-incorporated white racist attitudes which are present in Asian Americans. They take much false pride in their own economic progress and feel that blacks could succeed similarly if they only followed the Protestant ethic of hard work and education. Many Asians support S. I. Hayakawa, the so-called spokesman of yellow people, when he advises the black man to imitate the Nisei: "Go to school and get high grades, save one dollar out of every ten you earn to capitalize your business." But the fact is that the white power structure allowed Asian Americans to succeed through their own efforts while the same institutions persist in denying these opportunities to black Americans.

Certain basic changes in American society made it possible for many Asian Americans to improve their economic condition after the war. In the first place, black people became the target group of West Coast discrimination. During and after World War II, a huge influx of blacks migrated into the West, taking racist agitation away from the yellows and onto the blacks. From 1940 to 1950, there was a gain of 85.2 percent in the black population of the West and North; from 1950 to 1960, a gain of 71.6 percent; and from 1960 to 1966, a gain of 80.4 percent.

The other basic change in society was the shifting economic picture. In a largely agricultural and rural West, Asian Americans were able to find employment. First- and second-generation Japanese and Filipinos were hired as farm laborers and gar- deners, while Chinese were employed in laundries and restaurants. In marked con- trast is the highly technological and urban society which today faces unemployed black people. "The Negro migrant, unlike the immigrant, found little opportunity in the city; he had arrived too late, and the unskilled labor he had to offer was no longer needed." Moreover, blacks today are kept out of a shrinking labor market, which is also closing opportunities for white job-seekers.

Asian Americans are perpetuating white racism in the United States as they allow white America to hold up the "successful" Oriental image before other minority groups as the model to emulate. White America justifies the blacks' position by showing that other non-whites—yellow people—have been able to "adapt" to the system. The truth underlying both the yellows' history and that of the blacks has been distorted. In addi- tion, the claim that black citizens must "prove their rights to equality" is fundamentally racist.

Unfortunately, the yellow power movement is fighting a well-developed racism in Asian Americans who project their own frustrated attempts to gain white acceptance onto the black people. They nurse their own feelings of inferiority and insecurity by holding themselves as superior to the blacks. . . .

PART 2: THE RELEVANCE OF POWER FOR ASIANS IN AMERICA

The emerging movement among Asian Americans can be described as "yellow power" because it is seeking freedom from racial oppression through the power of a consoli- dated yellow people. As derived from the black power ideology, yellow power implies that Asian Americans must control the decision-making processes affecting their lives.

One basic premise of both black power and yellow power is that ethnic political power must be used to improve the economic and social conditions of blacks and yellows. In considering the relevance of power for Asian Americans, two common assumptions will be challenged: first, that the Asian Americans are completely pow- erless in the United States: and second, the assumption that Asian Americans have already obtained "economic" equality.

While the black power movement can conceivably bargain from a position of strength, yellow power has no such potential to draw from. A united black people would comprise over ten percent of the total American electorate; this is a significant enough proportion of the voting population to make it possible for blacks to be a con- trolling force in the power structure. In contrast, the political power of yellows would have little effect on state and national contests. The combined populations of Chinese, Japanese and Filipinos in the United States in 1960 was only 887,834—not even one- half percent of the total population.

However, Asian Americans are not completely weaponless, in the local political arena. For instance, in California, the combined strength of Chinese, Japanese, and Filipinos in 1960 was two percent of the state population. Their possible political sig- nificance lies in the fact that there are heavy concentrations of these groups in San

Francisco and Los Angeles. . . . In city and country government, a solid yellow voting bloc could make a difference. . . .

Even under the assumption that yellow political power could be significant, how will it improve the present economic situation of Asian Americans? Most yellow people have attained middle-class incomes and feel that they have no legitimate complaint against the existing capitalist structure. . . .

Although it is true that some Asian minorities lead all other colored groups in terms of economic progress, it is a fallacy that Asian Americans enjoy full economic opportunity. If the Protestant ethic is truly a formula for economic success, why don't Japanese and Chinese who work harder and have more education than whites earn just as much? . . .

The myth of Asian American success is most obvious in the economic and social position of Filipino Americans. In 1960, the 65,459 Filipino residents of California earned a median annual income of $2,925, as compared to $3,553 for blacks and $5,109 for whites. Over half of the total Filipino male working force was employed in farm labor and service work; over half of all Filipino males received less than 8.7 years of school education. Indeed, Filipinos are a forgotten minority in America. Like blacks, they have many legitimate complaints against American society.

A further example of the false economic and social picture of Asian Americans exists in the ghetto communities of Little Tokyo in Los Angeles and Chinatown in San Francisco. In the former, elderly Japanese live in run-down hotels in social and cultural isolation. And in the latter, Chinese families suffer the poor living conditions of a community that has the second highest tuberculosis rate in the nation.

Thus, the use of yellow political power is valid, for Asian Americans do have definite economic and social problems which must be improved. By organizing around these needs, Asian Americans can make the yellow power movement a viable political force in their lives.

Source: Amy Uyematsu, "The Emergence of Yellow Power in America" (reprinted from *Gidra*, October 1969), in *Roots: An Asian American Reader*, edited by Amy Tachiki, Eddie Wong, Franklin Odo, and Buck Wong (Los Angeles: UCLA Asian American Studies Center, 1971), 9–13.

Protest of Police Brutality in Chinatown, New York (1975)

In 1975, Peter Yew, a Chinese American, intervened in the police beating of a teenager in New York. The police then assaulted Yew and arrested him for assaulting an officer. Yew's beating and arrest sparked a protest by thousands of Asian Americans in Chinatown against police brutality and for better social services to address poverty among residents and discrimination against Asian Americans.

Source: Emile Bocian, *Protest of Police Brutality in Chinatown. Bilingual Chinese and English Banner Reads: "End all oppression! Fight Racial Discrimination. End Police Brutality. Support Yew Case,"* 1975, photograph, courtesy of Emile Bocian, Museum of Chinese in America (MOCA) Collection.

FURTHER READING

Bagley, Edythe Scott. *Desert Rose: The Life and Legacy of Coretta Scott King.* Tuscaloosa: University of Alabama Press, 2012.

Banks, Dennis, and Richard Erdoes. *Ojibwa Warrior: Dennis Banks and the Rise of the American Indian Movement.* Norman: University of Oklahoma Press, 2011.

Bates, Denise E. *The Other Movement: Indian Rights and Civil Rights in the Deep South.* Tuscaloosa: University of Alabama Press, 2012.

Borstelmann, Thomas. *The Cold War and the Color Line: American Race Relations in the Global Arena.* Cambridge, MA: Harvard University Press, 2001.

Davis, Flora. *Moving the Mountain: The Women's Movement in America since 1960.* Urbana: University of Illinois Press, 1999.

Davis, Mike, and John Wiener. *Set the Night on Fire: L.A. in the Sixties.* New York: Verso Books, 2020.

Duberman, Martin. *Stonewall: The Definitive Story of the LGBT Rights Uprising That Changed America.* Toronto: Plume Press, 2019.

Dudziak, Mary L. *Cold War Civil Rights: Race and the Image of American Democracy.* Princeton, NJ: Princeton University Press, 2002.

Echols, Alice. "Nothing Distant about It: Women's Liberation and Sixties Radicalism." In *The Sixties*, edited by David Farber, 149–74. Chapel Hill: University of North Carolina Press, 1994.

Gaines, Kevin. *American Africans in Ghana: Black Expatriates and the Civil Rights Era.* Chapel Hill: University of North Carolina Press, 2006.

———. "A World to Win: The International Dimension of the Black Freedom Movement." *OAH Magazine of History* 20, no. 5 (2006): 14–18.

Garcia, Mario T. *The Chicano Generation: Testimonios of the Movement.* Oakland: University of California Press, 2015.

Green, Venus. *Race on the Line: Gender, Labor, and Technology in the Bell System.* Durham, NC: Duke University Press, 2001.

Hall, Simon. *Rethinking the American Anti-war Movement.* New York: Routledge, 2011.

Hinnershitz, Stephanie. *A Different Shade of Justice: Asian American Civil Rights in the South.* Chapel Hill: University of North Carolina Press, 2020.

Hogan, Wesley C. *Many Minds, One Heart: SNCC's Dream for a New America.* Chapel Hill: University of North Carolina Press, 2007.

Joseph, Peniel. *The Sword and the Shield: The Revolutionary Lives of Malcolm X and Martin Luther King Jr.* New York: Basic Books, 2020.

King, Coretta Scott. *Coretta: My Life, My Love, My Legacy.* New York: Henry Holt, 2017.

Krochmal, Max. *Blue Texas: The Making of a Multiracial Democratic Coalition in the Civil Rights Era.* Chapel Hill: University of North Carolina Press, 2016.

Levy, Peter. *The New Left and Labor in the 1960s.* Urbana: University of Illinois Press, 1994.

Lewis, John. *Walking with the Wind: A Memoir of the Movement.* New York: Simon & Schuster, 2015.

Lopez, Ian Haney. *Racism on Trial: The Chicano Fight for Justice.* Cambridge, MA: Belknap Press of Harvard University Press, 2004.

Means, Russell, and Marvin J. Wolf. *Where White Men Fear to Tread: The Autobiography of Russell Means*. New York: St. Martin's Press, 1995.

Pawell, Miriam. *The Crusades of Cesar Chavez: A Biography*. London: Bloomsbury Press, 2014.

Plummer, Brenda Gayle. *In Search of Power: African Americans in the Era of Decolonization, 1956–1974*. Cambridge: Cambridge University Press, 2013.

Rosales, F. Arturo. *Chicano! The History of the Mexican American Civil Rights Movement*. Houston: Arte Publico Press, 1997.

Smith, Paul Chaat, and Robert Allan Warrior. *Like a Hurricane: The Indian Movement from Alcatraz to Wounded Knee*. New York: New Press, 1997.

Sowards, Stacey. *Sí, Ella Puede! The Rhetorical Legacy of Dolores Huerta and the United Farm Workers*. Austin: University of Texas Press, 2019.

Stein, Marc, ed. *The Stonewall Riots: A Documentary History*. New York: New York University Press, 2019.

Strain, Christopher B. *The Long Sixties: America, 1955—1973*. Hoboken, NJ: Wiley-Blackwell, 2016.

von Eschen, Penny M. *Race against Empire: Black Americans and Anticolonialism, 1937–1957*. Ithaca, NY: Cornell University Press, 1997.

13

The Black Freedom Movement in the Twenty-First Century

How reminiscent are current struggles to the 1950s and 1960s? What are the current issues? What do these issues reveal about the current nature and direction of the Black freedom movement? What do they reveal about the civil rights movement's legacy? What strategies are currently being employed? How, if at all, do they reflect those used in previous phases of the movement? In what ways are current movements—such as Black Lives Matters and MeToo—strikingly different from the mid-twentieth-century freedom movement?

While this reader explores the civil rights movement in an expansive context aligned with a larger Black freedom struggle, discussions of the civil rights movement still tend to be confined to the southern civil rights movement of the 1950s and 1960s. The civil rights movement remains fixed in the past. Monuments, celebrations, and mainstream retellings of the movement too often tell a story of American triumph, one in which racial injustices have been resolved and the playing field is now fair. The historian Jeanne Theoharis adds: "These tributes tell tales about the power of American values—of the disenfranchised's ability to use the lever of democracy and of the willingness of the powerful to change."[1] What is lost, however, are the radical aspects of the movement and the ways that struggle is unfinished.

From the 1990s through the first two decades of the twenty-first century, Black Americans continued to mobilize for a more just and democratic society, often in ways that highlighted the intersectionality of Black lived experiences. Both at the beginning of this era with the testimony of Anita Hill and at the end of this era with Tarana Burke's founding of #MeToo, Black women called attention to the painful realities of sexual harassment, abuse, and exploitation of their bodies. Echoing elements of Black feminism and the Combahee River Collective, Black queer women founded and led the movement for Black Lives Matter in protest of racially motivated murders of Black men and women, police brutality, bias in the criminal justice system, and mass incarceration. These issues continue to dominate the agenda of the Black freedom movement.

Public health and environmental racism have also played a more prominent role in Black freedom struggles since the 1980s. The HIV/AIDS crisis hit the African American community particularly hard. In the United States, the epidemic that began in the 1980s was not considered a public health crisis. Many public health practitioners, politicians, and community leaders linked the disease to high-risk behaviors such as drug abuse and homosexuality, though some high-profile cases of transmission occurred through blood transfusions. However, the disease spread beyond these groups, and by 1995, some fifty thousand Americans had died as a result of AIDS-related complications, and half of those who died were African American.

Concerns about public health and equitable access to public resources were starkly visible in the aftermath of Hurricane Katrina, a category 5 hurricane that touched down in New Orleans in late August 2005. While the hurricane itself battered the predominantly Black city, it was the breaching of the city's levees and immense flooding in the city's vulnerable and historical Black Ninth Ward that caused more than twelve hundred deaths, resulted in $125 billion in damages, and exposed the ugly truth of disinvestment in urban cities and inadequate government responses to crises. Similar concerns are evident in the ongoing water crisis in Flint, Michigan, a city with a majority Black population and where one out of every four falls below the poverty line. The crisis was exposed in 2014 after city officials changed the city's main water sources to the Flint River. Inadequate testing and treatment of the water exposed more than one hundred thousand of the city's residents to lead contamination. The COVID-19 pandemic also placed a spotlight on the public health crisis and racial, economic, and regional disparities in the U.S. health-care systems.

African Americans continue to call for change in a multitude of ways, from seeking reparations and the election of the nation's first Black president, Barack Obama, in 2008 and 2012, to the formation of new freedom movements like Black Lives Matters. Alicia Garza, Patrisse Cullors, and Opal Tometi were inspired to start the Black Lives Matters movement in 2013, when seventeen-year-old Travyon Martin was murdered. While taking a walk in his father's fiancée's gated community in Sanford, Florida, Martin was racially profiled and shot by George Zimmerman. Garza, Cullors, and Tometi "created the hashtag #BlackLivesMatter" to "articulate most clearly the overlapping oppressions confronting Black people in the struggle to end police violence and win justice."[2] BLM would arguably gain nationwide—and global—recognition after the murder of Michael Brown in Ferguson, Missouri. The movement has gone on to protest the state-sanctioned murders of African Americans, including Eric Garner, Tamir Rice, Breonna Taylor, and George Floyd, among others.

BLM is much like its predecessor the civil rights movement for two notable reasons. First, as Garza notes, the movement is "relationships and connections, exercising new forms of leadership, new tactics, and learning lessons from our elders—people like Bayard Rustin, Diane Nash, Linda Burnham, Assata Shakur and Angela Davis—who have been part of social movements before us."[3] And second, BLM is largely female. Keeanga-Yamahtta Taylor writes, "The Black women leading the movement against police brutality have worked to expand our understanding of the broad impact of police violence in Black communities. Sometimes this is articulated through the straightforward demand that society as a whole recognize that the police victimize Black women. . . . But Black women have also made a much more deliberate intervention to expose police brutality as part of a much larger system of oppression in the lives of all Black working-class and poor people."[4]

Black women have also taken action to call out symbols of white supremacy, like the Confederate flag. In an act of nonviolent direct action, activist Brittany "Bree" Newsome scaled a flagpole on the grounds of the South Carolina statehouse in 2015 to remove the Confederate flag, stating: "In the name of Jesus, this flag has to come down. You come against me with hatred and oppression and violence. I come against you in the name of God. This flag comes down today."[5] Newsome's actions came just over a week after the murders of nine African Americans attending a church service in Charleston, South Carolina, by a white supremacist. Newsome felt compelled to act in response to the Charleston church shooting but acknowledged that a much longer history of racial violence dating back to the civil rights movement and beyond also informed her decision to act.[6] Though Newsome and her accomplice were arrested, the South Carolina Legislature eventually voted to remove the flag less than one month after Newsome's action.

In the wake of ongoing domestic acts of racial terrorism and continued conversations about racism, dozens of city and state legislatures, colleges, and universities across the nation have weighed in on what to do with Confederate monuments. In one high-profile case, former mayor of New Orleans Mitch Landrieu decided to remove all Confederate statues from public spaces in the city in 2017. Landrieu argued that the Confederacy was a symbol of white supremacy and stated the following:

> The Confederacy was on the wrong side of history and humanity. It sought to tear apart our nation and subjugate our fellow Americans to slavery. This is the history we should never forget and one that we should never again put on a pedestal to be revered. As a community, we must recognize the significance of removing New Orleans' Confederate monuments. It is our acknowledgment that now is the time to take stock of, and then move past, a painful part of our history. Anything less would render generations of courageous struggle and soul-searching a truly lost cause.[7]

But the push to remove Confederate monuments and statues from public spaces and to erect monuments and statues to celebrate the civil rights movement must not stand in the way of true reform. The push to render the civil rights movement and the struggle against racial oppression as fixed in the past, and to remake the images and impact of the movement for political uses in the present, does significant harm to our own understandings of the movement and what it means to struggle for justice, dignity, and freedom. A national reckoning with racism, white supremacy, and the symbols used to memorialize our nation's history have too often been linked to the loss of Black life. As evidenced in the voices within this reader, the struggle for civil, political, economic, and social rights is ongoing. Progress must be measured by the strength of our democracy and the ability of all to live free from discrimination and oppression.

NOTES

1. Jeanne Theoharis, *A More Beautiful and Terrible History: The Uses and Misuses of Civil Rights History* (Boston: Beacon Press, 2018), 16.
2. Keeanga-Yamahtta Taylor, *From #BlackLivesMatter to Black Liberation* (Chicago: Haymarket Books, 2016), 166.

3. Taylor, *From #BlackLivesMatter to Black Liberation*, 166–67.

4. Taylor, *From #BlackLivesMatter to Black Liberation*, 166.

5. "Thank you, Bree, for Removing the Confederate Flag," *Evangelicals for Social Action* (online), June 27, 2015, https://web.archive.org/web/20150906121119/http://www.evangelicalsforsocialaction.org/nonviolence-and-peacemaking/thank-you-bree-for-removing-the-confederate-flag-2/.

6. "EXCLUSIVE: Bree Newsome Speaks for the First Time after Courageous Act of Civil Disobedience," *Blue Nation Review*, June 29, 2015, https://archives.bluenationreview.com/exclusive-bree-newsome-speaks-for-the-first-time-after-courageous-act-of-civil-disobedience/.

7. Mitch Landrieu, "On the Removal of Four Confederate Monuments in New Orleans" (speech, New Orleans, May 19, 2017), American Rhetoric, https://www.americanrhetoric.com/speeches/mitchlandrieuconfederatemonuments.htm.

DOCUMENT 13.1

Statement of Anita Hill to Senate Judiciary Committee (1991)

In 1991, when President George H. W. Bush nominated Clarence Thomas for Supreme Court justice, Thomas's sexual harassment of women came to the fore. Anita Hill, one of his accusers, was forced to recount her story before a televised congressional hearing. According to Hill, Thomas repeatedly asked her out on dates and made sexual overtures in the workplace. Given that Thomas was to become the second African American Supreme Court justice, Hill was doubted not only by U.S. senators but also by much of the African American community. In fact, many viewed Hill's testimony as a betrayal, as it could have potentially derailed what many considered another Black accomplishment. Thomas disputed her allegations by drawing on historical race and gender politics and was ultimately confirmed to the highest court in the land.

MS. HILL: Mr. Chairman, Senator Thurmond, members of the committee:

My name is Anita F. Hill, and I am a professor of law at the University of Oklahoma. I was born on a farm in Okmulgee County, Oklahoma, in 1956. I am the youngest of 13 children. I had my early education in Okmulgee County. My father, Albert Hill, is a farmer in that area. My mother's name is Irma Hill. She is also a farmer and a housewife.

My childhood was one of a lot of hard work and not much money, but it was one of solid family affection, as represented by my parents. I was reared in a religious atmosphere in the Baptist faith, and I have been a member of the Antioch Baptist Church in Tulsa, Oklahoma, since 1983. It is a very warm part of my life at the present time.

For my undergraduate work, I went to Oklahoma State University and graduated from there in 1977. I am attaching to this statement a copy of my resume for further details of my education.

SENATOR BIDEN: It will be included in the record as if read.

MS. HILL: Thank you. I graduated from the university with academic honors and proceeded to the Yale Law School, where I received my JD degree in 1980. Upon graduation from law school, I became a practicing lawyer with the Washington, DC, firm of Ward, Hardraker, and Ross.

In 1981, I was introduced to now Judge Thomas by a mutual friend. Judge Thomas told me that he was anticipating a political appointment, and he asked if I would be interested in working with him. He was, in fact, appointed as Assistant Secretary of Education for Civil Rights. After he had taken that post, he asked if I would become his assistant, and I accepted that position.

In my early period there, I had two major projects. The first was an article I wrote for Judge Thomas's signature on the education of minority students. The second was the organization of a seminar on high-risk students which was abandoned because Judge Thomas transferred to the EEOC where he became the chairman of that office.

During this period at the Department of Education, my working relationship with Judge Thomas was positive. I had a good deal of responsibility and independence. I thought he respected my work and that he trusted my judgment. After approximately three months of working there, he asked me to go out socially with him.

What happened next and telling the world about it are the two most difficult experiences of my life. It is only after a great deal of agonizing consideration and a great number of sleepless nights that I am able to talk of these unpleasant matters to anyone but my close friends.

I declined the invitation to go out socially with him and explained to him that I thought it would jeopardize at what at the time I considered to be a very good working relationship. I had a normal social life with other men outside of the office. I believed then, as now, that having a social relationship with a person who was supervising my work would be ill-advised. I was very uncomfortable with the idea and told him so.

I thought that by saying no and explaining my reasons my employer would abandon his social suggestions. However, to my regret, in the following few weeks, he continued to ask me out on several occasions. He pressed me to justify my reasons for saying no to him. These incidents took place in his office or mine. They were in the form of private conversations which would not have been overheard by anyone else.

My working relationship became even more strained when Judge Thomas began to use work situations to discuss sex. On these occasions, he would call me into his office for reports on education issues and projects, or he might suggest that, because of the time pressures of his schedule, we go to lunch to a government cafeteria. After a brief discussion of work, he would turn the conversation to a discussion of sexual matters.

His conversations were very vivid. He spoke about acts that he had seen in pornographic films involving such matters as women having sex with animals and films showing group sex or rape scenes. He talked about pornographic materials depicting individuals with large penises or large breasts involved in various sex acts. On several occasions, Thomas told me graphically of his own sexual prowess.

Because I was extremely uncomfortable talking about sex with him at all, and particularly in such a graphic way, I told him that I did not want to talk about these subjects. I would also try to change the subject to education matters or to nonsexual personal matters such as his background or his beliefs. My efforts to change the subject were rarely successful.

Throughout the period of these conversations, he also, from time to time, asked me for social engagements. My reaction to these conversations was to avoid them by eliminating opportunities for us to engage in extended conversations. This was difficult because at the time I was his only assistant at the Office of Education—or Office for Civil Rights.

During the latter part of my time at the Department of Education, the social pressures and any conversation of his offensive behavior ended. I began both to believe and hope that our working relationship could be a proper, cordial, and professional one.

When Judge Thomas was made chair of the EEOC, I needed to face the question of whether to go with him. I was asked to do so, and I did. The work itself was interesting, and at that time it appeared that the sexual overtures which had so troubled me had ended. I also faced the realistic fact that I had no alternative job. While I might have gone back to private practice, perhaps in my old firm or at another, I was dedicated to civil rights work, and my first choice was to be in that field. Moreover, the Department of Education itself was a dubious venture. President Reagan was seeking to abolish the entire department.

For my first months at the EEOC, where I continued to be an assistant to Judge Thomas, there were no sexual conversations or overtures. However, during the fall and winter of 1982, these began again. The comments were random and ranged from pressing me about why I didn't go out with him to remarks about my personal appearance. I remember his saying that some day I would have to tell him the real reason that I wouldn't go out with him.

He began to show displeasure in his tone and voice and his demeanor and his continued pressure for an explanation. He commented on what I was wearing in terms of whether it made me more or less sexually attractive. The incidents occurred in his inner office at the EEOC.

One of the oddest episodes I remember was an occasion in which Thomas was drinking a Coke in his office. He got up from the table at which we were working, went over to his desk to get the Coke, looked at the can and asked, "Who has pubic hair on my Coke?" On other occasions, he referred to the size of his own penis as being larger than normal, and he also spoke on some occasions of the pleasures he had given to women with oral sex.

At this point, late 1982, I began to feel severe stress on the job. I began to be concerned that Clarence Thomas might take out his anger with me by degrading me or not giving me important assignments. I also thought that he might find an excuse for dismissing me.

In January of 1983, I began looking for another job. I was handicapped because I feared that, if he found out, he might make it difficult for me to find other employment and I might be dismissed from the job I had. Another factor that made my search more difficult was that there was a period—this was during a period of a hiring freeze in the government. In February 1983, I was hospitalized for five days on an emergency basis for an acute—for acute stomach pain, which I attributed to stress on the job.

Once out of the hospital, I became more committed to find other employment and sought further to minimize my contact with Thomas. This became easier when Allison Duncan became office director, because most of my work was then funneled through her and I had contact with Clarence Thomas mostly in staff meetings.

In the spring of 1983, an opportunity to teach at Oral Roberts University opened up. I taught an afternoon session and seminar at Oral Roberts University. The dean of the university saw me teaching and inquired as to whether I would be interested in pursuing a career in teaching, beginning at Oral Roberts University. I agreed to take the job in large part because of my desire to escape the pressures I felt at the EEOC, due to Judge Thomas.

When I informed him that I was leaving in July, I recall that his response was that now I would no longer have an excuse for not going out with him. I told him that I still preferred not to do so. At some time after that meeting, he asked if he could take me to dinner at the end of the term. When I declined, he assured me that the dinner was a professional courtesy only and not a social invitation. I reluctantly agreed to accept that invitation, but only if it was at the very end of a working day.

On, as I recall, the last day of my employment at the EEOC in the summer of 1983, I did have dinner with Clarence Thomas. We went directly from work to a restaurant near the office. We talked about the work I had done, both at Education and at the EEOC. He told me that he was pleased with all of it except for an article and speech that I had done for him while we were at the Office for Civil Rights. Finally, he made a comment that I will vividly remember. He said that if I ever told anyone of his behavior that it would ruin his career. This was not an apology, nor was it an explanation. That was his last remark about the possibility of our going out or reference to his behavior.

In July of 1983, I left Washington, D.C. area and I've had minimal contacts with Judge Clarence Thomas since. I am of course aware from the Press that some questions have been raised about conversations I had with Judge Clarence Thomas after I left the EEOC. From 1983 until today, I have seen Judge Thomas only twice. On one occasion, I needed to get a reference from him, and on another he made a public appearance in Tulsa.

On one occasion he called me at home and we had an inconsequential conversation. On one occasion he called me without reaching me, and I returned the call without reaching him, and nothing came of it. I have, on at least three occasions, been asked to [act] as a conduit to him for others.

I knew his secretary, Diane Holt. We had worked together at both EEOC and Education. There were occasions on which I spoke to her, and on some of these occasions undoubtedly I passed on some casual comment to then Chairman Thomas. There were a series of calls in the first three months of 1985, occasioned by a group in Tulsa, which wished to have a civil rights conference. They wanted Judge Thomas to be the speaker and enlisted my assistance for this purpose.

I did call in January and February to no effect, and finally suggested to the person directly involved, Susan Cahall, that she put the matter into her own hands and call directly. She did so in March of 1985. In connection with that March invitation, Ms. Cahall wanted conference materials for the seminar and some research was needed. I was asked to try to get the information and did attempt to do so.

There was another call about another possible conference in July of 1985. In August of 1987, I was in Washington, D.C. and I did call Diane Holt. In the course of this conversation, she asked me how long I was going to be in town and I told her. It is recorded in the message as August 15. It was, in fact, August 20th. She told me about Judge Thomas's marriage and I did say, "Congratulate him."

It is only after a great deal of agonizing consideration that I am able to talk of these unpleasant matters to anyone except my closest friends. As I've said before these last few days have been very trying and very hard for me, and it hasn't just been the last few days this week. It has actually been over a month now that I have been under the strain of this issue.

Telling the world is the most difficult experience of my life, but it is very close to having to live through the experience that occasion this meeting. I may have used poor judgment early on in my relationship with this issue. I was aware, however, that telling at any point in my career could adversely affect my future career. And I did not want early on to burn all the bridges to the EEOC.

As I said, I may have used poor judgment. Perhaps I should have taken angry or even militant steps, both when I was in the agency, or after I left it. But I must confess to the world that the course that I took seemed the better as well as the easier approach.

I declined any comment to newspapers, but later when Senate staff asked me about these matters I felt I had a duty to report. I have no personal vendetta against Clarence Thomas. I seek only to provide the committee with information which it may regard as relevant.

It would have been more comfortable to remain silent. I took no initiative to inform anyone. But when I was asked by a representative of this committee to report my experience, I felt that I had to tell the truth. I could not keep silent.

Source: Anita Hill, "Opening Statement to the Senate Judiciary Committee" (speech, Washington, D.C., October 11, 1991), American Rhetoric, https://americanrhetoric.com/speeches/anitahillsenatejudiciarystatement.htm.

DOCUMENT 13.2

Statement of Clarence Thomas to Senate Judiciary Committee (1991)

Clarence Thomas was the second African American to sit on the U.S. Supreme Court, having succeeded Thurgood Marshall. Whereas Marshall added a liberal presence to the Court, backing an expansion of civil rights and affirmative action, Thomas brought a conservative voice to the Court. Throughout his career, both before and after his appointment to the highest court in the land, Thomas often opposed civil rights and affirmative action policies, imploring African Americans and others to see beyond race. Yet he readily invoked race to defend himself in the confirmation hearings when he accused Hill and Senate Judiciary Committee of committing a "high-tech lynching" against him.

SENATOR BIDEN: . . . The committee will please come to order. Judge, tough day and tough night for you, I know. Let me ask, do you have anything you'd like to say before we begin? And I understand that your preference is—which is totally and completely understandable—that we go one hour tonight, 30 minutes on each side. Is—Am I correct in that?

JUDGE THOMAS: That's right.

SENATOR BIDEN: Do you have anything you'd like to say?

JUDGE THOMAS: Senator, I would like to start by saying unequivocally, uncategorically, that I deny each and every single allegation against me today that suggested in any way that I had conversations of a sexual nature or about pornographic material with Anita Hill, that I ever attempted to date her, that I ever had any personal sexual interest in her, or that I in any way ever harassed her.

A second, and I think more important point. I think that this today is a travesty. I think that it is disgusting. I think that this hearing should never occur in America. This is a case in which this sleaze, this dirt, was searched for by staffers of members of this committee, was then leaked to the media, and this committee and this body validated it and displayed it at prime time over our entire nation. How would any member on this committee, any person in this room, or any person in this country, would like sleaze said about him or her in this fashion? Or this dirt dredged up and this gossip and these lies displayed in this manner? How would any person like it?

The Supreme Court is not worth it. No job is worth it. I am not here for that. I am here for my name, my family, my life, and my integrity. I think something is dreadfully wrong with this country when any person, any person in this free country would be subjected to this.

This is not a closed room. There was an FBI investigation. This is not an opportunity to talk about difficult matters privately or in a closed environment. This is a circus. It's a national disgrace.

And from my standpoint as a black American, as far as I'm concerned, it is a high-tech lynching for uppity blacks who in any way deign to think for themselves, to do for themselves, to have different ideas, and it is a message that unless you kowtow to an old order, this is what will happen to you. You will be lynched, destroyed, caricatured by a committee of the U.S. Senate, rather than hung from a tree.

Source: Clarence Thomas, "Statement before the Senate Judiciary Committee"
(speech, Washington, D.C., October 11, 1991), American Rhetoric,
https://americanrhetoric.com/speeches/clarencethomashightechlynching.htm.

DOCUMENT 13.3

LA Police Chiefs and Civil Rights Attorney on LA Riots (2001)

Police brutality against African Americans rose to the fore once again following the beating of a Black man, Rodney King, by four officers of the Los Angeles Police Department (LAPD). The beating was videotaped by a resident in a nearby building and was later aired by local, national, and even international television news outlets. Despite this, the police officers were acquitted. Their acquittal, along with other incidents of police brutality and racial tensions in the city, led to the 1992 Los Angeles Riots. The following document provides the perspectives of members of the LAPD and other legal officials, each addressing the police beating and its impact on policing in the city, including the late 1990s Rampart Scandal that uncovered widespread corruption in the antigang unit of the LAPD.

FMR. CHIEF DARYL GATES
Chief of L.A.P.D., 1978–1992

[Immediately after the Rodney King beating,] the image of the L.A.P.D. that was sent out to the world was this racist organization that took this opportunity to express its racism by brutalizing a black guy.

The media, particularly the electronic media, began giving that impression by playing that tape over and over again. And then, of course, everybody that had an opinion about what took place out there; they came in, they chimed in, and they gave their opinion; and it did look like racism. "My goodness, here is this black person who is being beaten. It looks like the Old South." That's the impression that was given, but a totally false impression, because there was nothing racist about it. No one knew what Rodney King had done beforehand to be stopped. No one realized that he was a parolee and that he was violating his parole. No one knew any of those things. All they saw was this grainy film and police officers hitting him over the head. . . .

Do you believe, in retrospect—and putting yourself back at that moment—that there were forces interested in exploiting that tape, that moment—forces that had an ax to grind with the L.A.P.D.?

I don't think there is any question about it. It was a great opportunity, a great opportunity. They had the Reverend Jesse Jackson coming out here every week. He didn't even know me, and he stood up and denounced me, over and over again. He knew nothing about me, knew nothing about the policies of the Los Angeles Police Department or what we had done in all communities throughout the city—our community relations, our community efforts. He knew none of this. He just blasted Daryl Gates and the Los Angeles Police Department. Al Sharpton came out. He knew nothing about the Los Angeles Police Department, knew nothing about me. These people . . . filled the atmosphere with hate: hate, hate, hate. Those poor Los Angeles police officers. I know—I talk to them, day in and day out. They sat back and said, "Hey, what did we do? What did we do? We go out every day. We try to do the job in the best way we know how. We know what service is all about. We know. We try to help people. We try to keep them safe. What did we do? What did we do?" All I could tell them is, "You didn't do anything. You did your job. You've done a good job. You're damn fine police officers, and this is a political thing, pure politics." . . .

You believed that the L.A.P.D. was a righteous department, that it was a good department. It wasn't a corrupt department. You were proud of the department. Why did you leave?

I've looked back and I've asked the same question, "Why did I leave?" And I left really because there was so much political pressure on the department, the Christopher Commission, and all of these things. I thought, OK. As you probably remember, in the last days, I was very, very critical of politicians. I was in the newspapers every single day, criticizing somebody. And I finally thought, "Hey, it will be better for my police officers if I get out of here. The focus of attention will not be so much on me. Maybe people will recognize what fine police officers they have out there, and maybe all of this will go away."

I really believed that I was hurting my police officers by staying, so I reluctantly retired. To this day, I think back, I should have stayed another year and straightened out things. I think I would have been better off if I had stayed another year. . . .

They brought in a chief of police from outside. That was a mistake. They brought in a chief of police from the East Coast. That was a mistake. . . . He came in, a very nice guy, and all of that. But he was an individual who did not understand the Los Angeles Police Department, did not have what people ridicule and say—very divisively—"the L.A.P.D. mentality," which is really a wonderful mentality. It's a mentality of police officers out there wanting to do the job.

He came in and didn't understand any of that. He didn't understand the structure of the Los Angeles Police Department, and he undermined that structure, because he didn't understand it. As a result of that, you set the stage for what happened in Rampart.

How?

He took away an awful lot of the kinds of things that are necessary in order to make sure that you don't have police officers doing things that they ought not to do. You have audits. You have inspections. You have close supervision, particularly of specialized units, like gang units. You have very, very close supervision. You need that supervision. It's important to have that supervision. He took all of that away. I had a lieutenant in charge. I had sergeants that understood what all of this was about, what gang investigations were all about. They are the ones that supervised and took pride in the supervision of the CRASH officers. He took all of that away, and he put them in the various areas. He put them into Rampart and didn't give them the supervision. He had the regular uniformed sergeants supervising. Uniformed sergeants don't understand the gang activity, and they don't understand how the CRASH units operate.

And then he really screwed up by taking the CRASH units away from the supervision, and putting them down at another location outside of Rampart, where they were on their own. What in the hell did anybody expect was going to happen? And it happened. It happened.

CHIEF BERNARD PARKS
Chief of L.A.P.D.

As a cop, you saw the Rodney King beating video tape. What was your reaction?

The first time I saw it, I thought it was bad. There was nothing that you could justify it or explain it. Even when I went to roll calls, and officers wanted to talk about what happened, that was not on the film. And you had to explain to them, no matter what happened that we didn't have a visual on, could we justify what we saw on the tape? Because there were enough officers present to subdue that situation early on without the significant number of baton strokes. And you could see from the body language of many of the officers, there was not a tense altercation going on there. Most of the officers were somewhat relaxed. There were a large number of them there. . . .

Was it racial?

I don't know, and I don't think we've seen anything in the sense that it is, per se, racial. I can't get in the heads of the officers [involved]. I think it was a breakdown in leadership and supervision, and I think it [the officers involved] lost track of what they were there for. They got more involved and engaged in swinging the baton than bringing this to a conclusion, and I think that's where the downside is.

People, in essence, justify that arrest, that scene, from a variety of perspectives, including, "Well, you have to look at the whole tape." Why is there that insistence on providing a rationale?

I think you find a lot of officers that, no matter what, want to be able to be supportive of other officers. And I think, unfortunately, they're not objective, often. But I don't believe, in the sense of our own credibility to the community, that you can sit there and look at that tape, just as the community looks at it, and find rationales that could justify what occurred. . . .

We certainly were not in a deadly force situation. With the number of officers there, it was time for someone to make a decision that the baton strikes weren't working. He was not being any more cooperative. Just sheer body weight would have taken him into control in the sense of the number of officers that were present. . . .

And you felt this way, presumably, more or less at the time? You didn't have to study the tape 42 times to come to that conclusion?

No, I think it was pretty obvious. And I think that's where, from the perspective of the community, that we lost credibility; when they sensed that there were comments being made that there was some justification for that. . . .

[After the riots in response to the acquittal of the officers involved in the Rodney King beating], Chief Gates's exit was prompted, and the Los Angeles Police Department gets a new chief, and then another one, both of them black. What does it mean to this city to have a black chief of police?

Although it may mean a lot to the black community, I basically don't think in general this city, because it's such a diverse city, takes it as it relates to being black is anything more significant than being white. They just want a productive chief of police. . . . They want a chief of police that they feel is going to be fair and provide service, and they don't much care what height, weight, or color they are. And I think it's a very narrow perspective. The meaningfulness of it is very localized to maybe a community.

. . . Is it fair to say that, on some level, Willie Williams first, and then you, got the job because of your race?

You know, I don't believe so. You don't get this job for one single purpose. The issue is that you have to have some skills that you bring to the table. The powers that be are looking at this issue much broader than a black person is going to solve it.

Do you think your race was irrelevant?

It's too obvious to be irrelevant. I think the issue is that it certainly . . . it may be value-added, but it's not something that is a situation that says you get the job, versus you don't get the job. . . .

GERALD CHALEFF
Former President of the L.A. Police Commission

When you saw the Rodney King tape—that endless loop that played forever—when you saw that, what did you see?

I was horrified. I thought that it was clearly officers out of control. Clearly, if this was the climate of the Los Angeles Police Department, then we were in serious trouble, and something had to be done.

Did some part of you say, "That's not the L.A.P.D. I know?"

No, and the reason being is not because that's not the individual officers I know. Certainly I know a lot of police officers, and they're all hard working, honest, thoughtful police officers trying to do a good job. Being a police officer is not an easy job, and I think we all have to understand the pressures.

Certainly you could argue that, in the Rodney King case, the adrenaline is flowing, and they're chasing someone, and then this incident occurs. But was I surprised that this happened in Los Angeles? No. Because as a defense lawyer, you know that there are situations that you've heard about where people arrested, or accused, or roughed up. Was I surprised at the violence of it and the length of it? Yes. . . .

On some level, did the Rodney King incident afford an opportunity to examine the way L.A. policing is done?

Sure, absolutely. . . . The old adage about a picture being worth a thousand words—when you see somebody on the ground being beaten, or appear to be being beaten by four or five officers, with other officers standing around—and then some of the comments that were made afterwards and how it was handled, it certainly conveys an image. . . . When you have a symbol like that of that's how your police department operates, of course it's going to lead to people saying that we have to evaluate what we're doing.

GREGORY YATES

Los Angeles civil rights attorney representing numerous Rampart clients in civil suits stemming from Perez's allegations

Give me a sense of what the Rodney King case said about the L.A.P.D. and its effect on Los Angeles.

Well, the obvious effect was that there was a riot, and I watched the city burn. But there was still some optimism that maybe this was just a select crew that had gone bad, so to speak. There were the racial implications, obviously. In 1988, the 39th and Dalton incident was another eye-opener, where they went into what they believed or had information was gang territory, drug-dealing territory. They just basically knocked houses down and arrested innocent citizens.

So the two things combined, Rodney King, 39th and Dalton, and then the findings of the Christopher Commission made it very evident in the early 1990s there were some serious problems. And more so outside of Los Angeles, the public began to view L.A.P.D. as being a corrupt, an almost SS troop kind of organization. I think the people that lived here wanted to deny it as long as they could, because you have to feel that you're protected. Who are you going to go to if you're in trouble? . . . I don't think that, until about 1994 or 1995, did I became completely convinced that it was an institutional problem.

Give me some sense of this department's place in the community.

Unfortunately, the image right now of the L.A.P.D. is at an all-time low. It's very tarnished. And I say "unfortunately," because I think it's important to the community to feel safe, to feel pride in their protectors.

Had it always been thus? When you began, what was the reputation of the L.A.P.D.?

I started practicing in 1974. I noticed that there was a certain "us versus them" attitude about the police. It's almost a Gestapo kind of approach—something totally different from the Midwest, where I went to school and was raised. That was the first thing that caught my attention about the L.A.P.D. . . .

It wasn't until I really got involved in the plaintiff's end of the practice, that I started handling the police misconduct cases, and always really wanted to believe that I'm seeing an exception to the rule, while knowing that there's bad cops just like there are bad lawyers, bad doctors. But I found out, I would say in the early 1990s, that the L.A.P.D. certainly had some very deep-rooted problems.

Source: Daryl Gates, Judge Larry Fidler, Bernard Parks, Gerald Chaleff, and Gregory Yates, "Race and Policing: The Legacy of Rodney King," interviews with PBS, *Frontline*, 2001, From *FRONTLINE #1915, LAPD Blues* (https://www.pbs.org/wgbh/pages/frontline /shows/lapd/race/king.html), © 1995–2022. WGBH Educational Foundation.

DOCUMENT 13.4

Charisse Jones, "Crack and Punishment: Is Race the Issue?" (1995)

The Violent Crime Control and Law Enforcement Act, perhaps better known as the 1994 Crime Bill, was signed into law by President Bill Clinton and signaled his administration's commitment to the ongoing War on Drugs. While intended to curb violent crime, the bill had a significant impact on nonviolent crime, as many states adopted mandatory minimums in order to receive federal funding to build new prisons, which dramatically increased incarceration rates. In the following *New York Times* article, Charisse Jones examines the troubling connection between the 1994 Crime Bill and its harsh punishments for those committing crack offenses (mostly Black and Brown) to those who commit cocaine offenses (mostly whites).

The drug-sentencing bill attracted little notice in Washington, compared with the attention focused on the pitched debate over the future of health care and welfare. But prisoner rights groups say word of its passage flashed through Federal prisons, and soon after there were rumblings of possible disturbances.

Prison officials will not say if they believe the uprisings that followed at five sites were related to the vote in Congress. But the disturbances have suddenly drawn attention to the debate over mandatory Federal sentencing laws for crack cocaine offenses. These laws, which Congress voted to maintain in the bill, are harsher than those for crimes involving powdered cocaine, and many lawyers and legislators say they have a disproportionate impact on poor black men.

It is both unfair, impractical, and unwarranted," said Laura Murphy, director of the Washington, D.C., chapter of the American Civil Liberties Union, who called race issues in the criminal justice system "the new frontier" of civil rights. "How can you go to an inner-city family and tell them their son is given 20 years, while someone in the suburbs who's using powdered cocaine in greater quantities can get off with 90 days' probation? When people understand the truth about the way these laws are imposed, the fact they've had no deterrent, and the race-based nature of these prosecutions, then I think a sleeping giant is going to roar."

But others say the violence and addiction that lie in the crack epidemic's wake explain why such offenses are more harshly punished.

"What about the gangs, the rivalries, the shootings, the killings?" said Jim Shedd, an agent and spokesman for the Drug Enforcement Administration in Miami. "Everybody's forgotten about the amount of violence that goes with crack cocaine. It's not a racist thing, but unfortunately that's what it's turned into."

Last week, during the march on Washington by hundreds of thousands of black men, and later in an emotional debate on the floor of the House of Representatives, speakers decried Federal laws that say it takes 100 times more powdered cocaine to draw the same mandatory minimum sentence of five years in prison that awaits a person convicted of possessing five grams of crack.

The United States Sentencing Commission, created by Congress to draft, monitor and amend sentencing guidelines for the Federal courts, recommended that legislators scrap the 100-to-1 ratio, and make equal the amounts of crack and cocaine powder that draw the same base sentences. It suggested a number of enhancements that would more severely punish offenders who had also used a weapon, or committed other crimes. But instead lawmakers passed legislation that rejected those recommendations, and urged the body to re-examine its findings.

This week, the Congressional Black Caucus sent a letter to President Bill Clinton urging him to veto Congress's bill. Representative Maxine Waters, Democrat of California, who attacked the sentencing laws during the House debate, has written to prison wardens asking them to relay to Attorney General Janet Reno their concerns about the impact of the uneven penalties.

Challenges to the penalties have never been upheld in Federal courts. But in 1991, the Minnesota Supreme Court struck down a state mandatory sentencing law that mirrored the disparities in the Federal statutes. And in Miami, some Federal prosecutors say they have chosen not to charge some crack suspects because they believe the punishment they will face is unduly harsh.

With a set of mandatory minimum sentencing laws passed in 1986, Congress for the first time distinguished between crack and powder cocaine. Crack, which emerged in the mid-1980's, had been deemed a new drug plague, blamed for escalating gang violence and for a surge in the number of neglected children flooding the child welfare system.

Crack is the only drug that carries a mandatory prison term for possession, whether or not the intent is to distribute, said Paul Martin, deputy staff director for the sentencing commission. Possession of heroin or powdered cocaine, without intent to sell, is a misdemeanor carrying a maximum of one year in jail. The commission had also sought to make punishment for simple crack possession equal to that of other drugs.

Although Federal statistics find that half of crack users are white, the sale and use of the substance, a cheaper form of cocaine, is often concentrated in poor, urban, minority communities, experts say. Last year, 90 percent of those convicted of Federal crack offenses were black, and 3.5 percent were white, sentencing commission officials say. By contrast, 25.9 percent of those convicted on Federal powdered cocaine charges were white, 29.7 percent were black and 42.8 percent were Hispanic.

"When we saw those statistics," said Judge Richard P. Conaboy, the sentencing commission's chairman, "our theory was a law, no matter how well-intentioned it was, if it's causing such discrepant results, then the law has to be changed and a new method has to be installed."

The commission's recommendations grew out of a study requested by Congress, said the judge, who added he was not surprised by last week's prison unrest.

Commissioners often spoke with prison officials, he said, and "in the course of our dialogue with them, we learned that a lot of their prison inmates are serving time under drug sentences, and that many of the families of these young black men in particular are concerned and hopeful that there will be some change made in that particular statute. And if the change was not made it might lead to problems."

But others say crack deserves its harsher penalties. While most experts agree that cocaine, be it a crystallized pellet or powder, does not cause its user to become violent, many law-enforcement officials say crack's bustling street trade is particularly vicious.

"The closer we get to the crack dealers on the street," said Los Angeles Deputy District Attorney Curtis Hazell, who heads the major narcotics unit, "the more likely they are to have a past history of violence."

Of those convicted in 1993 of Federal offenses involving powdered cocaine, 15.1 percent were given additional time for using a weapon, as compared with 28 percent of crack offenders, commission officials said.

"Crack clearly causes more trouble than powdered cocaine," said Dr. Robert Byck, professor of psychiatry and pharmacology at the Yale University School of Medicine. "When rock was introduced, the number of hospitalizations for cocaine impairment went way up, and the number of people addicted went way up."

But some sociologists argue that many of the ills associated with crack have as much to do with poverty, unemployment and homelessness as the drug itself, and that society should focus on creating more jobs and treatment programs.

Others say there are negligible pharmacological differences between crack and powdered cocaine. Though smoking crack makes the drug's high quicker and stronger, some doctors note that powdered cocaine can also be smoked, when it is concentrated using the technique known as free-basing. Powdered cocaine can also be injected, they point out, which is more likely to lead to addiction.

"The potency, dangerousness and risk depends on multiple factors," said Dr. Mitchell S. Rosenthal, president of the Phoenix House Foundation, a national drug treatment organization. "A person who is selling cocaine in the powdered form or crack form will both bring about a great deal of harm in the user. So does it make sense for a sentencing disparity? Probably not."

The primary difference between crack and powdered cocaine, some say, is the public perception of the user and seller—the white suburbanite usually linked with powdered cocaine, and the young, urban black man connected to crack.

"If these were young white men going to jail, this would not exist," said William Moffitt, a lawyer and treasurer of the National Association of Criminal Defense Lawyers, which has challenged the mandatory sentences in court. "So the war on drugs is essentially being borne by the black community."

The Sentencing Project, a national nonprofit organization that deals with criminal justice issues, recently released a report finding that one in three black men between the ages of 20 and 29 are in the grasp of the criminal justice system.

Marc Mauer, the project's assistant director, said the nation's drug policies were one of the primary reasons for this.

"Every middle-class parent knows that if their son or daughter started using drugs, the first response would be to find the best treatment program they could afford," Mr. Mauer said. "It would never occur to them to write out a check for $20,000 and reserve a space in the prison system for their kid's problem. We have the same problem, yet the responses are different—one a public health response, the other a criminal justice response—largely due to the individual who's affected by it."

Mr. Mauer and others said no one had proved that the stringent crack penalties have reduced other crimes or slowed addiction. And he and several others contended that the mandatory laws are too broad, punishing a small-time dealer caught with a few grams of crack as harshly as a drug kingpin.

But some law-enforcement officials argue that more blacks are being jailed for crack offenses because they are the ones committing the crimes.

"It's not disproportionate considering who's dealing," said Mr. Hazell, the prosecutor in Los Angeles. "It's like complaining that not enough Chinese are being prosecuted. But that's because it's not the Chinese that are doing that crime."

Source: Charisse Jones, "Crack and Punishment: Is Race the Issue?," *New York Times*, October 28, 1995, https://www.nytimes.com/1995/10/28/us/crack-and-punishment-is-race-the-issue.html. © 1995 The New York Times Company. All rights reserved. Used under license.

DOCUMENT 13.5

Louis Farrakhan, Address at the Million Man March (1995)

Minister Louis Farrakhan came to the fore of the Nation of Islam in the late 1970s and early 1980s. He relocated its headquarters to Mosque Maryam in Chicago. Farrakhan was one of the organizers of the Million Man March in 1995, one of the largest gatherings of African Americans in the history of the United States. At the march, Farrakhan implored Black men to abstain from violence, drugs, and alcohol and to step into a place of leadership within their families and communities.

. . . Right here on this mall where we are standing, according to books written on Washington, D.C., slaves used to be brought right here on this Mall in chains to be sold up and down the eastern seaboard.

Right along this mall, going over to the White House, our fathers were sold into slavery. But, George Washington, the first president of the United States, said he feared that before too many years passed over his head, this slave would prove to become a most troublesome species of property.

Thomas Jefferson said he trembled for this country when he reflected that God was just and that His justice could not sleep forever.

Well, the day that these presidents feared has now come to pass, for on this mall, here we stand in the capital of America, and the layout of this great city, laid out by a Black man, Benjamin Banneker. This is all placed and based in a secret Masonic ritual. And at the core of the secret of that ritual is the Black man. Not far from here is the White House.

And the first president of this land, George Washington, who was a grand master of the Masonic order, laid the foundation, the cornerstone of this capitol building where we stand. George was a slave owner. George was a slave owner. Now, the President spoke today and he wanted to heal the great divide. But I respectfully suggest to the President, you did not dig deep enough at the malady that divides Black and White in order to affect a solution to the problem. And so, today, we have to deal with the root so that perhaps a healing can take place.

. . . So, we stand here today at this historic moment. We are standing in the place of those who couldn't make it here today. We are standing on the blood of our ancestors. We are standing on the blood of those who died in the middle passage, who died in the fields and swamps of America, who died hanging from trees in the South, who died in the cells of their jailers, who died on the highways and who died in the fratricidal conflict that rages within our community.

We are standing on the sacrifice of the lives of our heroes, our great men and women that we today may accept the responsibility that life imposes upon each traveler who comes this way.

We must accept the responsibility that God has put upon us, not only to be good husbands and fathers and builders of our community, but God is now calling upon the despised and the rejected to become the cornerstone and the builders of a new world.

And so, our brief subject today is taken from the American Constitution. In these words, Toward a more union. Toward a more perfect union.

. . . We're not gathered here to say all of the evils of this nation. But we are gathered here to collect ourselves for a responsibility that God is placing on our shoulders to move this nation toward a more perfect union. Now, when you look at the word "toward," "toward," it means in the direction of, in furtherance or partial fulfillment of, with the view to obtaining or having shortly before coming soon, eminent, going on in progress. Well, that's right. We're in progress toward a perfect union. Union means bringing elements or components into unity.

It is something formed by uniting two or more things. It is a number of persons, states, etcetera, which are joined or associated together for some common purpose. We're not here to tear down America.

America is tearing itself down. We are here to rebuild the wasted cities. . . .

White supremacy is the enemy of both White people and Black people because the idea of White supremacy means you should rule because you're White, that makes you sick. And you've produced a sick society and a sick world. The founding fathers meant well, but they said, "toward a more perfect union."

So, the Bible says, we know in part, we prophesy in part, but when that which is perfect is to come, that which is in part shall be done away with.

So either, Mr. Clinton, we're going to do away with the mind-set of the founding fathers. You don't have to repudiate them like you've asked my brothers to do me. You don't have to say they were malicious, hate filled people. But you must evolve out of their mind-set.

You see their mind was limited to those six European nations out of which this country was founded. But you've got Asians here. How are you going to handle that? You've got children of Africa here. How are you going to handle that?

You've got Arabs here. You've got Hispanics here. I know you call them illegal aliens, but hell, you took Texas from them by flooding Texas with people that got your mind. And now they're coming back across the border to what is Northern Mexico, Texas, Arizona, New Mexico, and California. They don't see themselves as illegal aliens. I think they might see you as an illegal alien. You have to be careful how you talk to people. You have to be careful how you deal with people. The Native American is suffering today. He's suffering almost complete extinction. Now, he learned about bingo. You taught him. He learned about black jack. You taught him. He learned about playing roulette. You taught him. Now, he's making a lot of money.

You're upset with him because he's adopted your ways. What makes you like this? See, you're like this because you're not well. You're not well. And in the light of today's global village, you can never harmonize with the Asians. You can't harmonize with the islands of the Pacific. You can't harmonize with the dark people of the world who outnumber you 11 to 1, if you're going to stand in the mind of white supremacy. White supremacy has to die in order for humanity to live.

. . . Now, brothers, moral and spiritual renewal is a necessity. Every one of you must go back home and join some church, synagogue or temple or mosque that is teaching spiritual and moral uplift. I want you, brothers, there's no men in the church, in the mosque.

The men are in the streets and we got to get back to the houses of God. But preachers, we have to revive religion in America.

We have to revive the houses of God that they're not personal thiefdoms of those of us who are their preachers and pastors. But we got to be more like Jesus, more like Mohammed, more like Moses and become servants of the people in fulfilling their needs.

Brothers, when you go home, we've got to register eight million, eligible but unregistered brothers, sisters. So you go home and find eight more like yourself. You register and get them to register.

Well how shoul I register? Should I register as a Democrat? Should I register as a Republican? Should I register as independent?

If you're an independent, that's fine. If you're a Democrat, that's fine. If you're a Republican, that's OK. Because in local elections you have to do that which is in the best interest of your local community. But what we want is not necessarily a third party, but a third force.

Which means that we're going to collect Democrats, Republicans and independents around an agenda that is in the best interest of our people. And then all of us can stand on that agenda and in 1996, whoever the standard bearer is for the Democratic, the Republican, or the independent party should one come into existence. They've got to speak to our agenda.

. . . Now brothers, in closing, I want you to take this pledge. When I say I, I want you to say I, and I'll say your name. I know that there's so many names, but I want you to shout your name out so that the ancestors can hear it.

Take this pledge with me. Say with me please, I, say your name, pledge that from this day forward I will strive to love my brother as I love myself. I, say your name, from this day forward will strive to improve myself spiritually, morally, mentally, socially, politically, and economically for the benefit of myself, my family, and my people.

I, say your name, pledge that I will strive to build business, build houses, build hospitals, build factories, and then to enter international trade for the good of myself, my family, and my people. I, say your name, pledge that from this day forward I will never raise my hand with a knife or a gun to beat, cut, or shoot any member of my family or any human being, except in self-defense.

I, say your name, pledge from this day forward I will never abuse my wife by striking her, disrespecting her for she is the mother of my children and the producer of my future. I, say your name, pledge that from this day forward I will never engage in the abuse of children, little boys, or little girls for sexual gratification.

But I will let them grow in peace to be strong men and women for the future of our people. I, say your name, will never again use the B word to describe any female, but particularly my own Black sister.

I, say your name, pledge from this day forward that I will not poison my body with drugs or that which is destructive to my health and my well being. I, say your name, pledge from this day forward, I will support Black newspapers, Black radio, Black television. I will support Black artists, who clean up their acts to show respect for themselves and respect for their people, and respect for the ears of the human family.

I, say your name, will do all of this so help me God. . . .

Source: Minister Louis Farrakhan, "Million Man March Speech," speech (Washington, D.C., October 16, 1995), as recorded by CNN, https://voicesofdemocracy.umd.edu/farrakhan-million-man-march-speech-text/.

ACT UP New York HIV/AIDS Awareness Poster (1989)

Grassroots and activist groups stepped into the vacuum of leadership and failure of the Reagan administration to see the HIV/AIDS epidemic as a public health crisis. The AIDS Coalition to Unleash Power (ACT UP) was founded in 1987 to fight the epidemic through political advocacy, medical research, political advocacy, direct action, and solidarity with those living with the disease.

OUR GOVERNMENT CONTINUES TO IGNORE THE LIVES, DEATHS AND SUFFERING OF PEOPLE WITH HIV INFECTION BECAUSE THEY ARE GAY, BLACK, HISPANIC OR POOR. BY JULY 4, 1989 OVER 55 THOUSAND WILL BE DEAD. TAKE DIRECT ACTION NOW. FIGHT BACK. FIGHT AIDS.

Source: ACT UP New York, "American Flag [Our Government Continues to Ignore the Lives, Deaths and Suffering of People with HIV Infection . . .]," 1989, ink on paper, Manuscripts and Archives Division, New York Public Library Digital Collections, https://digitalcollections.nypl.org/items/510d47e3-68d3-a3d9-e040-e00a18064a99.

Malik Rahim, "'This Is Criminal': Report from New Orleans" (2(

Poverty was a determining factor in the decisions of roughly one hundred thou... Orleans residents who lacked the physical or economic means to leave the city in the wake of Hurricane Katrina and subsequent flooding that put nearly 80 percent of the city underwater. The slow response of the federal government and negligence in maintaining the city's levees, which fell under the pressure of hurricane water, led to a disastrous catastrophe. In the national media, images of whites "foraging" and "searching" for food were often juxtaposed with Blacks engaged in similar survival tactics, yet their actions were referred to as "looting." The following document reveals the frustration of Malik Rahim, an organizer on the ground in New Orleans in the days after the hurricane.

"THIS IS CRIMINAL"

It's criminal. From what you're hearing, the people trapped in New Orleans are nothing but looters. We're told we should be more "neighborly." But nobody talked about being neighborly until after the people who could afford to leave . . . left.

If you ain't got no money in America, you're on your own. People were told to go to the Superdome, but they have no food, no water there. And before they could get in, people had to stand in line for 4–5 hours in the rain because everybody was being searched one by one at the entrance.

I can understand the chaos that happened after the tsunami, because they had no warning, but here there was plenty of warning. In the three days before the hurricane hit, we knew it was coming and everyone could have been evacuated.

We have Amtrak here that could have carried everybody out of town. There were enough school buses that could have evacuated 20,000 people easily, but they just let them be flooded. My son watched 40 buses go underwater—they just wouldn't move them, afraid they'd be stolen.

People who could afford to leave were so afraid someone would steal what they own that they just let it all be flooded. They could have let a family without a vehicle borrow their extra car, but instead they left it behind to be destroyed.

There are gangs of white vigilantes near here riding around in pickup trucks, all of them armed, and any young Black they see who they figure doesn't belong in their community, they shoot him. I tell them, "Stop! You're going to start a riot."

When you see all the poor people with no place to go, feeling alone and helpless and angry, I say this is a consequence of HOPE VI. New Orleans took all the HUD money it could get to tear down public housing, and families and neighbors who'd relied on each other for generations were uprooted and torn apart.

Most of the people who are going through this now had already lost touch with the only community they'd ever known. Their community was torn down and they were scattered. They'd already lost their real homes, the only place where they knew everybody, and now the places they've been staying are destroyed.

But nobody cares. They're just lawless looters . . . dangerous.

The hurricane hit at the end of the month, the time when poor people are most vulnerable. Food stamps don't buy enough but for about three weeks of the month, and by the end of the month everyone runs out. Now they have no way to get their food stamps or any money, so they just have to take what they can to survive.

Many people are getting sick and very weak. From the toxic water that people are walking through, little scratches and sores are turning into major wounds.

People whose homes and families were not destroyed went into the city right away with boats to bring the survivors out, but law enforcement told them they weren't needed. They are willing and able to rescue thousands, but they're not allowed to.

Every day countless volunteers are trying to help, but they're turned back. Almost all the rescue that's been done has been done by volunteers anyway.

My son and his family—his wife and kids, ages 1, 5 and 8—were flooded out of their home when the levee broke. They had to swim out until they found an abandoned building with two rooms above water level.

There were 21 people in those two rooms for a day and a half. A guy in a boat who just said "I'm going to help regardless" rescued them and took them to Highway I-10 and dropped them there.

They sat on the freeway for about three hours, because someone said they'd be rescued and taken to the Superdome. Finally they just started walking, had to walk six and a half miles.

When they got to the Superdome, my son wasn't allowed in—I don't know why —so his wife and kids wouldn't go in. They kept walking, and they happened to run across a guy with a tow truck that they knew, and he gave them his own personal truck.

When they got here, they had no gas, so I had to punch a hole in my gas tank to give them some gas, and now I'm trapped. I'm getting around by bicycle.

People from Placquemine Parish were rescued on a ferry and dropped off on a dock near here. All day they were sitting on the dock in the hot sun with no food, no water. Many were in a daze; they've lost everything.

They were all sitting there surrounded by armed guards. We asked the guards could we bring them water and food. My mother and all the other church ladies were cooking for them, and we have plenty of good water.

But the guards said, "No. If you don't have enough water and food for everybody, you can't give anything." Finally the people were hauled off on school buses from other parishes.

You know Robert King Wilkerson (the only one of the Angola 3 political prisoners who's been released). He's been back in New Orleans working hard, organizing, helping people. Now nobody knows where he is. His house was destroyed. Knowing him, I think he's out trying to save lives, but I'm worried.

The people who could help are being shipped out. People who want to stay, who have the skills to save lives and rebuild are being forced to go to Houston.

It's not like New Orleans was caught off guard. This could have been prevented.

There's military right here in New Orleans, but for three days they weren't even mobilized. You'd think this was a Third World country.

I'm in the Algiers neighborhood of New Orleans, the only part that isn't flooded. The water is good. Our parks and schools could easily hold 40,000 people, and they're not using any of it.

This is criminal. These people are dying for no other reason than the lack of organization.

Everything is needed, but we're still too disorganized. I'm asking people to go ahead and gather donations and relief supplies but to hold on to them for a few days until we have a way to put them to good use.

I'm challenging my party, the Green Party, to come down here and help us just as soon as things are a little more organized. The Republicans and Democrats didn't do anything to prevent this or plan for it and don't seem to care if everyone dies.

Source: Malik Rahim with Mary Ratcliff, "'This Is Criminal': Malik Rahim Reports from New Orleans," *San Francisco Bay View*, September 1, 2005, https://sfbayview.com/2008/11/this-is-criminal/. Courtesy of Malik Rahim.

DOCUMENT 13.8

Report on the Flint Water Crisis (2017)

In its 2017 report on the Flint water crisis, the Michigan Civil Rights Commission implicated government malfeasance, environmental injustice, and systemic racism as core factors in a crisis that exposed thousands of children and families to lead contamination. Flint government officials failed to acknowledge complaints about the water and resulting illnesses from city residents, a majority of whom are Black and about 40 percent of whom are impoverished. The crisis, brought to light by residents in 2014, would last another two years following the publication of this report.

2010–TODAY: THE CRISIS

The current Flint Water Crisis is the direct result of decisions and actions made in the last several years. From an engineering perspective, it probably began in 2000 when the city's contract for water supplied by Detroit ended. Around that time decisions needed to be made about whether it was in Flint's interest to continue to source its water from Detroit, or to explore any other available options. From a liability perspective, the crisis timeline might more appropriately begin around 2010 when decisions were made that led Flint away from purchasing water from Detroit.

Neither timeline is wrong, though the 2010 timeline is particularly important. At this time, decisions were made not just about the water supply itself, but also about who the decisionmakers would be, what their goals would be, and to whom they would answer. If we set back the clock to prevent the current crisis, 2010 would be far enough. Certainly, with the wisdom only hindsight provides, it would be possible to prevent this crisis by changing decisions and actions that occurred between 2010 and the Governor's emergency declaration in January 2016.

Though always cognizant of the pain and suffering endured by the people of Flint, the Commission's goal in looking back is to also determine how to prevent the NEXT crisis. The roots of the Flint Water Crisis run much deeper than decisions made in the last ten years. Preventing the 'next Flint' requires going deeper as well. We must not only examine the decisions, but also why they were necessary. We believe that the Flint Water Crisis is a symptom of a deeper disease. Simply fixing the water system, like removing a tumor, is a critical step, but it won't help the people of Flint if the cancer remains.

This Commission hopes that investigations currently underway by the Attorney General's Office identify all those individuals whose decisions and actions, whether by neglect or malfeasance, were direct causes of the lead poisoning of Flint residents, and that where appropriate these individuals are held accountable. We support these efforts and will not engage in actions that might hinder those investigations. We equally support the right of the water contamination victims to pursue legal remedies and compensation through the courts. But as important as these actions are, they are not enough.

The causes of the Flint Water Crisis are not limited to events in the present decade. Similarly, fault for the crisis cannot be laid *solely* on the decisions and actions taken during this time, or *solely* on the individuals responsible for them. Preventing the 'next Flint' will not be that easy.

We agree with the conclusion reached by the Governor's Flint Water Advisory Task Force: "The Flint Water Crisis is a story of government failure, intransigence, unpreparedness, delay, inaction and environmental injustice." And although the story of government failure the Task Force told may be accurate, we believe it is incomplete. The story they told is only the most recent chapter. We believe the government failures that caused the Flint Water Crisis are much broader, more complex and require the additional chapters outlined in this report. If we are to prevent government's failures from causing similar crises in the future, our responses must be broader, deeper and more complex as well.

As noted earlier, fixing the problems that originated in Flint's latest chapter will address the tumor but not the cancer. We must address the systemic problems, and must acknowledge the role that race and racism played in producing and reproducing them. Left unaddressed, this systemic racism will continue to produce racialized results.

Government, particularly state government, was slow to recognize the emergency that existed in Flint's lead-poisoned water. Evidence was ignored and facts denied. Victims were ignored, advocates demeaned. Delay in responding exacerbated the harm significantly. But in time the state did recognize there was a problem that needed to be fixed.

Government addressed the problem, by doing what it could to minimize the damage caused. People needed fresh water, and the state began to supply it. There were many challenges. Communication, language, filter installation, supply, location, transportation, delivery, and countless other issues arose. Some were predictable and could have been avoided, others not. Many were acknowledged and corrected quickly, others took more prompting, and others are still being worked on. Thus, while imperfect, the Commission finds the state's response to the crisis following the declaration of emergency has been appropriately directed at addressing the immediate needs of Flint residents.

The governments involved (principally the state, but also local and federal), could have tried to get by doing less. But, the Commission also believes that Michiganders (including those not in Flint), would not have accepted anything less.

We cannot help but ask ourselves whether this goodwill and moral acceptance of responsibility will continue for the lifetime of all those who were harmed? Will Michigan be there for Flint's residents and their children as they continue [to] deal with the ills resulting from the current crisis in the next 10, 20, or 40 years?

Our review of Flint's history does not suggest optimism, but the present resolve of state, local, and federal leaders does provide hope.

A FINAL THOUGHT ON THE HARM CAUSED BY SPATIAL RACISM

Our review of Flint's history clearly establishes that past racism played an important role in creating the conditions that allowed the water contamination crisis to occur. The overtly racist practices and racialized 'neutral' policies (particularly housing policies) created the two Americas described in the Kerner report, and that the Commission finds still exist in Flint today. These practices and policies lay at the heart of this water crisis.

These policies and practices fostered separation and creation of a majority black city with an outsized and decaying infrastructure and mostly white suburban communities. The mostly white suburban communities were built with a combination of wealth largely generated in the city and racially unequal distribution of government financing. People and wealth left the city supported by racialized government policies, and formed separate political entities for reasons that may not have been racist, but were certainly racialized.

The fact that civil rights laws were not violated does not mean practices implemented over the past 50 plus years did not result in *de facto* discrimination and disparate impact.

Race, racialization, racism (particularly spatial), and *de facto* discrimination are the heart and soul of this crisis.

What does this mean for the white people who live in Flint who are victims of this water crisis every much as their black neighbors? Why should the skin color of someone who works or spent time in Flint and consumed the poisoned water matter?

Simply stated, they too are victims of racism by association.

White families who stayed behind while others fled lost the value of their real estate investments the same way the black families moving in did. Their lost retirement nest egg, or lost inheritance is no less harmful to them than it is to the African Americans who had no choice about living elsewhere.

White victims of racist acts and policies based on malice or disregard for blacks are victims of racism.

Whether the victim is black or white, racism isn't fixed by not repeating it; it is like a plague that engulfs everyone in its path.

Source: Michigan Civil Rights Commission, "The Flint Water Crisis: Systemic Racism through the Lens of Flint," Report of the Michigan Civil Rights Commission, February 17, 2017, https://www.michigan.gov/documents/mdcr/VFlintCrisisRep-F-Edited3-13-17_554317_7.pdf.

National Coalition of Blacks for Reparations in America Outlines the Reparations Campaign (2000)

The National Coalition of Blacks for Reparations in America was founded in 1987 with the goal of securing reparations for centuries of racial, economic, and social injustice against Black Americans. N'COBRA champions HR 40, a congressional bill aimed at opening a national discussion on reparations that was introduced by Representative John Conyers (D-MI) in 1989 and reintroduced in Congress every year through his death in 2019. Representative Sheila Jackson Lee (D-TX) reintroduced HR 40 to Congress that same year. The following document lists the reasons Americans of African descent should receive reparations and in what forms.

The Reparations Campaign, for Black people in the United States, emerged more than one hundred years ago as the U.S. Federal Government was trying to survive the ravages of warfare among its citizen [sic]. In the wake of the bitter hostilities from the Civil War a decision was made to release from bondage millions of then enslaved Africans.

As U.S. political, civil and business leaders grappled with the pressing question of "what to do with the Negroes?" the newly freed Africans cried out immediately for restitution—payback for centuries of stolen labor, cultural degradation and dehumanizations. Indeed, Africans held as slaves have been struggling for a restored sense of wholeness since being brought to this country as chattel.

Other organizations and individuals have carried the demand for reparations farther into the twentieth century. Many of them have become a part of today's Reparations Campaign which is being spearheaded by N'COBRA.

WHAT DO WE WANT?

We want our just inheritance: the trillions of dollars due us for the labor of our ancestors who worked for hundreds of years without pay. We demand the resources required removing all badges and indicia of slavery.

WHY DO WE WANT IT?

We must prepare African people and communities for the demands of the new millennium. Reparations are needed to repair the wrongs, injury, and damage done to us by the U.S. federal and State governments, their agents, and representatives. These have proved that their vision for African people in America is joblessness, more prisons (more killer kkkops), more black women and men in private prisons, aids and violence.

The U.S. Eurocentric educational system has failed to prepare African children for liberation, nation-building, and self-determination. This educational system produces people who are anti-black, including many blacks who are self-alienated and anti-black. We want our resources, our inheritance, to do for ourselves without U.S. Federal and State involvement.

WHEN DO WE WANT IT?

We want it NOW! We know that preparatory steps must be taken before we can receive reparations even when the U.S. Government agrees to pay us everything we demand. But NOW is the time to prepare for reparations.

How do we prepare for reparations? In order for reparations to make us whole, it must remove blacks from dependence on others (the government, and the descendants of slave owners and colonizers), to create our jobs, manufacture the goods we consume, feed, clothe, and shelter us, build our institutions, and oversee our money. There are many things we must do to prepare; only a few will be discussed here. We must determine what is required to enable us as a people, as a community, and as individuals to be self-determining. We need to learn the difference between wealth and money, and more about making money than spending it. And, have that we spend [sic], we need to learn how to keep it in our communities. There are too many of our entertainers, recording artists, athletes, lottery winners, etc., who earn millions of dollars and have nothing to show for it after a few years, but a memory of good times past.

We must study how reparations can be used for our liberation for seven generations to come, and not for a one time shopping spree. We must use this time to develop ways to keep the billions of dollars, which we now earn, in the black community.

HOW MUCH IS OWED?

Once we know how much damage has been done to us, and what is required to repair the damage, we will know how much is owed. We cannot allow anyone to offer, or accept on our behalf, some arbitrary figure based on some other peoples' reparations settlement. For example, the four year internment of Japanese in America, or the five year holocaust of Jewish people in Europe may require a different set of remedies than the 500 years holocaust of Africans in America. The nature and extent of the damage and the number of people impacted will dictate the type, duration, and amount of reparations owed. Some estimate eight trillion dollars.

HOW WOULD REPARATIONS BE PAID?

Payment may include all of the following: land, equipment, factories, licenses, banks, ships, airplanes, various forms of tax relief, education and training, to name a few. A good academic exercise would be to develop a plan for how reparations could be used collectively to enable the African community to become independent from racist institutions and economically self-sufficient for at least seven generations.

WHO WOULD PAY REPARATIONS?

The U.S. Government would pay reparations in the same manner as they voted for and paid billions to Europe through the Marshall Plan after WWII, or billions to Israel every year since WWII, or to Russia, or Eastern Europe, or to prop up some puppet African Government. Just as Americans did not, as individuals, pay for aid to those countries, they will not pay for the debt owed to Africans in America. Nor are we blaming individual Americans, we are simply holding the U.S. Government accountable for its wrongs.

WHO WOULD RECEIVE REPARATIONS?

People identified as Negro, Colored, black, African American, New Afrikan, black American who are the descendants of persons enslaved in the United States. Of course, those who feel that they are not due reparations, or do not need reparations will not be forced to accept it. What about Africans enslaved in other countries? Black reparations is an international movement. The descendants of Africans in Canada, Barbados, Haiti, Jamaica, and Brazil, West Indies, Caribbean, etc., are due reparations, but from their particular European colonizer. Colonized African countries too are due reparations. We recognize that although we were colonized and enslaved by different European colonizers and slavers, we are one people with many family members dispersed to different countries.

WHAT CAN WE DO TO HELP?

Make black reparations a household word. Learn to spell, define, and defend it. If we learn how to spell reparations, we will easily say it. Once we learn how to defend it we will raise the issue every time someone talks about affirmative action, welfare reform, jobs, education, housing, health care, prison, building, police brutality, and so on. N'COBRA members have developed books and other informational resources to enable each of us to become able defenders of black reparations. When people talk about building more prisons to deal with the crimes of today, we need to talk about reparations to deal with the effects of 500 years of crimes against the African community that led to the crimes today. We need reparations to keep our people out of prison. When people talk about how criminals must pay for their wrongdoing we must talk about how the U.S. Government must pay reparations for its wrongs.

Second : Support HR 40. This bill has been reintroduced in Congress by Congressman John Conyers of Michigan. It is a first formal step toward reparations in studying the impact of slavery and proposals for remedies. Work with organizations, churches, local governments, and State legislatures to pass a resolution in support of HR 40. Send a copy of each resolution to Mr. Conyers' office and to N'COBRA's National Office.

Third : Join a reparations organization. Have that organization or any organization to which you belong, become a member of N'COBRA. Or, you may join N'COBRA directly.

Fourth: Attend the local, regional, and national meetings on reparations to learn more about what you can do to help. How can I join? Attend an N'COBRA meeting and submit a membership application form, or request an application from the *National office*. Membership is open to organizations and individuals of good moral character who believe that black people in the USA, the descendants of enslaved Africans, are due reparations from the U.S. Government and various State governments.

Source: National Coalition of Blacks for Reparations in America, "The Reparations Campaign," in *Redress for Historical Injustices in the United States: On Reparations for Slavery, Jim Crow, and Their Legacies*, edited by Michael T. Martin and Marilyn Yaquinto (Durham, NC: Duke University Press, 2007), 625–28. Courtesy of N'COBRA.

U.S. Senate Resolution against Lynching (2005)

Senate Resolution 39 was sponsored by Senator Mary Landrieu (D-LA) and adopted in 2005. Lynching became a tool of domestic terrorism and white supremacy after Reconstruction to limit the freedoms and control the mobility of Black people. Despite campaigns by antilynching activists and the introduction of antilynching legislation at a multiple points since the late nineteenth century, these campaigns failed, most often due to the resistance of southern white political leaders. Since S. Res. 39, the House of Representatives and the Senate have gone beyond apology and each passed their own antilynching legislation. In March 2022, President Joe Biden signed the Emmett Till Antilynching Act (HR 55), which makes lynching a federal hate crime for the first time in American history.

109TH CONGRESS
1ST SESSION

S. RES. 39

Apologizing to the victims of lynching and the descendants of those victims
for the failure of the Senate to enact anti-lynching legislation.

IN THE SENATE OF THE UNITED STATES
February 7, 2005

Ms. Landrieu (for herself, Mr. Allen, Mr. Levin, Mr. Frist, Mr. Reid, Mr. Allard, Mr. Akaka, Mr. Brownback, Mr. Bayh, Ms. Collins, Mr. Biden, Mr. Ensign, Mrs. Boxer, Mr. Hagel, Mr. Corzine, Mr. Lugar, Mr. Dayton, Mr. McCain, Mr. Dodd, Ms. Snowe, Mr. Durbin, Mr. Specter, Mr. Feingold, Mr. stevens, Mrs. Feinstein, Mr. talent, mr. harkin, Mr. Jeffords, Mr. Johnson, Mr. Kennedy, Mr. Kohl, Mr. Lautenberg, Mr. leahy, Mr. Lieberman, Mr. nelson of Florida, Mr. Pryor, Mr. Schumer, Mr. stabenow, Mr. Salazar, Mr. Vitter, Mr. Obama, Mrs. Lincoln, Mr. Santorum, Mr. Sarbanes, Mr. Kerry, Mr. Byrd, Mr. coburn, Mr. coleman, Mr. craig, Mr. Mikulski, Mrs. Murray, Ms. Cantwell, Mr. Demint, Mr. Domenici, Mr. dorgan, Mr. Inouye, Mrs. Clinton, Mr. Nelson of Nebraska, Mr. Carper, Mr. Graham, Mr. Burr, Mr. McConnell, Mr. Bunning, Mr. Martinez, Mr. Burns, Mr. Dewine, Mrs. Dole, Mr. Rockefeller, Mr. Thune, Mr. wyden, Mr. Warner, Mr. Baucus, Mr. Roberts, Mr. Chafee, Mr. Sessions, Mr. Bond, Mr. Chambliss, Mr. Isakson, and Mr. Inhofe) submitted the following resolution; which was referred to the Committee on the Judiciary

June 13, 2005

Committee discharged; considered and agreed to

RESOLUTION

Apologizing to the victims of lynching and the descendants of those victims
for the failure of the Senate to enact anti-lynching legislation.

Whereas the crime of lynching succeeded slavery as the ultimate expression of racism in the United States following Reconstruction;

Whereas lynching was a widely acknowledged practice in the United States until the middle of the 20th century;

Whereas lynching was a crime that occurred throughout the United States, with documented incidents in all but 4 States;

Whereas at least 4,742 people, predominantly African-Americans, were reported lynched in the United States between 1882 and 1968;

Whereas 99 percent of all perpetrators of lynching escaped from punishment by State or local officials;

Whereas lynching prompted African-Americans to form the National Association for the Advancement of Colored People (NAACP) and prompted members of B'nai B'rith to found the Anti-Defamation League;

Whereas nearly 200 anti-lynching bills were introduced in Congress during the first half of the 20th century;

Whereas, between 1890 and 1952, 7 Presidents petitioned Congress to end lynching;

Whereas, between 1920 and 1940, the House of Representatives passed 3 strong anti-lynching measures;

Whereas protection against lynching was the minimum and most basic of Federal responsibilities, and the Senate considered but failed to enact anti-lynching legislation despite repeated requests by civil rights groups, Presidents, and the House of Representatives to do so;

Whereas the recent publication of "Without Sanctuary: Lynching Photography in America" helped bring greater awareness and proper recognition of the victims of lynching;

Whereas only by coming to terms with history can the United States effectively champion human rights abroad; and

Whereas an apology offered in the spirit of true repentance moves the United States toward reconciliation and may become central to a new understanding, on which improved racial relations can be forged: Now, therefore, be it

Resolved, That the Senate—

(1) apologizes to the victims of lynching for the failure of the Senate to enact anti-lynching legislation;

(2) expresses the deepest sympathies and most solemn regrets of the Senate to the descendants of victims of lynching, the ancestors of whom were deprived of life, human dignity, and the constitutional protections accorded all citizens of the United States; and

(3) remembers the history of lynching, to ensure that these tragedies will be neither forgotten nor repeated.

Source: Senate Resolution 39 (109th): Lynching Victims Senate Apology Resolution, Agreed upon June 13, 2005, https://www.govtrack.us/congress/bills/109/sres39/text.

Barack Obama, "A More Perfect Union" (2008)

In 2008, Barack Obama was elected the first African American president of the United States. He was reelected for a second term in 2012. During his two terms, Obama articulated and legitimated the experiences of African Americans, although several critics pressed him to do more. In the following speech, delivered on the campaign trail at the National Constitution Center in Philadelphia in March 2008, Obama explicitly engaged the role of race in his campaign as well as the ways in which racial tensions, white privilege and resentment, and racial inequality shaped American politics and society.

"We the people, in order to form a more perfect union."

Two hundred and twenty one years ago, in a hall that still stands across the street, a group of men gathered and, with these simple words, launched America's improbable experiment in democracy. Farmers and scholars; statesmen and patriots who had traveled across an ocean to escape tyranny and persecution finally made real their declaration of independence at a Philadelphia convention that lasted through the spring of 1787.

The document they produced was eventually signed but ultimately unfinished. It was stained by this nation's original sin of slavery, a question that divided the colonies and brought the convention to a stalemate until the founders chose to allow the slave trade to continue for at least twenty more years, and to leave any final resolution to future generations.

Of course, the answer to the slavery question was already embedded within our Constitution—a Constitution that had at is very core the ideal of equal citizenship under the law; a Constitution that promised its people liberty, and justice, and a union that could be and should be perfected over time.

And yet words on a parchment would not be enough to deliver slaves from bondage, or provide men and women of every color and creed their full rights and obligations as citizens of the United States. What would be needed were Americans in successive generations who were willing to do their part—through protests and struggle, on the streets and in the courts, through a civil war and civil disobedience and always at great risk—to narrow that gap between the promise of our ideals and the reality of their time.

This was one of the tasks we set forth at the beginning of this campaign—to continue the long march of those who came before us, a march for a more just, more equal, more free, more caring and more prosperous America. I chose to run for the presidency at this moment in history because I believe deeply that we cannot solve the challenges of our time unless we solve them together—unless we perfect our union by understanding that we may have different stories, but we hold common hopes; that we may not look the same and we may not have come from the same place, but we all want to move in the same direction—towards a better future for of children and our grandchildren.

This belief comes from my unyielding faith in the decency and generosity of the American people. But it also comes from my own story.

I am the son of a black man from Kenya and a white woman from Kansas. I was raised with the help of a white grandfather who survived a Depression to serve in Patton's Army during World War II and a white grandmother who worked on a bomber assembly line at Fort Leavenworth while he was overseas. I've gone to some of the best schools in America and lived in one of the world's poorest nations. I am married to a black American who carries within her the blood of slaves and slave-owners—an inheritance we pass on to our two precious daughters. I have brothers, sisters, nieces, nephews, uncles and cousins, of every race and every hue, scattered across three continents, and for as long as I live, I will never forget that in no other country on Earth is my story even possible.

It's a story that hasn't made me the most conventional candidate. But it is a story that has seared into my genetic makeup the idea that this nation is more than the sum of its parts—that out of many, we are truly one.

Throughout the first year of this campaign, against all predictions to the contrary, we saw how hungry the American people were for this message of unity. Despite the temptation to view my candidacy through a purely racial lens, we won commanding victories in states with some of the whitest populations in the country. In South Carolina, where the Confederate Flag still flies, we built a powerful coalition of African Americans and white Americans.

This is not to say that race has not been an issue in the campaign. At various stages in the campaign, some commentators have deemed me either "too black" or "not black enough." We saw racial tensions bubble to the surface during the week before the South Carolina primary. The press has scoured every exit poll for the latest evidence of racial polarization, not just in terms of white and black, but black and brown as well.

And yet, it has only been in the last couple of weeks that the discussion of race in this campaign has taken a particularly divisive turn.

On one end of the spectrum, we've heard the implication that my candidacy is somehow an exercise in affirmative action; that it's based solely on the desire of wide-eyed liberals to purchase racial reconciliation on the cheap. On the other end, we've heard my former pastor, Reverend Jeremiah Wright, use incendiary language to express views that have the potential not only to widen the racial divide, but views that denigrate both the greatness and the goodness of our nation; that rightly offend white and black alike.

I have already condemned, in unequivocal terms, the statements of Reverend Wright that have caused such controversy. For some, nagging questions remain. Did I know him to be an occasionally fierce critic of American domestic and foreign policy? Of course. Did I ever hear him make remarks that could be considered controversial while I sat in church? Yes. Did I strongly disagree with many of his political views? Absolutely—just as I'm sure many of you have heard remarks from your pastors, priests, or rabbis with which you strongly disagreed.

But the remarks that have caused this recent firestorm weren't simply controversial. They weren't simply a religious leader's effort to speak out against perceived injustice. Instead, they expressed a profoundly distorted view of this country—a view that sees white racism as endemic, and that elevates what is wrong with America above all that we know is right with America; a view that sees the conflicts in the Middle East as rooted primarily in the actions of stalwart allies like Israel, instead of emanating from the perverse and hateful ideologies of radical Islam.

As such, Reverend Wright's comments were not only wrong but divisive, divisive at a time when we need unity; racially charged at a time when we need to come together to solve a set of monumental problems—two wars, a terrorist threat, a falling economy, a chronic health care crisis and potentially devastating climate change; problems that are neither black or white or Latino or Asian, but rather problems that confront us all.

Given my background, my politics, and my professed values and ideals, there will no doubt be those for whom my statements of condemnation are not enough. Why associate myself with Reverend Wright in the first place, they may ask? Why not join another church? And I confess that if all that I knew of Reverend Wright were the snippets of those sermons that have run in an endless loop on the television and You Tube, or if Trinity United Church of Christ conformed to the caricatures being peddled by some commentators, there is no doubt that I would react in much the same way.

But the truth is, that isn't all that I know of the man. The man I met more than twenty years ago is a man who helped introduce me to my Christian faith, a man who spoke to me about our obligations to love one another; to care for the sick and lift up the poor. He is a man who served his country as a U.S. Marine; who has studied and lectured at some of the finest universities and seminaries in the country, and who for over thirty years led a church that serves the community by doing God's work here on Earth—by housing the homeless, ministering to the needy, providing day care services and scholarships and prison ministries, and reaching out to those suffering from HIV/AIDS.

In my first book, *Dreams From My Father,* I described the experience of my first service at Trinity:

"People began to shout, to rise from their seats and clap and cry out, a forceful wind carrying the reverend's voice up into the rafters.... And in that single note—hope!—I heard something else; at the foot of that cross, inside the thousands of churches across the city, I imagined the stories of ordinary black people merging with the stories of David and Goliath, Moses and Pharaoh, the Christians in the lion's den, Ezekiel's field of dry bones. Those stories—of survival, and freedom, and hope—became our story, my story; the blood that had spilled was our blood, the tears our tears; until this black church, on this bright day, seemed once more a vessel carrying the story of a people into future generations and into a larger world. Our trials and triumphs became at once unique and universal, black and more than black; in chronicling our journey, the stories and songs gave us a means to reclaim memories that we didn't need to feel shame about . . . memories that all people might study and cherish—and with which we could start to rebuild."

That has been my experience at Trinity. Like other predominantly black churches across the country, Trinity embodies the black community in its entirety—the doctor and the welfare mom, the model student and the former gang-banger. Like other black churches, Trinity's services are full of raucous laughter and sometimes bawdy humor. They are full of dancing, clapping, screaming and shouting that may seem jarring to the untrained ear. The church contains in full the kindness and cruelty, the fierce intelligence and the shocking ignorance, the struggles and successes, the love and yes, the bitterness and bias that make up the black experience in America.

And this helps explain, perhaps, my relationship with Reverend Wright. As imperfect as he may be, he has been like family to me. He strengthened my faith, officiated my wedding, and baptized my children. Not once in my conversations with him have I heard him talk about any ethnic group in derogatory terms, or treat whites with whom he interacted with anything but courtesy and respect. He contains within him the contradictions—the good and the bad—of the community that he has served diligently for so many years.

I can no more disown him than I can disown the black community. I can no more disown him than I can my white grandmother—a woman who helped raise me, a woman who sacrificed again and again for me, a woman who loves me as much as she loves anything in this world, but a woman who once confessed her fear of black men who passed by her on the street, and who on more than one occasion has uttered racial or ethnic stereotypes that made me cringe.

These people are a part of me. And they are a part of America, this country that I love.

Some will see this as an attempt to justify or excuse comments that are simply inexcusable. I can assure you it is not. I suppose the politically safe thing would be to move on from this episode and just hope that it fades into the woodwork. We can dismiss Reverend Wright as a crank or a demagogue, just as some have dismissed Geraldine Ferraro, in the aftermath of her recent statements, as harboring some deep-seated racial bias.

But race is an issue that I believe this nation cannot afford to ignore right now. We would be making the same mistake that Reverend Wright made in his offending sermons about America—to simplify and stereotype and amplify the negative to the point that it distorts reality.

The fact is that the comments that have been made and the issues that have surfaced over the last few weeks reflect the complexities of race in this country that we've never really worked through—a part of our union that we have yet to perfect. And if we walk away now, if we simply retreat into our respective corners, we will never be able to come together and solve challenges like health care, or education, or the need to find good jobs for every American.

We do not need to recite here the history of racial injustice in this country. But we do need to remind ourselves that so many of the disparities that exist in the African-American community today can be directly traced to inequalities passed on from an earlier generation that suffered under the brutal legacy of slavery and Jim Crow.

Segregated schools were, and are, inferior schools; we still haven't fixed them, fifty years after Brown v. Board of Education, and the inferior education they provided, then and now, helps explain the pervasive achievement gap between today's black and white students.

Legalized discrimination—where blacks were prevented, often through violence, from owning property, or loans were not granted to African-American business owners, or black homeowners could not access FHA mortgages, or blacks were excluded from unions, or the police force, or fire departments—meant that black families could not amass any meaningful wealth to bequeath to future generations. That history helps explain the wealth and income gap between black and white, and the concentrated pockets of poverty that persists in so many of today's urban and rural communities.

A lack of economic opportunity among black men, and the shame and frustration that came from not being able to provide for one's family, contributed to the erosion of black families—a problem that welfare policies for many years may have worsened. And the lack of basic services in so many urban black neighborhoods—parks for kids to play in, police walking the beat, regular garbage pick-up and building code enforcement—all helped create a cycle of violence, blight and neglect that continue to haunt us.

This is the reality in which Reverend Wright and other African-Americans of his generation grew up. They came of age in the late fifties and early sixties, a time when segregation was still the law of the land and opportunity was systematically constricted. What's remarkable is not how many failed in the face of discrimination, but rather how many men and women overcame the odds; how many were able to make a way out of no way for those like me who would come after them.

But for all those who scratched and clawed their way to get a piece of the American Dream, there were many who didn't make it—those who were ultimately defeated, in one way or another, by discrimination. That legacy of defeat was passed on to future generations—those young men and increasingly young women who we see standing on street corners or languishing in our prisons, without hope or prospects for the future. Even for those blacks who did make it, questions of race, and racism, continue to define their worldview in fundamental ways. For the men and women of Reverend Wright's generation, the memories of humiliation and doubt and fear have not gone away; nor has the anger and the bitterness of those years. That anger may not get expressed in public, in front of white co-workers or white friends. But it does find voice in the barbershop or around the kitchen table. At times, that anger is exploited by politicians, to gin up votes along racial lines, or to make up for a politician's own failings.

And occasionally it finds voice in the church on Sunday morning, in the pulpit and in the pews. The fact that so many people are surprised to hear that anger in some of Reverend Wright's sermons simply reminds us of the old truism that the most segregated hour in American life occurs on Sunday morning. That anger is not always productive; indeed, all too often it distracts attention from solving real problems; it keeps us from squarely facing our own complicity in our condition, and prevents the African-American community from forging the alliances it needs to bring about real change. But the anger is real; it is powerful; and to simply wish it away, to condemn it without understanding its roots, only serves to widen the chasm of misunderstanding that exists between the races.

In fact, a similar anger exists within segments of the white community. Most working- and middle-class white Americans don't feel that they have been particularly privileged by their race. Their experience is the immigrant experience—as far as they're concerned, no one's handed them anything, they've built it from scratch. They've worked hard all their lives, many times only to see their jobs shipped overseas or their pension dumped after a lifetime of labor. They are anxious about their futures, and feel their dreams slipping away; in an era of stagnant wages and global competition, opportunity comes to be seen as a zero sum game, in which your dreams come at my expense. So when they are told to bus their children to a school across town; when they hear that an African American is getting an advantage in landing a good job or a spot in a good college because of an injustice that they themselves never committed; when they're told that their fears about crime in urban neighborhoods are somehow prejudiced, resentment builds over time.

Like the anger within the black community, these resentments aren't always expressed in polite company. But they have helped shape the political landscape for at least a generation. Anger over welfare and affirmative action helped forge the Reagan Coalition. Politicians routinely exploited fears of crime for their own electoral ends. Talk show hosts and conservative commentators built entire careers unmasking bogus claims of racism while dismissing legitimate discussions of racial injustice and inequality as mere political correctness or reverse racism.

Just as black anger often proved counterproductive, so have these white resentments distracted attention from the real culprits of the middle class squeeze—a corporate culture rife with inside dealing, questionable accounting practices, and short-term greed; a Washington dominated by lobbyists and special interests; economic policies that favor the few over the many. And yet, to wish away the resentments of white Americans, to label them as misguided or even racist, without recognizing they are grounded in legitimate concerns—this too widens the racial divide, and blocks the path to understanding.

This is where we are right now. It's a racial stalemate we've been stuck in for years. Contrary to the claims of some of my critics, black and white, I have never been so naïve as to believe that we can get beyond our racial divisions in a single election cycle, or with a single candidacy—particularly a candidacy as imperfect as my own.

But I have asserted a firm conviction—a conviction rooted in my faith in God and my faith in the American people—that working together we can move beyond some of our old racial wounds, and that in fact we have no choice if we are to continue on the path of a more perfect union.

For the African-American community, that path means embracing the burdens of our past without becoming victims of our past. It means continuing to insist on a full measure of justice in every aspect of American life. But it also means binding our particular grievances—for better health care, and better schools, and better jobs—to the larger aspirations of all Americans—the white woman struggling to break the glass ceiling, the white man whose been laid off, the immigrant trying to feed his family. And it means taking full responsibility for own lives—by demanding more from our fathers, and spending more time with our children, and reading to them, and teaching them that while they may face challenges and discrimination in their own lives, they must never succumb to despair or cynicism; they must always believe that they can write their own destiny.

Ironically, this quintessentially American—and yes, conservative—notion of self-help found frequent expression in Reverend Wright's sermons. But what my former pastor too often failed to understand is that embarking on a program of self-help also requires a belief that society can change.

The profound mistake of Reverend Wright's sermons is not that he spoke about racism in our society. It's that he spoke as if our society was static; as if no progress has been made; as if this country—a country that has made it possible for one of his own members to run for the highest office in the land and build a coalition of white and black; Latino and Asian, rich and poor, young and old—is still irrevocably bound to a tragic past. But what we know—what we have seen—is that America can change. That is true genius of this nation. What we have already achieved gives us hope—the audacity to hope—for what we can and must achieve tomorrow.

In the white community, the path to a more perfect union means acknowledging that what ails the African-American community does not just exist in the minds of black people; that the legacy of discrimination—and current incidents of discrimination, while less overt than in the past—are real and must be addressed. Not just with words, but with deeds—by investing in our schools and our communities; by enforcing our civil rights laws and ensuring fairness in our criminal justice system; by providing this generation with ladders of opportunity that were unavailable for previous generations. It requires all Americans to realize that your dreams do not have to come at the expense of my dreams; that investing in the health, welfare, and education of black and brown and white children will ultimately help all of America prosper.

In the end, then, what is called for is nothing more, and nothing less, than what all the world's great religions demand—that we do unto others as we would have them do unto us. Let us be our brother's keeper, Scripture tells us. Let us be our sister's keeper. Let us find that common stake we all have in one another, and let our politics reflect that spirit as well.

. . . This union may never be perfect, but generation after generation has shown that it can always be perfected. And today, whenever I find myself feeling doubtful or cynical about this possibility, what gives me the most hope is the next generation—the young people whose attitudes and beliefs and openness to change have already made history in this election. . . .

Source: Barack Obama, "A More Perfect Union" (speech, Philadelphia, March 18, 2008), National Constitution Center, https://constitutioncenter.org /amoreperfectunion/docs/Race_Speech_Transcript.pdf.

Trayvon Martin Photograph (ca. 2010)

On February 26, 2012, seventeen-year-old Martin was shot and killed by George Zimmerman in Miami Gardens, Florida. Martin was walking through the neighborhood after visiting a nearby store. Zimmerman, who was suspicious of Martin, called local police and was told not to approach Martin. Zimmerman refused to follow orders and confronted Martin, eventually killing the Black teenager. Zimmerman was arrested for second-degree murder, but acquitted in 2013 after claiming self-defense. The murder of Trayvon Martin sparked a national debate about racial profiling and Florida's controversial Stand Your Ground laws. It also led to the formation of several antiracist groups like Dream Defenders, Million Hoodies Movement for Justice, and Black Lives Matter.

Source: Trayvon Martin, photograph, ca. 2010, CNN, https://www.cnn.com/2013/06/05/us /trayvon-martin-shooting-fast-facts/index.html.

Alicia Garza, "A Herstory of the Black Lives Matter Movement" (2014)

Arguably the most prominent social justice movement in the United States in the twenty-first century, Black Lives Matter was originally founded as a Twitter hashtag but quickly became a movement, galvanizing millions against systemic racism, police brutality, racially motivated murders of Black people, and mass incarceration. Three Black queer women, Alicia Garza, Patrisse Cullors, and Opal Tometi founded Black Lives Matter. In the following essay, Alicia Garza discusses how the movement came to be, the importance of Black people becoming free, and the ways in which "All Lives Matters" problematically erases the movement and efforts to call out system racism and anti-Blackness.

I created #BlackLivesMatter with Patrisse Cullors and Opal Tometi, two of my sisters, as a call to action for Black people after 17-year-old Trayvon Martin was posthumously placed on trial for his own murder and the killer, George Zimmerman, was not held accountable for the crime he committed. It was a response to the anti-Black racism that permeates our society and also, unfortunately, our movements.

Black Lives Matter is an ideological and political intervention in a world where Black lives are systematically and intentionally targeted for demise. It is an affirmation of Black folks' contributions to this society, our humanity, and our resilience in the face of deadly oppression.

We were humbled when cultural workers, artists, designers and techies offered their labor and love to expand #BlackLivesMatter beyond a social media hashtag. Opal, Patrisse, and I created the infrastructure for this movement project—moving the hashtag from social media to the streets. Our team grew through a very successful Black Lives Matter ride, led and designed by Patrisse Cullors and Darnell L. Moore, organized to support the movement that is growing in St. Louis, MO, after 18-year old Mike Brown was killed at the hands of Ferguson Police Officer Darren Wilson. We've hosted national conference calls focused on issues of critical importance to Black people working hard for the liberation of our people. We've connected people across the country working to end the various forms of injustice impacting our people. We've created space for the celebration and humanization of Black lives.

THE THEFT OF BLACK QUEER WOMEN'S WORK

As people took the #BlackLivesMatter demand into the streets, mainstream media and corporations also took up the call, #BlackLivesMatter appeared in an episode of *Law & Order: SVU* in a mash up containing the Paula Deen racism scandal and the tragedy of the murder of Trayvon Martin.

Suddenly, we began to come across varied adaptations of our work—all lives matter, brown lives matter, migrant lives matter, women's lives matter, and on and on. While imitation is said to be the highest form of flattery, I was surprised when an organization called to ask if they could use "Black Lives Matter" in one of their campaigns. We agreed to it, with the caveat that a) as a team, we preferred that we not use the meme to celebrate the imprisonment of any individual and b) that it was important to us they acknowledged the genesis of #BlackLivesMatter. I was surprised when they did exactly the opposite and then justified their actions by saying they hadn't used the "exact" slogan and, therefore, they deemed it okay to take our work, use it as their own, fail to credit where it came from, and then use it to applaud incarceration.

I was surprised when a community institution wrote asking us to provide materials and action steps for an art show they were curating, entitled "Our Lives Matter." When questioned about who was involved and why they felt the need to change the very specific call and demand around Black lives to "our lives," I was told the artists decided it needed to be more inclusive of all people of color. I was even more surprised when, in the promotion of their event, one of the artists conducted an interview that completely erased the origins of their work—rooted in the labor and love of queer Black women.

Pause.

When you design an event / campaign / et cetera based on the work of queer Black women, don't invite them to participate in shaping it, but ask them to provide materials and ideas for next steps for said event, that is racism in practice. It's also heteropatriarchal. Straight men, unintentionally or intentionally, have taken the work of queer Black women and erased our contributions. Perhaps if we were the charismatic Black men many are rallying around these days, it would have been a different story, but being Black queer women in this society (and apparently within these movements) tends to equal invisibility and non-relevancy.

We completely expect those who benefit directly and improperly from White supremacy to try and erase our existence. We fight that every day. But when it happens amongst our allies, we are baffled, we are saddened, and we are enraged. And it's time to have the political conversation about why that's not okay.

We are grateful to our allies who have stepped up to the call that Black lives matter, and taken it as an opportunity to not just stand in solidarity with us, but to investigate the ways in which anti-Black racism is perpetuated in their own communities. We are also grateful to those allies who were willing to engage in critical dialogue with us about this unfortunate and problematic dynamic. And for those who we have not yet had the opportunity to engage with around the adaptations of the Black Lives Matter call, please consider the following points.

BROADENING THE CONVERSATION TO INCLUDE BLACK LIFE

Black Lives Matter is a unique contribution that goes beyond extrajudicial killings of Black people by police and vigilantes. It goes beyond the narrow nationalism that can be prevalent within some Black communities, which merely call on Black people to love Black, live Black and buy Black, keeping straight cis Black men in the front of the movement while our sisters, queer and trans and disabled folk take up roles in the background or not at all. Black Lives Matter affirms the lives of Black queer and trans folks, disabled folks, Black-undocumented folks, folks with records, women and all Black lives along the gender spectrum. It centers those that have been marginalized within Black liberation movements. It is a tactic to (re)build the Black liberation movement.

When we say Black Lives Matter, we are talking about the ways in which Black people are deprived of our basic human rights and dignity. It is an acknowledgement

Black poverty and genocide is state violence. It is an acknowledgment that 1 million Black people are locked in cages in this country—one half of all people in prisons or jails—is an act of state violence. It is an acknowledgment that Black women continue to bear the burden of a relentless assault on our children and our families and that assault is an act of state violence. Black queer and trans folks bearing a unique burden in a hetero-patriarchal society that disposes of us like garbage and simultaneously fetishizes us and profits off of us is state violence; the fact that 500,000 Black people in the US are undocumented immigrants and relegated to the shadows is state violence;.the fact that Black girls are used as negotiating chips during times of conflict and war is state violence; Black folks living with disabilities and different abilities bear the burden of state-sponsored Darwinian experiments that attempt to squeeze us into boxes of normality defined by White supremacy is state violence. And the fact is that the lives of Black people—not ALL people—exist within these conditions is consequence of state violence.

When Black people get free, everybody gets free

#BlackLivesMatter doesn't mean your life isn't important—it means that Black lives, which are seen as without value within White supremacy, are important to your liberation. Given the disproportionate impact state violence has on Black lives, we understand that when Black people in this country get free, the benefits will be wide reaching and transformative for society as a whole. When we are able to end hyper-criminalization and sexualization of Black people and end the poverty, control, and surveillance of Black people, every single person in this world has a better shot at getting and staying free. When Black people get free, everybody gets free. This is why we call on Black people and our allies to take up the call that Black lives matter. We're not saying Black lives are more important than other lives, or that other lives are not criminalized and oppressed in various ways. We remain in active solidarity with all oppressed people who are fighting for their liberation and we know that our destinies are intertwined.

And, to keep it real—it is appropriate and necessary to have strategy and action centered around Blackness without other non-Black communities of color, or White folks for that matter, needing to find a place and a way to center themselves within it. It is appropriate and necessary for us to acknowledge the critical role that Black lives and struggles for Black liberation have played in inspiring and anchoring, through practice and theory, social movements for the liberation of all people. The women's movement, the Chicano liberation movement, queer movements, and many more have adopted the strategies, tactics and theory of the Black liberation movement. And if we are committed to a world where all lives matter, we are called to support the very movement that inspired and activated so many more. That means supporting and acknowledging Black lives.

Progressive movements in the United States have made some unfortunate errors when they push for unity at the expense of really understanding the concrete differences in context, experience and oppression. In other words, some want unity without struggle. As people who have our minds stayed on freedom, we can learn to fight anti-Black racism by examining the ways in which we participate in it, even unintentionally, instead of the worn out and sloppy practice of drawing lazy parallels of unity between peoples with vastly different experiences and histories.

When we deploy "All Lives Matter" as to correct an intervention specifically created to address anti-blackness, we lose the ways in which the state apparatus has built a program of genocide and repression mostly on the backs of Black people—beginning with the theft of millions of people for free labor—and then adapted it to control, murder, and profit off of other communities of color and immigrant communities. We perpetuate a level of White supremacist domination by reproducing a tired trope that we are all the same, rather than acknowledging that non-Black oppressed people in this country are both impacted by racism and domination, and simultaneously, BENEFIT from anti-black racism.

When you drop "Black" from the equation of whose lives matter, and then fail to acknowledge it came from somewhere, you further a legacy of erasing Black lives and Black contributions from our movement legacy. And consider whether or not when dropping the Black you are, intentionally or unintentionally, erasing Black folks from the conversation or homogenizing very different experiences. The legacy and prevalence of anti-Black racism and hetero-patriarchy is a lynch pin holding together this unsustainable economy. And that's not an accidental analogy.

In 2014, hetero-patriarchy and anti-Black racism within our movement is real and felt. It's killing us and it's killing our potential to build power for transformative social change. When you adopt the work of queer women of color, don't name or recognize it, and promote it as if it has no history of its own such actions are problematic. When I use Assata's powerful demand in my organizing work, I always begin by sharing where it comes from, sharing about Assata's significance to the Black Liberation Movement, what it's political purpose and message is, and why it's important in our context.

When you adopt Black Lives Matter and transform it into something else (if you feel you really need to do that—see above for the arguments not to), it's appropriate politically to credit the lineage from which your adapted work derived. It's important that we work together to build and acknowledge the legacy of Black contributions to the struggle for human rights. If you adapt Black Lives Matter, use the opportunity to talk about its inception and political framing. Lift up Black lives as an opportunity to connect struggles across race, class, gender, nationality, sexuality and disability.

And, perhaps more importantly, when Black people cry out in defense of our lives, which are uniquely, systematically, and savagely targeted by the state, we are asking you, our family, to stand with us in affirming Black lives. Not just all lives. Black lives. Please do not change the conversation by talking about how your life matters, too. It does, but we need less watered down unity and a more active solidarities with us, Black people, unwaveringly, in defense of our humanity. Our collective futures depend on it.

Source: Alicia Garza, "A Herstory of the Black Lives Matter Movement," *Feminist Wire*, October 7, 2014, http://www.thefeministwire.com/2014/10/blacklivesmatter-2/.

Bree Newsome Removes Confederate Flag from South Carolina Legislature (2015)

In the wake of Travyon Martin's death and the killings of unarmed Black men and women by police and white supremacists, the symbols of white supremacy also came under attack. In the following photograph, activist Brittany Newsome scales a flagpole on the grounds of the South Carolina statehouse in 2015 to remove the Confederate flag, stating: "In the name of Jesus, this flag has to come down. You come against me with hatred and oppression and violence. I come against you in the name of God. This flag comes down today." Newsome's nonviolent direct action came just over a week after the murders of nine African Americans attending a church service in Charleston, South Carolina, by a white supremacist.

Source: Adam Anderson, Brittany "Bree" Newsome removes the Confederate flag from the statehouse in Columbia, photograph, 2015. Adam Anderson / Reuters Pictures.

Interview with Tarana Burke on the MeToo Movement (2018)

The MeToo campaign emerged in 2006 but gained notoriety in 2017. As a survivor of sexual abuse, movement founder Tarana Burke used "me too" as a way to connect with young women of color with similar experiences and find collective and individual spaces of healing. In the piece below, Burke reflects on how and why #MeToo became a movement.

. . . What the world recognizes as the #MeToo movement was built on the labor of everyday people who survived sexual violence in a number of forms. Some were harassed, some survived child sexual abuse or other kinds of sexual assault, but all of them endeavored to stand in their truth. All at once starting last October, millions of people raised their hands and voices to be counted among the number of people who had experienced sexual harassment, assault and abuse. More than 12 million in 24 hours on Facebook. Half a million in 12 hours on Twitter. And the numbers kept growing. . . .

. . . Everyday people—queer, trans, disabled, men and women—are living in the aftermath of a trauma that tried, at the very worst, to take away their humanity. This movement at its core is about the restoration of that humanity.

This is one reason that the weaponization of #MeToo has been so shocking. Several men and some women, many of whom are rich and powerful, have mischaracterized this movement out of their own fears and inability to hold a nuanced perspective. . . .

It has been a year of great liberation and empowerment. Every day I meet people who have moved from victim to survivor by simply adding their own "Me too" to the chorus of voices. They have freed themselves from the burden that holding on to these traumas often creates and stepped into the power of release, the power of empathy and the power of truth. They have looked their demons in the face and lived to see another day, and they have become the empirical proof that we can win the fight to end sexual violence.

. . . This is a survivors' movement created for and by those of us who have endured sexual violence. The goal is to provide a mechanism to support survivors and move people to action. . . .

For our part we are building out our work both online with the October launch of our new comprehensive website and on the ground through programming and partnerships. We have also partnered with the New York Women's Foundation to create a #MeToo movement fund that will raise $25 million to put toward working to end sexual violence over the next five years. Our goal is to keep expanding the work and building the movement.

For too long women and others living on the margins have managed to survive without our full dignity intact. It can't continue to be our reality. The work of #MeToo builds on the existing efforts to dismantle systems of oppression that allow sexual violence, patriarchy, racism and sexism to persist. We know that this approach will make our society better for everyone, not just survivors, because creating pathways to healing and restoration moves us all closer to a world where everyone knows the peace of living without fear and the joy of living in your full dignity. I intend to keep doing this work, from within this amazing movement, until we get there.

DOCUMENT 13.16

Ibram X. Kendi, "The American Nightmare" (2020)

From *Stamped from the Beginning: The Definitive History of Racist Ideas in America* (2017) to *How to Be an Antiracist* (2019), Ibram X. Kendi's scholarship sheds light on the significance of race and racism in American history. In "The American Nightmare," Kendi positions the police murder of George Floyd, protests for racial justice, and the inequities in health care made stark by the COVID-19 pandemic not as anomalies, but on par with Black Americans' experiences of system racism in America. He implores Americans to choose the path of antiracism over racism.

It happened three months before the lynching of Isadora Moreley in Selma, Alabama, and two months before the lynching of Sidney Randolph near Rockville, Maryland.

On May 19, 1896, *The New York Times* allocated a single sentence on page three to reporting the U.S. Supreme Court's *Plessy v. Ferguson* decision. Constitutionalizing Jim Crow hardly made news in 1896. There was no there there. Americans already knew that equal rights had been lynched; *Plessy* was just the silently staged funeral.

Another racial text—published by the nation's premier social-science organization, the American Economic Association, and classified by the historian Evelynn Hammonds as "one of the most influential documents in social science at the turn of the 20th century"—elicited more shock in 1896.

"Nothing is more clearly shown from this investigation than that the southern black man at the time of emancipation was healthy in body and cheerful in mind," Frederick Hoffman wrote in *Race Traits and Tendencies of the American Negro*. "What are the conditions thirty years after?" Hoffman concluded from "the plain language of the facts" that black Americans were better off enslaved. They are now "on the downward grade," he wrote, headed toward "gradual extinction."

Hoffman's *Race Traits* helped legitimize two nascent fields that are now converging on black lives: public health and criminology.

Hoffman knew his work was "a most severe condemnation of moderate attempts of superior races to lift inferior races to their elevated positions." He rejected that sort of assimilationist racism, in favor of his own segregationist racism. The data "speak for themselves," he wrote. White Americans had been naturally selected for health, life, and evolution. Black Americans had been naturally selected for disease, death, and extinction. "Gradual extinction," the book concluded, "is only a question of time."

Let them die, Hoffman seemed to be saying. That thought has echoed through time, down to our deadly moment in time, when police officers in Minneapolis let George Floyd die.

With its pages and pages of statistical charts, *Race Traits* helped catapult Hoffman into national and international prominence as the "dean" of American statisticians. In his day, Hoffman "achieved greatness," assessed his biographer. "His career illustrates the fulfillment of the 'American dream.'"

Actually, his career illustrates the fulfillment of the American nightmare—a nightmare still being experienced 124 years later from Minneapolis to Louisville, from Central Park to untold numbers of black coronavirus patients parked in hospitals, on unemployment lines, and in graves.

"We don't see any American dream," Malcolm X said in 1964. "We've experienced only the American nightmare."

A nightmare is essentially a horror story of danger, but it is not wholly a horror story. Black people experience joy, love, peace, safety. But as in any horror story, those unforgettable moments of toil, terror, and trauma have made danger essential to the black experience in racist America. What one black American experiences, many black Americans experience. Black Americans are constantly stepping into the toil and terror and trauma of other black Americans. Black Americans are constantly stepping into the souls of the dead. Because they know: They could have been them; they are them. Because they know it is dangerous to be black in America, because racist Americans see blacks as dangerous.

To be black and conscious of anti-black racism is to stare into the mirror of your own extinction. Ask the souls of the 10,000 black victims of COVID-19 who might still be living if they had been white. Ask the souls of those who were told the pandemic was the "great equalizer." Ask the souls of those forced to choose between their low-wage jobs and their treasured life. Ask the souls of those blamed for their own death. Ask the souls of those who disproportionately lost their jobs and then their life as others disproportionately raged about losing their freedom to infect us all. Ask the souls of those ignored by the governors reopening their states.

The American nightmare has everything and nothing to do with the pandemic. Ask the souls of Breonna Taylor, Ahmaud Arbery, and George Floyd. *Step into their souls.*

No-knocking police officers rushed into your Louisville home and shot you to death, but your black boyfriend immediately got charged, and not the officers who killed you. Three white men hunted you, cornered you, and killed you on a Georgia road, but it took a cellphone video and national outrage for them to finally be charged. In Minneapolis, you did not hurt anyone, but when the police arrived, you found yourself pinned to the pavement, knee on your neck, crying out, "I can't breathe."

History ignored you. Hoffman ignored you. Racist America ignored you. The state did not want you to breathe. But your loved ones did not ignore you. They did not ignore your nightmare. They share the same nightmare.

Enraged, they took to the streets and nonviolently rallied. Some violently rebelled, burning and snatching property that the state protected instead of your life. And then they heard over America's loudspeaker, "When the looting starts, the shooting starts."

Your loved ones are protesting your murder, and the president calls for their murder, calls them "THUGS," calls them "OUT OF STATE" agitators. Others call the violence against property senseless—but not the police violence against you that drove them to violence. Others call both senseless, but take no immediate steps to stem police violence against you, only to stem the violence against property and police.

Mayors issue curfews. Governors rattle their sabers. The National Guard arrives to protect property and police. Where was the National Guard when you faced violent police officers, violent white terrorists, the violence of racial health disparities, the violence of COVID-19—all the racist power and policy and ideas that kept the black experience in the American nightmare for 400 years?

Too many Americans have been waiting for black extinction since Hoffman. *Let them die.*

The National Guard lines up alongside state and local police. But they—your loved ones mourning you and mourning justice—are not going home, since you are not at home. They don't back down, because they will never forget what happened to them, what happened to you!

You! You! You! The murdered black life that matters.

You are them. They are you. You are all the same person—all the murdered, all the living, all the infected, all the resisting—because racist America treats the whole black community and all of its anti-racist allies as dangerous, just as Hoffman did. What a nightmare. But perhaps the worst of the nightmare is knowing that racist Americans will never end it. Anti-racism is on you, and only you. Racist Americans deny your nightmare, deny their racism, claim you have a dream like a King, when even his dream in 1967 "turned into a nightmare."

In 1896, Frederick Hoffman deployed data to substantiate racist ideas that are still building caskets for black bodies today. Black people are supposed to be feared by all, murdered by police officers, lynched by citizens, and killed by COVID-19 and other lethal diseases. It has been proved. No there there. Black life is the "hopeless problem," as Hoffman wrote.

Black life is danger. Black life is death.

Hoffman's *Race Traits* was "arguably the most influential race and crime study of the first half of the twentieth century," wrote the historian Khalil Gibran Muhammad in *The Condemnation of Blackness*. It was also arguably the most influential race and public-health study of the period.

In the first nationwide compilation of racial crime data, Hoffman used the higher arrest and incarceration rates of black Americans to argue that they are, by their very nature and behavior, a dangerous and violent people—as racist Americans still say today. Hoffman compiled racial health disparities to argue that black Americans are, by their very nature and behavior, a diseased and dying people. Hoffman cataloged higher black mortality rates and showed that black Americans were more likely to suffer from syphilis, tuberculosis, and other infectious diseases than white Americans. The same disparities are visible today, as black Americans die of COVID-19 at a rate nearly two times their share of the national population, according to the COVID Racial Data Tracker.

Now step back into their souls.

You are sick and tired of the nightmare. And you are "sick and tired of being sick and tired," as Fannie Lou Hamer once said. But racist America stares at your sickness and tiredness, approaches you, looks past the jagged clothes of your history, looks past the scars of your trauma, and asks: *How does it feel to be the American nightmare?*

While black Americans view their experience as the American nightmare, racist Americans view black Americans as the American nightmare. Racist Americans, especially those racists who are white, view themselves as the embodiment of the American dream. All that makes America great. All that will make America great again. All that will keep America great.

But only the lies of racist Americans are great. Their American dream—that this is a land of equal opportunity, committed to freedom and equality, where police officers protect and serve—is a lie. Their American dream—that they have more because they are more, that when black people have more, they were given more—is a lie. Their American dream—that they have the civil right to kill black Americans with impunity and that black Americans do not have the human right to live—is a lie.

From the beginning, racist Americans have been perfectly content with turning nightmares into dreams, and dreams into nightmares; perfectly content with the law of racial killing, and the order of racial disparities. They can't fathom that racism is America's nightmare. There can be no American dream amid the American nightmare of anti-black racism—or of anti-Native, anti-Latino, anti-Asian racism—a racism that causes even white people to become fragile and die of whiteness.

Take Minneapolis. Black residents are more likely than white residents to be pulled over, arrested, and victimized by its police force. Even as black residents account for 20 percent of the city's population, they make up 64 percent of the people Minneapolis police restrained by the neck since 2018, and more than 60 percent of the victims of Minneapolis police shootings from late 2009 to May 2019. According to Samuel Sinyangwe of Mapping Police Violence, Minneapolis police are 13 times more likely to kill black residents than to kill white residents, one of the largest racial disparities in the nation. And these police officers rarely get prosecuted.

A typical black family in Minneapolis earns less than half as much as a typical white family—a $47,000 annual difference that is one of the largest racial disparities in the nation. Statewide, black residents are 6 percent of the Minnesota population, but 30 percent of the coronavirus cases as of Saturday, one of the largest black case disparities in the nation, according to the COVID Racial Data Tracker.

This is the racial pandemic within the viral pandemic—older than 1896, but as new as COVID-19 and the murder of George Floyd. But why is there such a pandemic of racial disparities in Minneapolis and beyond? "The pages of this work give but one answer," Hoffman concluded in 1896. "It is not in the conditions of life, but in race and hereditary that we find the explanation of the fact to be observed in all parts of the globe, in all times and among all peoples, namely, the superiority of one race over another, and of the Aryan race over all."

The two explanations available to Hoffman more than a century ago remain the two options for explaining racial disparities today, from COVID-19 to police violence: the anti-racist explanation or the racist explanation. Either there is something superior or inferior about the races, something dangerous and deathly about black people, and black people are the American nightmare; or there is something wrong with society, something dangerous and deathly about racist policy, and black people are experiencing the American nightmare.

Hoffman popularized the racist explanation. Many Americans probably believe both explanations—and live the contradiction of the American dream and nightmare. Many Americans struggle to be anti-racist, to see the racism in racial disparities, to cease blaming black people for disproportionate black disease and death, to instead blame racist power and policy and racist ideas for normalizing all the carnage. They struggle to focus on securing anti-racist policies that will lead to life, health, equity, and justice for all, and to act from anti-racist ideas that value black lives, that equalize all the racial groups in all their aesthetic and cultural differences.

In April, many Americans chose the racist explanation: saying black people were not taking the coronavirus as seriously as white people, until challenged by survey data and majority-white demonstrations demanding that states reopen. Then they argued that black Americans were disproportionately dying from COVID-19 because they have more preexisting conditions, due to their uniquely unhealthy behaviors. But according to the Foundation for AIDS Research, structural factors such as employment, access to health insurance and medical care, and the air and water quality in neighborhoods are drivers of black infections and deaths, and not "intrinsic characteristics of black communities or individual-level factors."

There's also no clear relationship between violent-crime rates and police-violence rates. And there's no direct relationship between violent-crime rates and black people. If there were, higher-income black neighborhoods would have the same levels of violent crime as lower-income black neighborhoods. But that is hardly the case.

Americans should be asking: Why are so many unarmed black people being killed by police while armed white people are simply arrested? Why are officials addressing violent crime in poorer neighborhoods by adding more police instead of more jobs? Why are black (and Latino) people during this pandemic less likely to be working from home; less likely to be insured; more likely to live in trauma-care deserts, lacking access to advanced emergency care; and more likely to live in polluted neighborhoods? The answer is what the Frederick Hoffmans of today refuse to believe: racism.

Instead, they say, like Donald Trump—like all those raging against the destruction of property and not black life—that they are "not racist." Hoffman introduced *Race Traits* by declaring that he was "free from the taint of prejudice or sentimentality . . . free from a personal bias." He was merely offering a "statement of the facts." In fact, the racial disparities he recorded documented America's racist policies.

Hoffman advanced the American nightmare. What will we advance? Hoffman implied we should *let them die*. Will we fight for black people to live?

History is calling the future from the streets of protest. What choice will we make? What world will we create? What will we be?

There are only two choices: racist or anti-racist.

Source: Ibram X. Kendi, "The American Nightmare," *Atlantic*, June 1, 2020, https://www.theatlantic .com/ideas/archive/2020/06/american-nightmare/612457/. © 2020 The Atlantic Monthly Group, LLC. All rights reserved. Used under license.

FURTHER READING

Alexander, Michelle. *The New Jim Crow: Mass Incarceration in the Age of Colorblindness*. New York: New Press, 2010.

Baldassare, Mark. *The Los Angeles Riots: Lessons for the Urban Future*. Boulder, CO: Westview Press, 1994.

Burke, Tarana, and Brené Brown, eds. *You Are Your Best Thing: Vulnerability, Shame Resilience, and the Black Experience*. New York: Random House, 2021.

Carbado, Devon, ed. *Black Men on Race, Gender, and Sexuality: A Critical Reader*. New York: New York University Press, 1999.

Cohen, Cathy. *The Boundaries of Blackness: AIDS and the Breakdown of Black Politics*. Chicago: University of Chicago Press, 1999.

Collier Hillstrom, Laurie. *The #MeToo Movement*. Santa Barbara, CA: ABC-CLIO, 2018.

Darity, William, Jr., and A. Kirsten Mullen. *From Here to Equality: Reparations for Black Americans in the Twenty-First Century*. Chapel Hill: University of North Carolina Press, 2020.

Dyson, Michael Eric. *Come Hell or High Water: Hurricane Katrina and the Color of Disaster*. New York: Civitas Books, 2007.

Felker-Kantor, Max. *Policing Los Angeles: Race, Resistance, and the Rise of the LAPD*. Chapel Hill: University of North Carolina Press, 2020.

Forman, James, Jr. *Locking Up Our Own: Crime and Punishment in Black America*. New York: Farrar, Straus & Giroux, 2018.

Hinton, Elizabeth. *From the War on Poverty to the War on Crime: The Making of Mass Incarceration in America*. Cambridge, MA: Harvard University Press, 2017.

Kendi, Ibram X. *How to Be an Antiracist*. New York: One World, 2019.

Khan-Cullors, Patrisse, and Asha Bandale. *When They Call You a Terrorist: A Black Lives Matter Memoir*. New York: St. Martin's Press, 2018.

Landrieu, Mitch. *In the Shadow of Statues: A White Southerner Confronts History*. New York: Penguin Books, 2019.

Levitt, Jeremy, and Matthew Whitaker. *Hurricane Katrina: America's Unnatural Disaster*. Lincoln: University of Nebraska Press, 2009.

Martin, Michael, and Marilyn Yaquinto. *Redress for Historical Injustices in the United States: On Reparations for Slavery, Jim Crow, and Their Legacies*. Durham, NC: Duke University Press, 2007.

Morrison, Toni, ed. *Race-ing Justice, En-gendering Power: Essays on Anita Hill, Clarence Thomas, and the Construction of Social Reality*. New York: Pantheon Books, 1992.

Pauli, Benjamin. *Flint Fights Back: Environmental Justice and Democracy in the Flint Water Crisis*. Cambridge, MA: MIT Press, 2019.

Price, Melanye T. *The Race Whisperer: Barack Obama and the Political Uses of Race*. New York: New York University Press, 2016.

Provine, Doris Marie. *Unequal under Law: Race in the War on Drugs*. Chicago: University of Chicago Press, 2007.

Ransby, Barbara. *Making All Black Lives Matter: Reimagining Freedom in the Twenty-First Century*. Berkeley: University of California Press, 2018.

Romano, Renee, and Leigh Raiford, eds. *The Civil Rights Movement in American Memory*. Athens: University of Georgia Press, 2006.

Taylor, Keeanga-Yamahtta. *From #BlackLivesMatter to Black Liberation*. Chicago: Haymarket Books, 2016.

Theoharis, Jeanne. *A More Beautiful and Terrible History: The Uses and Misuses of Civil Rights History*. Boston: Beacon Press, 2018.

Walters, Ron. "Barack Obama and the Politics of Blackness." *Journal of Black Studies* 38, no. 1 (2007): 7–29.

"War on Drugs Stats, 1980–2000: Rates of Adult Drug Arrest by Race." In *Freedom on My Mind: A History of African Americans with Documents*, edited by Deborah Gray White, Mia Bay, and Waldo E. Martin Jr., 579. Boston: Bedford/St. Martin's Press, 2012.

Washington, Harriet. *A Terrible Thing to Waste: Environmental Racism and Its Assault on the American Mind*. New York: Little, Brown Spark, 2020.

Watkins-Hayes, Celeste. *Remaking a Life: How Women Living with HIV/AIDS Confront Inequality*. Berkeley: University of California Press, 2019.